Preserving Complex Digital Objects

Preserving Complex Digital Objects

Edited by
Janet Delve and David Anderson

Published by Facet Publishing,
7 Ridgmount Street, London WC1E 7AE
www.facetpublishing.co.uk

Facet Publishing is wholly owned by CILIP: the Chartered Institute of
Library and Information Professionals.

British Library Cataloguing in Publication Data
A catalogue record for this book is available from the British Library.

ISBN 978-1-85604- 958-0

First published 2014

Text printed on FSC accredited material.

Typeset from editors' files by Facet Publishing Production in 11.5/14 pt
Garamond and Frutiger
Printed and made in Great Britain by CPI Group (UK) Ltd, Croydon,
CR0 4YY.

Contents

Foreword

Over the past decade, a community of researchers, technologists and memory institutions such as libraries and archives have made substantial progress towards ensuring the long-term viability of digital content. Individuals routinely hold terabytes of material; organizations hold hundreds of terabytes. The ones that plan for the future have a reasonable level of confidence that they can, with vigilance and some good fortune, keep these collections safe and usable for the next generation. But these collections are fairly simple in form – images, photographs, office documents.

The digital age has seen a rush of change – creation, emergence, false starts and firsts. Digital content, software and technology have gone beyond creating documents, producing audio and video, capturing data or performing analysis. They mediate artistic creation, community, social interaction and the closest human bonds.

Perhaps the most remarkable of these inventions is the computer game, with its outstanding artistry, simulated worlds with rich physics, automated players, sophisticated narratives that reflect player choices, and real social interaction between human players. These deeply complex digital objects touch the lives of hundreds of millions of people and have given rise to major commercial enterprises and multi-billion dollar industries.

Digital art provides additional challenges. In part, this is due to the creative experimental nature of digital art. Artists often collaborate with data analysts, scientists and engineers. They encourage each other to push the boundaries of what can be done. For the current volume, this means that they challenge what can be replicated at all – much less preserved.

Simulations and their visualizations have become an essential component of policy formation and decision-making as well as the basis for understanding their consequences. They are also a key component of exploration and discovery in both scientific and commercial domains. In fields from archaeology to x-ray crystallography, both expert scientists and the general public rely on visualizations that they can manipulate to deepen their understanding. Every simulation and subsequent presentation, however, makes simplifying assumptions and approximations; has poorly understood boundary conditions; and is subject to misrepresenting a situation either intentionally or unintentionally. As a result, it is critical to preserve the simulation itself for future understanding and analysis of the results.

In spite of the importance of these artefacts, there are not yet effective methods of keeping and preserving them for future generations – or even re-commercialization and study today. Indeed, understanding and capturing the context in which they work or ensuring legal rights to do so make the challenge even greater.

To my knowledge, this is the first book to bring together a comprehensive collection of viewpoints to look at the arguments for, challenges to, and steps towards the preservation of these sorts of complex digital objects. I hope that it will help to drive future investment into establishing the appropriate legal framework, conceptual principles, commercial agreements and technical approaches for overcoming these challenges.

This is a timely and important book that addresses an essential problem.

Adam Farquhar
The British Library

Preface

Back in 2010 the often-expressed mantra was that bit preservation was a 'solved problem'. In the UK higher education (HE) sector, there was also a view that we now had all the digital repositories that we needed and therefore the preservation of simple digital objects (for instance, scholarly articles in PDF format) should – in theory, anyway – no longer be a problem. That may have been an over-simplification but regardless of its merits it did open up some space to start thinking about digital objects that were not so straightforward. Along with the problem of scale, the preservation of 'complex objects' was a regular topic of discussion when research challenges were being considered and it therefore seemed sensible for Jisc to try to help the community to address the issue of complexity when funding became available.

At the briefing meeting for the Jisc Infrastructure for Education and Research Programme, in October 2010, I set out the requirements for one of the areas of work in the programme. It invited proposals for a single collaborative project to 'to produce a definition and description of the effective preservation of complex visual digital materials and develop recommendations for practice'. Happily, we did receive proposals in response to this call; and even better, what transpired was the POCOS (Preservation of Complex Objects Symposia) project that organized a series of symposia and produced the original publications which form the basis of this book.

One of the original challenges of defining the work that became the POCOS project was to somehow limit the scope. Most disciplines and many domains of work have to deal with digital materials that are dynamic and have embedded material, or complex dependencies and behaviours, but the realm of preserving complex visual objects (particularly cultural objects) seemed under-researched. To break the work down into more manageable components and to give it some shape, one of the early decisions prior to announcing the call was to divide the territory into three sub-domains: simulations and visualizations; gaming environments and virtual worlds; and software-based art. It was far from certain at that early stage how meaningful, complementary and balanced those categories would be, particularly in terms of their relative maturity and the various levels of stakeholder interest, but it became clear as the project progressed that these categories *were* structurally useful and perhaps even helpful in terms of allowing practitioners to situate and describe their work, some of which featured in more than one sub-domain, and some of which was applicable to all.

It should be stressed that although this book *does* represent the culmination of several years of hard work on the part of the POCOS team, it is not simply the outcome of an initiative that began with a Jisc funding call. What it does is draw together into one volume many of the strands of work from across the digital preservation community that have relevance to the broad area of preserving complex objects. Some of this work (particularly in the area of significant properties and the preservation of software) has also been funded by Jisc but much of it also comes out of European Commission-funded initiatives (e.g. the KEEP and Planets projects) or is the result of ongoing work in Europe and the USA by groups and individuals who make it their business to engage with objects at the difficult end of the digital preservation spectrum.

The principal outcome of this book will hopefully be to set out what is currently understood about dealing with complex digital objects and will provide a broad framework for starting to manage and address relevant issues. It deals with multifaceted, difficult problems (only some of which are technical) and, irrespective of the various views that exist on the wisdom of preserving what some consider to be implicitly ephemeral materials, it should be clear that these problems test, stretch and sometimes exceed our capacity to deal with them. As a description of research at the boundaries of digital preservation, this alone makes it a valuable contribution to the literature. More than that though, it brings together some of the leading practitioners in the world today who are tackling issues in this space and provides a much-needed examination and commentary on why this material is of value and why continued investment is needed to preserve it for future generations.

Neil Grindley
Jisc

Contributors

Daisy Abbott started her career researching digital culture and digitization efforts across the world before moving into digital documentation of performing arts research. She worked as a digital curation advisor before moving to her current position at the Digital Design Studio, Glasgow School of Art, as a research developer specializing in 3D digital documentation and visualization technologies and methods across the heritage, arts and medical domains. She comes from a background in theatre, film and television studies and IT. Daisy's research interests span various aspects of the creation and continuing use of digital information. Specific areas of interest include: digital representations of ephemeral events and how these representations affect performing arts scholarship and curation methodologies; interaction design; performed heritage; use of digital documentation in education or recreation and the development of new digital pedagogies; information retrieval; standards for digital arts and humanities; digital curation; and serious games.

Professor David Anderson is Professor of Digital Humanities, CiTech Research Centre Director, and co-leader of the Future Proof Computing Group (FPCG) at the University of Portsmouth (UoP). He holds a BA Hons in philosophy (Queen's University Belfast, QUB) and a PhD in artificial intelligence (QUB). His research interests include digital preservation, history of computing, paraconsistent logic, epistemology, artificial intelligence and the philosophy of mind. He was the UoP Principal Investigator for the EC FP7 Project KEEP. In addition to being the Editor-in-Chief of the Taylor & Francis journal *The New Review of Information Networking*, David has served on numerous international committees, including the IEEE publications committee. He is a member of the Arts and Humanities Research Council (AHRC) Peer Review College.

Drew Baker is a Research Fellow within the Department of Digital Humanities, King's College London. One of the founding members of the King's Visualisation Lab (KVL), he has worked in the field of 3D visualization and interpretation of archaeology and history since 1997. He has specialized in the area of 3D modelling, specifically using interactive Virtual Reality Modeling Language (VRML) and virtual world technologies. His primary area of interest is in using 3D and advanced technology to bring cultural history from traditional passive media into interactive new media – transforming the user into an active participant though exploration of virtual worlds and artefacts – the process of developing such environments and interactions and the long-term preservation of digital cultural heritage. His personal research area is in the first century AD Campania region of Italy, focusing on the Roman colony of Pompeii, insula VIII.7, and the history of the rediscovery and archaeological excavations of the area since their destruction in 79 AD.

Andrew Ball is an experienced IT audit professional who spent 12 years with the UK Audit Commission, where he was Head of IT Audit. His professional background is in IT service, project and programme management, with over 20 years' experience. He holds a number of professional qualifications in PRINCE2, ITIL and MSP. Andrew is also a Certified Information Systems Auditor and a Chartered Member of the British Computer Society.

Professor Richard A. Bartle is Senior Lecturer and Honorary Professor of Computer Game Design at the University of Essex, UK. He is best known for having co-written in 1978 the first virtual world, MUD, and for his 1996 Player Types model, which has seen widespread adoption by the massively multiplayer online (MMO) games industry. His 2003 book *Designing Virtual Worlds* is the standard text on the subject, and he is an influential writer on all aspects of MMO design and development. In 2010 he was the first recipient of the prestigious Game Developer's Choice (GDC) 'Online Game Legend' award.

Winfried Bergmeyer studied art history, European ethnology and archaeology at the universities of Marburg and Zurich. He worked at the

Saxonian Cultural Heritage Service in Dresden. After advanced training as manager for online marketing in 1999 he worked as project co-ordinator at LuraTech GmbH in Berlin and thereafter as scientific assistant at the Institute for Museum Research. Since May 2009 he has worked at the Computerspielemuseum (Computer Games Museum) in Berlin. He is co-ordinator of the working group Langzeitbewahrung as part of the German Museums Association

Professor Simon Biggs was born in Australia in 1957 and moved to the UK in 1986, where he was Professor of Interdisciplinary Arts at Edinburgh College of Art. He has recently (2014) returned to Australia, where he is Professor of Art at the University of South Australia, Adelaide, while retaining an Honorary Professorship at Edinburgh College of Art. He has been making art with digital media since 1978, which has been presented at Tate Modern, Centre Georges Pompidou, Academie der Künste, Berlin, Rijksmuseum Twenthe, Enschede, Macau Arts Museum, San Francisco Cameraworks, Walker Art Center, Minneapolis and the Art Gallery of New South Wales. He has been a keynote speaker at many conferences, most recently Cornell University's 2010 Society for the Humanities Conference. Works include *Autopoeisis* (with James Leach, 2004), *Halo* (1998), *Magnet* (1997), *Book of Shadows* (1996) and *Great Wall of China* (1999) – see www.littlepig.org.uk.

Clive Billenness previously held the post of EC Project Management Expert at the British Library. He was the Project Manager for POCOS and also a work package lead on the EC FP7 Project KEEP, as well as a member of the British Library's project team on the EC FP7 Project SCAPE. Qualified in Prince2, MSP and Management of Risk (MoR), he was the Programme Manager of the Planets Project and a member of the team which created the Open Planets Foundation. He is a Certified Information Systems Auditor. As a Head of the Northern Region's Public Sector Information Risk Management Team at KPMG LLP, he was responsible for directing a review on behalf of the National Audit Office of the £30m project to update the Department of Work and Pensions computer systems. He also advised the UK Office of Government Commerce and the Office of the UK Deputy Prime Minister on a number of IT Projects. Before that, he was a Regional Service Lead for the Audit Commission, where he was frequently loaned to clients to assist with the recovery of projects which were in exception. Clive is a member of the Office of Government Commerce's Examining Board for Project, Programme and Risk Management examinations. He is also a Director of the UK Best Practice User Group for the same disciplines. He is a regularly published author on project management for the Chartered Institute of Public Finance and Accountancy (CIPFA).

boredomresearch (www.boredomresearch.net) is a collaboration between Southampton (UK)-based artists **Vicky Isley** and **Paul Smith**. The collective is internationally renowned for creating software-driven art that explores extended timeframes. Projects include generative objects, interactive online projects and installations. Based at the National Centre for Computer Animation at Bournemouth University (UK), its work benefits from a fine blend of art and science, allowing the artists to achieve art works underpinned by a deep appreciation of the creative possibilities of technology and expertise in artificial life programming. They are greatly inspired by the diversity that exists in nature. Using computational technology, they explore this diversity to simulate natural patterns, behaviours and intricate forms, which gradually change over time. boredomresearch's art works are in many international collections including the British Council and Borusan Contemporary Art Collection, Istanbul. The art work 'Ornamental Bug Garden 001' has been awarded honorary mentions in the Transmediale.05 festival, Berlin (2005), and the VIDA 7.0 Art & Artificial Life International Competition, Madrid (2004).

Paul Charisse is currently Senior Lecturer in Animation at Portsmouth University. He has worked for a variety of VFX companies over the past ten years including Weta Digital, where he worked on the *Lord of the Rings* trilogy animating the character Gollum. Since then he has worked as an animator, modeller, pre-viz artist and rigger on a number of films including *Prince Caspian, Stardust, Harry Potter and the Order of the Phoenix, Zorro II, Hellboy II* and *Brothers Grimm*. He has also designed a facial animation system for Lionhead studios. He is presently lecturing in animation at Portsmouth University and is directing a full length feature film using performance capture called *Stina and the Wolf*, due for release in 2017.

Neil Chue Hong completed an MPhys degree in computational physics from the University of Edinburgh. He is the Principal Investigator and

Director of the EPSRC-funded Software Sustainability Institute, a national facility based at the University of Edinburgh supporting research software users and developers, to drive the continued improvement and impact of research software. Neil began his career at Edinburgh Parallel Computing Centre, working on technology transfer to small businesses and large scale data access and integration projects. From 2007 to 2010, Neil was Director of OMII-UK at the University of Southampton, which provided and supported free, open-source scientific software to the UK e-research community. His current research interests are in software ecosystems, community engagement and development, cloud computing for science, and the role of software as a research object. He is editor of the *Journal of Open Research Software*, and an advocate for Software Carpentry.

Professor John R. Clarke, University of Texas, received his PhD from Yale University. In 1980 he began teaching at the University of Texas at Austin, where his teaching, research and publications cover ancient Roman art, art-historical methodology and contemporary art. His work has focused on the visual culture of ancient Rome, art-historical methodology, and contemporary art and criticism. He has published seven books; two appeared in 2007, *Looking at Laughter: humor, power, and transgression in Roman visual culture, 100 B.C.–A.D. 250* (University of California Press) and *Roman Life: 100 B.C.–A.D. 200* (Abrams). He has published numerous articles, chapters and reviews, including several on the mosaics and paintings of Villa A at Oplontis, Torre Annunziata, Italy. Currently John is co-director of the Oplontis Project, a collaboration with the Archaeological Superintendency of Pompeii, the Department of Art and Art History at UT Austin, and the King's Visualisation Lab, King's College London. The Oplontis Project will furnish a comprehensive publication of this huge luxury villa (50 BC–AD 79), with all the research findings keyed to a navigable, 3D digital model. Support for the project includes a collaborative research grant from the National Endowment for the Humanities.

Esther Conway is an Earth Observation Data Scientist at the Centre for Environmental Data Archival. She is an experienced researcher and analyst in the field of digital preservation, having worked on a variety of EU- and UK-based research projects. Her main area of research has been the development of methods and models to support the long-term exploitation of scientific research assets. Esther originally trained in physics at Imperial College London and subsequently acquired a Masters in information systems and technology from City University London.

Dr Angela Dappert (Digital Preservation Coalition) is Project Officer for the EU TIMBUS Project. TIMBUS is about digital preservation of timeless business processes. She also serves on the PREMIS editorial committee. In both capacities she is involved with modelling and defining metadata for computational environments. She has worked at the British Library on data carrier stabilization, digital asset registration, preservation planning and characterization, e-journal ingest and digital metadata standards. Before this she worked for Schlumberger, the University of California, Stanford University and Siemens. Angela holds a Diploma in Medical Informatics from the University of Heidelberg, an MSc in computer sciences from the University of Texas at Austin, and a PhD in Digital Preservation Modelling from the University of Portsmouth..

Dr Janet Delve is co-leader of the Future Proof Computing Group, one of the research clusters in the Centre for Cultural and Industrial Technologies Research (CiTech) at the University of Portsmouth. She holds degrees in mathematics (UCL), French (Southampton), together with a Masters degree in microwaves and modern optics (UCL), and a PhD in the history of mathematics (Middlesex University). Her research interests include: metadata modelling for digital preservation; data warehousing applied to cultural domains; and the crossover between the history of computing and digital preservation. The University of Portsmouth is a partner in the EC FP7 Project KEEP, in which Janet is responsible for the data modelling of complex digital objects and the development of the technical environment metadata database TOTEM. She is a member of the AHRC Peer Review College.

Dr Hugh Denard, Digital Humanities, King's College London, earned his BA in theatre and classical civilizations at Trinity College, Dublin, in 1992. He completed an MA in ancient drama and society in the Classics Department at the University of Exeter in 1993 and a PhD on versions of Greek tragedy by Irish writers, in the Department of Drama at Exeter, in 1997. He held a one-year Teaching Fellowship in the English Department at Trinity College Dublin (1997–8), before moving to the School of Theatre Studies at the

University of Warwick in 1998, where he taught students of theatre and performance studies, co-ordinated the Theatre, Media and Text degree and worked as a researcher on the AHRC Theatre of Pompey Project. Hugh moved to King's College London with the other members of the Visualisation Lab in September 2005. From January to March 2011 he was Visiting Research Fellow at the Long Room Hub, Trinity College Dublin, where he studied the early Abbey Theatre and produced a research-based, mixed-media performance at the Samuel Beckett Theatre.

Dr Adam Farquhar is Head of Digital Scholarship at The British Library, where he focuses on establishing for scholars and researchers services which take full advantage of the possibilities that digital collections present. He was previously Head of Digital Library Technology, at which time he co-founded the Library's Digital Preservation Team (www.bl.uk/aboutus/stratpolprog/digi) and initiated its Dataset Strategy and Programme (www.bl.uk/datasets). He was Co-ordinator and Scientific Director of the EU co-funded Planets Digital Preservation project (www.planets-project.eu) and was a lead architect on the BL's Digital Library System. He is President of DataCite (www.datacite.org), an international association dedicated to making it easier to identify, cite and re-use scientific data; founder and Chairman of the Open Planets Foundation (www.openplanetsfoundation.org); and serves on the Board of the Digital Preservation Coalition. Prior to joining The British Library, he was the principal knowledge management architect for Schlumberger (1998-2003) and research scientist at the Stanford Knowledge Systems Laboratory (1993-1998). He completed his PhD in Computer Sciences at the University of Texas at Austin (1993). His work focuses on improving the ways in which people can represent, find, share, use, exploit and preserve digitally encoded knowledge.

Neil Grindley is Head of Resource Discovery at Jisc. Whilst working in the role of Programme Manager with responsibility for digital preservation at Jisc, Neil was responsible for designing and commissioning the programme of work that ultimately spawned the Preservation of Complex Objects Symposia (POCOS) project. Jisc is an organization that invests in and supports technology-related projects and services for the UK higher and further education sector and is influential within and beyond the UK as an innovative agent of change. Prior to working at Jisc Neil was involved with promoting the use of advanced ICT methods in arts and humanities research; and before that was the IT Manager at the Courtauld Institute of Art.

Dr Perla Innocenti is a cultural heritage scholar and Research Fellow at the School of Culture and Creative Arts, University of Glasgow, where she is leading interdisciplinary research on cultural networks as Principal Investigator of the EU-funded FP7 SSH collaborative research project European Museums in an Age of Migrations (MeLa). Her main research interest is in the field of cultural and digital heritage, across the museum, library and archive sectors. In particular she has a passion for research in preserving tangible and intangible cultural heritage and scientific digital objects, cultural heritage informatics, the application of information technology to museums, libraries and archives, and innovative ways of representing information online. Perla contributed to and led research as Co-Investigator of EU-funded FP6, FP7 and PSP collaborative research projects (DPE, Planets, CASPAR, SHAMAN, DL.org, ECLAP) on digital preservation and digital libraries, and various national initiatives on digital heritage. She came to Glasgow from the Politecnico di Milano, Italy, where she held a research scholarship on information systems for industrial design and co-ordinated digital libraries activities and projects. Prior to that, she conducted research on museology and museography in Italy with Scuola Normale Superiore in Pisa, Goppion Laboratorio Museotecnico, Istituto Nazionale di Archeologia e Storia dell'Arte in Rome, and Pinacoteca Nazionale di Bologna. Perla's papers, projects and more can be found at www.gla.ac.uk/schools/cca/staff/perlainnocenti.

Dr William Kilbride is Executive Director of the Digital Preservation Coalition (DPC), a not-for-profit membership organization, which provides advocacy, knowledge exchange, workforce development, assurance and partnership on issues of digital preservation. The DPC has around 45 organizational members across the UK and Ireland and is active in a number of international research initiatives and partnerships. William started his career as an archaeologist in the early 1990s when the discipline's enthusiasm for using technology was not matched by the skills for looking after the resulting data. This gave him an early and practical introduction to the challenges of data management and preservation. He was previously a Lecturer in Archaeology at Glasgow University, where he retains an honorary position, Assistant Director of the Archaeology Data Service at the University of York and Research Manager with Glasgow Museums.

Dr Leo Konstantelos is Research Data Curator at the University of Melbourne. His work addresses the management, curation and preservation of research data, with a particular focus on social and cultural informatics. Previously, Leo has held positions at the University of Glasgow as a Principal Investigator for the POCOS project and as a Teaching Fellow in Digital Media and Information Management studies; and as a Research Fellow at the University of Portsmouth. He holds an MSc in Information Technology (2005) from the Department of Computing Science at the University of Glasgow and a PhD in Digital Humanities (2009) from the Humanities Advanced Technology & Information Institute (HATII). Leo has participated in a number of EU-funded projects, including Preservation and Long-term Access through NETworked Services (Planets), Sustaining Heritage Access through Multivalent ArchiviNg (SHAMAN) and Keeping Emulation Environments Portable (KEEP). His research interests lie in applying digital curation and digital preservation theory and practice to the born-digital arts.

Michael Takeo Magruder (www.takeo.org) is a visual artist and researcher based in the Department of Digital Humanities, King's College London, who works with digital and new media including real-time data, immersive environments, mobile devices and virtual worlds. His practice explores concepts ranging from media criticism and aesthetic journalism to digital formalism and computational aesthetics, deploying Information Age technologies and systems to examine our networked, media-rich world. In the last 15 years, Michael's projects have been showcased in over 250 exhibitions in 30 countries, including Circulo de Bellas Artes, Madrid; the Courtauld Institute of Art, London; EAST International, Norwich; Eastside Projects, Birmingham; FACT, Liverpool; Georges Pompidou Center, Paris; KIBLA Multimedijski Center, Maribor; QUAD, Derby; SESI' Cultural Centre, São Paulo; Tokyo Metropolitan Museum of Photography; and Trans-Media-Akademie, Hellerau. His art has been funded by the Andy Warhol Foundation for the Visual Arts; Arts Council England; the Esmée Fairbairn Foundation; the EU Culture Programme; the Leverhulme Trust; the National Endowment for the Arts, USA; and the National Lottery, UK. He has been commissioned by numerous public galleries in the UK and abroad and by the leading internet art portal Turbulence. In 2010, Michael was selected to represent the UK at *Manifesta 8: the European Biennial of Contemporary Art* and several of his most well-known digital art works were added to the Rose Goldsen Archive of New Media Art at Cornell University.

Dr Brian Matthews is Group Leader of the Research Data Group within the Science and Technology Facilities Council (STFC) Scientific Computing Department. He has worked on a wide range of different areas of computing and information technology. He gained his PhD on equational reasoning systems with Glasgow University, and worked in the area of formal methods for software engineering. He then worked on projects on structured documentation, data modelling and the web. He has been involved with the semantic web, developing early versions of the RDF format for thesauri and other knowledge organization systems, which has evolved into the *SKOS recommendation*. In recent years, Brian has become increasingly involved in developing technology and tools to support scientific research and collaboration. This has involved work in data management, preservation and distributed systems, especially building data cataloguing systems for scientific facilities and collaborations. He has also contributed to developing STFC's institutional repository ePubs, and has been involved in other projects in digital libraries, information management, digital curation and data publication.

Dr Jerome McDonough is an Associate Professor in the Graduate School of Library and Information Science (GSLIS) at the University of Illinois at Urbana-Champaign. He holds a PhD in library and information studies from the University of California at Berkeley and his current research focuses on metadata and digital preservation. He is currently the Principal Investigator for the Preserving Virtual Worlds 2 project, an investigation into the significant properties of computer games funded by the Institute of Museum & Library Services. Prior to joining the faculty at GSLIS, Jerome was the head of the Digital Library Development Team for New York University Libraries. He has served on the NISO Standards Development Committee, and on various metadata standards bodies for libraries, including the METS digital library standard and the PREMIS digital preservation metadata standard.

Dr Kenton McHenry received a PhD in computer science from the University of Illinois at Urbana-Champaign in 2008, after completing a BS degree from

California State University of San Bernardino. He is currently a senior research scientist at the National Center for Super-computing Applications (NCSA) and leader of the Image and Spatial Data Analysis (ISDA) division. Kenton's background is in computer vision, with interests in the areas of image segmentation, object/material recognition and 3D reconstruction. At NCSA he has applied this experience to the task of digital curation: specifically, digital preservation and access. In recent years he has worked on a series of tools focused around the need for file format conversions in digital archives. One such tool, NCSA Polyglot, is a file format conversion service that was designed as an extensible, distributed and practical solution to accessing data among the many contemporary (and legacy) file formats available. The Polyglot service is built on top of another tool developed by the ISDA group, the 'software server'. Software servers are background processes run on a machine to provide API-like access to installed applications. These servers essentially turn traditional desktop software into web-based services and allow Polyglot to carry out a potentially large number of format conversions.

Jenny Mitcham, a digital archivist at the University of York, was trained as a field archaeologist but after a few years working on excavations at home and abroad, decided that it would be kinder to her wrists and knees to move into the sphere of IT. After an MSc course in archaeological computing she worked in several different places, including serving as a Sites and Monuments Officer, before eventually moving to the Archaeology Data Service (ADS) in 2003, where she worked until 2012. One of the core functions of the ADS is to archive digital materials for the long term and make these objects available for re-use. She is familiar with the wide range of challenges that archaeological data provides, and has a particular interest in standards and certification in digital archiving and how we enable the reuse of data. The ADS works to preserve and disseminate the wide range of data types that archaeologists produce. These range from simple text reports, spreadsheets and digital photographs to far more complex 3D digital models. Although for the ADS the principles of digital archiving remain the same no matter what the data, complex data, which is often large in size and in proprietary formats, brings new challenges. In 2012 Jenny took on her new role at the University of York and is now involved with planning for the preservation of the wide range of data produced by research across the University as a whole.

Professor James Newman is Professor of Digital Media, Course Leader in Creative Media Practice and Director of the Media Futures Research Centre at Bath Spa University. He researches, writes and teaches on digital media, videogames and the cultures of play and has written numerous books on videogames and gaming cultures for publishers including Routledge and the BFI. He is a co-founder of the National Videogame Archive, which is a partnership with the National Media Museum, the UK's official collection of videogames and the ephemera of games culture, and a member of the European Federation of Game Archives, Museums and Preservation projects (EFGAMP). He is a co-producer on the GameCity international games festival and sits on the board of the gaming culture special collection of the UK Web Archive. James' latest book, *Best Before: videogames, supersession and obsolescence*, was published by Routledge in 2012 and is the first book-length project tackling issues of game history, heritage and digital media preservation.

Dr Dan Pinchbeck is Creative Director of thechineseroom, an independent game development studio based in Brighton and Portsmouth. Its first game, *Dear Esther*, was released on Steam on 14 February 2012. Beginning life as a research project, then a source mod, *Dear Esther* has gathered multiple international awards, critical acclaim and a dedicated following since it was first conceived in 2007. In 2013, thechineseroom released the cult horror game *Amnesia: a machine for pigs*. The studio is currently working on *Everybody's Gone to the Rapture*, an open world Playstation 4 exclusive title with Sony Santa Monica. This game began life as an AHRC-funded research project on commercialization of academic game research. Dan is also Reader in Computer Games at the University of Portsmouth, where he teaches game design. He holds a PhD in first-person gaming, and has published internationally on experimental game design, independent game development, story and gameplay, and game preservation. His first book, *DOOM: scarydarkfast*, was published by the University of Michigan Press as part of its Landmark Videogames Series in 2012.

Daniel Pletinckx trained as a civil engineer, with a specialization in information technology. He gained extensive experience in system design, quality assurance, digital image processing and synthesis, 3D and virtual reality through a career of 15 years in private industry. He is the author of several articles on computer graphics and cultural heritage presentation and has lectured extensively at major computer graphics and cultural heritage conferences. He was chief consultant to the Ename 974 project, a major heritage project in the historical village of Ename, Belgium, and founded the international Ename Center for Public Archaeology and Heritage Presentation, together with Dirk Callebaut and Neil Silberman. He designed four TimeScopes in Ename, which received three international awards (Golden Scarab award and Flemish Monument Award in 1998 for TimeScope1, the VGI ICT Award for best innovation in public outreach in cultural heritage for TimeScope3). Currently, Daniel is Director of Visual Dimension bvba, an SME dealing with consulting on and designing of new systems for cultural heritage and tourism. Visual Dimension provides consultation to major European heritage organizations on innovating and optimizing the use of ICT technology in tangible and intangible cultural heritage and tourism. Visual Dimension also specializes in new, efficient ways to digitize existing cultural heritage objects and monuments, and in virtual reconstruction of historical buildings and landscapes.

Dr Arif Shaon leads the technical team in the Library Repository Services unit of University of New South Wales (UNSW) Library. He provides technical leadership to development of information repositories that facilitate curation and preservation of UNSW research data collections. Prior to joining UNSW in September 2012, he worked as a Senior Research Scientist at the STFC in the UK, where he played leading roles in several European and UK projects in the field of advanced environmental informatics and digital preservation. He also has considerable experience in the emerging area of the semantic web, particularly in developing linked data approaches to support the UK Open Data initiative.

Iain Simons is the Director of the GameCity festival at Nottingham Trent University. He has written and talked about videogame culture for a wide variety of audiences and publications. In 2008 he co-founded the National Videogame Archive, a unique collection of videogame software, hardware and ephemera.

Paul Wheatley is a specialist in digital preservation and works for the University of Leeds. He is educated in computer science and has previously worked for the British Library and as a technology journalist and software developer. Paul has played a leading role in various collaborative digital preservation developments at the University of Leeds, including the Camileon project, which gained international recognition for helping to rescue the BBC Domesday system using emulation technology.

Tom Woolley became the National Media Museum's first Curator of New Media in 2007, responsible for the Museum's youngest collection. Before joining the curatorial team, he directed the Bradford Animation Festival (BAF). He has a background in multimedia design, having graduated from the University of Bradford in 2002 with a BSc in electronic imaging and media communications. He has been establishing and expanding the new media collection to illustrate the development of digital media, with particular focus on the internet, home computing and videogames. In 2010 he curated the exhibition *Immersion* by Robbie Cooper and the Games Lounge display in the Museum foyer. In 2008 he helped to establish the National Videogame Archive in partnership with Nottingham Trent University. Tom programs BAF Game, the games strand of the Bradford Animation Festival. BAF Game aims to help students connect with the videogames industry and showcases gaming's creative culture. He is lead curator on Life Online – a new permanent gallery, which explores the history and social impact of the internet.

Glossary

Access the process of turning an *AIP* into *DIP*, i.e. using data from a digital archive

ADF Amiga Disk File, a file format used by Amiga computers and emulators to store images of disks

ADF Opus a Microsoft Windows-based program to create *ADF*

ADS Archaeology Data Service, a digital archive specializing in archaeological data, based in York

AHDS Arts and Humanities Data Service, a data service for higher education, closed in 2008

AIMS a project funded by the Mellon Foundation to examine archival principles in the digita lage

AIP Archival Information Package, a package of information held within an *OAIS*

APA Alliance for Permanent Access, a European network, set up *APARSEN*

APARSEN a Network of Excellence funded by the *EC*, see *APA*

API an interface provided by a software program in order to interact with other software applications

Archival storage the *OAIS* entity that contains the services and functions used for the storage and retrieval of *AIP*

ARCOMEM ARchive COmmunities MEMories, an *EC*-funded project in digital preservation

ASCII American Standard Code for Information Interchange, a standard for electronic text

BADC British Atmospheric Data Centre

BL The British Library

BlogForever an *EC*-funded project working on robust digital preservation, management and dissemination facilities for weblogs

BLPAC British Library Preservation Advisory Centre, a service of the *BL* which promotes preservation

BS10008 a British standard pertaining to the evidential weight of digital objects

CARARE Connecting ARchaeology and ARchitecture in Europeana

CASPAR Cultural, Artistic and Scientific Knowledge for Preservation, Access and Retrieval

CAVE Computer Assisted Virtual Environment, or Cave Automatic Virtual Environment

CCAAA Co-ordinating Council of Audiovisual Archives Associations

CCSDS Consultative Committee for Space Data Systems, originators of the *OAIS* standard

CD-ROM Compact Disc Read Only Memory

Characterization stage of ingest processes where digital objects are analysed to assess their composition and validity

Checksum a unique numerical signature derived from a file, used to compare copies

CiTech Centre for Cultural and Industrial Technologies Research

Cloud (Cloud-computing, Cloud-based, etc.) on demand, offsite data storage and processing provided by a third party

CRT Cathode Ray Tube

CSP Compound Scholarly Publication

CVS Concurrent Versions System or Concurrent Versioning System, a client-server revision control system used in software

Data dictionary a formal repository of terms used to describe data

DCC Digital Curation Centre, a data management advisory service for research

DDC Dewey Decimal Classification

Designated community a group of users who should be able to understand a particular set of information

DigiCurVE Digital Curation in Vocational Education, an assessment project funded by EU on training provision in Europe

Digital Object a set of bit sequences, e.g. a single document such as a *PDF* file, or an image of a (console) game, etc.

DIP Dissemination Information Package, the data disseminated from an *OAIS*

DOCAM Documentation and Conservation of the Media Arts Heritage

DOS Disk Operations System

DP Digital Preservation

DPA Digital Preservation Award, biannual prize awarded by the *DPC*

DPC Digital Preservation Coalition, a membership body that supports digital preservation

DPTP Digital Preservation Training Programme, an intensive training course run by *ULCC*

DRIVER Digital Repository Infrastructure Vision for European Research

DROID a tool developed and distributed by *TNA* to identify file formats, based on *PRONOM*

DSA Data Seal of Approval, a process by which organizations can undertake self-evaluation of their *DP* practices

DVD Digital Versatile Disk; formerly the same abbreviation was used for Digital Video Disk

EC European Commission

Edina a national data centre based in Edinburgh University, mainly funded by *Jisc*

Emulation adapts a computer environment so that it can render a software artefact as if it were running on its original environment

Emulation framework a framework that offers emulation services for digital preservation

Encapsulation a process where digital objects are captured with information necessary to interpret them

ENSURE Enabling kNowledge Sustainability Usability and Recovery for Economic value, an *EC*-funded project

EPOCH European Network of Excellence in Open Cultural Heritage

EPSRC Engineering and Physical Sciences Research Council, UK

EU European Union

FOAF Friend of a Friend, machine-readable ontology describing persons

FRBR Functional Requirements for Bibliographic Records

GD-ROM Giga Disc Read Only Memory, proprietary optical storage medium for the game console Sega Dreamcast

GIF Graphic Interchange Format, an image which typically uses *lossy compression*

GIS Geographical Information System, a system that processes mapping and data together

HATII Humanities Advanced Technology and Information Institute at Glasgow University

HDD Hard Disk Drive

HEI Higher Education Institution

HTML Hypertext Markup Language, a format used to present text on the world wide web

ICA International Council on Archives

ICOM International Council of Museums

ICOMOS International Council on Monuments and Sites

IGDA International Game Developers Association

IIPC International Internet Preservation Consortium

Incremental a project funded by *Jisc* at *HATII* and Cambridge University

Ingest the process of turning an *SIP* into an *AIP*, i.e. putting data into a digital archive

ISO International Organization for Standardization, a body that promotes standards

Jisc Joint Information Systems Committee of the Higher Education Funding Councils

JPEG Joint Photographic Experts Group, a format for digital photographs which is *lossy*

JPEG 2000 a revision of the *JPEG* format which can use *lossless compression*

KB Koninklijke Bibliotheek, national library of the Netherlands, partner in *KEEP* and *APARSEN*; *APA* home to *LIBER and NCDD*

KEEP Keeping Emulation Environments Portable, an *EC*-funded project to develop *emulation* services to run on a virtual machine

KVL King's Visualisation Lab

LC Library of Congress

LCD Liquid Crystal Display

LED Light Emitting Diode

LIBER a network of European Research Libraries involved in *APARSEN* and *AP*, offices at the *KB*

LIDAR Light Detection and Ranging, an optical remote sensing technology used to measure properties of a target using light or laser.

LiWa Living Web Archives, an *EC*-funded project which developed web archiving tools

LOCKSS Lots of Copies Keeps Stuff Safe, a *DP* principle made into a toolkit for e-journal preservation, see *UKLA*

LOD Linked Open Data

Lossless compression a mechanism for reducing file sizes that retains all original data

Lossy compression a mechanism for reducing file sizes which typically discards data

MANS Media Art Notation System

Memento an innovative tool which allows time based discovery of web pages, winner of *DPA* 2010

METS Metadata Encoding and Transmission Standard, a standard for presenting metadata

Migration the process of moving data from one format to another

MP3 digital audio format (standing for both MPEG-1 or MPEG-2 Audio Layer III)

NARA US National Archives and Records Administration

NCDD Dutch national digital preservation coalition, closely aligned with *APA, DPC* and *Nestor* and hosted by *KB*

NDAD UK National Digital Archive of Datasets, formerly funded by *TNA* and operated by *ULCC*

NDIIPP National Digital Information Infrastructure and Preservation Programme, a major programme from the *LC*

Nestor German network of expertise in digital preservation, closely aligned to *APA* and *NCDD*

NRW North Rhine-Westphalia, state of Germany

OAI-ORE Open Archives Initiative Object Reuse and Exchange, a standard for description and exchange of web resources.

OAI-PMH Open Archives Initiative Protocol for Metadata Harvesting

OAIS Open Archival Information System, a reference model describing a digital archive

OCLC Online Computer Library Center, Inc., a US-based library and research group

OMII-UK an open-source organization that empowers the UK research community by providing software for use in all disciplines of research

Open source software in which the underlying code is available for free

OPF Open Planets Foundation, a membership organization which sustains outputs from the *PLANETS* project

OSS Open Source Software

Paradata information about human processes of understanding and interpretation of data objects, e.g. descriptions stored within a structured dataset of how evidence was used to interpret an artefact

PARSE.INSIGHT an *EC*-funded project that developed a roadmap for *DP* infrastructure in Europe

PDF Portable Document Format, a format for producing and sharing documents

PDF/A a version of the *PDF* standard intended for archives

PLANETS a project funded by the *EC* to develop a suite of *DP* tools including *PLATO*, now maintained by *OPF*

PLATO a *preservation planning* tool which was created by the *PLANETS* project

PNM Preservation Network Model

POCOS Preservation Of Complex Objects Symposia, a *Jisc*-funded project which

organized a series of three symposia on preservation of Visualizations and Simulations; Software Art; and Gaming Environments and Virtual Worlds in 2011–12

PREMIS Preservation Metadata: Information Strategies, a metadata standard

Preservation planning defining a series of preservation actions to address an identified risk for a given set of *digital objects*

PrestoPRIME an *EC*-funded project which develops tools and services for the preservation of digital audiovisual content

PRONOM a database of file formats with notes on associated issues, used with *DROID*

PROTAGE Preservation organizations using tools in agent environments, an *EC*-funded project

PSD Adobe PhotoShop file format

RCAHMS The Royal Commission on the Ancient and Historical Monuments of Scotland

RCAHMW The Royal Commission on the Ancient and Historical Monuments of Wales

RCUK Research Councils UK

RDF Resource Description Framework

RIN Research Information Network, a group that studies and reports on research needs

RLG Research Libraries Group, the US research group that produced *TDR*, now part of *OCLC*

RLUK Research Libraries UK

SaaS Software as a Service, architecture whereby software is managed remotely by a service provider (see also *Cloud*)

SCAPE Scalable Preservation Environments, an *EC*-funded project developing scalable preservation actions

SHAMAN Sustaining Heritage Access through Multivalent Archiving, an *EC*-funded project

SIARD Software-Independent Archiving of Relational Databases

Significant properties a concept whereby identifying the most important elements of a file will aid preservation

SIP Submission Information Package, data received into an *OAIS*

SKOS Simple Knowledge Organization System, specifications on a knowledge organization system, developed by *W3C*

SPEQS Significant Properties Editing and Querying for Software

SSMM Software Sustainability Maturity Model

STFC Science and Technology Facilities Council, UK

STM Science, Technology and Medicine, a major area of publishing, sometimes meaning the International Association of Scientific, Technical and Medical Publishers

SWISH joint venture between *RCAHMS* and *RCAHMW* to provide digital services, including long term preservation

TDR Trusted Digital Repository, a standard which characterizes 'trust' in a digital archive

TIFF Tagged Image File Format, a common format for images, typically *lossless*

TIMBUS an *EC*-funded project which is investigating the preservation of online services

TNA The National Archives, UK

TOTEM Trustworthy Online Technical Environment Metadata Database

TRAC Trusted Repository Audit and Certification, a toolkit for auditing a digital repository

UBS Universal Serial Bus

UKDA UK Data Archive University of Essex, a digital archive for social and economic data

UKLA UK *LOCKSS* Alliance, a service of *Edina* which offers e-journal preservation

UKWAC UK Web Archiving Consortium

ULCC University of London Computer Centre, host of *NDAD* and creators of *DPTP*

UMD Universal Media Disc, proprietary *CD-ROM* format of Sony Computer Entertainment

UML an industry standard for visualization, specification construction and documentation of artefacts of software systems

UNESCO United Nations Educational, Scientific and Cultural Organization: an agency of the United Nations supporting programmes to promote education, media and communication, the arts, etc.

VFX visual effects

VHS Video Home System, videocassette recording technology

Virtualization creation of a virtual rather than an actual instance of software or hardware (see also *Emulation*)

VRML Virtual Reality Modelling Language, file format for representing 3D graphics

W3C World Wide Web Consortium

WF4EVER Advanced Workflow Preservation Technologies for Enhanced Science, an *EC*-funded project

WinUAE Amiga emulator supporting 5.25" and 3.5" double density disks and 3.5" high density floppy disks

XML Extensible Markup Language, a widely used format for encoding information

Introduction

Janet Delve and David Anderson

Future Proof Computing Group, School of Creative Technologies,
University of Portsmouth, UK

The need to preserve complex digital objects

The latest stage (2010s) in the digital revolution has taken society to a new level in the 'information age', with the proliferation of social networking, Cloud computing, tablet computers and smartphones. Digital technologies are now truly affecting all walks of life: personal, social, business, academic, political, technological, etc. One wonders whether even Alan Mathison Turing (1912–54), the computing pioneer who first set down the range of possible uses for computers, could or would have anticipated their present ubiquity. Whilst memory institutions try to come to grips with preserving arguably 'more standard' digital material such as electronic records, e-books and e-journals from the business and academic communities, personal digital data is increasing at such a rate that it is likely to outstrip 'standard' archived material. The Digital Lives project neatly summarizes the situation:

> With society and humanity facing some very demanding challenges and changes in the coming years and decades it is imperative that analysis of the way people live their lives in relation to their cultural, social and natural environments can be conducted regularly and systematically, based on reliable sources of personal information – obtained and used ethically and legally with the full and ongoing support of participating individuals. Life information promises to be an invaluable resource in monitoring the natural environment, in capturing historical events and precedents as witnessed by people everywhere, and in comprehensive recording of literary, artistic, socio-political and scientific endeavour and enlightenment. At the

same time it represents a possible emancipation of people generally, allowing interested individuals of the digital populace to have their personal and family memories, creativity and unfolding lives, acknowledged as a persistent personal archive and through lasting digital objects.

John et al. (2010, vi)

The exhibition on Pompeii and Herculaneum at the British Museum in 2013 highlights the reality that we are indebted to the fact that we have a first-hand account of the eruption of Vesuvius recorded by Pliny, which has proved a seminal analysis of such events for posterity. Will we be so fortunate with today's digital historical, environmental and cultural heritage? Will the archaeological 3D representations that are fundamental to today's world be extant for future societies? For not only is digital material and accompanying technology seemingly omnipresent, it is also developing at an increasingly rapid rate, and it is becoming ever more complex. So how do we approach the analysis of such seemingly impenetrable material?

The preservation of such complex materials and the environments associated with them presents the digital preservation (DP) community in general and the Jisc community in particular with considerable intellectual and logistical challenges. While many of the techniques that have been developed within the context of migration-based DP approaches, where digital objects are migrated from one computer platform or file format to another, are of continuing value, others cannot be applied so well, given the extra complexity presented by, for example, interactive videogames. Recent work undertaken in the Planets and KEEP projects has shown that the problems involved in preserving such materials and their associated environments, while substantial, are by no means intractable.

An essential first step when considering the nature of complex digital objects is to recognize that there are *multiple layers of difficulty* encountered when attempting to analyse them. These layers could be superficially likened to Georg Cantor's 'levels of infinity'[1] in terms of mapping out the size of the problem space to be tackled. The first 'level of infinity' is that of scale. How do we try to preserve an interactive virtual world such as World of Warcraft, which has been played by millions of players in several continents over many years? 'Big data' is now a term on everybody's lips, defined by Gartner[2] as 'high-volume, high-velocity and high-variety information assets that demand cost-effective, innovative forms of information processing for enhanced insight and decision making'. How do public or private archives begin to tackle the gargantuan quantities of data involved?

The second 'level of infinity' is that of detail: the problem of drilling down through many layers of technical items which have various levels of interconnectedness, both within digital objects themselves and also with their technical environments. An example of such a challenge is that of using binary translation and virtualization to preserve software art and videogames, a subject investigated by Konstantelos (2010) under the aegis of the European Commission (EC) Planets project[3], where running interactive digital art using both emulation and virtualization techniques was examined in depth. The emulation process involves creating software that will emulate – that is, function the same as – hardware functions. In some cases software that has become obsolete is emulated as well. Using emulation to preserve videogames was also the subject of a broad, systematic, in-depth study in the EC KEEP project[4] (Pinchbeck et al., 2009).

Determining significant properties of digital objects encompasses both levels of infinity: detail and scale. The Planets project played an important role in both conducting and disseminating research in this area (Dappert and Farquhar, 2009) which involves recording each aspect of a complex digital object and then developing ontologies of significant properties. The issue of scale crops up again when carrying out emulation, as in practice it necessitates mapping out the necessary hardware, software, middleware, etc. that makes up the technical environment of each complex digital object. The work in Planets to characterize digital objects (Thaller, 2009), and the technical environment modelling activity (TOTEM) in KEEP thus represent important aspects of the state of the art in this problem space, and have provided a firm foundation from which to research the area further. So, from this springboard, how do we start to tackle the task of analysing the complex digital object *per se*?

Background to POCOS

First, there is the need to recognize the fact that these complex digital objects are used by a wide variety of stakeholders coming from a plethora of different user communities, which may or may not have any experience of digital preservation. Given the ubiquity of digital material outlined above, it clearly is not possible to research every possible type of object, so some realistic scope had to be determined. The starting point for the Jisc-funded POCOS project was thus to investigate the preservation of three distinct types/domains of complex digital object:

1   Simulations and visualizations
2   Software art
3   Gaming environments and virtual worlds.

The remit of the project encompassed exploring with international experts the research results achieved so far for each of these types/domains; presenting coherent pathfinder solutions; and clearly signposting areas where work remains to be done. A further step was to synthesize key findings across all three areas and emphasize synergies that can be built upon, and to disseminate these to the various stakeholder communities. These were the principal objectives that POCOS addressed, with the POCOS partners being well placed to tackle the problem space: the University of Portsmouth as overall co-ordinator, bringing research and technical input from KEEP; the British Library, supplying project management and research expertise from Planets; King's Virtualisation Laboratory, bringing specialist visualization and simulation knowledge and experience; and The Humanities Advanced Technology & Information Institute, contributing their specialist software art expertise from Planets.

So, POCOS brought together the leading researchers and practitioners in each field to present their findings, identify key unsolved problems, and map out the future research agenda for the preservation of complex digital materials and their related environments, in a series of three symposia presented across the UK:

*   Simulations and Visualisations, organized by the King's Virtualisation Laboratory (KVL) at King's College London on 16 and 17 June 2011
*   Software Art, organized by The Humanities Advanced Technology & Information Institute (HATII), the University of Glasgow, at the Lighthouse, Glasgow, on 11 and 12 October 2011
*   Gaming Environments and Virtual Worlds, organized by the Future Proof Computing Group, the University of Portsmouth, at the Novotel Hotel, Cardiff, on 26 and 27 January 2012.

Most importantly, the vehicle for these investigations was the *symposium*: a forum in which experts can share ideas and concepts. So POCOS did not start with a firm notion of a complex digital object, the idea being that the definition of such terms would evolve over the life of POCOS, and indeed are presented in the pathfinder solutions at the end of this book.

The fundamental task to be faced during these symposia lay in presenting specialist material of great technological, organizational and semantic complexity in a lucid, cogent, relevant and approachable manner, so as to engage UK higher education institution (HEI) researchers and practitioners in a wide variety of disciplines, as well as reaching those further afield in, for example, commerce, industry, cinema, government, games and films classification boards, and healthcare. There was also the added concern that the specialists in each field may not necessarily be aware of general trends in DP, and vice versa. Similarly, any differences in terminology needed to be carefully addressed. Hence, clarity of expression and good communication was paramount throughout all the exchanges and discussions.

To this end, a series of three e-books, one for the output of each symposium plus any additional salient material, is available from the POCOS website.[5] This book is the final compendium book covering all three symposia, together with a set of pathfinder solutions.

The nature of the objects in the three domains

First, it is important to note that simulations and visualizations are in a somewhat different category from software-based art, gaming environments and virtual worlds. The last two are each cognate disciplines in their own right: software-based art has dedicated artists, museums, techniques and commissioning procedures, and gaming environments and virtual worlds have their own games developers, games museums, conferences for the gaming community, etc. Simulations and visualizations, on the other hand, are generic techniques or outputs that are used in many different fields. The predominant field in which they are considered in POCOS is archaeology, with the King's Visualisation Laboratory, King's College London, leading the investigations. However, there are many other fields where such techniques and outputs are vital, and one suggestion that arose at the end of the first symposium was the use of simulations and visualizations in film, which led to Chapter 21 on preserving film animations. There is one important topic, however, that arises from considering the items from an archaeological perspective: that of the *hybrid digital object*,[5] part-artefact and part-simulation/visualization.

A similar issue arises in software art, owing to the fact that many of the art works are *composite hybrid digital objects*, being part physical and part digital, thus compounding the tasks for the DP community to take into account. For example, a software art work may be based on the movement of live snails (and this work has a truly long shelf life), or on the fluctuations of the stock exchange. So the work comprises complex elements linked together by mathematical or physical calculations, all of which must be meticulously preserved to retain the cultural and technological context of the work. A consideration that is unique for software art is the value aspect. Since there is no distinction between master copies and any others in software art, the problem of a museum commissioning and preserving *the* art work is contentious, to say the least. It is clear that artist, technology provider and curator need to work together right from the earliest moments of a commissioned software art work's life to ensure that steps are in place for its long-term preservation.

The preservation issues for the games community are different again. Only very recently have games been officially recognized as part of our cultural heritage, so up to now there have not been the official links in place between memory institutions and gaming communities. Thankfully this is changing, and more and more national libraries are starting to archive games and virtual worlds, and indeed a dedicated association, EFGAMP, the European Federation of Game Archives, Museums and Preservation projects[6] was set up in April 2013 to this end. The French National Library has been collecting computer games for many years, and has a sizeable collection. Its work has been really important in preserving games from France and beyond. The Royal Library, Copenhagen, Denmark, also has a sizeable games collection and the British Library holds games collections in its personal digital archives. Previously the only other groups leading games preservation were the games fans and developers themselves, and they did a good job of creating emulators for platforms in order to keep playing old games. However, there were some particular issues facing games preservation that were troublesome.

Particular problems revolve around the area of intellectual property rights (IPR) that leave some games 'orphaned', with no one knowing who owns them and thus how they can legally be preserved. IPR is even more difficult for virtual worlds, where permission is needed from the users to preserve their avatars. Not surprisingly, this is not readily forthcoming, and so at best, it is only possible to preserve incomplete virtual worlds. Another pressing topic is the technical complexity of the games and virtual worlds and their attendant environments. Saving the many parts of these games (mods, cracks, etc.), plus details of their computing environments so that they can be emulated or virtualized in future, poses a significant challenge. The founding of the dedicated New Media Museum, UK, has been a real boon in this respect, with their games environments and associated material, as has the Computer Games Museum in Berlin, Germany, which allows access to old games via the KEEP Emulation Framework.

All three domains thus have their particular challenges and ways of addressing them. This book has been put together in such a way that the synergies between them are drawn together so as to provide the reader with generic guidance, with case studies, etc., highlighting specialist problem areas.

The book's contents
Part 1: Why and what to preserve: creativity versus preservation

For many cultural heritage domains, it is often not clear that it is necessary to preserve digital material. With complex digital objects, it is frequently the case that preserving them is passed over as being just too difficult to contemplate. The domains and areas covered in this book encompass an interesting span in this respect: with simulations and visualizations, and computer games, it is not clear why or what to preserve. In summary, the opening chapter here eloquently elucidates *why* it is important to preserve such multifaceted digital artefacts, and the second chapter then leads us into considering what *can* be preserved. For digital art, the imperative to preserve is recognized, owing to the need to keep exhibiting the art work, and also for the conserving institution to preserve the art work's value. The discourse here is around the impact on creativity of the process of preservation. The third and fourth chapters tackle such matters from the digital art standpoint. Each chapter provides thought-provoking arguments that are relevant for general and specific audiences, and as a whole, this section provides a general introduction to the raison d'être of the book.

Dr Dan Pinchbeck of thechineseroom is a leader in games preservation, as well as being an award-winning games developer for *Dear Esther*. In his other life as Reader in Computer Games at the University of Portsmouth, Dan played a large part in shaping the program for the Gaming Environments and Virtual Worlds symposium. In Chapter 1 'Standing on the shoulders of heavily armed giants – why history matters for game development', he traces the history of first-person shooter games and highlights why games history is important for games developers. He then draws attention to the main problems facing games preservation today.

In Chapter 2, 'Archaeology versus anthropology: what can truly be preserved?', Professor Richard R. Bartle of the University of Essex examines the real difficulties of preserving virtual-world inhabitants as opposed to their environments, and emphasizes the need to gather these social aspects of the data right now.

Professor Simon Biggs, an art historian formerly working with software art at the Edinburgh College of Art, observes that for several decades now, redundancy has not been an unhappy coincidence. On the contrary, for some it has become part of a creative strategy and even a creative force for artists who have questioned permanence. In some cases transience is a deliberate attempt to subvert the art market or simplistic notions of value. So, he posits in Chapter 3, 'Make or break? Concerning the value of redundancy as a creative strategy', that crudely applied preservation actions may flout the creative process. In Chapter 4, 'Between code and space: the challenges of preserving complex digital creativity in contemporary arts practice', Michael Takeo Magruder of the Centre for Computing in the Humanities, King's College London, introduces art that takes real-time data and turns it into dynamic and constantly changing representations. In this context the software is only one part of an installation which is embedded in many other components, and has sophisticated interdependencies, sometimes involving distributed sources.

Part 2: The memory institution/data archival perspective

This section takes us from the general 'why and what to preserve' to the more specific 'how are memory institutions tackling the preservation of complex digital objects?' and comprises chapters for various subject areas delineating the preservation approach taken. In Chapter 5, 'Preservation of digital objects at the Archaeology Data Service', Jenny Mitcham considers the issues surrounding the preservation of hybrid digital objects and then delineates the practices and standards adopted at the Archaeology Data Service, where she was previously employed. In Chapter 6, 'Preserving games for museum collections and public display: the National Videogame Archive', Tom Woolley, previously Curator of New Media, National Media Museum, Professor James Newman, Bath Spa University, and Iain Simons, Nottingham Trent University, describe the scope, current work, holdings and access policy of the National Videogame Archive (NVA), and they reflect on proven solutions and plans for overcoming the challenges surrounding videogame preservation and display in the future.

In Chapter 7, 'Bridging the gap in digital art preservation: interdisciplinary reflections on authenticity, longevity and potential collaborations', Dr Perla Innocenti, from the School of Culture and Creative Arts, University of Glasgow, discusses issues of authenticity, longevity and collaboration in preserving digital art from an interdisciplinary perspective, explaining how embracing variability in preservation approaches can match the intrinsic variability and dynamic authenticity of digital arts. In Chapter 8, 'Laying a trail of breadcrumbs – preparing the path for preservation', Drew Baker of the KVL and David Anderson of the Future Proof Computing Group (FPCG), University of Portsmouth, set the scene for digital preservation from the visualization/simulation perspective.

Part 3: Digital preservation approaches, practice and tools

This section is split into three parts and provides practical details: the technical 'how-to' of preserving complex digital material. The first part is 'A good place to start: software preservation'. Complex digital objects comprise multiple pieces of software in various forms and guises, so a thorough examination of preserving software is of fundamental importance. Chapter 9, 'Digital preservation and curation: the danger of overlooking software', by Neil Chue Hong, Director of the Software Sustainability Institute, and Chapter 10, 'How do I know that I have preserved software?', by Dr Brian Matthews, Dr Arif Shaon and Esther Conway of the STFC Rutherford Appleton Laboratory, both come from presentations at a Jisc seminar in February 2011 on preserving software. They provide both an excellent introduction to digital preservation in general as well as solid guidelines for all stages of preserving software, including case studies. In particular, they provide a solid foundation in this respect: a thorough, comprehensive analysis of how to categorize and then preserve software.

The second part, 'Tools and techniques', covers approaches and tools used to preserve visualizations, simulations and 3D objects. As such objects can be present in archaeology, digital art or computer games, this area will be of general interest to many readers. Chapter 11, 'Digital preservation strategies for visualizations and simulations', by Janet Delve of the FPCG, Dr Hugh Denard, previously from the Centre for Computing in the Humanities, King's College London, and Dr William Kilbride, Executive Director, Digital Preservation Coalition, looks at DP techniques for preserving visualizations and simulations. The main theme that emerged in this chapter was the acknowledgement that emulation has now come of age as a suitable DP strategy to tackle preserving complex digital objects. In Chapter 12, 'The ISDA tools: preserving 3D digital content', Dr Kenton McHenry, Rob Kooper, Luigi Marini and Michael Ondrejcek from the National Center for Supercomputing Applications, University of Illinois at Urbana-Champaign, explore a plethora of cutting-edge tools and techniques in terms of their suitability for preserving 3D visualizations and simulations.

The third part, 'Metadata, paradata and documentation', encompasses these key issues for preserving complex digital material. The chapters in this section cover metadata and documentation for performance, digital art, computer games, and visualizations and simulations. In Chapter 13, 'Ecologies of research and performance: preservation challenges in the London Charter', Dr Hugh Denard elucidates the theory and practice of the London Charter – a fairly recent approach to preserving visualizations that was spearheaded by KVL and others, and that has now become standard. In Chapter 14, 'A tangled web: metadata and problems in game preservation', Dr Jerome McDonough of the Graduate School of Library & Information Science, University of Illinois at Urbana-Champaign, examines the unique challenges that games preservation presents as identified by the Preserving Virtual Worlds team from their work on metadata and web ontology language (OWL) ontologies. In Chapter 15, 'Metadata for preserving computing environments', Dr Angela Dappert, of the Digital Preservation Coalition TIMBUS project, continues the metadata challenges theme and takes a broader look at metadata needed for preserving business environments, including that of the games industry.

In Chapter 16, 'Preserving games environments via TOTEM, KEEP and

Bletchley Park', Janet Delve, Dr Dan Pinchbeck and Winfried Bergmeyer of the Computer Games Museum, Berlin, discuss the recent TOTEM technical registry work carried out in the KEEP project. The chapter outlines how TOTEM can be accessed to ascertain computing environment metadata for PC games and games consoles, and how the KEEP Emulation Framework, developed by the Koninklijke Bibliotek (KB – Dutch National Library) and Tessella, is being deployed at the Computer Games Museum to run old games via emulation. Attention is drawn to the wealth of computing environment material available at computer history museums worldwide, prompting closer collaboration with colleagues from this domain. In Chapter 17, 'Documenting the context of software art works through social theory: towards a vocabulary for context classification', Dr Leo Konstantclos, University of Melbourne, previously HATII, looks at documenting the context of software art works through social theory.

Part 4: Case studies

The case studies cover a variety of particular issues from real cases in archaeology, digital art and animation. In Chapter 18, 'The Villa of Oplontis: a "born digital" project', Professor John R. Clarke of the University of Texas at Austin enumerates the issues surrounding the preservation of hybrid digital objects in the field of archaeology. In Chapter 19, 'Preservation of complex cultural heritage objects – a practical implementation', Daniel Pletinckx, Director of Visual Dimension bvba, explores the DP difficulties faced by cultural heritage institutions in the same field. In Chapter 20, 'In homage of change', Vicky Isley and Paul Smith of boredomresearch note that the interactions and interdependencies between digital art elements are not always planned and not always obvious at the point of creation. For example, moving software from one processor to another can change the temporal performance of an art work dramatically. Paul Charisse is a Senior Lecturer in Animation, University of Portsmouth, and has worked on animation for the Harry Potter films and as part of the animation team behind Gollum in *The Lord of the Rings*. In Chapter 21, 'Archiving software and content in visual film effects: an insider's perspective', he gives us a glimpse of the difficulties peculiar to preserving animations in the film industry. Daisy Abbott of the Glasgow School of Art considers the topic of 'preserving interaction' in Chapter 22. Interaction amplifies the preservation challenge, especially when it comes to setting the extents of any preservation plan. She observes that interaction is at the core of much software art, and therefore there is no canonical form to be preserved as there might be with a dataset or a document. The extents of preservation actions necessary to protect such art works are thus unclear.

Part 5: A legal perspective

This section covers legal and security issues which are salient for all areas of DP. In Chapter 23, 'The impact of European copyright legislation on digital preservation activity: lessons learned from legal studies commissioned by the KEEP project', David Anderson summarizes the findings from the layman's guide to the KEEP legal studies on how the law affects DP issues surrounding media transfer and emulation for multimedia works. In Chapter 24, 'Issues of information security applicable to the preservation of digital objects', Andrew Ball, former head of IT Audit, the Audit Commission, and Clive Billenness of the FPCG consider the topic of information in the DP context.

Part 6: Pathfinder conclusions

In Chapter 25, 'Pathfinder conclusions', Janet Delve and David Anderson put forward concluding statements and a roadmap for each of the three key areas.

Notes

1   Developed at the end of the nineteenth century.
2   www.gartner.com/it-glossary/big-data.
3   www.planets-project.eu.
4   www.keep-project.eu/ezpub2/index.php. Keeping Emulation Environments Portable (KEEP) is a medium-scale research project which started on 1 February 2009 and is co-financed by the EC's 7th Framework Programme (ICT-3-4.3 Digital libraries and technology-enhanced learning priority).
5   www.pocos.org/index.php/publications.php.
6   www.efgamp.eu.

References

Dappert, A. and Farquhar, A. (2009) *Significance is in the Eye of the Stakeholder*, paper presented at ECDL 2009, www.planets-project.eu/docs/papers/Dappert_Significant_Characteristics_ECDL2009.pdf.

John, J. L., Rowlands, I., Williams, P. and Dean, K. (2010) *Digital Lives: personal digital archives for the 21st century: in initial synthesis* (Project Report), AHRC Digital Lives.

Konstantelos, L. (2010) *Preservation of Dynamic and Interactive Content by use of Binary Translation and Virtualisation – a methodology for experimentation*, HATII, University of Glasgow.

Pinchbeck, D., Anderson, D., Delve, J., Ciuffreda, A., Alemu, G. and Lange, A. (2009) *Emulation as a Strategy for the Preservation of Games: the KEEP project: breaking new ground: innovation in games, play, practice and theory*, paper presented at DiGRA 2009, Brunel University.

Thaller, M. (2009) *The eXtensible Characterisation Languages – XCL*, Hamburg, Verlag Dr Kovac.

PART 1

Why and what to preserve: creativity versus preservation

Standing on the shoulders of heavily armed giants – why history matters for game development

Dan Pinchbeck[1]

Creative Director, thechineseroom, Brighton, UK

Abstract

I examine the evolution of first-person shooter and role-playing games and consider how over the past 30 years the two genres have influenced one another. I trace their development from initial mainframe-based games, though their growth into multiple-player versions and finally the creation of immersive virtual reality environments encountered in current products, highlighting key moments in their evolution. I consider the motivations from the position of different people with an interest in computer games for seeking to preserve them in view of their cultural significance. Finally, I identify the weaknesses in the current arrangements for preservation and advocate a more structured approach in the future.

Introduction

When I was invited to attend the Preservation of Complex Objects Symposia (POCOS), my brief was to speak from a developer's perspective rather than that of an academic. I should explain, however, that I started out as a member of an academic research team considering matters relating to games history. Initially we focused on games history and tried to identify games design spaces which were not being exploited by the games industry.

In our role as academics, we were able to use research programmes to explore these topics, without the pressure that the games industry is normally under to produce a commercially successful game. Researchers have an ability to push the boundaries of design, as they have different objectives, and the production of 'interesting' data would still be considered a successful outcome, even if the game 'failed' as a cultural artefact. Fortunately, however, the game which we produced, *Dear Esther*,[2] also achieved praise from the games community leading on to a commercial release.

My topic here is to consider why games history and preservation are of great importance to contemporary games developers and what I, as a developer, would like to become available.

When *Dear Esther* was released, it received a high score from *Edge* magazine, but I noted one interesting comment from a reviewer who said that 'Piece by piece "Dear Esther" makes you forget all you have learned about games and reminds you of a time when genres were still young'.

A first-person shooter perspective

This is interesting in the context of *Dear Esther* which is a first-person game in which there is a direct perceptual mapping between the player and the avatar, and the player sees through the avatar's eyes, with no character on screen. This is a genre of game which is most associated with combat-style games involving (usually gun-) battles with various types of hostile creature within a labyrinth. Examples of this include *Doom*[3] and *Wolfenstein*.[4] It was here that the template for what first-person gaming could be like was first defined.

I would like to consider the history of how first-person games have developed. A debate has arisen about whether *Dear Esther* is an 'art game' or a logical extension of first-person shooter games. We, as the authors, have always seen *Dear Esther* as a natural progression from the original first-person shooter games, even though it does not have weapons, gameplay, action or a story. To understand the lineage and evolutionary history of how these games have developed is important for achieving an understanding of the future development path of these types of game.

For a developer, understanding of games history is also commercially important, because understanding what has proven successful (and unsuccessful) in the past will assist in future development. However radical a game like *Dear Esther* might initially feel, many of the core design challenges were defined – and solved – early in the evolution of the genre.

The earliest first-person shooter computer game was *Maze War*,[5] developed by Steve Colley and first released in 1973, and all the elements of contemporary first-person games can be found there at the very outset of the genre.

The game has a simple wire-frame maze which operates in a single horizontal plane in which players interact and shoot one another. All first-person (and also many third-person) games have their genesis here. And interestingly this game became multi-user almost immediately. Given the strength of multiple-player gaming worldwide, one can see that the concept of multiple-players interacting across a network was already present in *Maze War* right at the outset of computer games. Because game technology initially outpaced home networking technology, interest in non-arcade-based multiple-player gaming tailed off for a long time. Nevertheless, the core principle was established at the beginning that with first-person shooter games, players would play with each other.

When one considers analogies in other types of design, for example any kind of simple household object, even when the object diversifies or new functionality is added, by tracing back to the core function one can still understand something about how the object was developed and what its constraints are. The same is true for games. The fact that the original design was for one-to-one or one-to-many gaming, and not just a lone human player versus a computer, is really important to what one understands about the game. The whole environment is designed to create uncertainty, as the player has limited knowledge and does not know what they will confront next. The key principle is *immediacy* and this is essential to the gaming experience. This is intimately related to the inherent unpredictability of human players.

The foundation of first-person shooter games as a popular genre really began with *Doom* in 1993. This game is very similar in nature to *Maze War*. While the graphical appearance of the environment and the avatars is far more sophisticated than in *Maze War*, the gameplay is almost identical. *Doom* followed an earlier game called *Wolfenstein 3D*, itself a remake of a side-scrolling 1982 stealth game called *Castle Wolfenstein*, where the player tried to escape by hiding and moving bodies out of the way, but not shooting very much. This also replicated the core game experience of *Maze War*, but with added excitement provided by the addition of Adolf Hitler as a character, along with large guns and other violent accoutrements.

An emotional framework

Doom depended on state-of-the art technological knowledge, with which the developers combined virtual reality and graphical advances with classic 1970s arcade games. When I recently interviewed John Carmack (co-founder of id Software), he said of himself and the writing team:

> We were not innovators, we were vandals. We looked at what academics were doing with virtual reality and simulation and it was really beautiful, but it was also really slow. We said 'let's just rip the guts out of it and make it run really, really fast'. So we vandalized academic simulation research to get something which ran as fast as Space Invaders.
>
> DOOM (2013)[6]

Thus, technology provided an emotional framework for a human experience.

Doom is also significant because although the storyline is very simple (demons from Hell invade a space station), it has very significant content. The authors established a design principle that everything in the game existed purely to support gameplay. Thus the demons do not possess complex artificial intelligence, they simply charge and attack. There are no complex puzzles to solve in *Doom* – the player simply moves around the game shooting at things. Therefore, the content was pared down to enable the gameplay to be extremely fast paced, while the story meshed and supported the emotional content of the game. Many similar games followed *Doom*, but they are all almost identical apart from higher graphic resolution.

Interestingly this genre missed the 1980s almost entirely. During that decade, most of the first-person games were role-playing games with slower play. As a result, the emotional intensity of the game-playing experience is different, although game designers recognized that within the notion of first-person play there was 'something' which they wished to retain and use. And at the core of the development of the first-person game was the unique experience given to the player when the perception of the avatar is mapped to their own.

The emotional experience is changed when a game is perceived through the senses of the avatar. There is a sense of immediacy, and the gameplay is highly immersive. The game designer can foreshorten the player's natural sense of perception so they are unable to predict what will occur next, thereby heightening tension – first-person games lend themselves to tension like no other gaming medium. These games can also contain enormous drama of scale, with play moving from narrow corridors to immense vistas and back again. Although early role-playing games were very slow, what was understood was the unique emotional relationship between the player and the world that this genre of game creates.

First-person shooter (FPS) and role-playing game (RPG) crossovers

Moving into the late 1990s, role-playing games fell into the background for a while until a new set of titles appeared, which, like *Doom*, capitalized on the immediacy of the action and the emotional journey which the player experienced. These new titles also considered what had been lost through the simplification of the playing experience in games like *Doom*, and whether it was possible to recombine the 'configurative' activities from role-playing games in order to exploit the strengths of two different genres of game and create a new, third one.

This led to the birth of what are referred to as 'FPS/RPG crossovers', which continue to develop the relationship of the player with the world. These combine elements of arcade game play and configurative game play. The power of these games comes not just from the gameplay itself (which often retains much from the 1980s games) but also the scale and depth of the world which these offer. An excellent example of this scale and depth is to be found in *Skyrim*.[7]

It is difficult to decide whether to link *Skyrim* to role-playing games or to games like *Doom*. Even though *Skyrim* is a fantasy, role-playing game, the violence has been muted. The player does carry a weapon, but is not constantly confronted by opponents to kill, arcade-style. Instead, the game presents the player with a huge world to explore and to 'be' in. The gameplay is associated with the ability to travel around a beautifully rendered world where the player can immerse themself in the 'atmosphere' of the game.

This concept of 'soaking up the atmosphere' is actually fundamental to the genre, dating right back to *Maze War*. It is as much a part of the experience of playing the game to have an emotional reaction to the world of the game as to occupy oneself with pressing buttons on the controller repeatedly. In this genre, one sees a refinement of the concept of 'being in the world'. It is here that games and virtual reality have the greatest degree of crossover between academic and commercial approaches. There is the capacity to insert a player into an artificial environment and for them to have some form of complex emotional experience within it.

This is true even of games which seek to reintroduce more elements of arcade play. A game may even attract criticism in relation to aspects of its gameplay (e.g. unrealistic combat capabilities, flawed artificial intelligence algorithms, poor plot) but still receive positive comments for the overall environment in which it is executed. These criticisms are frequently encountered in first-person games, yet equally often it is observed that the relationship between the player's avatar and the game environment can overcome these apparent design weaknesses.

The birth of contemporary first-person games

One game which might be described as heralding the birth of contemporary first-person games is *Half Life*,[8] which represents a generational shift from *Doom*. Although much of the gameplay is familiar from predecessor games, *Half Life* reflects a greater focus than before on creating a deeper relationship between the player and their environment. 'Cut scenes', which link action scenes together, were discarded. Instead, characters within the world interact with the player, driving the story forwards without breaking play. This encourages the player to engage with the story more deeply if they wish to. Additional minor details are added to the game environment to reflect more closely the way humans acquire information about the world around them. Examples of this are a passenger missing a tram and a vending machine failing to dispense drinks. This approach is more engaging for the player.

While technology was insufficiently advanced for this to be implemented in *Doom*, this new approach also reflects an evolution in the sophistication of design. Awareness of this kind of sophistication is often disregarded outside the community of games designers and specialists when discussing games. These aspects are, however, fundamental to the consideration of the evolution of games. They represent a quantum leap in the conceptualization of this genre of games.

For example, one also sees game designers beginning to explore complex themes from traditional literature. One example of this is *Far Cry 2*,[9] which explicitly frames its action within a reference to Joseph Conrad's novella *Heart of Darkness*. High-culture reference points are being introduced into these games, which permits a new level of discussion about the content of a game, which might otherwise be dismissed as simple, relatively mindless entertainment. In games such as this, literature combines with arcade game play. This approach also makes complex philosophical ideas more accessible. Young teenagers are now being exposed to the works of such media practitioners, authors, film-makers and theorists, from Conrad to Tarkovsky and even Ann Rand.

Pushing the boundaries – thechineseroom

In 2007 we released *Dear Esther* (originally as a *Half Life* 2mod, then as a standalone commercial game in 2012). Although nominated for international games awards, *Dear Esther* has removed elements formerly considered essential to first-person gaming. However, it is observable that while first-person gameplay has seen some refinement and modification over time, the major sophistication that has occurred over the years is that of the relationship between the player and their environment. The core gameplay of earlier games like *Maze War* and *Doom* can still be recognized in modern games; the evolution has really been about the sophistication of game worlds as immersive fictional spaces. Modern games such as *Dear Esther* are a logical extension of this aspect of the history of this genre.

It may appear that these historical issues are only of academic interest. They are, however, very important to game developers. Contemporary game designers should and frequently do consider the roots of elements they are introducing into their new games. Their concerns are twofold:

- Historically does this element work in game play?
- Is this innovation really as innovative as we might first think?

Compared to many other forms of media, game players are phenomenally literate about their subject, to an extent which greatly exceeds that of film and book enthusiasts. Games players have a high degree of awareness and understanding of the technology which enables their experience. Claims by games developers to have innovated in a specific area of play are liable to rapid challenge from within this expert community.

Aside from intellectual property considerations, when designing a game which might exploit others' approaches there are issues both of personal professional pride and reputational impact if similarities are identified. It is therefore important for authors to be aware of their games history not only to seek evidence of prior success of an approach, but also to check whether another author has already written something identical. Today's authors are keen to learn from their predecessors – to stand on the shoulders of giants (heavily armed or not). It is therefore critically important to have access to the history of games.

In addition, from a teaching perspective, it is important that students have awareness of game history, but it is sometimes difficult to gain access to this material. For example, the history of first-person shooter games and that of role-playing games are fundamentally linked. It is even likely that first-person shooter games owe more to role-playing games than to arcade games, although this is often not the primary direction in which one might look. If, therefore, students intend to evolve those genres further, they need to possess a good understanding of the history. This history is, however, hard to access. This is partly because of weaknesses in games preservation.

First, games preservation is largely illegal. There is little formal games preservation, and we are instead reliant on private collectors with 'abandonware' or simply pirated copies of games running under emulation, which itself often relies on illegal, reverse engineered technology. It is therefore hard for an educator to advise students to study a particular game when this might involve them participating in illegal acts and breach of copyright. This may be the only source, however; the alternative is simply accepting knowledge gaps, which is equally unacceptable.

Likewise, games developers are at similar risk if they wish to reference historic material when creating a new game. This contrasts harshly with the situation with books and films, which remain easily accessible. Risks of criminal or civil liability arising from the improper access to historic games material can be a substantial source of concern to games publishers and distributors and so may inhibit commercial development. However, a lack of awareness of design history and inability to preserve older titles also exposes IP owners to increased risk of cloning or uncredited adoption of an older title idea.

Another consideration is not simply the content of the game but also the underlying technology. An example of this is the id Tech engine used to create *Doom*. This was a ground-breaking piece of software that fundamentally impacts on the game *Doom* became, and is therefore fundamental to the genre. In order to best understand the game and its design, I should really seek a detailed understanding about how this engine works. Preservation of the games experience is not sufficient: we should strive to preserve the entire development environment that enabled the experience.

Leadership

There is a need for leadership. There needs to be an alternative to this community-led, semi-legal preservation. Without this community-led approach, the situation today would be dire, with little or no preservation of games material, but it's not enough. Equally, institutions like the National Videogame Archive are working very hard in this area of preservation, but more needs to be done.

I also think that the case is already made that computer games should be preserved as cultural objects. They are items of cultural worth. They are no less part of our cultural heritage than cartoons, movies, music or literature. Computer games are played by millions of people, and they make a considerable contribution to the economy. The most important issue to be considered is how almost three decades of cultural material has become endangered owing to the lack of formal preservation structures, to the extent that those preservation activities which are taking place are frequently illegal.

This demonstrates the importance of initiatives like the POCOS symposia. In my multiple roles of game player, game developer and academic, I need to be able to access games history, to be able to play games dating back to the 1970s, and to understand what techniques and approaches worked and how the build tools worked. Finally, there is a natural human curiosity to understand how things work, and if this curiosity is shared by only a small percentage of gamers in the world, this is still a need common to a very large number of individuals.

Therefore, if preservation is to be applied to different types of object on the basis that there is an identified audience for this material, then there are likely to be many games enthusiasts who will be grateful if they are not compelled to engage in potentially illegal preservation practices in order to engage with their medium.

Notes

1   Thanks here to Clive Billenness, Visiting Research Fellow, Future Proof
    Computing Group, School of Creative Technologies, University of
    Portsmouth, for his support in writing this chapter.
2   http://dear-esther.com.
3   www.idsoftware.com/games/doom/doom-final.
4   www.idsoftware.com/games/wolfenstein/wolf3d.
5   *Maze War* on Xerox Alto–YouTube:
    www.youtube.com/watch?v=7chDIySXK2Q.
6   Doom: Scarydarkfast, Dan Pinchbeck Series: Landmark Video Games, doi:
    http://dx.doi.org/10.3998/lvg.11878639.0001.001, Ann Arbor, MI,
    University of Michigan Press, 2013.
7   www.elderscrolls.com/skyrim.
8   http://planethalflife.gamespy.com/hl.
9   www.ubi.com/US/Games/Info.aspx?pId=5925.

CHAPTER 2

Archaeology versus anthropology: what can truly be preserved?

Richard A. Bartle

Honorary Professor of Computer Game Design,
School of Computer Science and Electronic Engineering,
University of Essex, UK

Introduction

This chapter concerns what it means to 'preserve' a virtual world. Virtual worlds are shared online environments exemplified by *World of Warcraft* (Pardo et al., 2004), which is a game world, and *Second Life* (Rosedale et al., 2003), which is a social world. All virtual worlds bring together a particular collection of six features to create a radically different experience for the player than would be the case if any single one of these features were omitted. These are the features (Bartle, 2003):

1   An automated rule set (the *physics*) enables players to effect changes to the virtual world.
2   Players represent individuals 'in' the virtual world through which they act (their *character* or *avatar*).
3   Interaction with the world takes place in real time.
4   The world is shared, so other players can be encountered in it and the changes made by any one player affect all players.
5   The world is relatively persistent: if you stop playing, the world continues.
6   It is not the real world (i.e. reality)!

Most virtual worlds are game worlds, and as such are often referred to as *massively multiple-player online role-playing games* (MMORPGs, or MMOs for short). Although what I discuss here applies to all virtual worlds, players of game worlds so outnumber players of social worlds that virtual worlds as a genre are usually sold as a form of computer game. This suggests that if we were to preserve them, the techniques used to preserve other types of computer game can readily be applied. As we shall see, however, virtual worlds differ from computer games in some important ways that impact on their preservational demands.

Preservation

There is much to virtual worlds. Before delving into what we should preserve of them and how we should preserve it, we should first consider why we would want to preserve anything at all.

The initial response to the non-expert's question 'Why do we want to preserve X?' is 'So that future generations can learn from X'. Learn *what*, though? There are three basic responses as to what the people of the future can learn from what we present to them through preservation:

1   They can learn about us.
2   They can learn about themselves.
3   They can learn why important things are important.

Put another way: history, literature and art.

History

Historians aim to understand the old meanings of old artefacts – what the past meant to the people of the past. Preservation is important to historians because it gives them a source. From multiple sources, they can reconstruct the past. They can then explain the past in ways relevant to their present. These explanations in turn act as historical documents for the generations of historians that follow. For computer games, the primary artefacts that require preservation are the games themselves.

Suppose a game historian today is playing the decades-old arcade game, *Galaxian* (Sawano et al., 1979). The historian can only imagine what it must have been like to play the game when it first came out,[1] but this *is* actually possible: the historian puts aside his or her present-day self and tries to play as their 'period' self, based on their accumulated knowledge of what the games landscape was like back in 1979. This can help the historian understand what games meant to people back in the day. Strictly speaking, game historians don't *have* to play the games they study, any more than the historians of Ancient Rome have to participate in gladiatorial combat; however, if we preserve the games for them anyway, at least they have the option of trying them out or not.

To preserve a game for use by the historians of the future, the task is similar to that faced by a library in possession of a collection of ancient texts. The physical source is maintained whenever possible, but its content is made available in a more accessible and less fragile form. For example, if a historian today wants to read the Magna Carta, typically they will have no need to touch the actual document – a transcript or a scan will suffice. An examination of the original copy would only be necessitated if the medium itself was the subject of the research, rather than the message (to compare the quality of its vellum to that of other documents of the era, say).

So it is with computer games. The original hardware should be preserved in working order, if at all possible, for the benefit of researchers for whom the hardware is itself their chief focus. Unfortunately, repeated use of aging hardware will inevitably degrade it. Researchers who are primarily interested in the content have no need to use creaking old pieces of electronics, so ought therefore to be provided with a simulation (of the hardware, running the original software) or a facsimile (in which the hardware and software are both non-original, but the content they implement is by and large indistinguishable from the original content). The advantage of digital preservation this way is that if the original form perishes, the copies can live on; this is why we can still read Homer's *Odyssey* today even though the last remaining original copies decayed thousands of years ago.[2]

Literature

Students of literature begin with the fact that a text does not mean today what it meant in the past. They are concerned almost entirely with examination of the content of preserved artefacts, as opposed to the form. When they do look at what an author 'meant' by what was written, it is only as one of many techniques for finding new ways of interpreting the content; the 'real' meaning of the content to the author and the readers of the past is not directly relevant.

The central thrust of this approach is that texts are situated in their historical context but their content is open to new interpretation. Language and symbols change meaning over time. More importantly, *readers* change over time. Jane Austen 2012 is not Jane Austen 1816. The same applies whether the artefact is literature, music, dance – or computer games.

Games studies experts looking at an old computer game aren't trying to extract old meaning from old symbols: they're trying to extract new symbols from it, to which they attribute new meaning. The designer of the game ceded authorial control over his work the moment it was published: it became an artefact, for people in general to interpret how they will. How many children who play Snakes and Ladders either know or care that it's a centuries-old Indian game created to convey the notion of fate? They play it simply because (for them) it's fun. If someone plays a 1985 computer game for fun, does it matter whether it's 1985-player fun? Isn't the fact that it's today-fun more important to that player?

Preservation of games for the benefit of future players is, in this scenario, a case of presenting them with an artefact that was useful in the past in the hope that they can find some use for it in the future. It presents itself as a flawed mirror: the past is like the present, but different in small ways. In interpreting its imperfect reflections, the users of the future notice differences compared to the contemporary reflections they are used to seeing; in reconciling these, they learn more about who they are and about the society in which they live.

In practical terms, this means that content is more important to preserve than form. Physical hardware is only important as an object of fetish, in that its existence as a connection to the past might inspire certain players to take an interest in the historical aspects of the work. However, it should be remembered that for multiple-player games, 'content' doesn't simply mean the embodiment of rules in software: other players are content, too.

Art

The *Mona Lisa*[3] can be looked upon as a document of life in 16th-century Tuscany – that is, from an historical perspective. It can also be seen as an enigmatic image of a beautiful woman, or an admirable work of high craftsmanship – that is, from a literature perspective.

A third way of looking at it is as an expression of artistic intent. In this perspective, the artist is attempting to convey a message through (in the case of *Mona Lisa*) his work. By experiencing the work, an individual can pick up what the artist was trying to say.

Whether a game is old or new, its players can't help but gain some insight into the mind of its designer as they play. The more they play, the more they see how ideas develop and change over time, and pick up signature design tropes; they can tell a Molyneux game from a Meiers game as easily as they can tell a Mozart piece from a Lady Gaga piece. In gaining this understanding, such players are better able to create their own games, should they have something they want to say that they can't express better some other way.

Preserving games is important because it allows the designers and critics of the future to understand how things got to be how they are, so they can better understand the trajectory of where they are going. Only by understanding the rules can you wilfully break them; only by understanding what has been said can you disagree; only by reading can you learn to write.

For a game critic or a game designer of the future, games from the past should be preserved because they are saying something important that can't be separated from what they are. As to what those important things *are*, well you'd have to play the games to find out: that's the point.

Virtual worlds

All this would be fine if virtual worlds were games, but they're not. Even game worlds aren't games: they're places. Just like places in real life, the people who live there are part of the place. You can't talk about Leicester without considering the inhabitants of Leicester; you can't talk about *Star Wars: the Old Republic* (Ohlen et al., 2011) without considering the players of *Star Wars: the Old Republic*.

What virtual worlds *are* is bound up with who inhabits them. You can't separate the two without missing half the picture. The players of a virtual world are an intrinsic part of the historical context, the artefact created and the medium through which any authorial message is being delivered. Without them, you have an environment but no virtual world.

Preserving only the software of a virtual world is like preserving only the buildings of a city. That's better than nothing, but it basically leads only to future archaeology. The space is saved, but the space is only part of what a city is. Historians have to reconstruct what the people who lived there might have been like; students of literature can repurpose the ruins but not the culture; artists can see the empty streets but only imagine what the players who travelled them meant.

If we are preserving virtual worlds for a purpose, we should strive to help people make use of what we preserve for that purpose. For virtual worlds, this means preserving the players as well as the software and hardware that constitute the world.

Of course, cryogenically preserving a representative sample of players is neither morally not technically feasible. Given that we can't preserve actual players, the next best thing is to preserve studies of them. As it happens, there is a discipline for studying cultures, communities and the social relations between people: anthropology. Unfortunately, anthropological studies can only be undertaken while a virtual world is alive and vibrant; as in real life, it's no use writing an ethnographic study of Pompeii *after* it has been buried in ash – it has to be done beforehand if it is to capture the essence of the place.

Expense aside, there are practical problems with creating ongoing studies of virtual worlds:

- The worlds themselves can change. *World of Warcraft* today is not the same as the *World of Warcraft* that launched in 2004,[4] as a result of which casual players now greatly outnumber hard-core players.
- Individual players themselves mellow over time and behave differently.
- Operators run multiple copies of the same virtual world code on separate servers. There can be cultural differences between players across servers. Some of these may reflect real-life cultural differences,[5] but some don't.[6]
- Studies tend to last months, but perhaps ought to last years.

That said, anthropological studies of virtual worlds do exist. To get a sense of what *Second Life* was like in its heyday, look no further than Boellstorff (2008). Perhaps more poignantly, Rosenberg's (1992) ethnography of *WolfMOO* is all that remains of a once energetic and effervescent virtual world. Such works of scholarship are few and far between, however, in part as a result of the time and effort it takes to collect the data and in part due to a (not entirely unfounded) suspicion among senior anthropologists that the people who want to study virtual worlds are merely using that as an excuse to play them more. It would help if major virtual world development companies had anthropologists on their payroll, but unfortunately trained fieldworkers are not at the forefront of many hiring strategies right now.

Nevertheless, we could do more in other ways to help the people for whom we are preserving virtual worlds. Examples include:

- video recordings of people (actually players, not academics) playing at various stages in their playing career
- interviews with players, designers and developers
- design documents.

We should archive what we think the people 200 years from now will need to know in order to make sense or use of what we're preserving. We should also leave notes telling them *why* we think they'll need what we're preserving for them (and perhaps apologizing for obvious omissions . . .).

Conclusion

If something is worth saving, it's worth saving for a reason. We should anticipate that reason and provide as much supporting material as we can to aid the researchers of the future.

For virtual worlds, *of course* this would mean the hardware and the software – that goes without saying. However, it would ideally *also* include anthropological studies. Virtual worlds are designed to be inhabited, and the inhabitants are *part of the design*. To overlook them is to overlook what virtual worlds *are*.

Indeed, the same applies to some extent to all computer games. They are more than just the hardware and the software: they are also the players. Designers of games don't merely design for the direct behaviour of players, they design for the emergent behaviour of players: because games are interactive, players are akin to necessary components that have to be designed for. To preserve what a game *is*, in any sense, the players must be included.

The hardware and software is, nonetheless, probably the best place to start preservation, though.

Notes

1 It was like playing *Space Invaders*, except I could get to the second screen . . .

2 If indeed the 'original' oral tale was ever written down anyway.

3 Or *La Gioconda*.

4 Especially following the *Cataclysm* expansion that rewrote the map.

5 Players from the Far East can play the same game very differently from players in the West.

6 For example, there may be two routes through a large room. On one server, players take the right route; on another, they take the left route.

References

Bartle, R. A. (2003) *Designing Virtual Worlds*, Indianapolis, IN, New Riders.

Boellstorff, T. (2008) *Coming of Age in Second Life*, Princeton, Princeton University Press.

Ohlen, J. [lead designer] (2011) *Star Wars: the Old Republic*, Austin, BioWare.

Pardo, R. [lead designer] (2004) *World of Warcraft*, Irvine, Blizzard Entertainment.

Rosedale, P. [lead designer] (2003) *Second Life*, San Francisco, CA, Linden Research.

Rosenberg, M. (1992) *Virtual Reality: reflections of life, dreams, and technology. An ethnography of a computer society*,
ftp://sunsite.unc.edu/pub/academic/communications/papers/muds/muds/Ethnography-of-a-Computer-Society.

Sawano, K. et al. (1979) *Galaxian*, Tokyo, Namco.

CHAPTER 3

Make or break? Concerning the value of redundancy as a creative strategy

Simon Biggs

Professor of Art, School of Art, Architecture and Design,
University of South Australia

Introduction

There is a contradiction at the heart of digital art making, regarding its temporal mediality and relationship with a mainstream visual arts practice that values permanence. Why do we wish to preserve something temporal and fleeting? Will the preservation of digital works contribute to a process of commodification that many media artists have sought to avoid by embracing the ephemeral nature of digital media? Are there reasons that would justify preserving digital works of art when, for some artists, redundancy is a key principle in their practice?

A cultural determinacy?

Art is generally valued according to a set of established criteria that include authenticity, originality, craft skill, uniqueness, rarity, provenance and state of preservation. Modernist artists, as early as Dada but more often since, have sought to question or overturn these criteria and establish alternative value systems, where mass production, appropriation, temporality, decay and transience are foregrounded. Established artists as diverse as Tristan Tzara, Kurt Schwitters, Andy Warhol, Judy Chicago, Donald Judd, Robert Smithson, Joseph Beuys, Carolee Schneeman and Nam June Paik have, through various strategies of production, contextualization and mediation, proffered alternative models of artistic value.

Smithson's *Spiral Jetty* stands as an emblematic work in this regard –

unownable, more or less impossible to preserve, being subject to the vagaries of its environment, produced employing heavy earth-moving equipment and regularly transformed through natural weathering and chemical processes – perhaps the only conventional criterion of value such a work sustains is its singularity and thus rarity value. *Spiral Jetty* stands as one of the iconic post-war American art works, a touchstone for generations of artists since, probably because it breaches so many of the established values we conventionally associate with art objects.

The digital arts share many characteristics with work like Smithson's. The digital and media arts have their roots in 1970s post-modern culture – the first generation of media artists, including Robert Breer (recently deceased), Pauline Oliveros, Stan van der Beek, the Whitneys, Paik and many others, often members of Fluxus, emerged during the 1960s and were central to an artistic culture that would prove influential beyond its domain, feeding into conventional visual art practices as well as other disciplines, such as music, literature and performance, and facilitating the emergence of novel art forms. These artists focused on process and action, not craft and the final artefact. They were, admittedly, often obsessive in their use of materials, but they generally avoided fetishistic strategies, often choosing the abject and quotidian over the rare and rarefied. Many of these artists used materials that, by their nature, could not be preserved. Their rationale for such choices was not just aesthetic but often socio-economic.

A second generation of digital artists can trace their origins to this same cultural milieu. Larry Cuba, Jeffrey Shaw, Roy Ascott and others have produced works that employ media platforms that are by their nature unstable and unfixed, focusing value on transience and momentary experience. For these artists the attraction of digital media was not just the potential of such systems and tools, or how these systems allowed reflection upon what was rapidly becoming a mediatized culture, but also the innately fleeting character of the art works and experiences that could be produced. Their artistic rationale was to circumvent the traditional values of the visual arts and, especially, the art market. This was, in many cases, a political imperative.

Today we have a fourth generation of digital arts practitioners, following on from an intermediary generation including artists as diverse as Bill Seaman, Vuk Cosic and Toshio Iwai, in a domain of the creative arts with a 50-year history. At risk of generalizing, this latest generation of artists is arguably more pragmatic than its forebears. However, it is the case that much digital arts activity remains focused on unstable media and is undertaken at either the margins of the mainstream visual arts world or outwith it altogether.

Why is this? Could it be that the ideals of generations of experimental artists have had limited impact and the traditional values we earlier identified, as underpinning the commodification of art, sustain the determination of the canon? It seems that few collectors are willing to invest in art works that might survive for only a few years – or even minutes or seconds. Few private collectors are keen to get involved in the expense of developing novel preservation techniques for those digital art works that may have the potential to be conserved. The art market and thus, to a considerable degree, mainstream visual arts practice is driven by private collectors' cheque books. You have to 'follow the money' to find 'where the action is', and it is not in digital art. This was publicly affirmed by Ekow Eshun, when he announced the closure of London's Institute of Contemporary Arts' Live and Media Arts department, citing its 'lack of cultural urgency' (Gardner, 2008), by which he meant mainstream (*née* market-determined) interest. Eshun's subsequent departure from the ICA was possibly not unconnected with the political fallout of that decision but was mainly due to the parlous state of the ICA's finances. In this there is a comforting irony for artists engaged in the media arts.

Nevertheless, the ICA aside, there are a number of public museums investing in developing media arts (including digital) conservation programmes. Tate, MoMA, the Stedlijk, SFMoMA, the Pompidou and a few others are leading on this work. A smaller number of specialist institutions, such as ZKM, the Daniel Langlois Foundation (which has recently announced it is donating its entire collection to the Québecois Film Council as its founder ceases engagement with the sector), the Netherlands Media Arts Institute (until its recent closure) and the BFI, are also doing important work in this area, as are a number of academic research programmes. The work of Jon Ippolito, previously curator at the Guggenheim responsible for media arts and now Professor at the University of Maine (Depocas, Ippolito and Jones, 2003), on the Variable Media Initiative, is notable, as is that of Steve Partridge, with the Video Rewind project at Dundee University, and Scott Rettberg at the University of Bergen, with the European Electronic Literature Knowledge Base. This is all important work but it largely focuses, quite reasonably, on developing conservational techniques for works that the institutions involved have in their collections. By definition, most of these works are by artists who are part of the canon of contemporary art, if only because these institutions have collected their work. As we have observed, much of the activity in the digital arts remains at the margins of, or outside of, the mainstream art world and very few digital works are in such collections.

Most digital art work produced is never likely to be collected, privately or institutionally. Many of the most important works in the field will escape their clutches, often because, as previously noted, artists choose to employ creative strategies to ensure this will be the case. What will happen to this work? If it is lost then it will never be part of the documented history of the domain and, as we know, history consists of what we document. Does it matter if this work is lost? If it does matter, then will it fall to future archaeologists, those whose job it is to reveal what has been lost to history, to recover what they can of such works? If so, then what will they recover?

Errki Huhtamo's and Jussi Parikka's recently released book, *Media Archaeology* (Huhtamo and Parikka, 2011), indicates that this is not a problem of the future but of the present and, even, the recent past. Many digital art works have already been lost as the media platforms and other dependencies they rely on are superseded by new operating systems, chip-sets and entirely new kinds of media. Some artists speculated that the internet would function as an eternal proxy preservation medium but many works that have network software or hardware dependencies or employ network protocols have been lost as the technology of the internet has evolved. Many net art projects are no longer accessible, are often poorly documented and references to them might only exist in third-party media. Igor Štromajer, for example, has just completed deleting most of his online work from his server, removing it from the internet (Štromajer, 2011). Works such as Štromajer's would seem to present a class of art that now requires the attention of archaeologists rather than historians.

There are some who are suggesting that we are witnessing the demise of the home computer and the evolution of a new platform that offers an experience that, while highly interactive, does not possess the profoundly adaptable and interactive characteristics of a fully programmable computer. These new devices are typified by the smartphones, tablets and iPads that proliferate in consumer culture. Core to the design of these devices is the separation of reading and writing. By this, I do not mean conventional writing, as it is possible to undertake word processing on these devices – although that may involve purchasing add-on hardware, such as keyboards, to render the writing experience tolerable. I am using the word 'writing' here in the profound sense of being able to 'write the machine' and make the medium. This is one understanding of what media art can be – not art that employs media but art that fashions media.

A technological interdependency

Alan Turing's original conception of the computer was of a symbolic machine – a machine that exists as a symbolic description operating on those symbols according to the descriptions, thus operating on itself and the symbols and descriptions that compose it. Turing's machine is a writing machine that can write and rewrite itself. In this sense it is a machine with inherent agency. All computers, to a greater or lesser extent, are instances of Turing's original vision. Some programming languages have been developed in order to render these symbolic ontology's explicit as they are 'written' (for example, Prolog). Most computer operating systems are designed to be highly configurable and reprogrammable, either by easy to use drag-and-drop or clickable preference panes or through the rewriting of the 'boot' algorithms that run during the start-up of the computer. These 'preferences' are symbolic descriptions of what the computer is – its capabilities, processes, dependencies and properties. Within the scope of the hardware it is possible to create many different types of computer by manipulating these algorithms. It is also possible to automate this process, so that symbolic systems (for example, computer programs) are able to create their own descriptions of what a computer might be. Many computer viruses are designed to do this.

Generally, the more configurable a machine is, especially at a low level approaching hardware dependencies, the less easy it is to use, requiring, as you would expect, a significant knowledge of computational theory and technology. However, as computers have become pervasive in our society and used for a wider range of activities they have also become easier to use. This is, generally, a good thing, enhancing our productivity, experience of things and even facilitating novel forms of expression and experience.

However, computers become progressively easier to use at the risk of denying the user the capability to reprogram or reconfigure the machine. This is the case with many consumer-oriented devices, such as consoles, smartphones and tablets. These machines remain computers in so far as they can run software, perform calculations and interact with external phenomena, like the user's touch. However, they are not 'writing machines' in the sense of Turing's vision. It is true that software can be written to be used on these devices – but such software is not written on the device. Rather, it is written on a computer and installed on the client device. Thus it becomes difficult to describe a smartphone or tablet as a 'writing machine', in the sense Turing conceived the computer, and thus equally difficult to consider such devices as computers. Their precise status is somewhat unclear.

Is this a problem? It can be argued that it is. As smart mobile devices replace computers, as current sales projections suggest they will, those who exclusively use such devices will be unable to 'write' their own machines. On many levels this may not appear a significant issue. Most current computer users do not seek to build their own computers or learn computer programming. However, this emerging scenario evokes the classic dichotomy between production and consumption, the chasm between user and producer. Karl Marx, and numerous other socio-economic thinkers, have written on what happens when people have no access to or power over the means of production. Ted Nelson (Nelson, 2003) has argued that the computer is an inherently revolutionary device as it offers users access to the means of production, allowing them to redefine those means by reconfiguring the machine itself. For such apostles of computer liberation the arrival of the smart device popularizes the technology they helped develop whilst sounding the beginning of the end for their utopian vision. What has this to do the preservation of digital art?

A reading and a writing

The issue here is literacy and being able to read and write; where it is important to be enabled to create something – a text, a machine, a world. This is what artists do. They are people who, through high levels of literacy, are able to create shared experiences, both imaginary and real, symbolic and material. To my mind interesting art works are those that enable the reader to participate in this process of making and becoming, whether by the exercise of their imagination, through the process of interpretation, or by materially or symbolically changing the work itself in some manner. In the case of digital art this interplay of reading and writing has been enabled at the level of the symbolic codes that describe the machine, the medium, that materializes the work. In these works the explicit processes of 'writing' are as dynamic and motile as their potential 'readings'.

It could be argued that to appreciate writing one needs to know not only how to read but also be a writer – if only for the quotidian task of composing an e-mail or school essay. Like the book, the computer is a platform that is as good for writing as it is for reading, that invites a two-way engagement with its potential, such that the reader/writer is able to intervene in and determine what that might be. What would our culture be like if most of us could only read, and gaining access to the instruments for making texts was the preserve of professional 'writers'? If we lose the ability to write we will, as non-writers, lose the ability to read, becoming illiterate. Denied the ability to operate in the symbolic universe our capacity to imagine alternative worlds or selves and, ultimately, to make ourselves, will be compromised. We would be 'written' by, and become the property of, others. There is deep meaning in the claim that literacy liberates and transforms. In this context digital literacy is also transformational.

Does it matter if many of us lose the capacity to read and write with computers? Arguably it does, if we accept that we live in a progressively mediatized world, a society where our relationships with knowledge, information, work, play and one another are mediated by digital systems at every level. If we wish to be active participants in this culture, rather than passive consumers, then we do need to retain literacy with the dominant media, computers. In this respect the proliferation of consumer smart devices is a threat to our literacy and capacity for creative engagement. Those who are, for whatever reason, excluded from the 'digerati' will be confined to the role of consumers of digital culture.

Sherry Turkle has observed, in her recent book *Alone Together* (Turkle, 2011), that we no longer ask what we use computers for but what we do not. The computer has become essential not only in our practical lives but also in our social and emotional lives. Computer literacy is no longer just a requirement for getting the right job but for navigating and understanding our social relations. However, the social media that have enabled this would appear to be part of the same ilk of technologies as the consumer devices we have already been discussing. We have to ask, are social media part of a drift away from digital literacy or are we witnessing a new form of literacy emerge, an 'emotional' literacy, digitally mediated, where we 'write' ourselves into being within information space? If we are to accept Turkle's argument, the answer to this latter question is a, not unproblematic, no. However, if we accept this is a new form of literacy then we can ask whether we are witnessing an evolutionary step in the human–machine interface, where our capacity to create has become both a materially and socially symbolic operation? If so, we can conceive of media being social in a profound sense; of media platforms enabling the making of social relations, cultures and people. Arguably, it is, as yet, too early to know which is the likely outcome, if either.

Tim Ingold notes that creativity is often considered as an imposition of order by an agent of some kind (Ingold, 2009) but has argued that we can alternatively view it as 'an ongoing generative movement that is at once itinerant, improvisatory and rhythmic', weaving with and through the many agents involved – human, material and technological. This is a participative and inclusive comprehension of creativity and, although Ingold does not cite Mauss, this generous approach could be considered to be related to the notion of creativity as 'gift', evoking creativity's key role in social formation. At the heart of Ingold's argument is the principle that creativity is an activity, not a thing, and, quoting Paul Klee, he observes that when embodied in an artefact the living dynamic that is creativity expires. In this vision the work of art appears as no more than the dead and decaying remains of what was the living creative activity.

This returns us to the original conjecture of this text, that many media (and other contemporary) artists have chosen the path they have in order to maintain their focus on art as something you do, not something you make. Many artists have chosen to produce work that defies conservation and collection, existing only for as long as the work is in 'play' amongst all those engaged in its making – the author, the reader and others. For many this has not been an aesthetic strategy but pursued out of a particular apprehension of the role of creativity in the weaving (or 'writing') of society. Ingold uses the term 'textility', with diligence, suggesting not only the archaic process of weaving but also the process of 'writing'. It is tempting here to consider one of the earliest examples of automation, and its role in the development of computing, the punch-card programmable Jacquard Loom, used extensively, from the 19th century onwards, in the textile industries. In this machine we have 'writing' and weaving as functions of one another and a mechanical model for how people are made – as necessary attendants to the machine and subjects of the Industrial Revolution, a metaphor for how we are 'written' and 'woven' as a social fabric. The question remains – who is being made, by whom and to what purpose? We are reminded why literacy is so important.

The risk inherent in a strategy of artistic redundancy, where art works are made to decay, fail or be lost, as the systems they depend on evolve into other forms, is that of forgetting and subsequent illiteracy. Should we seek to preserve works of digital art not because we wish them, as artefacts, to participate in the socio-economic milieu that is the contemporary art world but because, by allowing these works to die without trace, we are contributing to a cultural forgetting that may ultimately lead us to risk losing our capacity to 'write' and thus to read. 'Writing' is something we do, not something we make – but it is also something we read, our capacity to write being directly linked to our ability to read, and vice versa. If we lose the possibility of one, we will lose the capacity for the other. If we were to treat all art in this manner, allowing it to decay as soon as its existence as a vital 'becoming' is complete, then we would have nothing to read. This risks ignoring the generative potential in reading that which 'remains'. In this sense no art work is ever complete or dead. No matter how they are made, or how inert they might appear, art works remain alive and open to new completions. The question is how this is informed by those who are reading? At the same time we recognize that without forgetting, without decay and death, there is no new life, there are no new experiences and no new memories.

References

Depocas, A., Ippolito, J. and Jones, C. (2003) *Permanence through Change: the variable media approach*, www.variablemedia.net/pdf/Permanence.pdf.

Gardner, L. (2008) Ekow Eshun and the ICA's Death Blow to Live Art, *Guardian*, 23 October, www.guardian.co.uk/stage/theatreblog/2008/oct/23/ica-live-arts-closure.

Huhtamo, E. and Parikka, J. (2011) *Media Archaeology : approaches, applications, and implications*, Berkeley, CA, University of California Press.

Ingold, T. (2009) The Textility of Making, *Cambridge Journal of Economics*, **34** (1), 91–102.

Nelson, T. (2003) From Computer Lib/Dream Machines (originally published 1974). In Montfort, N. and Wardrip-Fruin, N. (eds), *The New Media Reader*, Cambridge, MA, MIT Press, 301–38.

Štromajer, I. (2011) *What Is Expunction?*, www.intima.org/expunction.

Turkle, S. (2011) *Alone Together: why we expect more from technology and less from each other*, New York, NY, Basic Books.

CHAPTER 4

Between code and space: the challenges of preserving complex digital creativity in contemporary arts practice

Michael Takeo Magruder

Department of Digital Humanities, King's College London, UK

Introduction

Society's technological advancements have always inspired wider creativity and provided new frameworks for artistic expression. As artists often seek to assimilate the cutting-edge technologies of their time, the history of art has needed to progress alongside a history of preservation in which improved strategies and mechanisms for conservation have been devised in order to safeguard emerging forms of art deemed culturally significant. At present, the pervasive growth of digital media and its rapid uptake by artists has created different, currently problematic sets of challenges for those aiming to preserve the myriad of technology-based art works being realized by contemporary practitioners.

Now that the experimental use of digital technologies in art has fully expanded outside its previous confines of self-contained software and hardware systems, digital creativity has become firmly enmeshed within wider, complex and often non-digital contexts. Progressive work in this area commonly relies upon hybrid means of creation such as tapping into external sources of live data, exploiting user-generated media repositories, blending digital constructs with traditional analogue materials, distributing processes and outputs across varying combinations of virtual, physical and networked space, incorporating seemingly endless permutations for interaction and dialogue with spectators and participants, and engaging in interdisciplinary collaborations that are firmly rooted in non-arts subjects. The adoption of such possibilities, while opening new terrains for artistic exploration, has also necessitated a fundamental rethinking of historically straightforward issues regarding preservation, in particular, (re)defining what constitutes the actual art work that is to be documented and preserved.

Shifting from the digital to the hybrid

Given the current situation and its undeniable impact on artists using the latest technologies within their practice, it is important to acknowledge and address the apparent shortcomings that arise when traditional methods (or mindsets) of long-term preservation for material art objects are applied to creations that are either wholly or partially digital in nature. In terms of safeguarding the specific software and hardware components that comprise such work, it is certainly useful (if not essential) to gain insights from the technology sector and adopt industry-standard methodologies that have been devised to archive digital infrastructures securely. However, it is equally crucial to understand that technologically based art works are often not merely amalgamations of 0s and 1s or unique collections of integrated circuit boards, and, as such, cannot be defined (much less preserved) by only retaining these discrete digital elements.

Unlike many of my peers, I do not consider myself a *digital* or *new media* artist, but rather, a *contemporary* practitioner who happens to integrate various digital structures within the art-making process. Conversely, such is the importance and extent of my use of digital media, none of my projects produced within the past decade would exist if their computational aspects were removed. Employing technologies usually associated with high-performance computing and visualization, I appropriate (and also derive immense creative inspiration from) numerous types of display systems ranging from broadcast media façades and immersive CAVEs (computer assisted virtual environments) to spherical projection setups and full-dome (360°) environments. However, I often blend these bespoke combinations of software and hardware with a wide selection of analogue ingredients. Traditional fine art materials are intermixed with lines of code and grids of pixels in ways that are as conceptually refined and aesthetically prominent as their digital counterparts.

Similarly to most visual artists working within the contemporary scene, the greater majority of my projects are in some way related to and displayed within traditional gallery spaces such as the white cube and the black box. It is within these surroundings that I strive to liberate the born-digital aspects of my creations from the rigid confines of 'the screen', translating them into tangible forms that are more visceral and engaging for spectators and participants alike. But as with the hybrid forms themselves, such physical manifestations comprise only one channel within a wide gamut of distribution possibilities. Embracing the infinitely reconfigurable quality of new media, I simultaneously release projects across networked and virtual spaces like the world wide web and the online metaverse of *Second Life*. Individual art works mutate through various iterations and formats in a manner that is not too dissimilar from the current production/distribution model of the digital entertainment industry.

There is no question that such variability greatly complicates the preservation of art created within these contexts. In an ideal scenario, each of my individual projects would benefit from a conservation strategy that is as customized as the work itself. However, adopting this type of highly granular approach is often not practical or even possible, since it requires committing substantial resources that are usually beyond the scope of what institutions (or artists themselves) can realistically provide. Given this difficult position, it is crucial to highlight common issues that arise when attempting to preserve these kinds of art works. For this reason, I will now outline a series of case studies taken from my own practice in order to consider some of the many questions that must be addressed by researchers seeking to develop new frameworks which will help facilitate the preservation of contemporary 'digital' art.

Case study I: incorporating live external data streams

For the past two decades, artists working with new media have employed computational systems to examine and critique the rise of ubiquitous information structures within society. Unsurprisingly, advanced work in this area has rapidly progressed from using static internalized datasets to appropriating external streams of real-time data. These projects frequently use data sources that are related to our increasingly complex digital lives in order to construct aesthetic forms and environments that echo ever-changing forces within the real world.

One such example is *Data_Plex (economy)* (Magruder, 2009a), a networked, real-time art installation that is generated from and evolves with the financial markets. The work reflects on the unpredictability of the global economy and the capitalist institutions of which it is comprised. It is created from a single live feed of the Dow Jones Industrial Average (DJIA), the most cited international stock index, which is compiled from the share prices of 30 of the largest and most widely owned public companies based in the USA.

From a technological standpoint, the art work is constructed from a hybrid software pairing consisting of a server-side Java application and a client-side Virtual Reality Modelling Language (VRML) framework that translates the stream of fluctuating stock information into a metaphorical cityscape based on modernist aesthetics of skyscrapers and urban grids. Each corporation is represented in the virtual environment by a series of cubic forms that are proportioned according to factors such as its stock price, market capitalization and percentage of the DJIA. Current positions drift alongside ghosted (grey) structures of the recent past – dissolving traces from the previous four days of trading. Manifestations of historical (blue) highs, (red) lows and (green) volumes express the fortunes of the market in colour, while each company's representation is textured by a unique image that has been generated by its own financial data. The virtual world ebbs and flows at an erratic pace as vast volumes of capital are shifted during the trading day, while after hours, the realm sleeps in anticipation of the opening bell.

The art work's highly structured technical framework makes it incredibly simple to capture a static moment within the virtual space and save the resulting collection of (.wrl) geometry and (.gif) image files that constitute the complete environment. However, can even such a perfect three-dimensional 'snapshot' adequately convey the fundamental qualities of the piece? *Data_Plex (economy)* was conceived during the immediate aftermath of the 2008 global financial crash, and was intentionally realized in a way that would allow individuals the opportunity to interact with a live embodiment of the financial market and witness its volatile fluctuations in real time. For this reason, should we not also attempt to record and preserve the data timeline of the DJIA, since it both represents and can be used to fully reconstruct the work's evolutionary path? If so, capturing a finite period of this data is readily achievable, even if we must delve into the past and data-mine the DJIA archives. We can reclaim and store a day, a week, a month or perhaps even a year of such information, but considering that the art work's history continues to unfold as long as the DJIA exists, how can we preserve something that is still being created and whose life expectancy is yet to be determined?

Case study II: linking to unstable media repositories

If preserving art with elements of live data is incredibly problematic, then what additional issues arise when the integrated data source is continuously affected by the actions of its users? Software-based artists have developed many sophisticated methods for producing generative digital forms, but the complexity of these systems often pales in comparison to those drawing upon the decision-making intricacies of the human mind. For these reasons, I find it far more artistically compelling to tap into data that possesses humanistic qualities and connections. For example, instead of creating a virtual blossom from predefined sets of algorithms and texture libraries, it is more conceptually provocative to construct such an entity from actual representations of flowers that have been uploaded into the public domain by living people.

Data Flower (Prototype I) (Magruder, 2010b) explores this possibility of creating unpredictable and ephemeral synthetic flora within the deterministic constraints of the digital realm. As with *Data_Plex (economy)*, the 3D structure of the work is produced by a set of VRML files that define the core geometry of the artificial forms within the environment. Similar to previous generations of software art using codified artificial life mechanics, a series of algorithms instigates and directs an endless cycle of emergence, growth and decay upon the virtual blossoms. Randomization of certain parameters at the onset of each new cycle causes subtle mutations within the petal formations and ensures that every flower develops in a slightly different manner.

However, unlike conventional artificial life systems that are solely based upon unchanging internalized code, the art work integrates an external, non-deterministic element directly into its creation process. The surface textures of the synthetic blossoms are programmatically constructed each day by a server-side Java application that parses the image repository Flickr and selects 100 of the most recent photographs which have been uploaded with the tag 'flower'. The sampled pictures are then algorithmically prepared and stored as a temporary dataset that is linked to the art work's VRML structure. On each loop of the flowering cycle, a randomly selected image from the dataset is applied across the growing virtual geometry, thus completing the flower's ephemeral form. As in real life, every virtual blossom the art work generates is unique, since its internal 'genetic' codes induce a perpetual state of flux and its external 'developmental' influence is derived from an ever-changing pool of user-generated media.

As regards preserving the software framework of *Data Flower (Prototype I)*, the VRML component is extremely simple to conserve since it only consists of a pair of unchanging (.wrl) text files. Furthermore, the Java application and source code can be archived using industry standard protocols, and the programmatically generated images can easily be preserved since they are ISO-compliant JPEGs. As a consequence, it is very straightforward to capture a viable instance of the art work comprising the two VRML files and the current set of 100 unique JPEGs. This approach would constitute an important first step in preservation, but in such a state the work would lose its unpredictable and highly ephemeral qualities and exist as a stripped-down approximation of its true self. To archive a more artistically accurate version of the piece would require the inclusion of data that could translate these important characteristics. An obvious solution would be to capture and use the work's past trajectory to simulate these features. However, reconstructing even a small fragment of its data timeline is practically impossible. There is no means to obtain the necessary information from the art work's own internal software framework because the source image data is not permanently stored within a database and the resulting JPEGs are overwritten on a 24-hour cycle. Attempting to extract the required historical data from Flickr would prove equally futile since its media assets are constantly being altered and removed by its users. To further complicate matters, even if data-mining Flickr in this way was technically possible, would it be legal (or ethical) to attempt to create a data archive from a commercial organization's digital infrastructure that contains assets which are owned (in terms of copyright) by millions of different independent users?

Case study III: introducing analogue materials and processes

The secure preservation of many kinds of archived data clearly is an important part of any general conservation strategy for software-based art. However, given the current trends surrounding post-digital arts production and the rising enthusiasm for bringing data into the real world, it is not surprising that artists manipulating data within their practice are increasingly interested in developing processes which translate their born-digital creations into tangible forms within physical space. Although such artefacts are often very similar to traditional art objects and can arguably be preserved using standard conservation methods for analogue materials, it should not be assumed that the digital precursors of these creations are redundant and do not need to be retained.

In 2010 I was commissioned to undertake a major research-based arts project for *Manifesta 8: the European Biennial of Contemporary Art* in Murcia, Spain. The resulting body of work, entitled *(in)Remembrance [11-M]* (Magruder, 2010a), was a series of interrelated artistic interventions and art works reflecting on the 11 March 2004 (11-M) train bombings in Madrid, which killed 191 civilians and wounded over 1800 people. The project was exhibited at the biennial in the Museo Regional de Arts Moderno (MURAM), Cartagena, as a site-specific installation within one of the museum's white cube gallery spaces and consisted of various material artefacts interspersed with a few projection/screen-based components.

The exhibition was very well received, and most visitors seemed to categorize and interface with the work as a conventional – not a digital or new media – contemporary arts project. Although each of the separate elements comprising the installation could be related to a traditional visual arts format (such as photography, print, sculpture or video) and appeared to be far removed from any digital creation processes, the reality was quite the opposite. Over a year-long period of research, I had data-mined source materials pertaining to the 11-M attacks from numerous internet-based public and news media repositories in order to compile an extensive digital archive consisting of approximately 12.5GB of data and nearly 8500 individual files. This archive was then used to formulate all of the installation's eight bespoke components by algorithmically processing various portions of its data into digital forms that could be rendered into physical objects within the gallery space.

The project's source data archive and many algorithmic processes provided the fundamental basis for the art work to such an extent that if any of these software-based elements were withdrawn, it would not have been possible to synthesize any of the exhibited artefacts. For example, one of the works included in the *(in)Remembrance [11-M]* installation was a large collection of black-and-white photographic prints displayed atop a long rectangular white plinth in the centre of the gallery space. These prints showed various remediated images relating to the 11-M attacks and were produced from a set of several thousand digital photographs contained within the project archive. These photographs were uniformly batch-processed with a custom algorithmic protocol that generated a series of master images, which were then output to thousands of physical 7 x 5 inch prints via a commercial digital photographic lab service. In the installation, the finished prints were arranged in a seemingly random manner that encouraged visitors to peruse them and choose some to take away. Over the three-month exhibition period the selection of prints changed on a daily basis as visitors removed them from the plinth and gallery attendants replenished the assortment.

In terms of preservation, is it the analogue or digital form of these prints that represents the true artefact? Is it more important to retain the physical photographic prints that were specially created for and displayed within MURAM, since their exact material qualities could never be perfectly reproduced? Or is it the master set of digital files that holds the most practical (and perhaps conceptual) significance, since it could be used to generate a new version of the work at some future point in time?

Another even more complex example from the *(in)Remembrance [11-M]* body of work is a series of five photo-mosaics that also comprised part of the installation. As with the photographic prints, the photo-mosaics were exclusively created from the source data archive. The digital files were algorithmically assembled from a library containing thousands of image tiles created from news media photographs showing the immediate aftermath of the bombings. Over the sequence of five photo-mosaics, the tiles became smaller and greater in number, and gradually composited a picture of a 11-M remembrance shrine that had been taken by a member of the public and posted on Flickr. Each finished photo-mosaic was then incorporated into an intricately designed broadsheet layout and exported to a standard print-ready PDF format for litho printing. The set of PDFs was given to the newspaper *La Opinión de Murcia* to publish sequentially as full-page prints over a five-day period. At the end of each publication day, I ventured into the city and retrieved a single copy of that day's print from the garbage. I then returned to the museum with the copy, signed it, encased it within a museum-quality frame and added it to the installation.

With regard to this piece, again the question arises as to what constitutes the actual work that needs to be preserved. Is it the digital source files such as the TIFF photo-mosaics or the PDF page designs? Is it the physical artefacts such as either the several hundred thousand mass-produced newsprints or the single degraded copy that I retrieved and signed? Or perhaps, is it the sum of the artistic process itself that now only persists within stories and documentation surrounding the project?

Case study IV: blending virtual, physical and networked spaces

The challenge of preserving art works consisting of both analogue and digital elements becomes further complicated when notions of variable space and time are layered into the creative process. As individuals are increasingly fascinated with extending their digital lives across a growing range of virtual and networked environments made possible through the latest technologies, it is logical that many artists working within the digital domain have adopted similar approaches within their practice.

Although the production of mixed-reality art works constructed from varying combinations of virtual, physical and networked space coming together in real time is not a 21st-century development, the launch of the online 3D virtual world product *Second Life* in 2003 by Linden Lab opened a seemingly infinite range of new possibilities for artistic exploration in this area. In February 2008 Turbulence, a leading international portal and commissioner of networked art, curated a seminal exhibition and symposium, entitled *Mixed Realities*, which showcased five art works which simultaneously engaged visitors across *Second Life*, a traditional gallery space and the internet. Collaborating with two of my long-standing colleagues, Drew Baker (Research Fellow in the Department of Digital Humanities, King's College London) and David Steele (Senior Technical Consultant based in Arlington, Virginia), I was awarded a commission to create a new work for the show. Our project, entitled *The Vitruvian World* (Magruder, Baker and Steele, 2007), combined my ongoing interests in using *Second Life* as platform for mixed-reality art with Baker's expertise in 3D modelling within virtual worlds and Steele's extensive knowledge of advanced web programming and architecture.

The Vitruvian World was a multinodal installation based upon the architectural theories and principles of the first-century BC Roman architect, engineer and writer Vitruvius. Using Vitruvius's formulae for ideal temple construction contained within his text *De Architectura (Ten Books on Architecture)*, we devised a mixed-reality art work that interconnected the three distinct spaces. Within the virtual environment of *Second Life*, we transformed a full 256m² public simulator (sim) of land into an aesthetic realm made from 'natural' and 'architectural' features that were precisely built and arranged according to Vitruvian proportions. The synthetic landscape and its contents existed in a continuous state of change as the objects within the world responded to the presence of visiting avatars. In the architectural centre of the realm there was an enclosed area containing a lone human form that seemed to be made from the same material as its surroundings. This *puppet* body was linked to the physical gallery space and could be controlled by real-world visitors to the exhibition. The puppet's audiovisual senses were rendered in the gallery as a high-definition corner projection and surround-sound environment that would immerse the users and allow them to explore the realm. A third type of figure was also located within the virtual world, hidden beneath the ever-shifting landscape. This inanimate *doll* was devoid of human agency and only existed to document the passage of time within the space. The doll's aerial view of the virtual realm was captured and transmitted across the internet to a server-side application that processed the live datastream into sequential images which were then reconstituted into an algorithmic (Flash) video montage. This ever-changing piece of networked art was projected in the gallery exhibition and accessible on the Turbulence website, and allowed both local and remote passers-by a chance to observe remediated 'painterly' glimpses of the virtual world before the data was then reflexively looped back into *Second Life* and aesthetically layered onto the area of the virtual landscape being recorded by the *doll*.

Given the proprietary, closed nature of *Second Life* and the draconian terms and conditions of service imposed by Linden Lab, it has always been unclear how projects created within the platform might be fully preserved. In terms of the virtual forms, compositional elements of *Second Life* creations like geometry, textures and scripts are notoriously difficult to extract successfully from the system, and such processes are usually dependent on having full permissions on every aspect of every item within a targeted build (a highly unlikely scenario, considering that building in *Second Life* is based upon a collaborative and 'buy-to-use' mentality). Potential solutions for securely archiving *Second Life* content do exist – most notably the open-source 3D application server *OpenSimulator* – but these options have yet to be adequately explored by the wider research community. Additionally, if an art work is also partially comprised of physical and networked spaces and layers that exist outside *Second Life*, the situation (and its effect on preservation) becomes exponentially more complex.

To further complicate matters, the appeal and impact of art works like *The Vitruvian World* are hugely related to their innovative approach and placement at the forefront of current artistic-technological boundaries. These projects will consequently require a sense of historical context in order to be fully appreciated once their leading-edge qualities become outdated. However, as *Second Life* is a 'living' metaverse that is defined in many ways by social activities and conventions, which evolve at a much faster rate than in real life, it can be extremely difficult (and sometimes impossible) to capture these contextual aspects before they change or disappear.

For these reasons, the residual legacy of many art projects using *Second Life* is often limited to documentation. But can even a comprehensive collection of images, stories, videos and other relevant materials properly communicate the conceptual, technological and aesthetic intricacies of these kinds of ephemeral work? Can such traces be used to reconstruct or at least reimagine the actual artistic experiences that they provided? If not, and given the apparent lack of other viable options and strategies at present, must it simply be accepted that such art works cannot be adequately preserved at this point in time?

Case study V: integrating time-based, collaborative content

The rising use of virtual environments like *Second Life* as platforms for artistic practice is not surprising, given the vast creative possibilities that they offer. One of the most exciting aspects of these systems is an underlying social dimension that in many ways exemplifies the collective ethos of current online culture. Within these realms, communities of users regularly collaborate on numerous activities, ranging from the generation of in-world content and resources to the production of virtual performances and serious games. For artists creating work within such settings, the emphasis on individual effort is often replaced by a focus on group relationships and achievements. As a result, traditional standards based upon the notion of a sole creator have become outmoded, since they usually lack the facility to properly acknowledge the varying contributions of multiple individuals working towards a common goal. Given that issues concerning authorship and ownership greatly inform any conservation strategy for art, careful consideration must be given to understand how these factors might alter the preservation requirements for art works created within such collaborative frameworks.

Changing Room v1.0 (Magruder, 2009b) is an example of a collaborative art installation reflecting on the transitory nature of mixed-reality environments and the creative potential of working within these liminal spaces. The art work was undertaken in partnership with Eastside Projects, a leading contemporary arts venue based in Birmingham, UK, with an international reputation for producing highly experimental exhibitions and events. *Changing Room* linked the organization's real-world premises to a virtual simulacrum constructed in *Second Life* in order to facilitate the curation, realization and documentation of distinct – yet interrelated – art projects arising from a common pool of virtual and physical resources. Over a seven-week period, a group of resident artists was invited to use the environments and materials to create works of their own conceptual and aesthetic design. Each project lasted for a single week, after which the spaces and communal assets were handed over to the next artist for repurposing.

Changing Room's primary virtual component was a set of 128 translucent green columns located within Eastside Projects' virtual gallery. Each column was constructed from a single primitive object (*prim*) that could be fully modified using the standard in-world toolset. Resident artists were given exclusive rights to transform and program these digital structures, but could not generate their own objects within the space. If any of the art work's prims were deleted or removed from the area, a series of scripts would instantly regenerate them in their original state.

The installation's corresponding physical environment was situated in Eastside Projects' second gallery and was constructed from recycled materials that had been collected from the organization's previous exhibitions. Live audiovisual feeds from the virtual world were streamed into the physical space and displayed on a large projection set-up and set of three LCD screens. Visitors entering the physical gallery were tracked by a hidden motion sensor that relayed its data to the virtual realm. The presence of spectators in the physical space caused translucent blue spheres to be generated within the virtual world. Resident artists could use these prims as additional building materials within their projects; however, as each sphere only had a 12-hour lifespan, they would soon disappear and leave no trace of their existence.

As the project's lead artist, I constructed and exhibited the art work's initial configuration for a period of one week, after which I relinquished control over the virtual and physical resources to the first resident artist who then continued the process. In terms of documenting the installation, at the conclusion of each artist's session photographic, video and textual materials were collected both virtually and physically. In addition, an exact copy of the 128 permanent prims was captured in order to archive a 3D 'snapshot' of the artist's virtual creation.

Although these archived states can be perfectly preserved and reformed within the virtual world (as long as *Second Life* persists), they lack most of the important artistic qualities that I associate with the installation. These arrangements of virtual objects do not communicate how the individual projects slowly evolved over time, nor do they relay any sense of the complex interrelationships between the artists' works. Likewise, the fundamental connection to the physical environment and its material contents is lost. As such, the more traditional documentation assets collected by the participants provide a far more compelling representation of the total project. If documentation can more accurately embody an art work's significance, is it the actual digital artefacts of that work which should ultimately be preserved?

Another serious consideration in preserving an art work like *Changing Room* relates to its profoundly collaborative nature. Although I conceived the project and therefore have been designated as the artist who 'owns' the overall intellectual capital of the work, if the contributions of the six other participants were to be removed, then the art work would not exist. Furthermore, as I had requested my collaborators to realize their own independent ideas within the overarching environment that I had envisaged, is my role in the project actually more akin to that of a curator supporting the creativity of others within the context of a live event? If so, should a preservation strategy for the project be founded upon methods that are more suitable for archiving exhibitions and performances than individual art works?

Case study VI: creating within interdisciplinary contexts

The integration of emerging virtual-world platforms and technologies within practice-based research is not unique to the arts, but rather has permeated numerous other academic disciplines and contexts. As a consequence, such environments have brought together a wide range of individuals with a variety of interests and expertise. Given this situation, it is not surprising that artists working within these spaces have begun to engage in new types of collaborations with practitioners not normally associated with contemporary arts practice.

In 2010, I was commissioned by the organizers of the Digital Humanities conference in London to realize an interdisciplinary project that would explore creative collisions and collaborative possibilities between contemporary arts discourse and digital humanities scholarship. I chose to undertake this work with my close colleague Dr Hugh Denard (Lecturer in the Department of Digital Humanities, King's College London), a specialist in Greek and Roman theatre history with interests in using advanced visualization technologies within academic research.

Over an intensive three-month period of dialogue and exchange, we conceived a site-specific installation for the event that conjoined my long-standing use of real-time virtual environments as platforms for artistic expression and Denard's extensive research concerning the playfully illusionistic and fantastical worlds of Roman fresco art. The resulting art work, entitled *Vanishing Point(s)* (Magruder and Denard, 2010), was a virtual/physical project that blended the principles of ancient Roman art with digital virtual worlds in the idiom of stained glass.

In designing the primary virtual component of the installation, we drew upon the conceptual and compositional principles of theatrically inspired Roman frescoes to compose a classically influenced virtual garden that occupied an entire public sim within *Second Life*. The synthetic garden was built from a selection of beautifully detailed and intricately constructed 'natural' and 'architectural' elements. A single statuesque *doll* rested atop an ornate pedestal in the centre of a lush expanse of grass, while perfectly positioned arrangements of trees and sculpted hedges were framed between a pair of grand colonnades receding towards the horizon. Visiting avatars could wander within the space and relax in the company of strutting peacocks and small doves resting in the light of the artificial sun.

The art work's physical manifestation was embedded within the Great Hall of the Grade I listed King's Building, created in 1831 by English architect Sir Robert Smirke (1781–1867). A scenic view of the virtual landscape was captured by the doll's gaze and saved as a single ultra-high resolution TIFF image that was used as the primary source material for the real-world installation. The digital image was algorithmically processed and divided into plates conforming to the 108 rectangular window panes of the Great Hall's end wall. These image files were printed onto Duratrans (a large-format digital transparency film) and attached to the individual windows in a manner reminiscent of the spatial-pictorial traditions of stained glass. *Vanishing Point(s)* supplanted an elegant, uncanny view of the virtual garden into the enclosed urban space between the King's Building and the adjacent East Range. The work called upon the daily rhythms of natural light to animate, through the semi-translucent film, a magically poised moment, while the composition's subtle framing elements teased viewers with playful elisions of physical and virtual space.

As with the other previously discussed case studies, it is debatable what should be considered the primary form of the art work. In this instance, is it the virtual garden landscape that still (for now) exists within the 'living' metaverse of *Second Life*; the digital set of large-format images and derivative plates that are currently stored within the project's data archive; or the physical site-specific manifestation in the Great Hall, which will remain until it is removed or until the Duratrans degrade? Furthermore, even if it is decided that these three discrete elements are all part of the actual art work and will therefore be adequately preserved, what about the underlying humanities scholarship that fundamentally relates to the piece? Given that Denard's in-depth research concerning ancient Roman wall painting directly informs the art work's core concept and compositional structure, is not such an important contextual aspect inherently part of the complete work? If so, can the preservation of an art work like *Vanishing Point(s)* still be considered from only an arts perspective, or must it embrace a more interdisciplinary approach that reflects the project's non-arts related discourses and hybrid research nature?

Conclusion: retaining the essence of 'digital' art

Although I am an artist whose practice is absolutely dependent on digital media and processes, in reflecting upon issues of preservation I keep returning to the thought that it is not really the software or the hardware aspects of my projects which truly define my work. Of course these elements are crucial, and without them, my art would simply cease to exist. But even though my creations use technology, the essence of what they are resides well beyond the sum of their digital parts, and for this reason I feel it is vital to consider carefully the greater nature and significance of the art works themselves.

If any path of artistic creation begins with concepts and ends in outputs, there will be various structures and contexts along this sequential journey that certainly need to be retained. For artists like myself, many of these will indeed be digitally based, but undoubtedly many others will not, and as such we must be mindful not to take a technologically deterministic approach to conservation that inhibits us from securing all the essential ingredients – both digital and non-digital – that comprise the art works we are attempting to safeguard.

The protection of art for future generations must surely be the ultimate goal of any dialogue concerning preservation. Given the considerable challenges faced by those seeking to preserve today's digitally based art forms, perhaps initiatives like the Preservation of Complex Objects Symposia can sustain a common forum that not only acknowledges but, more importantly, potentially establishes a collective foundation for realizing practical solutions which will provide the means to help save these legacies of our contemporary digital culture.

Acknowledgments

I wish to express my warmest thanks to my long-time collaborators Drew Baker and David Steele, whose technical expertise and assistance over the last ten years has not only made the production of these and many other art works possible but, more importantly, has deeply informed my approach to using computational media.

References

Magruder, M. Takeo (2009a) *Data_Plex (economy)*, art work, www.takeo.org/nspace/ns031 [accessed 1 April 2012].

Magruder, M. Takeo (2009b) *Changing Room v1.0*, art work, www.takeo.org/nspace/sl007 [accessed 1 April 2012].

Magruder, M. Takeo (2010a) *Data Flower (Prototype I)*, art work, www.takeo.org/nspace/ns034 [accessed 1 April 2012].

Magruder, M. Takeo (2010b) *(in)Remembrance [11-M]*, art work, www.takeo.org/nspace/2010-(in)remembrance_11m [accessed 1 April 2012].

Magruder, M. Takeo, Baker, D. and Steele, D. (2007) *The Vitruvian World*, art work, www.turbulence.org/Works/vitruvianworld [accessed 1 April 2012].

Magruder, M. Takeo and Denard, H. (2010) *Vanishing Point(s)*, art work, www.takeo.org/nspace/sl005 [accessed 1 April 2012].

PART 2

The memory institution/data archival perspective

CHAPTER 5

Preservation of digital objects at the Archaeology Data Service

Jenny Mitcham

Archaeology Data Service, the University of York

Background to the ADS

The Archaeology Data Service (ADS) was founded in 1996 for the purpose of preserving digital data produced by archaeologists based in the UK, and making it available for scholarly re-use. The ADS was initially established as part of the Arts and Humanities Data Service (AHDS), with sister services covering other disciplines within the arts and humanities. Data is archived to ensure long-term preservation, but it is also made available free of charge for download or via online interfaces to encourage re-use.[1]

The digital archive at the Archaeology Data Service was established several years prior to the acceptance of the Open Archival Information System (OAIS) model as an ISO standard in 2002 (Lavoie, 2004). ADS archival procedures and policies have evolved over time as the organization itself and the wider world of digital archiving have grown and matured. We have now adopted the OAIS reference model approach and mapped our archival practices to it.

ADS preservation strategy is based on the migration of submitted files into archival formats suitable for preservation. This strategy is detailed in our formal preservation policy, which, along with all ADS advice and guidance, is available online.[2] File formats for preservation are selected using a number of criteria as described in the DPC Technology Watch Report *File Formats for Preservation* (Todd, 2009).

It is important for the ADS to be able to demonstrate that it can be trusted as a digital archive. Researchers who have invested time and effort in creating a dataset needs to trust that we will take care of their data in the long term. They also need to trust that they will be able to locate their files whenever they need to access them in the future. In order to further enhance the level of trust that our depositors put in us as an appropriate repository for their data, we successfully applied for the Data Seal of Approval (DSA)[3] at the start of 2011. Undergoing the DSA peer review process has benefited the ADS in many ways (Mitcham and Hardman, 2011), but the opportunity it gave us to reflect on and further formalize ADS archival procedures was a valuable outcome in its own right.

ADS collections policy

The ADS has a collections policy which describes the types of data that we accept for deposit.[4] Data has to relate in some way to archaeology or the historic environment for it to be of interest to our designated community (as per the OAIS model). Our collections policy describes in some detail the types of data that we accept. Regarding visualizations and 3D reconstructions it reads as follows:

> 2.2.8. Visualisation.
> 3D reconstructions, including computer-generated solid models, VRML, and other visualisations will be collected where it is feasible to maintain them and where they are considered to be capable of re-use and restudy or are seen as being of importance for the history of the discipline in accordance with the procedures defined in the AHDS Guide to Good Practice for Virtual Reality. In general the ADS will also preserve the data from which the model is derived, and sufficient metadata in accordance with the principles of the London Charter (2009).[5]

While visualizations produced by archaeologists are clearly within our collections remit, it is important to highlight the caveats mentioned in the collections policy. Data must be 'capable of re-use' or be 'of importance for the history of the discipline'. These factors can be quite subjective and difficult to quantify. There is mention of 'sufficient metadata' and this is one of the challenges that we frequently face in our day-to-day archiving work. We believe that the single biggest barrier to the future re-use of data is inadequate documentation (Austin and Mitcham, 2007). This goes for all types of data that we receive, not just visualizations, but it is often the case that the more complex the dataset, the more metadata is required to archive it successfully.

Despite the variety of data types mentioned in our collections policy, much of the data that we ingest into our digital archive is not of a complex nature: the most commonly ingested formats are all widely understood data types with fairly straightforward migration paths to suitable archival file formats. However, there have been a number of projects that we have worked on over the last few years which have brought complex data to the forefront of our minds and enabled us to formulate and put into practice strategies for managing them.

The Big Data project

In 2005-6 the ADS carried out a project for English Heritage entitled 'Preservation and Management Strategies for Exceptionally Large Data Formats' but more informally known as 'The Big Data project'.[6] This project aimed to investigate preservation, re-use and dissemination strategies for, what were then considered, exceptionally large data files generated by archaeologists undertaking fieldwork and other research. The project focused on data collection techniques capable of producing large quantities of data during the course of a single survey. These include techniques that result in 3D datasets which are frequently the starting point for the creation of 3D models and visualizations. The techniques highlighted by the project case studies were laser scanning, lidar (a remote sensing technology that measures distance by illuminating a target with a laser and analysing the reflected light) and maritime and terrestrial geophysics, but project recommendations could be applied to all large datasets.

One of the first deliverables of the Big Data project was the creation of an online survey for creators and users of 'big data' in archaeology. The survey questions were wide-ranging and covered data creation and re-use, selection and retention policies, file formats, software, archiving strategies and storage. Though the questionnaire was targeted at a relatively small community, the results were interesting and in many cases confirmed existing assumptions. A full report on the findings of the Big Data project survey is available online[7] but some of the key findings are as follows:

• A wide range of proprietary software packages is in use.

- About half of respondents did not have any policy in place for archiving their data.
- The majority of respondents would be happy to let others access their data.
- The desire for re-use of these types of datasets is considerable.

This project looked specifically at what we termed 'big data', but perhaps one of the conclusions that could be drawn from the project is that it is not so much the size of the data that matters, it is the complexity. Though the logistics of moving large files around can be a problem, hardware storage is becoming cheaper over time, computers have increasing processing power, and many archiving tasks can be batch-processed or run as background tasks. It is complex digital objects that can be more challenging to a digital archivist than files which are large in size yet relatively simple in structure.

The VENUS project

The ADS was involved in another project investigating the creation and archiving of large and complex datasets in 2008–9. The European Commission funded the VENUS project,[8] seeking to look at methods and tools for the virtual exploration of deep underwater archaeology sites. Underwater sites, normally accessible to just a small number of experienced divers, are an excellent use case for 3D modelling where visualization techniques can help others experience them too. The VENUS project team used underwater recording techniques such as sonar and photogrammetry to collect huge quantities of information about the Roman shipwreck at Port-Miou C off the coast of the Calanques, between Marseilles and Cassis in the south of France. This information was then used to create visualizations of the site that could be made available to a wider audience. The role of the ADS in this project was first to give guidance on how the data should be collected and managed in order to facilitate long-term archiving and re-use, and second to create an exemplar archive of the data and disseminate the results online.

The advice and guidance produced as part of this project is now freely available, both in the form of a VENUS preservation handbook[9] and a guide to good practice for marine remote sensing and photogrammetry.[10]

The exemplar archive published from VENUS project can be viewed on the ADS website[11] and gives an example of how complex datasets can be archived and disseminated in a relatively simple way. Raw multibeam sonar survey data is available to download as a series of XYZ files. Virtual Reality Modelling Language (VRML) files are available to download in a compressed (zipped) format, and an animation of the VRML model is also provided as a streamed video to allow researchers to preview the model before they commit to downloading a large file. Other supporting data (including photographs, database files and reports) is also presented online.

ADS archival strategy for complex datasets

The VENUS project exemplar archive as described above is a useful illustration of our strategy for archiving complex datasets. Our primary concern is to archive the raw data from which a model is derived. This data should be accompanied by adequate documentation and metadata to ensure its independent utility. OAIS states that an archive should:

> Ensure that the information to be preserved is Independently Understandable to the Designated Community. In particular, the Designated Community should be able to understand the information without needing special resources such as the assistance of the experts who produced the information.
>
> Consultative Committee for Space Data Systems (2012)

Raw data and documentation should therefore go hand in hand. There is little value in us preserving a raw dataset from a laser scanning or geophysical survey without the contextual information that makes that data meaningful and suitable for re-use by others.

Our focus on the raw data may sometimes be at odds with the focus of the data depositor, who may consider their 3D model to have more value and interest for others than raw, unprocessed output. We would argue however that it is the raw data which has the greatest long-term re-use potential. It may be used for creating alternative interpretations of a site, or be repurposed to answer entirely different research questions long after the platform and software for displaying the visualization has become obsolete.

Where appropriate, the ADS is also keen to archive other types of data produced by a project where a suitable preservation path can be found. These may include processed data, derived data, decimated data, 3D models, visualizations and fly-throughs. We are often inhibited in this field by the large numbers of proprietary and binary file formats used to analyse, process and visualize 3D data, and a stable and open preservation format may not always be available to us.[12] Sometimes these files can only be preserved on a 'best efforts' basis with no guarantee that we would be able to maintain their functionality over time. In these situations the depositor should supply 'snapshots' of the model (image and movie files for example) alongside full documentation, so that future researchers can view the model even if they are not able to explore it at first hand.

When planning selection and retention strategies for data prior to archiving, we find 'preservation intervention points' a useful approach. Preservation intervention points, or PIPs, are a concept that came out of the VENUS project. They represent points across the lifecycle of the data at which the data creator may want to submit data for archiving. Preservation intervention points will occur at data capture, after processing, post-processing and analysis and at the point of the creation of dissemination outputs. At the end of each of these processes, the data may have been altered in some way to produce a derived dataset worthy of preservation in its own right. Data creation and analysis can be a complex series of processes and this model highlights the fact that preservation copies of the data may need to be created at a variety of different points through the lifecycle of the project.

At each potential preservation intervention point, an assessment must be made to establish whether the data at this stage is worthy of preservation. The criteria for making this assessment are as follows:[13]

- **Preservation metadata** There should exist appropriate levels of preservation metadata so that the data is made re-usable rather than simply preservable.
- **Resource discovery metadata** There should be appropriate levels of resource discovery metadata so that data from each point can be meaningfully differentiated and distinguished from other parts of the dataset (this mostly applies to legacy data).
- **Identifiable migration paths** There should be clear migration options for data at all stages.
- **Re-use cases** This is probably both the most important criterion and occasionally the most difficult to judge. Where the data is in a form that

can obviously be used by other researchers, or in other contexts, then the question is simply whether re-use is likely to occur. The other complication is that, for certain types of data, a re-use case can be imagined as feasible even if it is currently not being enacted. An example of this would be a form of data that might lend itself to a post-processing technique under development, or merely envisaged as possible in the future (or an enhancement to an existing technique).

- **Repeatability** Is the process that created this data repeatable? If so, an earlier stage may be an appropriate PIP; if not, then this intervention point should be selected.
- **Retention policy** The data should match the retention policy of the target archive.
- **Value** The cost of intervening to preserve data at this particular point, given that no project has an unlimited budget. 'Value' here also means the value of the material to be archived, e.g., it might be worth preserving data produced by a repeatable process if that process were particularly expensive and difficult to reproduce. Value, therefore, has to do with balancing the perceived worth of the data against the cost of archiving.

Using this approach to work through and formalize selection and retention decision-making demands a certain amount of intellectual engagement with the preservation process from the data producers. By encouraging them to think about the 'value' of the data they hold, they can start to collate a subset of files for archiving for which a re-use case can be envisaged.

Guides to good practice

The importance of submitting adequate metadata alongside the data to be archived has already been stressed. One of the core functions of the ADS is to offer advice and guidance to data creators and depositors on preparing and documenting a dataset prior to archiving. One of the ways that we achieve this is through our Guides to Good Practice.[14] These Guides were originally published by the ADS and the AHDS from 1998 onwards and were available in hard copy and also free of charge as static online publications. Since January 2009 we have been working with both English Heritage[15] and Digital Antiquity[16] to refresh and enhance the Guides to Good Practice series.

Through this new, collaborative project we have updated and restructured the original Guides, making them available in an online wiki environment to allow easy and quick collaboration and also more frequent future updates. The original Guides included subjects such as excavation, geophysics, geographic information systems (GIS), computer aided design (CAD) and virtual reality, but a range of new Guides has now been added to the existing set, on subjects including 3D laser scanning, lidar and photogrammetry.

The aim of the Guides is to provide practical advice on the creation, preservation and re-use of digital resources, including valuable guidance on metadata creation. The level of metadata and documentation that should accompany a project archive will vary depending on the nature of the data to be deposited. Metadata for visualizations and simulations should include following:[17]

- a description of the project as a whole (title, dates, funders, copyright, creators, etc.)
- a description of the audience and level of interaction (who is the model aimed at and how can they interact with it?)
- methods and techniques used to create the model (application format, specification, hardware platform, authoring tools, etc.)
- details of datasets that have been incorporated into the model: laser scanning, geophysics, lidar for example (note that separate guidance on the level of metadata required for each of these techniques will be listed in the appropriate Guide to Good Practice)
- details of which features of the model are based on hypothesis rather than evidence
- details of delivery platform (OS, web browser, plug-in, hardware, scripting language, etc.)
- a description of the look and feel of the model, and what it feels like to experience it.

The last of these points is possibly the hardest to get right. Virtual worlds are notoriously difficult to describe, as our experiences of them can be quite subjective – different people may view and explore them in different ways.

Where is all the complex data?

At the ADS the framework for the archiving of complex digital datasets is firmly in place. We are a trustworthy digital archive with many years of experience behind us. Our research work over recent years includes projects that have specifically looked at large and complex 3D datasets and we have a published set of guidance documents aimed at data creators who are working in this field. However, an analysis of our actual data holdings would show only a small number of datasets that include visualizations, simulations and 3D models. We know that archaeologists are often early adopters of new technologies and techniques for visualizing their datasets, but there are a number of reasons why the results of their work are not routinely deposited with us.

At the ADS we charge the data depositor for our services as a digital archive. This is a one-off charge that covers the cost of ingest, storage, dissemination, administration and any ongoing file migrations that may be carried out to guard against future obsolescence. Our charging policy is available to view online[18] and is based not only on the number of files deposited with us but also on their size and complexity. Larger and more complex files are more time-consuming to work with and more expensive to store thus will cost more to deposit with us. The benefit of this approach is that people are encouraged to think about selection and retention and consider where the preservation intervention points should be rather than giving us every file that has been created as part of a project. The downside, however, is that if archiving costs have not been budgeted for, when a project ends there may be little money left to cover archiving of the full dataset, so a selection of smaller and less complex files such as project reports and images may be prioritized.

As discussed above, adequate metadata is essential if we are to archive complex data successfully. Situations may arise where a researcher wishes to deposit a dataset with us but does not have (and cannot produce retrospectively) suitably detailed metadata. This is particularly true of complex data that may require a more detailed set of technical metadata as well as contextual and resource discovery metadata. As part of the ingest process, digital archivists at the ADS perform various checks on data submitted to ensure that it is independently understandable and suitable for re-use. Where crucial documentation is missing, we may have to discuss with the depositor what elements of the dataset are not suitable for inclusion in the archive.

Another issue that sometimes contributes to the problem is that of copyright and ownership. An archaeological researcher is unlikely to have the equipment and expertise required to carry out an airborne lidar survey of their study area. If they wish to use lidar data to create a 3D model of a landscape, they need to acquire that data from elsewhere. At the end of the project this data cannot then be submitted to the ADS for archiving if copyright is not held by the project team. The owners of the lidar dataset may not accede to our terms and conditions for making the data (or datasets derived from it) freely available online. An example of this can be seen in the University of Birmingham's North Sea Palaeolandscape Project[19] – a digital archive published by the ADS in 2011. This was an interesting re-use of 3D seismic survey data to generate information on the Mesolithic landscape of the North Sea. The primary dataset that they used to create their 3D model was a mapping of the seabed compiled by Petroleum Geo-Services.[20] This seismic data is commercially very sensitive and for this reason could not be widely disseminated by the ADS. Similarly, the models the project created based on this data also could not be made publicly available.

Conclusion

The ADS is a digital archive with many years' experience of preserving and disseminating the digital data that archaeologists produce. Our OAIS and migration-based archival strategy is openly documented[21] and well established. The approach that we take to archiving remains the same whether the data is simple or complex. There are, however, particular challenges that we are faced with when handling complex data.

When archiving 3D models and visualizations, the many different technologies used to create and display them can be a problem. This is a fast-evolving field, with many different proprietary file formats in use. Sometimes, there will be no obvious migration pathway that will adequately preserve the significant properties[22] of a model. There is no one-size-fits-all preservation strategy for data of this type and individual projects need to be assessed on a case-by-case basis. These problems, however, should not be insurmountable. A key element in tackling these issues is to ensure that digital archiving is an essential part of a project plan and that funding for it is built into a project budget from the start. The project team need to start a dialogue with the digital archive as early as possible to ensure that a suitable preservation strategy can be agreed and that adequate metadata and documentation is created along the way.

There are many reasons why we feel that visualizations and 3D models should be preserved. Archaeological remains are regularly described as being a finite and non-renewable resource and due to natural and man-made processes some sites and monuments will not be with us forever in their current physical form. Thus a 3D visualization of a panel of rock art which may be gradually weathering and eroding over time may be the best way we have of experiencing that rock art 100 years from now. Other archaeological remains are accessible only to a small minority (for example cave or underwater sites) and visualizations are the only way that the majority of archaeologists, and the public, will ever be able to experience them. Many more sites we know about as archaeologists are no longer in existence or are entirely ruinous and a digital reconstruction that allows people to explore how they might have once appeared is an extremely valuable tool for understanding the past. Preservation of models and visualizations such as these is important to the discipline as a whole and very much within the remit of the ADS.

Notes

1 http://archaeologydataservice.ac.uk/about/background.
2 http://archaeologydataservice.ac.uk/attach/preservation/PreservationPolicyV1.3.1.pdf.
3 www.datasealofapproval.org.
4 http://archaeologydataservice.ac.uk/advice/collectionsPolicy.
5 http://archaeologydataservice.ac.uk/advice/collectionsPolicy#section-collectionsPolicy-2.2.CollectionDataTypes.
6 http://archaeologydataservice.ac.uk/research/bigData.
7 http://archaeologydataservice.ac.uk/research/bigDataQuestionnaire.
8 http://archaeologydataservice.ac.uk/research/venus.
9 http://archaeologydataservice.ac.uk/attach/venus/VENUS_Preservation_Handbook.pdf.
10 http://guides.archaeologydataservice.ac.uk/g2gp/RSMarine_Toc.
11 http://archaeologydataservice.ac.uk/archives/view/venus_eu_2009.
12 For examples of situations where a suitable migration path cannot be found, see Jeffrey (2010).

13   These criteria are taken from the Guides to Good Practice:
     http://guides.archaeologydataservice.ac.uk/g2gp/ArchivalStrat_1-3.
14   http://guides.archaeologydataservice.ac.uk.
15   www.english-heritage.org.uk.
16   www.digitalantiquity.org.
17   For further guidance on appropriate levels of metadata and documentation
     see the London Charter (www.londoncharter.org) and Chapter 13 below.
18   http://archaeologydataservice.ac.uk/advice/chargingPolicy.
19   http://archaeologydataservice.ac.uk/archives/view/nspp_eh_2011.
20   www.pgs.com.
21   http://archaeologydataservice.ac.uk/advice/preservation.
22   The InSPECT project defines significant properties as follows: 'The
     characteristics of digital objects that must be preserved over time in order to
     ensure the continued accessibility, usability, and meaning of the objects, and
     their capacity to be accepted as evidence of what they purport to record.'
     (Grace, Knight and Montague, 2009).

References

Austin, T. and Mitcham, J. (2007) *Preservation and Management Strategies for Exceptionally Large Data Formats: 'Big Data' final report 1.03*, 28 September,
     http://archaeologydataservice.ac.uk/attach/bigData/bigdata_final_report_1.3.pdf.
Consultative Committee for Space Data Systems (2012) *Reference Model for an Open Archival Information System. Recommendation for Space Data Systems Standard*,
     CCSDS Magenta Book,
     http://public.ccsds.org/publications/archive/650x0m2.pdf.
Grace, S., Knight, G. and Montague, L. (2009) *Investigating the Significant Properties of Electronic Content over Time: final report*,
     www.significantproperties.org.uk/inspect-finalreport.pdf.
Jeffrey, S. (2010) Resource Discovery and Curation of Complex and Interactive Digital Datasets. In Bailey, C. and Gardiner, H. (eds), *Revisualizing Visual Culture*, Farnham, Ashgate Publishing, 45–60.
Lavoie, B. F. (2004) *The Open Archival Information System Reference Model: introductory guide*, Digital Preservation Coalition Technology Watch Series, Report 04-01, www.dpconline.org/component/docman/doc_download/91-introduction-to-oais.
Mitcham, J. and Hardman, C. (2011) *ADS and the Data Seal of Approval – case study*

for the DCC, www.dcc.ac.uk/resources/case-studies/ads-dsa.

Todd, M. (2009) *File Formats for Preservation*, Digital Preservation Coalition Technology Watch Series Report 09-02, www.dpconline.org/component/docman/doc_download/375-file-formats-for-preservation.

CHAPTER 6

Preserving games for museum collections and public display: the National Videogame Archive

Tom Woolley
Formerly New Media, National Media Museum, UK

James Newman
Professor of Digital Media, Bath Spa University, UK

Iain Simons
Nottingham Trent University, UK

Introduction to the National Videogame Archive

Formed in 2008 as a partnership between the National Media Museum in Bradford, West Yorkshire, and Nottingham Trent University (NTU) and drawing on expertise from colleagues at Bath Spa University, the National Videogame Archive (NVA) aims to collect, interpret, make accessible for study and research and, where possible, exhibit videogames and the associated ephemera of videogame cultures.

Formerly known as the National Museum of Photography, Film and Television, the National Media Museum changed its name in 2006 to encompass wider forms of media and reflect the radical impact of digital technology. As a key part of this refocusing, in 2007 the Museum created a new Curator of New Media role to widen the collection within the areas of internet and computing technology, videogames and digital art. At the same time, researchers at Nottingham Trent University and Bath Spa University were conducting feasibility research to investigate the efficacy of formal preservation and exhibition strategies and environments for UK videogames. Following consultation, the NVA – a sub-division of the Museum's National New Media Collection – was launched in October 2008 (National Media Museum, 2010)

The NVA aims to preserve, analyse and display the products of the global videogame industry by placing the games in their historical, social, political and cultural contexts. This means treating videogames as more than digital code that can be dissected and emulated or as a system of rules or representations. At the heart of the NVA is a respect for the material form of the game as well as the box art, manuals, advertising, marketing and merchandizing materials that support it and give it meaning and context.

In addition to collecting, curating and archiving these vital parts of popular culture, the ongoing research of the NVA is oriented around exploring and devising innovative and engaging ways to exhibit and analyse videogames for a general audience. This involves considering the interpretation and display of videogame experiences for diverse audiences that might include adepts and non-adepts alike, and exhibition in environments such as museum galleries which are not normally conducive to videogame play (see e.g. Newman, 2009, 2011, 2012; Newman and Woolley, 2009).

Types of material within the NVA

The NVA is the Museum's youngest collection. It includes more than 2000 individual items, ranging from software and hardware through to fan-made maps, developer documentation, prototype hardware interfaces and controllers, and assorted ephemera, including magazines and other computing and gaming publications. At present, the majority of the items in the collection have been donated by the British public but the collection also includes objects gifted by members of the international games industry (including prototype Rock Band controllers donated by Harmonix, the first prototype EyeToy PlayStation USB camera donated by Sony London Studios, and development sketches and designs for Samarost donated by the game's developer, Jakub Dvorsky) In addition, in 2011 the NVA acquired a large number of objects from the British Film Institute, which had amassed a collection of gaming hardware, software and ephemera during the 1990s.

Importantly, unlike many amateur collecting projects such as the High Voltage SID Collection (HVSC), for example, the NVA does not and cannot aim to be a completist collection. As such, decisions are informed by the collecting policy, which identifies key areas and narratives around which directed collecting takes place.

As its mission statement and collecting policy indicate, the NVA's aims are wide-reaching. Centring on the moments of creation and development, the texts themselves, and the reception of games by fans, journalists and critics, the collection seeks to document the complete lifecycle of videogames. In order to put this vision into practice, the NVA aims to collect around the following areas.

Hardware

The NVA has a comprehensive collection of gaming consoles, computers and peripherals that have shaped the way we consume and play videogames. From the Magnavox Odyssey, the world's first home games console, released in 1972, to the latest hardware releases, the NVA aims to preserve devices that have influenced the way the public have experienced games in the best condition possible. As well as mass-produced consumer services, the NVA also includes several unique prototypes that have been donated by members of the international game development and journalism communities.

Software

Most of the NVA's collection comprises games software. Currently, software programs are stored on their original, portable media and include compact cassettes, floppy disks, CDs and DVDs, as well as other proprietary formats that include various cartridge and disc-based systems. The NVA aims to collect landmark titles that have captured the UK public's attention and demonstrated innovation that has pushed the medium of games forward. The NVA currently holds a large collection of Sinclair Spectrum, BBC Micro and Commodore 64 cassette tapes from the 1980s.

Marketing materials

Alongside the games and consoles, the NVA is also building a collection of games industry marketing materials that aim to place the medium within a cultural context and preserve the way games have been advertised and sold to the public. This section includes posters, magazines, television commercials and websites.

Games creation and design

To explore the production of videogames the NVA also includes design documentation – from the earliest ideas scrawled in a notepad through to concept art, character and level design. A key aim of the NVA is to build a collection of games production material that tracks the development cycle of key titles. In addition to collecting materials already in existence, a key strategy for documenting development practice has been the instigation of the

'Director's Commentaries' project. Drawing on the collaboration with colleagues at NTU and, in particular, the GameCity international videogames festival, the project mimics the DVD extra format by inviting game developers to reflect critically on their professional practice by narrating playthroughs of their games. Commentaries are presented both as live events and video-recorded pieces and form a key interpretative resource and a means of capturing the development stories of key games, studios and individuals.

Community materials

The vibrant and passionate fan communities that surround many games aims to be recorded by the NVA to help illustrate and preserve this incredibly rich and valuable resource. This area includes player-generated walkthroughs, fanzines, fan fiction, fan art, speedruns and websites. The collection of fan-generated ephemera is key to the NVA's mission, as it is these materials that reveal much of the meaning of videogames to their players. The diversity of fan-produced materials such as superplay videos, walkthroughs and machinima speak to the malleability of videogames and their ability to be remade and played with by players. Videos of gameplay, for instance, illustrate the use of specific techniques (including the exploitation of bugs, glitches, and other inconsistencies in the operation of gameplay) that may be central to the use of games within particular communities and contexts.

Challenges of games preservation

The challenges surrounding the preservation of videogames are extensive and the NVA is working to provide successful case studies that explore how games can be preserved so they can be experienced by future generations. The Museum's 'Games Lounge' has proved to be a key site for information gathering, particularly in relation to questions of objects handling, resilience and durability.

Hardware preservation

To begin with, the plastics that are used to produce many items of hardware and software within the collection are fragile and easily degradable. In recognition of the severity of material deterioration, the Museum stores all

NVA items within an environmentally controlled space with the following specifications (see Brain and David, 2006):

- 18–22°C
- relative humidity 45–55%
- UV under 10 microwatts per lumen
- visible light – less than 50 lux.

Nevertheless, there is more to the material care of videogames than the deterioration of plastics. The electrical components of videogames hardware (and software in the case of cartridges) may also prove to be extremely fragile and typically systems require considerable maintenance to keep them running. Many of the items within the NVA collection are working models but are never turned on, in an attempt to preserve their original condition. However, while such precautions may preserve the outward appearance of these objects, not running the machines or plugging/unplugging cartridges may, in certain circumstances, accelerate the ageing process, as specific electronic components lose charge, corrode and may ultimately become inoperable. Ideally, and in common with other similar collections, the NVA aims to build an accompanying handling collection of objects that are designed to be switched on and used by patrons.

Software preservation

The National Media Museum, together with the wider Science Museum Group, is currently working towards a sustainable solution to preserving digital assets. The fragility of portable magnetic media and the effects of bit-rot are well documented, even if their true extent is not yet fully understood or predictable (Lowood et al., 2009) and the NVA is collaborating with other institutions already working within this area to build a secure and reliable digital repository of videogames, while retaining the software in its original formats in the best conditions possible. Digital images are currently being preserved within the National Media Museum's image archive and manageable solutions for preserving video and audio assets are being assessed.

In recognition of the importance of the fan cultures that support and sustain games, as well as the desire to understand 'gaming' in its widest context, the NVA has developed a partnership with the British Library to build a special collection of websites as part of the UK Web Archiving project. Announced in 2012, the gaming special collection will build a collection of industry- and community-produced websites that illustrate the impact and influence of videogames on society.

Public exhibitions

Whilst the various objects in the NVA's collection are available to view and research at the National Media Museum (the Museum operates a system whereby patrons may request access to specific objects from the collection), in order to showcase the NVA and reflect the new digital culture remit of the Museum, the Games Lounge public gallery opened in February 2010. Initially sited in the foyer entrance of the Museum but now relocated to a larger gallery space, the Games Lounge includes a selection of playable original arcade and console games as well as titles playable under emulation, alongside key items of contextualizing ephemera.

- **Arcade cabinets** Space Invaders, Asteroids, Galaxian, Pac-Man, Defender, Centipede, Donkey Kong, Frogger, Gauntlet, Street Fighter II, Point Blank
- **Emulation** Manic Miner (ZX Spectrum), Prince of Persia (DOS)
- **Original console and controllers** Pong (Atari VCS 2600), Mario Kart (Super Nintendo), Sonic the Hedgehog 2 (Sega Megadrive), GoldenEye 007 (Nintendo 64), Actua Soccer (Playstation 1).

All of the games are heavily used by the public. Confounding initial expectations, the arcade cabinets have proved to be comparatively problematic and require regular maintenance. Given their original intention, location and apparently robust design, the fragility of the arcade cabinets in the collection was unexpected. Numerous problems have been encountered by transporting and moving the original cabinets. This has highlighted loose connections and fragile circuit boards. The cathode ray tube (CRT) monitors contained within the arcade cabinets have also demonstrated signs of age through several cases of image strobing/flickering and display malfunction through extensive use and overheating. Another regular symptom has also been malfunctions and blockages in the coin operation system, created by visitors using the incorrect coins.

Conversely, while modern emulations making use of custom controllers but running emulated code on generic PCs have proved to be as reliable as anticipated, the robustness of 1980s and 1990s consoles has been similarly high. As such, putatively fragile devices have required only very minimal input from the Museum's gallery maintenance team. The team will continue to monitor and report on the situation.

The use of emulation is obviously somewhat controversial in relation to videogames. First, and most widely discussed, emulation and, in particular, the acquisition and use of commercial ROMs (the generic name for extracted game code), is typically categorized as software piracy, as it requires circumventing technical measures of protection such as DRM (digital rights management). Second, given the importance of the 'feel' of gameplay, emulation poses problems for those sensitive to the presentation of playable games. As Newman (2011) notes, 'even the most seemingly minor variations in the operation, look and feel of digital games have considerable impacts on the experience of play'.

Moreover, as McDonough et al. (2010) have noted in *Preserving Virtual Worlds Final Report*, there are not only considerable variations between the audiovisual and interface operation of different emulators even when running the same extracted code, there are manifest differences between even the qualitatively 'best' emulators and the original hardware/software combinations (assuming a definable original can be identified, which is particularly problematic in the case of PC games or even consoles requiring connection to TV displays, as the specificities of audio and video output are highly contingent on display technologies – see also Montfort and Bogost, 2009).

At this stage in the development of the NVA's exhibition strategy, the development and assessment of practical solutions to emulation is key. The Games Lounge presents a vital testbed within which to evaluate the efficacy of emulation for specific audiences. We might tentatively suggest that while the specificities of the CRT blurring and scanline interference that Montfort and Bogost (2009) note, or the importance of frame-accurate emulation for expert players of *Street Fighter IV*, as Newman (2012) notes in relation to play performances such as frame reading, will be important for serious game players, for more general audiences such nuances will be comparatively insignificant if not unnoticeable. This certainly raises important questions about identifying audience(s) and their particular needs for any game archive or collection (Bogost, 2007).

For the Games Lounge, the emulated titles have been developed with the user experience in mind, and patron feedback suggests that the current solution is a successful compromise between an accurate, genuine experience and a robust, maintainable working exhibit. To create a truly authentic experience, the Museum could have used an original ZX Spectrum computer running *Manic Miner* from cassette tape. This would have to have been loaded every day before the public arrive and reloaded if the fragile system ever crashed. The emulated solution works from a Windows PC running a ZX Spectrum emulator and simply boots up automatically every morning. The PC keyboard micro controller has been rewired into an original ZX Spectrum keyboard in an attempt to re-create the authentic experience. Just as Bogost (n.d.) has invited us to consider the importance of visual displays, we should perhaps also muse on the potential significance of the anticipation and expectation that is built through the cassette loading process and question whether this forms part of the experience to capture and communicate.

The current selection of titles included in the Games Lounge has been guided by a desire to show the evolution of games across different platforms, hardware and genres. Multiple-player experience and quick bursts of enjoyment were also considered to create a gallery that demonstrates a broad spectrum of games that are easy, fun, intuitive and quick to play. As such, we must recognize the specific context in which the Games Lounge activity takes place and the intersection between the ambitions of curatorial teams, researchers and the strategic, operational and managerial imperatives of a national institution.

It was of vital importance for each game in the Games Lounge that the Museum sought permission from the copyright holder to display the game free of charge within the gallery. The significance of this endeavour should not be underestimated and the sheer amount of time and effort involved in just the process of identifying rights holders in this most complex field of co-owned and licensed intellectual property may prove to limit the scalability of such an initiative. Strategies for dealing with IP in relation to formal preservation practice continue to present themselves as among the most urgently needed in the sector. In part, this motivates the NVA's partnership in the European Federation of Game Archives, Museums and Preservation projects (EFGAMP) coalition.

The Games Lounge is soon to be relaunched in a new permanent space within the Museum. This allows the NVA a larger public space to try new and different games and experiment with strategies for displaying and engaging with videogames in a gallery setting. The Games Lounge and other temporary exhibition spaces can also be used as a catalyst to drive the collection forward and acquire new material to help the NVA grow.

Note

Since this chapter was originally written, and following restructuring at the National Media Museum, curatorial responsibility for the NVA collection now resides with the Science Museum in London.

References

Bogost, I. (n.d.) *A Television Simulator: CRT emulation for the Atari VCS*, www.bogost.com/games/a_television_simulator.shtml [accessed 10 April 2012].

Bogost, I. (2007) *Persuasive Games: the expressive power of videogames*, Cambridge, MA, MIT Press.

Brain, D. and David, F. (2006) *Specifications for New Showcases: Ingenious Plastics Centenary 2007*, London, Science Museum.

Lowood, H., Armstrong, A., Monnens, D., Vowell, Z., Ruggill, J., McAllister, K., Donahue, R. and Pinchbeck, D. (2009) *Before It's Too Late: preserving games across the industry/academia divide*, http://wiki.igda.org/images/4/43/State_of_Play_Before_Its_Too_Late.pdf [accessed 10 April 2012].

McDonough, J., Olendorf, R., Kirschenbaum, M., Kraus, K., Reside, D., Donahue, R., Phelps, A., Egert, C., Lowood, H. and Rojo, S. (2010) *Preserving Virtual Worlds Final Report*, University of Illinois, http://hdl.handle.net/2142/17097 [accessed 10 April 2012].

Montfort, N. and Bogost, I. (2009) *Racing the Beam: the Atari Video Computer System*, MIT Press.

National Media Museum (2010) *National Media Museum Collecting Policy Statement*, NMSI, www.nationalmediamuseum.org.uk/AboutUs/ReportsPlansPolicies/CollectingPolicy.aspx [accessed 22 April 2014].

Newman, J. (2009) Save the Videogame! The National Videogame Archive: preservation, supersession and obsolescence, *M/C Journal*, **12** (3), July.

Newman, J. (2011) (Not) Playing Games: player-produced walkthroughs as archival documents of digital gameplay, *International Journal of Digital Curation*, **2** (6), 109–27.

Newman, J. (2012) Ports and Patches: digital games as unstable objects, *Convergence: the international journal of research into new media*, **18** (2), 135-42.

Newman, J. and Woolley, T. (2009) Make Videogames History: game preservation and the National Videogame Archive. In *Proceedings of DiGRA 2009*, Brunel University, London.

CHAPTER 7

Bridging the gap in digital art preservation: interdisciplinary reflections on authenticity, longevity and potential collaborations

Perla Innocenti

History of Art, School of Culture and Creative Arts,
University of Glasgow, UK

Digital casualties: challenges for digital art preservation

Born-digital art is fundamentally art produced and mediated by a computer. It is an art form within the more general 'media art' category (Altshuler, 2005; Paul, 2008a, 2008b; Depocas et al., 2003; Grau, 2007; Graham and Cook, 2010; Lieser, 2010) and includes software art, computer-mediated installations, internet art and other heterogeneous art types.

The boundaries of digital art are particularly fluid, as it merges art, science and technology to a great extent. The technological landscape in which digital art is created and used challenges its long-term accessibility, the potentiality of its integrity, and the likelihood that it will retain authenticity over time. Digital objects – including digital art works – are fragile and susceptible to technological change. We must act to keep digital art alive, but there are practical problems associated with its preservation, documentation, access, function, context and meaning. Preservation risks for digital art are real: they are technological but also social, organizational and cultural.[1]

Digital and media art works have challenged 'traditional museological approaches to documentation and preservation because of their ephemeral, documentary, technical, and multi-part nature' (Rinehart, 2007b, 181). The technological environment in which digital art lives is constantly changing, which makes it very difficult to preserve this kind of art work. All art is subject to change. This can occur at art object level and at context level. In most circumstances change is very slow, but in digital art this isn't the case anymore because it is happening so quickly, owing to the pace of technological development.

Surely the increased pace of technological development has more implications than just things happening faster. Digital art, in particular, questions many of the most fundamental assumptions of the art world: what is a work of art in the digital age? What should be retained for the future? Which aspects of a given work can be changed and which must remain fixed for the work to retain the artist's intent? How do museums collect and preserve? Is a digital work as fragile as its weakest components? What is ownership? What is the context of digital art? What is a viewer? It is not feasible for the arts community to preserve over the centuries working original equipment and software. And industry has no incentive to reproduce old parts or to make current parts backwards compatible. Furthermore, as Richard Rinehart noted, because of lack of formal documentation methods and the goal of bypassing traditional art world's values and practices, media art works are 'becoming victims to their own volatile intent' (Rinehart, 2007b, 181). Museums have long played a critical role in the creation and transmission of knowledge, culture and identity (Bennett, 2009; Knell, Macleod and Watson, 2007). As they undergo a metamorphosis from the physical to the virtual, museums continue to serve this custodial role, although their nature and reach might be very different in the future. In particular, as museums invest in collecting digital works, they come to recognize that these works are fragile and may require substantial and continued investment in finance and effort to keep them accessible over time.

Long-term accessibility of digital art: previous work

Digital art may seem less physical than traditional art. But as the novelist Bruce Sterling noted, 'very little materiality, is very, very far from no materiality at all.' (Sterling, 2003, 15). The bitstream might be composed of numbers, but the device – the computer – has similar conservation problems to those of a painting (e.g. humidity, heat, physical damage), plus a whole set of new ones.

Digital preservation is not only about keeping the bits that we use to represent information, but to keep these bits alive, as an ongoing activity to ensure recurring value and performance of digital objects, including digital art works. As Seamus Ross clarified, digital preservation is about 'maintaining the semantic meaning of the digital object and its content, about maintaining its provenance and authenticity, about retaining its interrelatedness, and about securing information about the context of its creation and use' (Ross, 2007, 2). Conservation and restoration are relevant; however, they are part of a larger group of activities to ensure longevity for digital objects: collection and repository management, selection and appraisal, destruction, risk management, preserving the context, interpretation and functionality of objects, ensuring a collection's cohesion and interoperability, enhancement, updating and annotating, scalability and automation; storage technologies and methods.

In the last decades much work has been done towards establishing the long-term accessibility of electronic, media and digital art, as well as documenting media and digital art in order to keep it accessible in the future. Some of the key projects and initiatives in this area had already begun in the 1970s (for example, the Electronic Art Intermix [EAI] and the Netherlands Media Art Institute [NIMk] and Montevideo/Time Based Arts) and further initiatives developed through the following decades, including V2, Matters in Media Art, Forging the Future and DOCAM.[2]

These projects and initiatives have contributed to raising awareness of some of the challenges of digital art preservation, examined media and digital art works, and explored some specific documentation aspects and initiated collaborations with other institutions. Nevertheless, much of this work has been survey-like and not particularly well founded from either a theoretical or methodological perspective. So far, the theoretical aspects of the problem of digital art preservation and curation have been examined without much grounding particularly in experimentation, and without responding to the theoretical and methodological dilemmas posed by digital art (e.g. transience, emergence and lack of fixity). Also the long-term preservation of documentation for digital art has not yet been systematically addressed. Documentation for digital art is at risk as much as digital art works themselves, and needs sustainable business and organizational models to be preserved in the long term. It is evident that digital art is a new phenomenon that requires a new suite of methodologies.

An interdisciplinary methodological approach to the preservation of digital art

The goal of the research project Preserving Computer-Generated Imagery: Art Theory, Methods and Experimental Applications that I am conducting at the University of Glasgow is to contribute to laying the foundations for a preservation framework of digital art and identifying interdisciplinary synergies with areas such as digital preservation, philosophy of art, museology, archival science and information management. Digital art is, after all, data designed to be constructed (represented, viewed, experienced) in particular ways, whose theoretical implications need consideration. The methodology that I have chosen to take is bottom up, to try to understand how digital art works. That is: I am starting with the works, the conservators and the creators. So I have decided to adopt a two-step approach, described below: on-site visits to major international collectors of digital art and in-depth interviews with their staff and experimentation with testbeds to assess preservation methods and processes.

I am using a mixed method of humanistic, social science and engineering approaches, described below.

The humanistic element of it is the art history element, and the reflection on what is a work of art in the digital age and what is the context of digital art. I am presenting some 'Reflections on authenticity and longevity for digital art' in the following section of this paper, ideas which have been further shaped by my social science approach, discussed in the next section.

Social science approach

From a social science perspective I have visited and talked with some of the most important collectors of digital art, conducting a whole series of interviews, which have provided me a window on the practices of different organizations that are working with digital art. I have borrowed methods from anthropology and grounded theory. Ethnography has become a common feature in social studies of scientific knowledge and technology, in particular thanks to Stephen Woolgar (Woolgar, 1996; Cooper et al., 1995). In my ethnographic process of observation of digital art, I am looking at key digital art organizations and how they are collecting, curating, preserving, displaying, and financing digital art. I am conducting on-site in-depth interviews, visits and observations because what I am told is sometimes at variance with what is being done. The organizations that I am targeting and selecting for my case studies are major international collectors of digital art works and digital art documentation. I visited ZKM | Media Museum at the ZKM | Center for Art and Media Karlsruhe (Germany), Ars Electronica

Centre – AEC (Linz, Austria), Hirshhorn Museum and Sculpture Garden (Washington, DC, USA), Smithsonian American Art Museum and Lunder Conservation Center (Washington, DC, USA), Museum of Modern Art in San Francisco – SFMOMA (San Francisco, CA, USA), Berkeley Art Museum – BAM (Berkeley, CA, USA), Museum of Modern Art – MOMA (New York, NY, USA), Whitney Museum of American Art (New York, NY, USA) and the Netherlands Media Art Institute – NIMk (Amsterdam, the Netherlands).

The complexity of maintaining the object longevity and the myriad of change that can occur over time means that we need to talk with organizations that have decades of experiences to understand what needs to be done in this area. Interviews with stakeholders of digital art preservation (museum directors, conservators, curators, registrars, technicians) are a new approach in this area. I have also conducted interviews and observations with selected digital artists (John Gerrard, Studio Azzurro, Maurice Benayoun) for an additional analysis of relevant aspects of preservation for digital art works.

Engineering approach

Preservation for computer-based art is more than just a question of trying to understand the problem. We also need to take a little time to see what might be possible because – as I concluded after my first visit at ZKM – preservation and curation of digital art is as much an art historical problem as it is an engineering problem. One of the fundamental challenges in the preservation of digital art is that the work of the conservators tends to be ad hoc. It is also based upon responsiveness to unique situations and not constructed on a body of theory and practice, as other aspects of art management and restoration tend to be. This should hardly surprise us, though, as digital art is a new phenomenon. So in the second phase of my investigation I decided to design engineering experiments to advance the understanding of the processes and methods by which digital art can be preserved and handled. For example, to preserve digital objects we need to be able to extract essential characteristics – the significant properties (see, e.g., Guttenbrunner et al., 2010; Hedstrom and Lee, 2002) – of the digital object from a file, to decide whether approaches such as migration and emulation will work for maintaining digital objects in accessible form. This is a new approach to research in this area.

Reflections on authenticity and longevity of digital art

Two aspects emerged from the first phase of my investigation that strike me as key for digital art preservation: the intrinsic performing nature of digital art, and the dynamic nature of digital art authenticity.

Digital art as a process of components interactions

The ability to establish authenticity in a digital object is crucial for its preservation (Ross, 2002). Even if the concept of authenticity is highly nuanced in the digital age, it is still a starting point for discussion of digital art. But to talk about authenticity we need to look at how digital art is created and rendered. For example, the image of the work *Bubbles* (2001), by Muench and Furukawa, is a process of interaction of many components: for this example, particularly, the file in which the data matrix representing the image is stored, and the software capable of interpreting and rendering this data form. If we were to explore this example in full, we would also need to discuss the hardware, the data projector, the screen, and the relationships (including intended effects) that all this has with the viewer.

Digital art as performance

This interaction of components leads me to think that all digital art is a performance, and more than a performance between the viewer and the object. In this particular instance, the performance that I am actually talking about is the performance of the work: because a digital art work consists of a set of code, and for the art work to become, it must be performed. Before the viewer interacts with the digital art work, this process of becoming has to occur. For example in the case of John Gerrard's 3D real-time work *Grow Finish Unit* (near Elkhart, Kansas) (2008), the algorithm developed by Gerrard needs to be performed in order for the work itself – the real-time 3D – to come to life.

Actually, this problem isn't unique to digital art. For example, within the AktiveArchive project, Johanna Phillips and Johannes Gfeller wrote interesting reflections about reconstruction and well informed re-performances of video art (Phillips, 2009; Gfeller, 2009). But in the field of digital art, it is nearly another construct. Some ground-breaking work in the documentation of performances has been done by Richard Rinehart, former digital media artist and director of the UC Berkeley Art Museum/Pacific Film Archive. Rinehart produced a promising theoretical approach based on a formal notation system for digital and media art creation, documentation and preservation: the Media Art Notation System (MANS) (Rinehart, 2007b). He compared media art to the performing arts, because media art works do not exist in a stable medium, and are inherently variable and computational. Their preservation is thus an interpretive act. Given the similar variability of music and media arts, Rinehart considers it appropriate to adopt a mechanism like a musical score for binding the integrity of media art works apart from specific instruments.

Instantiations, authenticities and documentation in digital art

Considering digital art as performance leads to some interesting reflections about its instantiations. As Seamus Ross observed, the

> first renderings of digital objects might best be referred to as an initial 'representation or instantiation'. The problem is: how can we record the functionality and behaviour as well as the content of that Initial Instantiation (II) so that we can validate subsequent instantiations? Where Subsequent Instantiations (SI) share precision of resemblance in content, functionality, and behaviour with the initial instantiations, the 'SIs' can be said to have the same authenticity and integrity as the 'IIs'.
>
> Ross (2006)

This notion of precision of resemblance is intended to reflect the fact that initial instantiations of digital objects and subsequent ones will not be precisely the same, but will have a degree of sameness. This degree of sameness will vary over time – in fact in the case of digital objects it is likely to decline as the distance between the initial instantiation and each subsequent one becomes greater, although this degree of variation may be mitigated by such circumstances as, for example, the frequency at which the digital object is instantiated. So each time a digital work of art is instantiated, it has a greater or lesser precision of resemblance to the initial instantiation that the artist created. The subsequent instantiations represent with greater or lesser degrees of accuracy the intentionality of the artist. Whether they have greater or lesser degrees of authenticity is a separate but fundamentally important question and needs to be considered in the context of, for example, the authenticity of performances. The UNESCO *Guidelines for the Preservation of Digital Heritage* mentions the question of assessing an acceptable level of variance of such instantiations (National Library of Australia and UNESCO, 2003, section 16.7) . This was also more recently highlighted by Richard Rinehart, in relation to the ecological balance of changes in the technological environment of digital art.

The intrinsic performing nature of digital art works makes them allographic rather than autographic works, along the distinction described by Nelson Goodman (Goodman, 1969). So I would like to draw a parallel between the instantiation of the code in a digital work, and the instantiation of the notation in a music performance, as described by John Butt (2002) and Dennis Dutton (2003).

We often assume that music notation is a rigid set of instructions. In reality, sometimes notation is the result of performance, sometimes it is a reminder, and sometimes it is just an example. There is no single process from notation to performance. The notation is going in all directions, with a complex relationship between sender and receiver. In his seminal book *Playing with History: the historical approach to musical performance* (Butt, 2002), John Butt has questioned whether 'authenticity' is still an appropriate term for music performance given that, in performance terms, it tends to condemn its negative to a sort of fake status. In music, partly through Butt's efforts, we now tend to use the term 'historically informed performance'. In his reflection on nominal authenticity in the arts, Dutton writes,

> the best attitude towards authenticity in music performance is that in which careful
> attention is paid to the historic conventions and limitations of a composer's age,
> but where one also tries to determine the artistic potential of a musical work,
> including implicit meanings that go beyond the understanding that the composer's
> age might have derived from it.
>
> Dutton (2003)

The dynamic notion of authenticity of digital art might seem to be in contrast with the notion of material authenticity that has been constructed for historical art works. If we look at authenticity in object conservation in museums, authenticity is a term associated with the original material components and process in an object, and its authorship or intention. For example, in his critique of traditional conservation ethics, Jonathan Kemp describes 'authenticity in the sense of "original material", traditionally one aspect of an object charged with the assignation of a "truth value" that legitimizes some aesthetic experiences' (Kemp, 2009, 60–1). However, these conservation principles are socially constructed processes mediated by technology-based practices, whereas the object keeps changing: it deteriorates, its context might change, and the way in which it is conserved and redisplayed will change. The role of conservators and of museums also changes over time. Therefore the conservators are caught between reconciling fidelity to the original artist intention and fidelity to the passage of time. Joseph Grigely also argued that any work of art is subject to a 'continuous and discontinuous transience' (Grigely, 1995, 1), that is integral to its authenticity. This means that any work of art – I would add, including digital art – is not fixed in a single point in time, but it is rather in a 'continuous state of becoming', as Heather MacNeil and Bonnie Mak elegantly pointed out (MacNeil and Mak, 2007, 33). As in Penelope's tale, conservators are actively constructing, deconstructing and reconstructing the authenticity of a work based on their understanding of its nature and the current conventions and assumptions for conserving it.

These reflections on instantiations and authenticity led my attention to the concept of authenticity in electronic records. As Jennifer Trant noted, 'archives have been challenged to manage electronic records as evidence for several decades' (Trant, 2009, 373). Like art conservators, archivists and record keepers are concerned with issues of fidelity. The trustworthiness of a record rests primarily on its fidelity to the original event, from which the record arises. The concept of provenance – a well documented chain of custody – is thus a fundamental archival principle, which helps to establish authenticity.

This has parallels with my reflections on instantiations of digital art works. If we look at computer-based art from the point of view of performance and archival authenticity, what is then really important is a trustworthy chain of documentary evidence about the work's genuine origins, custody and ownership in the museum collection. Authenticity is not an original condition, but it is rather a dynamic process. Digital art works are pushing the boundaries of traditional conservation practices and the notion of historicity. For example, let's look at the ongoing preservation strategy devised within the

Digital Art Conservation project for the interactive media art work *The Legible City, 1989–1991* in the ZKM | Media Museum.[3] This strategy could be seen as the equivalent of rewriting an older music score to adapt it to a modern or different instrument. On one hand, this iconic interactive installation is based on proprietary, work-specific software; on the other, it uses obsolete hardware and custom-made components. Such combination makes the preservation of *Legible City* a costly and risky business, both in the cost of maintaining its Indigo 2 computer (no longer produced by Silicon Graphics) and because of the potential weak point represented by its specially built analog-digital transformer. Conservators at ZKM examined, documented and created a fully functional replica of this transformer (the interactivity intended as part of the installation was also recorded), and software porting to another operating system is currently being evaluated by the ZKM as a more sustainable long-term preservation solution for the Indigo 2 computer.

Some conservators and curators might argue that the replacement of the historical software and transformer challenges the historicity and originality of the art work. However, digital art collectors need to come to terms with the fact that it will not be possible to guarantee original working equipment forever: in order to be kept alive, digital art works will need to be adapted to a new technology. This art work at ZKM is in the state of becoming. This idea of becoming is clearly referenced in the work of Heather Marie MacNeil and Bonnie Mak about constructions of authenticity, and this goes back to the notion that digital art becomes, which I mentioned earlier. Digital works are in a state of evolution.

Cultural institutions and cross-sectoral collaborations in digital preservation

Digital preservation is characterized by a wide range of activities to ensure longevity for digital objects, as mentioned at the beginning of this paper. It is thus an interdisciplinary area, in which diverse disciplines – for example archival science, library science, information management, computer forensics – are converging to support organizations in making their digital assets available to future users. The results of my research on digital art preservation confirm the potential benefits of cross-sectoral digital preservation partnerships and collaborations between cultural institutions (Innocenti, 2014; also for digital preservation Walker, 2006; Hingley, 2009;

Timms, 2009; Rodger, Jorgesen and D'Elia, 2011).

The term 'cultural institution' can be characterized by a number of specific features: the presence of a collection, offered to users within the frame of a systematic, continuous, organized knowledge structure and encompassed by scholarship, information and thought. Cultural institutions typically address public knowledge and memory, in a culture of inquiry and learning, and with interdisciplinary dynamic connections. They also deal with the need to create a coherent narrative, a story of who we are and what our cultural, historical and social contexts are. In modern Western society, cultural institutions include but are not limited to museums, libraries, archives (sometimes jointly defined as LAMs – libraries, archives and museums – see Zorich et al., 2008), galleries, and other heritage and cultural organizations.

Their histories are often intertwined, although their interrelations have not always led to a consolidated path of collaboration. For example, although often originating as unified 'universal museums', museums and libraries have developed separate institutional contexts and distinct cultures. Jennifer Trant noted how philosophies and policies of museums, archives and libraries now reflect their different approach to interpreting, collecting, preserving and providing access to objects in their care (Trant, 2009). Liz Bishoff remarked that:

> libraries believe in resource sharing, are committed to freely available information, value the preservation of collections, and focus on access to information. Museums believe in preservation of collections, often create their identity based on these collections, are committed to community education, and frequently operate in a strongly competitive environment.
>
> Bishoff (2004)

In the last century policy-makers have attempted to group and bridge these communities of practices through 'their similar role as part of the informal educational structures supported by the public, and their common governance' (Trant, 2009, 369).

Such commonalities are increasingly important to the sustainability of museums, libraries and public cultural institutions in a globalized world. The International Federation of Libraries Association (IFLA) remarked that museums and libraries are often natural partners for collaboration and co-operation (Yarrow, Clubb and Draper, 2008). One of the IFLA groups,

Libraries, Archives, Museums, Monuments and Sites (LAMMS), unites the five international organizations for cultural heritage, IFLA (libraries), ICA (archives), ICOM (museums), ICOMOS (monuments and sites) and CCAAA (audiovisual archives), to intensify co-operation in areas of common interest. In this context, a study in the USA observed that 'collaboration may enable . . . museums and libraries to strengthen their public standing, improve their services and programs, and better meet the needs of a larger and more diverse cross–sections of learners' (Institute of Museum and Library Services, 2004, 9). Archives have often been a virtuous third player in museum and library collaborations. For example, Rick Rinehart with Tim Hoyer secured a grant from the California Digital Library, National Leadership Program, for a project on integrating museums, libraries and archives access in the Online Archive of California (MOAC) (Rinehart, 2003; Rinehart, 2007a).

Some studies of museum and library collaborations have highlighted the benefits of joining forces and resources in a variety of areas, including but not limited to library activities and programmes related to museum exhibits; travelling museum exhibitions hosted in libraries; links between web-based resources in library and museum websites; library programmes including passes to museums; collaborative digitization and digital library projects enhancing access to resources in both museums and libraries; collaborative initiatives to bring in authors as speakers; and museum and library partnerships with other cultural and educational organizations. Partnerships in digital preservation research, practical applications and training would be a natural and mutually beneficial addition to such a portfolio of collaborations, as shown by the few but slowly increasing number of partnerships in this area.

The fruitful convergence between museums and libraries faces a number of challenges with respect to their different missions, cultures and organizational and funding structures. The nature of this collaboration can be multifaceted and varied, and the terminology itself is interpreted with diverse meanings, in particular regarding the degree of intensity of the collaboration and its transformational capacity, as noted by Hannah Gibson, Anne Morris and Marigold Cleeve (2007) and Betsy Diamant-Cohen and Dina Sherman (2003). However, the numerous opportunities for improving access to collections and leveraging funding, and also for partnerships in digital preservation, seem worth the challenge.

Conclusions: for a dynamic preservation model of digital art

With this paper, I hope to stimulate discussions about current and future approaches for digital art preservation, and contribute to the interdisciplinary foundations of a scientific framework for digital art preservation.

Authenticity – as MacNeil and Mak clearly pointed out – is a social construct, whose parameters and contents are always changing and under negotiation. Authenticity allows us to author stability in our disciplines. The current fast-paced digital environment defies the traditional structures of stability that have been authored for traditional art. Therefore, our approach to digital art works should be variable and digital object-responsive, with a level of tolerance of variability to match digital art's intrinsic variability and dynamic authenticity, as outlined in this paper. The designated community for whom we are preserving digital art should also be identified, together with the modality of restaging digital works and of preserving the related digital documentation. In conclusion, if conservation for digital art is a moving target, then our scientific methodology should be a moving gun.

Acknowledgments

I am deeply indebted to Professor Seamus Ross at the Faculty of Information, University of Toronto, for his precious suggestions, guidance and support throughout this research, and more recently to Professor John Butt at the University of Glasgow, for sharing his knowledge and experience of musical performance. I am also very grateful to all my interviewees for the time and helpful insights that they have shared with me regarding conservation and preservation for digital art.

The aspects related to cross-domain partnerships between cultural institutions are part of an ongoing investigation of networks of museums, libraries and public cultural institutions, which I am leading within the EU-funded project European Museums in an Age of Migrations (MeLa), funded within the European Union's Seventh Framework Programme (SSH-2010-5.2.2), Grant Agreement n. 266757.

Note

1   See, for example, the work done in the DRAMBORA (Digital Repository

Audit Method Based On Risk Assessment), created and developed by DigitalPreservationEurope and the UK Digital Curation Centre (see www.repositoryaudit.eu, accessed 6 August 2012). Among other benefits, using this tool allows one to build a detailed catalogue of prioritized pertinent risks, categorized according to type and inter-risk relationships, that includes not only technical but also, for example, organizational and legal risks, in relation to the organization's mission, objectives, activities and assets. See also Innocenti, McHugh and Ross (2008).

2   Documentation and Conservation of the Media Arts Heritage.

3   An image of this interactive work by Jeffrey Shaw, together with ZKM digital art conservation approach, is available at http://www02.zkm.de/digitalartconservation/index.php/en/exhibitions/zkm-exhibition/nnnnnjeffrey-shaw.html. See also Serexhe, B. (2013).

References

Altshuler, B. (2005) Collecting the New: a historical introduction. In Altshuler, B. (ed.) *Collecting the New: museums and contemporary art*, Princeton, NJ, Princeton University Press.

Bennett, T. (2009) *The Birth of the Museum: history, theory, politics*, reprint, London, Routledge.

Bishoff, L. (2004) The Collaboration Imperative, *Library Journal*, **129** (1), 34–5.

Butt, J. (2002) *Playing with History: the historical approach to musical performance*, Cambridge, Cambridge University Press.

Cooper, G., Hine, C., Rachel, J. and Woolgar, S. (1995) Ethnography and Human-Computer Interaction. In Thomas, P. J. (ed.), *The Social and Interactional Dimensions of Human-Computer Interfaces*, Cambridge, Cambridge University Press, 11–36.

Depocas, A., Ippolito, J., Jones, C. and Daniel Langlois Foundation for Art, Science and Technology (2003) *Permanence Through Change: the variable media approach (La Permanence par le Changement: l'approche des médias variables)*, New York, NY, Guggenheim Museum Publications.

Diamant-Cohen, B. and Sherman, D. (2003) Hand in Hand – museums and libraries working together, *Public Libraries*, **42** (2), 102.

Dutton, D. (2003) Authenticity in Art. In Levinson, J. (ed.), *The Oxford Handbook of Aesthetics*, Oxford, Oxford University Press.

Gfeller, J. (2009) The Reference Hardware Pool of AktiveArchive at Bern

University of Arts: a basis for a historically well informed re-performance of media art. In Schubiger, I. (ed.), *Reconstructing Swiss Video Art from the 1970s and 1980s*, Zurich, J. R. P. Ringier, 166–74.

Gibson, H., Morris, A. and Cleeve, M. (2007) Links Between Libraries and Museums: investigating museum-library collaboration in England and the USA, *Libri*, **57** (2), 53–64.

Goodman, N. (1969) *Languages of Art: an approach to a history of symbols*, London, Oxford University Press.

Graham, B. and Cook, S. (2010) *Rethinking Curating: art after new media*, Cambridge, MA, MIT Press.

Grau, O. (2007) *MediaArtHistories*, Cambridge, MA, MIT Press.

Grigely, J. (1995) *Textualterity: art, theory and textual criticism*, Ann Arbor, MI, University of Michigan Press.

Guttenbrunner, M., Wieners, J., Rauber, A. and Thaller, M. (2010) Same But Different – comparing rendering environments for interactive digital objects. In Ioannides, M., Fellner, D., Georgopoulos, A. and Hadjimitsis, D. G. (eds), *Digital Heritage*, paper presented at the Third International Conference, EuroMed 2010, Lemessos, Cyprus, 8–13 November.

Hedstrom, M. and Lee, C. A. (2002) Significant Properties of Digital Objects: definitions, applications, implications. In *Proceedings of the DLM-Forum 2002: @ccess and preservation of electronic information, best practices and solutions*, Barcelona, 6–8 May, European Communities, Luxembourg, 218–23.

Hingley, S. (2009) Preservation: the benefits of partnership working, paper presented at Doing More With Less, Preservation Advisory Centre forum on skills development, 30 November, British Library Conference Centre, www.bl.uk/blpac/pdf/forumpartnerships.pdf.

Innocenti, P. (ed.) (2014) *Migrating Heritage: experiences of cultural networks and cultural dialogue in Europe*, Aldershot, Ashgate.

Innocenti, P., McHugh, A. and Ross, S. (2008) Tackling the Risk Challenge: DRAMBORA Interactive. In Cunningham, P. and Cunningham, M. (eds), *Collaboration and the Knowledge Economy: issues, applications, case studies*, Amsterdam, IOS Press.

Institute of Museum and Library Services (2004) *Charting the Landscape, Mapping New Paths: museums, libraries, and K-12 learning*, Washington, DC.

Kemp, J. (2009) Practical Ethics v2.0. In Richmond, A. and Bracker, A. (eds), *Conservation: principles, dilemmas and uncomfortable truths*, Burlington, MA, Elsevier, 60–72.

Knell, S. J., Macleod, S. and Watson, S. E. R. (2007) *Museum Revolutions: how museums change and are changed*, London, Routledge.

Lieser, W. (2010) *Digital Art: Neue Wege in der Kunst*, Potsdam, H. F. Ullmann.

MacNeil, H. M. and Mak, B. (2007). Constructions of Authenticity, *Library Trends*, **56** (1), 26–52.

National Library of Australia and UNESCO (2003) *Guidelines for the Preservation of Digital Heritage*, Paris, Information Society Division, UNESCO.

Paul, C. (2008a) *Digital Art*, London, Thames & Hudson.

Paul, C. (2008b) *New Media in the White Cube and Beyond: curatorial models for digital art*, Berkeley, CA, University of California Press.

Phillips, J. (2009) The Reconstruction of Video Art: a fine line between authorised re-performance and historically informed interpretation. In Schubiger, I. (ed.), *Reconstructing Swiss Video Art from the 1970s and 1980s*, Zurich, J. R. P. Ringier, 158–65.

Rinehart, R. (2003) MOAC – a report on integrating museum and archive access in the online archive of California, *D-lib Magazine*, **9** (1).

Rinehart, R. (2007a) *Museums and Online Archives Collaboration: Digital Asset Management Database*, www.bampfa.berkeley.edu/media/DAMD_Online_Documentation.pdf [accessed 27 March 2012].

Rinehart, R. (2007b). The Media Art Notation System: documenting and preserving digital/media art, *Leonardo*, **40** (2), 181–7.

Rodger, E., Jorgensen, C. and D'Elia, G. (2011) Partnerships and Collaboration among Public Libraries, Public Broadcast Media and Museums: current context and future press stable, *Library Quarterly*, **75** (1), 42–66.

Ross, S. (2002) Position Paper on Integrity and Authenticity of Digital Cultural Heritage Objects, *Digicult: integrity and authenticity of digital cultural heritage objects*, **1**, 6–8.

Ross, S. (2006) Approaching Digital Preservation Holistically. In Tough, A. G. and Moss, M. S. (eds), *Record Keeping in a Hybrid Environment: managing the creation, use, preservation and disposal of unpublished information objects in context*, Oxford, Chandos Press, 115–53.

Ross, S. (2007) Digital Preservation, Archival Science and Methodological Foundations for Digital Libraries, keynote address at the *European Conference on Research and Advanced Technology for Digital Libraries* (ECDL), Budapest, Hungary, 17 September, www.ecdl2007.org/Keynote_ECDL2007_SROSS.pdf.

Serexhe, B. (ed.) (2013) *Preservation of Digital Art: theory and practice*, The Digital Art

Conservation Project, Vienna, Ambra Verlag.

Sterling, B. (2003) Digital Decay. In Depocas, A., Ippolito, J., Jones, C. and Daniel Langlois Foundation for Art, Science and Technology (eds), *Permanence Through Change: the variable media approach (La Permanence par le Changement : l'approche des médias variables)*, New York, NY, Guggenheim Museum Publications, 10–22.

Timms, K. (2009) New Partnerships for Old Sibling Rivals: the development of integrated access systems for the holdings of archives, libraries and museums, *Archivaria*, **68**, 67–96.

Trant, J. (2009) Emerging Convergence? Thoughts on museums, archives, libraries, and professional training, *Museum Management and Curatorship*, **24** (4), 369–87.

Walker, A. (2006) Preservation. In Bowman, J. H. (ed.), *British Librarianship and Information Work 2001–2005*, Farnham, Ashgate Publications, 501–18.

Woolgar, S. (1996) Technologies as Cultural Artefacts. In Dutton, W. H. and Peltu, M. (eds), *Information and Communication Technologies: visions and realities*, Oxford, Oxford University Press, 87–102.

Yarrow, A., Clubb, B. and Draper, J-L. (2008) *Public Libraries, Archives and Museums: trends in collaboration and cooperation*, The Hague: International Federation of Library Associations and Institutions.

Zorich, D., Waibel, G., Erway, R. and OCLC (2008) *Beyond the Silos of the LAMs: collaboration among libraries, archives and museums*, Dublin, OH, OCLC Programs and Research.

CHAPTER 8

Laying a trail of breadcrumbs – preparing the path for preservation

Drew Baker
King's Visualisation Lab,
Department of Digital Humanities,
King's College London, UK

David Anderson
Professor of Digital Humanities and
CiTECH Research Centre Director,
University of Portsmouth, UK

Introduction

Recent decades have seen an exponential increase in the use of computer systems in academic disciplines traditionally thought of as being non-technical. This has partly been driven by the opportunities which computational tools and techniques make possible, and partly by a perceived need to position research at the 'cutting edge' of technology. The use of computing is seen as enhancing research funding applications and improving institutional profiles. The rapid uptake of computing has not, however, been accompanied by a commensurate attention to ensuring that digital-based research and deliverables are preserved in the long term.

The process of ensuring long-term access to non-digital material is well understood and while not always fully implemented, it is nevertheless relatively uncomplicated. The situation is markedly different when dealing with material that is wholly, or partly, digital. The preservation of, and provision for long-term access to, even the simplest digital object typically involves marshalling a surprisingly large number of technologies and specialized curatorial skills and tools, and no small degree of expense. In the case of complex digital objects, or hybrid objects, there are only a handful of centres in the UK or internationally which possess the knowledge or resources to tackle the preservation issues involved.

In this introductory chapter we will set out very briefly, and in fairly general terms, the overall preservation landscape as it applies to digital objects. We will try to give some sense of the main approaches available, and their strengths and weaknesses.

Traditional objects and the digital counterparts

Before looking at the principal preservation approaches currently in use, it is probably worth mentioning a fundamental difference between traditional objects and their digital counterparts. A standard textbook is capable of being read and understood by anyone who has sufficient intellectual capability, language skills, comprehension and so on, together with physical access to the material. The very same material in digital form requires something more – a facilitating layer of technology through which access to the content must always be mediated. It is usually possible to access the contents of digital files using more than one particular technology – one might use a Kindle or a PC, for example – but direct unmediated access is not possible. The increasing digitization of material opens up very many opportunities for knowledge to be disseminated and accessed in new ways, and for new audiences, but the price of these potential benefits is that without available technology there can be no access to information stored in digital form.

This opens up the question of what happens when new and incompatible devices on which one wishes to access preserved digital objects supersede the technology originally used to create them. If some preservation action is not taken, the answer is simple: the old digital material will gradually be accessible on fewer and fewer platforms, and, when the last compatible device ceases to work, the digital objects will be inaccessible.

Preservation approaches

Two main techniques have emerged for retaining long-term access to preserved digital objects. The first of these, and by far the more commonly used, is migration, or format shifting. The focus of this approach is the actual digital object to be preserved, and migration requires that preserved files are converted so as to be compatible with whatever hardware platform is available to access them. Thus, files originally written in 1960 on a DEC PDP-1 machine and solely intended for use on that system may be converted to run on a VAX machine in the 1970s or on an iPAD2 in 2012. For simple file types the process of developing file conversion tools is not a particularly complicated one. However, there are a relatively large number of known file types in existence (somewhere in excess of 6000) and some of these are so intimately bound up with the particularities of their originally intended hardware that the conversion process becomes more tricky. So, in addition to potentially needing to develop thousands of individual file conversion programs each time a new computer system is invented, one must check each of these very carefully to see the effect it has on the content of preserved files.

Even when a great deal of care has been exercised, it is not uncommon for files originally written for one computer system to appear slightly differently on a new system: colours, fonts or pagination may be all altered, sometimes so slightly that detection is hard to guarantee. While in some cases this may not be important, in others it may crucially alter the intellectual content or meaning in ways which are not systematically predictable. Moreover, these conversion errors gradually accumulate as a file moves from one system to the next, leaving open the very distinct possibility that over a relatively short time it will be nearly impossible to view the digital material in its original form. Furthermore, the substantial expense involved in digital storage is such that, within an institutional context, it is by no means assured that a copy of the original files will be preserved after conversion has taken place. In very many cases this will mean that post-conversion there will be no route back to the original material.

Migration is a technique best applied to simple file types, such as ASCII, or PDF 1.0. When faced with more complex digital objects, such as modern videogames, virtualizations or computer-based art works, migration is not a viable option, particularly within an institutional context. Large-scale preservation activity is always expensive, but the time, equipment and expertise required to migrate (or port), for example, interactive videogames from one hardware system to another and to ensure that they look and behave exactly the same on each platform is completely beyond the means of any library or archive in the world. This is quite aside from any legal restrictions which might apply to the activity.

A second approach to digital preservation moves attention away from digital objects and concentrates instead on the hardware platforms on which they were originally intended to run – their environments. This so-called 'emulation' approach attempts to develop software that when run on one hardware platform makes it behave as if it were another. Thus, one might run a 'PC Emulator' on an iMac, thereby enabling one to access PC files on Apple hardware. The principal advantages of emulation are that, if done properly, it completely bypasses any concerns about file-format inflation and complexity. If the emulator performs as it should, then any file which ran on the original platform, whatever its format or complexity, should perform under emulation exactly as it did on the original.

For most people emulation as a preservation approach is poorly understood to the point of being technologically intimidating, and it is not uncommon even within the digital preservation community for mention of emulation to be met with incomprehension, where it is not actually resisted. The complexities of producing an emulator are certainly great, and within a preservation context it is necessary not only to capture all the officially documented characteristics of a hardware system, but also to incorporate undocumented aspects of the original platform. This extra requirement is not only prompted by some sense of intellectual completeness but reflects the fact that a great deal of high-performance software depends on exploiting (deliberately or otherwise) undocumented hardware features. The technical understanding required to produce such a completely faithful emulator is not widely available and in the case of some machines may not any longer exist. Therefore, while an emulation-based approach to digital preservation has definite attractions, it cannot be considered an easy alternative. Furthermore, emulators are digital objects in their own right, and are just as subject to being rendered inaccessible when the hardware platform on which they were designed to run becomes obsolete, as are any other digital objects.

As new hybrid disciplines, such as the digital humanities, start to emerge and mature, and as information technology enables researchers to conduct their work in virtual environments, the need to understand what is meant by 'preservation', what constitutes a 'digital object' and how digital research creates artefacts in their own right is becoming ever more critical. There are many myths, assumptions and implementation failures surrounding digital preservation and this chapter will examine some of these.

Digital ubiquity: a preservation challenge

Digital objects and the data with which they are entwined have within a generation become not only commonplace but ubiquitous. The silicon revolution now gives anyone with access to a computing device the ability to access, create, manipulate and comment upon data, once the domain of specialist equipment, skills and tasks. It can be argued that this familiarity, while not breeding contempt, has somewhat devalued our perception of data. While Moore's Law predicts a doubling of processing power every two years, Rock's

Law (also known as Moore's Second Law) observes that the cost of producing the components doubles every four years, reflecting the expanding market for new and innovative products requiring capital investment, which in turn perpetuates new products. This cycle is ultimately dependent on the marketing of new product to the masses and a high obsolescence attrition rate, especially when combined with software that takes advantage of innovations and the repurposing of earlier developments into other ancillary hardware.

If tangible objects, from computer workstations to smartphones, monitors to mass storage devices, have a relatively fixed commercial lifespan and are considered almost as consumable goods – often not considered as items requiring accounted depreciation (at least in terms of components) – then what hope is there for intangible assets such as data? The loss of an MP3 player may be inconvenient but a new and better model can be purchased at a similar, if not better, price than that paid for the older model, and the albums downloaded from the internet. To replace a sound system that would allow one to play a vinyl collection, or even cassette tape, would cost significantly more.

An unspoken promise

If there is a commercial imperative, then, to sell product to the mass market there is an implied promise that the newer, faster, better, easier version will provide some form of integration with existing systems. While clearly if there is a radical change, for example for videotape to compact disc, one cannot expect the media to work (although one is always surprised to hear that someone cannot watch their wedding video anymore, as they disposed of their VHS recorder some years ago), but anyone faced with connecting, for example, a flat-screen LED television to existing DVD players, game consoles, media stations, online services and/or home computer networks soon finds themself lost in the different combination of cables and input/output options.

To some extent this naivety extends to the digital domain; we assume that someone is 'looking after' the internet and we are upset when our favourite website or service is taken down or unavailable, a DVD fails to play on our new system, a CD-ROM supposed to be able to store data for 100 years is corrupted or the latest update to a piece of software changes the way we work. And yet at the heart of this complex system of disposable parts lies the very thing which is set up to allow us to access – the data, the ghost in the machine, without which the whole system would be useless. If any part of this complex digital object fails then the integrity of the whole cannot be guaranteed: preservation of complex digital objects then is much more than ensuring that your files are backed up.

The *Oxford English Dictionary* defines preservation as 'the act of maintaining (something) in its original or existing state'; this implies that the object of preservation is both stable and that there is a process of ensuring that its stability is continued. We do not commonly think of 'digital' as implying *statis* or stability; the idea that digital objects are dynamic, interactive, customizable and available on demand has more to do with good marketing for products than describing the actual data that it uses in novel ways. Data, when taken as a whole, is for the most part static.

So if data is primarily static or at least if it can be captured at a point in time, a snapshot if you will, then the data could be hived off and kept somewhere safe ready for when it might be needed. While this is to some extent true, such a viewpoint focuses on the data, and as such data on its own is not of much use: it needs to be organized in some way, stored in some format and accessible by some method in order to be useful rather than just a series of bits and bytes. These additional properties when bundled with the data denote a data object (or record or file).

Much like a series of characters organized together as a piece of text, these bundles make sense of the words that they form and organize them into a comprehensible communication. This piece of text, however, is only comprehensible if it obeys the rules of the language it is written in and if the person reading it can understand that language. Our conceptual piece of text therefore must have some standards applied to it in order to be understood and the mechanism for reading the text must be available in order for the text to be actually read.

It is remarkable that so much tacit or assumed understanding of how data is organized and why formats and standards are important is unacknowledged or undocumented in many digital projects. Whether this is a direct result of the ease of access and use of information technology, or whether the drive to use information technology in new and innovative ways means that such considerations are sidelined, is open to debate.

Wherever the problem may lie, the greatest criticism of research utilizing visualization and simulation as part of its methodology is that it is not 'scientific', or rather that it does not follow the principles of scientific methodology and, in particular, that results cannot be readily reproduced. It does not mean that the data used to create the visualization is necessarily flawed; rather, that the results are different because the environment in which the data exists has changed. If, then, we can ensure that not only is the data, the characters of our text, recorded but also the entire digital object is described (to extend the metaphor, how the book containing the text is organized, the conventions it uses and its dependencies), then the meaning of the text can be understood within the context of its environment (within the context of the book, to continue the metaphor). The object book can be preserved in a library, reprinted, translated, scanned from paper to a data file or even emulated as an e-book but the knowledge that is created through the interaction between the data and its object is maintained, preserved and repeatable. Understanding this complexity and being able to communicate this with data therefore is fundamental to preservation. It is this symbiotic relationship between data and the digital object, and how that complexity can be managed, documented and safeguarded, that we will now consider in practical ways.

Preservation planning

The first step in planning the preservation of a digital object (of whatever complexity) is to apply a known standard to the component parts of that object. As an object may have many different components it may be necessary to apply different standards to each different part, and it may be necessary to apply multiple standards to a specific media type, depending on the circumstances. While the application of standards is crucial to the preservation process it is equally important to record the standard that is being used as part of the metadata record of the object. The application of standards does not guarantee that digital object preservation is assured, but it greatly enhances the probability that the data will be comprehensible and usable long term.

Where proprietary formats cannot be avoided, then the preservation plan should strongly consider the use of a parallel standard that can be included within the preservation process as an ancillary archive item. A number of projects conducted by King's College London's King's Visualisation Lab (KVL) utilized the online persistent virtual world platform of Linden Lab's

Second Life.[1] While the platform offers the user the functionality to construct digital artefacts natively within the *Second Life* environment, the decision was taken to conduct the modelling phase of the project offline wherever possible, using 3D Studio Max.

The 3D Studio Max file created to describe the geometry and the associated texture files (mostly held in Adobe's Photoshop .PSD format as working files) were converted into a form that could be imported into the online virtual world environment. In addition to the .max and transfer format the files describing the geometry were also exported into VRML97 ISO/IEC 14772-1:1997[2] format for archiving along with the original source files. The decision to build offline was primarily informed by the absence from the *Second Life* platform of any mechanism for saving or export from the virtual world (the environment is persistent) or provision of version control for development (and recovery). In addition, there was an identified risk in the nature of the platform; Linden Lab is a commercial company and charges for renting virtual land and could change the terms and conditions of usage or close-down, thus rendering the work inaccessible, and because of the persistent nature of the development of the platform, the system is, in effect, in a state of perpetual beta testing with no single point that could be selected for a baseline of preservation.

At first glance the process of producing a 'data double' may seem superfluous but such redundancy can be seen as an extension to the quality control process in ensuring that a build has interoperability between platforms, as well as producing a data recovery strategy as part of a project's overall security procedures. For those in the visualization community this concept will not be new; the creation of independent digital objects or data artefacts is common best practice. Each component will have the geometry, properties and behaviour for each artefact as well as any metadata and paradata stored as an integral part of the data load for that artefact. The construction of a data artefact is in itself an act of preservation and while it may seem time-consuming, it does not necessarily have to be, especially if the artefact is intended to be re-used, software engineering principles are applied and the appropriate resources have been allocated to the development cycle for the project.

The specification document

The starting point for creating any data artefact is the specification document, which will describe the object, its behaviour and requirements and any subordinate objects. From this all geometry, code, component parts, metadata and paradata will be derived. When the inclusion of a data double is required then it should be included in the specification document and its relationship shown in the entity relationship diagram. Whether the data double should itself reference other standardized data double types or not is a matter of preference but should be clear from the documentation. If the data double has graceful failure functionality (that enables its system to continue operating in the event of the failure of some of its components), such as looking for a resource in multiple locations via URL, then this can be used both to add robustness to the integrity of the object and identify the standard resource.

Documentation is the scourge of many projects but is vital to communicate purpose, structure and process between the different team members and end users, which includes those who will be involved with the maintenance of digital objects. Again, just having good documentation will not preserve a visualization or even a digital object but it will help to ensure that the concepts and direction are detailed and provide a record of what was supposed to be included even if the digital object integrity has failed. It should be noted that inline comments within source code and house style are also documentation in their own right and care should be taken when finalizing code to ensure that unnecessary comments are removed and that house styles are applied throughout.

Good documentation and data artefact creation can only be achieved when there is an understanding of the benefits of doing so and where there is an institutional willingness to invest the time and resource in their creation. It is estimated that correct application of paradata and data artefact creation will add up to 50% to the total planned time of the development cycle, and further that this must be planned as an integrated activity of development. Regrettably, additional development time for this process is rarely included in the original project schedule or considered an additional process that can be slotted in at the end of the project. As project timetables get squeezed, clients change specifications, time is spent developing feature creep functionality or it simply happens that the development cycle has been under-resourced, the paradata process is abandoned in favour of meeting delivery schedules.

Maintaining good documentation and adhering to standards may not be very exciting, especially to those who are used to working in visual media with almost real-time results. However, failing to do so will cause long-term problems for preservation. It is not difficult to find examples of projects where noncompliance with standards and documentation have caused significant problems, either when maintenance was required or archived work was revived for inclusion in later projects. In one case, the source code for an entire content management system written by a commercial external partner that closed down at the end of the project was handed over in a mixture of English and Dutch, with no visible conventions and no documentation; eventually the entire back end had to be rewritten.

One possible conclusion that can be drawn from the previous example is that it was not the absence of standards and documentation that caused the failure of the system and subsequent work, but rather that a change in a third-party piece of software required alterations in the system which, if properly documented, would have been relatively straightforward to implement. When considering preservation it is all too easy to focus only on just the data or the bespoke software that has been created as part of a project and make the assumption that everything else will remain the same or at least be compatible. If we recall the definition of preservation, the phrase 'original or existing state' is a useful reminder to include provision for ancillary software and hardware on which the system is dependent.

Upgrades, upgrades

To misquote Benjamin Franklin: 'In this world nothing can be said to be certain, except death and taxes and upgrades'. Generally upgrades are considered a good thing, often bringing new functionality and productivity, but when seen through the lens of preservation these benefits are not relevant, as the systems and data objects have been built to utilize known functionality at the time of creation, and rarely have over-specified affordances that offer even medium-term future-proofing.

In some projects it is the case that although standards are applied to data objects and their properties and interconnections understood and described, the systems that supported them are external to the project. Of these one of the longest-running, THEATRON, an online e-learning suite for theatre history, was constructed around HTML and VRML data objects enhanced by a variety of rich media. The output of the project was launched to the general public in 1999 to both critical and popular acclaim and still attracts around 300 unique users each month. Over a decade after its launch, the system has suffered numerous problems with changes in third-party software: web browsers have changed the way that they display information, perform operations and allow access to resources; VRML has not achieved the predicted uptake for 3D display on the internet; component software has been deleted from catalogues, restricting availability and functionality; and codecs and media players have changed, rendering movies unplayable.

Not only must developers consider and prepare for how they will ensure their data is fit for archiving, but they must also preserve how that data will be accessed. The digital objects and systems to run THEATRON exist in a 'perfect' archive state, as the project still holds a fallback server which was created at time of publication. As such, this server is a 'closed' digital object, and apart from hardware failure and data loss could be seen by some as representative of digital preservation. However this perfect-state archive of the digital object is relatively useless, apart from providing a reference point should that project ever be revisited (simply providing a data 'quarry' for a reworking of the application) as no client system that would be required to connect to and access the held data has been archived along with the server.

Even if a system is considered to be closed and not requiring additional software there will be, in almost every case, software components outside the control of the developer. For example, operating systems, device drivers, network and communications software (not to mention lower-level firmware) all form part of the electronic ecosystem within which digital objects reside. Preserving all of this software may not be viable as part of the preservation process (see Chapter 23) but as a minimum the versions of all software used by the final system should be documented, giving name, version and release and, if appropriate, any additional information such as customized settings.

If the digital object is utilizing external objects from the internet, such as web page links or resources, then once again we must consider that these are volatile and may not either be available or contain the same information as originally held. One project contained links to websites from which useful tools had been acquired only to discover some time later that many of these were no longer available and had been removed by the provider, and in one case the domain name had expired and been bought and reissued as an adult entertainment site. Wherever possible, linking to online web resources should take full advantage of alternative location descriptors and it is recommended that within the documentation all web-linked resources carry a citation similar to those used when authoring written papers giving a retrieval date of known accessibility.

Similarly the preservation of systems may be compromised by changes in hardware technologies, which cannot be predicted. For the visualization community these are arguably the graphics processors and display technologies. While graphics cards usually provide some basic functionality and backwards compatibility, this cannot be assumed, especially where specific affordance of hardware is being exploited. The recent uptake of LCD and LED screens over CRT has implications, too, for preservation of the integrity of the visual image. Screen resolutions have changed as have refresh rates, and applications designed with older resolutions in mind may find unexpected results such as image distortion when run though new displays. Where image quality is important, for instance in lighting simulations, calibration may no longer be possible or may provide less than optimum results.

For both hardware and software the minimum specifications for the system will be provided by the project's requirement documents, which can be supplemented by the quality assurance testing reports prior to release. While such documentation will not protect the system from the progress of technology, it will ensure that future investigators can understand the base requirements of the system and the range of functionality that was available over a range of different test combinations. All information of a technical nature will help in understanding what functionality is required in reconstructing the system either physically or through emulation.

It should go without saying that specialist hardware built specifically for, or utilizing features of, specific hardware components will not necessarily work or be able to use the intended functionality of newer hardware. KVL had experience of this in a proof of concept pilot project using early consumer market 3D shutter glasses. The system required to run the proof of concept application depended on a specific combination of graphics card, drivers and a high refresh rate CRT monitor. Changes to any of these individual components resulted in unexpected results and failure; most notably, the drivers which contained an exploit used by the shutter glasses were reissued, closing out the functionality and requiring the use of older additional software that in turn excluded affordances to other, newer software. In all of this the data component of the digital object still exists, uncompromised by the failure of the hardware component, but is useless, as it is bound to the hardware environment.

Human factors

The third part of the system trinity is the human component, sometimes referred to as 'wetware', and constitutes the knowledge of how to operate a system of hardware and software. Preserving that knowledge and those skill sets is probably the hardest of all of the components of the system; users tend to learn by building on tacit knowledge of systems which retain familiarity over generations of software/hardware, but seldom consider reading the operation manual for the latest piece of equipment unless they need specific information about new or changed functionality. However, such a continuity of understanding cannot be assumed when looking to the future. We have already touched on the importance of documentation for systems specification and functional requirements and as a minimum these should be incorporated into the digital object. Furthermore, any operation documentation for the system and, if appropriate, links to online support or community-derived resources should be included.

Having looked at ways in which the developer and project can prepare complex digital objects for a process of preservation, or at least understand and document the boundaries of preservable items, we must consider the implications of the preservation process. This book discusses many different approaches to the practicalities of preservation, from best practice through to third-party hosting and archiving, which give a project the opportunity to consider and lay down plans at the start of the development process. The book also contains links to organizations and best-practice resources that will help guide readers in ensuring that their complex digital objects have the best chance of being preserved in a state which will be suitable for future generations to access, use and build upon.

There is, however, one critical obstacle that must be overcome if preservation is to occur, and that is the institutional support and vision. There appears to be a perception that preservation of digital objects is simply achieved by ensuring that data can be placed onto storage media, put on the shelves of an archive and, much like physical books, will be there in perpetuity for all. We have seen that complex digital objects are much more than simply the data; if it were just that then the solution to preservation would be as simple as printing the data out onto paper and archiving it applying the knowledge, techniques and wisdom of the archive curator and librarian, who have centuries of understanding the medium and how best to manage it. However, the complexity that arises from the interaction between data, software and hardware is much more subtle and ephemeral than crude methods (with apologies to archivists and librarians everywhere) and with such a dynamic and volatile set of variables a traditional, and often intuitional, view of preservation cannot apply to the digital domain.

If the institution is not prepared to accept the value of digital objects, it will not accept the cost and effort in preserving them. Digital is not disposable anymore; as we start the migration from the physical to the virtual experience and experimentation, both the intellectual capital and cash price invested in producing digital objects is increasing. With the ever-diminishing pot of funding both institutionally and from sponsors, provision is seldom made for preservation post-completion of a project or, if there is, it is at a fixed term. If such a commitment is not forthcoming, then the preservation of complex digital objects will rely on the level of care that the developers have built into the object in the hope that some day someone will be able to resurrect it.

There are alternative possibilities that could be considered. Funding could be sought explicitly for preservation purposes; although this is unlikely to cover everything, it may preserve specific components. Funding to extend the initial project or refresh digital objects to the latest benchmarks is possible but traps the project in a constant recycling of material that does little more than explore the functionality and affordances of new technical developments unless new research questions and directions can be developed from the existing objects.

As a discipline, computer science has been in existence for around 60 years, widely accessible personal computing for 30 and the internet and world wide web as we recognise it today less than 20. Digital preservation is a young but vital field which demands that we understand what is possible in the present and at the same time plan and predict for the future. We must practise *Ruinenwerttheorie*, the theory of ruin value, building digital monuments today while trying to visualize their future use and relevance to posterity.

Notes

1 http://secondlife.com.

2 ISO/IEC 14772-1:1997 *Information technology – computer graphics and image processing – the Virtual Reality Modeling Language – Part 1: Functional specification and UTF-8 encoding*, www.iso.org/iso/catalogue_detail.htm?csnumber=25508.

PART 3

Digital preservation approaches, practice and tools

A good place to start: software preservation

CHAPTER 9

Digital preservation and curation: the danger of overlooking software

Neil Chue Hong

Software Sustainability Institute,
University of Edinburgh, UK

Introduction

From preserving research results to storing photos for the benefit of future generations, the importance of preserving digital data is gaining widespread acceptance. But what about software?

It is easy to focus on the preservation of data and other digital objects, such as images and music samples, because they are generally seen as end products. The software that is needed to access the preserved data is frequently overlooked in the preservation process. But without the right software it could be impossible to access the preserved data – which undermines the reason for storing the data in the first place.

A key challenge in digital preservation is being able to articulate, and ideally prove, the need for preservation. There are different purposes and benefits which facilitate making the case for preservation. These should be combined with preservation plans regarding data and hardware: digital preservation should be considered in an integrated manner. For example, media obsolescence and recovery is often as much a part of a software preservation project as a data preservation project.

The Software Sustainability Institute (SSI)[1] in partnership with Curtis+ Cartwright Consulting[2] have developed a series of outputs to support the sector by raising awareness of software sustainability and preservation issues, as part of a Jisc-funded initiative. In particular a benefits framework[3] has been published that can help groups understand and gauge the benefits or drawbacks of allocating effort to ensuring that preservation measures are built into processes, and to promote actively preserving legacy software. The rest of this chapter provides a summary of advice based on this work.

When should you consider software preservation?

Software is used to create, interpret, present, manipulate and manage data. There is no simple and universally applicable formula for determining if your software needs to be preserved, and how to go about preserving it. Instead there are a range of questions and factors which should be taken into account. In particular, curators should consider software preservation whenever one or more of the following statements is/are true:

The software cannot be separated from the data or digital object

In an ideal world, data can be isolated and preserved independently of the software used to create or access it. Sometimes this is not possible. For example, if the software and the data form an integrated model, the data by itself is meaningless. This means that the software must be preserved with the data to ensure continued access.

If data is stored in a format that is open and human-readable, then any software that follows that format can be used to read the data. If the data is stored in a format that is closed and arcane, then you must also preserve the software that is used to access it.

The software is classified as a research output

The software could fall under a research funders' preservation policy. This means that the software must be preserved as a condition of its funding. It may also be the case that software must be preserved to achieve legal compliance.

The software has intrinsic value

Software can be a valuable historical resource. If the software was the first example of its type, or it was a fundamental part of a historically significant event, then the software has inherent heritage value and should be preserved.

How should I approach software preservation?

When considering software preservation, the following should be considered:

- Is there still knowledge and expertise to handle and run the software?
- How much access do you have to the:
  — owners
  — developers
  — source code
  — hardware
  — users?
- Do you have the necessary intellectual property rights (IPR)? See Chapter 23.
- How authentic does the preserved software need to be?
- What is the maintainability of underlying hardware?
- Is maintaining integrity or authenticity an important requirement?
- Is the software covered by a preservation policy or strategy?
- Is there a clear purpose in preserving the software?
- Is there a clear time period for preservation?
- Do the predicted benefit(s) exceed the predicted cost(s)?
- Is there motivation for preserving the software?
- Are you also interested in further development or maintenance?
- Are the necessary capability, capacity and resources available?

Preserving the knowledge behind software is as critical as the software itself. Good documentation is important, as is having access to the developers of the software. A project undertaken by the Science and Technologies Facilities Council (STFC) identified a set of significant properties of software,[4] which can be used as a structured framework to elicit key information from the development team.

Purposes and benefits of software preservation

A key challenge in digital preservation is being able to articulate, and ideally prove, the need for preservation. The benefits framework developed by the SSI and Curtis+Cartwright identifies four main purposes to software preservation, along with their associated benefits. A summary of these benefits and a range of illustrative scenarios for each purpose are listed in Table 9.1.

Table 9.1 Benefits and scenarios of software preservation

Purpose	Benefits	Scenarios
Achieve legal compliance and accountability	Reduced exposure to legal risks Avoidance of liability actions Easily demonstrable compliance lessens audit burden Improved institutional governance Enhanced reputation	Maintaining records or audit trail Demonstrating integrity and authenticity of data and systems Addressing specific or regulatory requirements Resolving copyright or patent disputes Addressing the need to revert back to earlier versions due to IP settlements Publishing research openly for transparency or as a condition of funding
Create heritage value	(Heritage value is generally considered to be of intrinsic value)	Ensuring a complete record of research outputs where software is an intermediate or final output Preserving computing capabilities (software with or without hardware) considered to have intrinsic value Supporting museums and archives
Enable continued access to data and services	For research data and business intelligence: • fewer unintentional errors due to increased scrutiny • reduced research fraud • new insight and knowledge • increased assurance in results For systems and services: • current operations maintained • opportunity for improved operations via corrective maintenance • reduced vendor lock-in • improved disaster recovery • increased organizational resilience • increased reliability	Reproducing /repeating/verifying research results Reanalysing data in the light of new theories Re-using data in combination with future data 'Squeezing' additional value from data Verifying data integrity Identifying new use cases Maintaining legacy systems (including hardware) Ensuring business continuity Avoiding software obsolescence Supporting forensics analysis (e.g. for security or data protection purposes) Tracking down errors in results arising from flawed analysis
Encourage software re-use	Reduced development cost Reduced development risk Accelerated development Increased quality and dependability Focused use of specialists Standards compliance Reduced duplication Learning from others Opportunities for commercialization	Continuing operational use in institution Increasing uptake elsewhere Promoting good software

Seven approaches to software preservation

We observed seven distinct approaches, characterized by what is being preserved and passed on. The approaches set out are an extended set from those traditionally covered. This is done to give proper coverage of approaches specific to open-source software, to give additional flexibility and to include a 'default' option for a baseline. The different approaches are:

1 Technical preservation (techno-centric) – preserve original hardware and software in same state
2 Emulation (data-centric) – emulate original hardware and operating environment, keeping software in same state
3 Migration (functionality-centric) – update software as required to maintain same functionality
4 Cultivation (process-centric) – keep software 'alive' by moving to a more open development model
5 Hibernation (knowledge-centric) – preserve the knowledge of how to re-create the exact functionality of the software at a later date
6 Deprecation – formally retire the software without leaving the option of resuscitation or re-creation
7 Procrastination – do nothing.

Some approaches are better suited than others to each purpose. Table 9.2 provides an indicative mapping between the four purposes and appropriate approaches. We do not consider procrastination to be an appropriate approach to any software. Deprecation involves the explicit decision that there is no longer a case to preserve the software based on any of the purposes.

Each approach is provided with a description, a set of activities, and notes on costs. Some metrics (or more general indicators) are also proposed to determine if the approach is going to plan. These will need to be tailored to the specific software preservation plan being used. Migration is not included in detail here as it is covered comprehensively in Chapter 10.

Table 9.2 Preservation approaches

	Technical Preservation	Emulation	Migration	Cultivation	Hibernation
Legal compliance and accountability	✓	✓	✓		
Create heritage value	✓	✓			
Continued access to data and services	✓	✓	✓	✓	✓
Software re-use			✓	✓	✓

Technical preservation

Technical preservation is a planned and intentional decision to keep the software and hardware running in the same state. There is also the option of purchasing spares so that components can be replaced as they fail. It is important to bear in mind that no obsolete technology can be kept functional indefinitely.

Technical preservation is easy in principle: you simply continue business as usual. However, there are drawbacks to this approach, the first being maintenance. Over time, hardware components will wear out and must be replaced. When hardware is no longer manufactured, components become scarce, expensive and ultimately unobtainable. The second drawback is isolation. Your software only works with very specific hardware, which limits your users to those people with the right hardware. Specific activities within this approach are likely to include:

- purchasing spares
- regular checking that the system works
- maintaining hardware
- replacing hardware elements as they fail
- scheduling review points in the calendar.

There are some points to factor in about the costs of this approach:

- Some upfront costs to purchase spares.
- Low cost initially (maintenance only) to keep the hardware and software running.

- Costs likely to rise over time as maintenance gradually becomes more difficult.
- At some point a large cost will be incurred as hardware fails and a replacement approach is necessary.

Some metrics or indicators to monitor how well this approach is proceeding could be designed around one or more of the following:

- continued executability
- ongoing maintenance overheads
- number of remaining spares
- expected cost of a replacement system.

Emulation

An emulator is a software package that mimics the old hardware and/or operating environment, and can be run on a different computer, giving your software a new lease of life. As always, there are drawbacks. You need to find an emulator, which, in some cases may not be possible, meaning that you either have to write an emulator yourself, which requires specialist skills and could be expensive, or explore another of the sustainability approaches. It is difficult to write an emulator that perfectly mimics the old hardware. This can lead to differences between the operation of the old hardware and the new emulator, which could manifest themselves in annoying quirks or more serious problems. Specific activities within this approach are likely to include:

- regular checking that the system works
- regression testing
- verifying and validating results
- updating and maintaining the emulator
- scheduling review points in the calendar.

There are some points to factor in about the costs of this approach:

- It will be low cost if an emulator exists, as costs of emulator development are borne by someone else.
- Emulators themselves need sustaining (it may be prudent to contribute

effort to the emulator development, thereby incurring some costs).
- At some point a large cost may be incurred as the emulator ceases to work and a replacement approach is necessary.

Some metrics or indicators to monitor how well this approach is proceeding could be designed around one or more of the following:

- continued executability
- frequency of updates
- cost of emulation
- emulation performance.

Cultivation

Cultivation is the process of opening development of your software, by allowing developers licensed access to your code so that they can work with you. Thus, outside developers can develop your software so that it meets their exact needs, and in doing so any bugs they fix or new functionality they add can be given back to your project. With more widespread knowledge about your software the departure of one person is less likely to affect the software's future.

Cultivation is a long-term process which is unsuitable as a quick fix to ensure short-term sustainability; it requires effort and planning over many months and years. Moving to open development is not as simple as making your source code publicly available. You also need to build a community around the software, and this requires work to understand your community and how to appeal to them. Once in place, your community could become self-sustaining, so that the future of your software is assured. Specific activities within this approach are likely to include:

- choosing an appropriate open-source licence
- applying an open-source licence to an existing codebase
- moving code to an open-source repository
- setting up a development website, mailing list, etc.
- cleaning code to make it presentable for new comers
- providing test data to use to validate functionality
- establishing governance for the software

- engaging with users and contributors
- scheduling review points in the calendar.

There are some points to factor in about the costs of this approach:

- Ensuring software maturity could add significant costs.
- Cultivation involves sustained effort.
- The costs and likelihood of success are difficult to predict.
- If successful, it spreads costs.
- Ideally it becomes financially self-sustaining.

Some metrics or indicators to monitor how well this approach is proceeding could be designed around one or more of the following:

- Open Source Software (OSS) Watch Software Sustainability Maturity Model[5]
- the Community Roundtable's Community Maturity Model[6]
- size of user community: rocketing, increasing, a 'known' community, decreasing, plummeting
- spread of user community: internal, external, cross-domain
- number and spread of contributors
- continued executability and compilability.

Hibernation

Hibernation is suitable for software which has come to the end of its useful life, but may need to resurrected to double-check analysis or prove a result. Alternatively, there may not be a user community for your software, but you believe one will occur in the future. Hibernation allows you to preserve the knowledge about software so that it can be resurrected in the future.

Unlike sustainability, hibernation can be a one-off process, with a beginning and – importantly – an end. Preparing software for hibernation can be resource-heavy, and if the software is never resurrected, those resources were wasted. Specific activities within this approach may include:

- reviewing and improving documentation
- recording the significant properties of the software

- archiving the software along with all documentation
- scheduling review points in the calendar.

If the software is already OSS then hibernation should be relatively straightforward, since there ought to be a code repository, up-to-date documentation and a means to contact user and contributors (if any).

There are some points to factor in about the costs of this approach:

- At its simplest, hibernation involves documenting pseudo-code (e.g. publishing the algorithm in a research paper) – this is inexpensive.
- However, ensuring rigorous documentation is time-consuming.
- There is a small ongoing cost to ensure discoverability, accessibility, etc., of hibernated software and materials.
- Hibernation should significantly reduce future development costs.

Typical performance metrics include:

- completeness of documentation (code, design, testing, etc.)[7]
- currency of programming language, middleware and operating environment
- archive availability and resilience
- compilability and executability at review points.

Deprecation

If software lacks a community, the resources to continue or a developer, then the only alternative is deprecation. All software development comes to an end, but, unlike hibernation, no effort is invested in preparing the software beforehand. If, in the future, someone wants to use the software, they may not be able to find a stored copy and it might be expensive or impossible to resurrect the software.

Deprecation is easy to perform, but often marks the end of a software package's life and is typically only chosen when no other option is available. Specific activities within this approach are likely to include:

- deciding on a timeframe for deprecation

- notifying users and contributors of the intent to deprecate
- archiving the software along with all documentation.

There are some points to factor in about the costs of this approach:

- There are costs in formally shutting down development.
- Deprecation generally assumes software has been superseded and no emergency recovery effort is needed.

Some metrics or indicators to monitor how well this approach is proceeding could be designed around one or more of the following:

- infrequency of user engagement
- completeness of documentation (e.g. see those defined in the section on hibernation, above)
- archive availability and resilience (e.g. see those defined in the section on hibernation, above).

Procrastination

Procrastination is the default (but not recommended) option. It does not require any changes to the current working practices, and it does not involve any additional effort at the current time. However, it can result in large amounts of effort needing to be expended in the future to continue to use the software, or end up wasting effort if the software is not required.

Building it into the process

A principle from other areas of digital preservation is that considering preservation and sustainability upfront (and regularly) is important. This would imply that building preservation measures into software development and digital curation measures is good practice. Two 'preservation measures' are apparent:

1 *Software engineering* Being able to encourage better software engineering practice early in the lifecycle will benefit software preservation if and when required.

2   *Identifying explicit preservation requirements* Requirements capture and management is an upfront activity in software development, and preservation requirements should be considered along with other requirements.

This suggests that it is important that there is a link between digital curators and software developers. The extent to which software engineering practice and preservation requirements should be a priority depends on the intended functionality of the software (i.e. whether it fits one or more of the four purposes) and the nature of the software itself. For example, is the software meant to be a proof-of-concept demonstrator, something more heavyweight like a pilot, or perhaps an operational service for a defined set of users? Each allows a different approach to be taken with different expectations of robustness and longevity.

It is important to understand all facets of software and choose the best route for its preservation as part of a broader preservation and development strategy. In this way, we can ensure that important software is preserved for future generations.

Acknowledgements

This work has been funded by the Jisc as part of the Clarifying the Purposes and Benefits of Preserving Software study, carried out by Matt Shreeve (Curtis+Cartwright Consulting Ltd) and Neil Chue Hong, Steve Crouch, Simon Hettrick and Tim Parkinson (Software Sustainability Institute). The SSI is funded by the EPSRC (Engineering and Physical Sciences Research Council) under grant EP/H043160/1. Parts of this work build on the Jisc-funded Significant Properties of Software study carried out by Brian Matthews et al. at STFC.

Notes

1   www.software.ac.uk.
2   www.curtiscartwright.co.uk.
3   www.software.ac.uk/attach/SoftwarePreservationBenefitsFramework.pdf.
4   www.jisc.ac.uk/media/documents/programmes/preservation/spsoftware_report_redacted.pdf.

5   www.oss-watch.ac.uk/resources/ssmm.xml.
6   http://community-roundtable.com/2009/06/the-community-maturity-model.
7   http://escholarship.org/uc/item/8089m1v1.pdf.

Further reading

Berman, F. et al. (2010) *Sustainable Economics for a Digital Planet: ensuring long-term access to digital information. Final report of the Blue Ribbon Task Force on Sustainable Digital Preservation and Access*,
http://brtf.sdsc.edu/biblio/BRTF_Final_Report.pdf.

Chue Hong, N., Crouch, S., Hettrick, S., Parkinson, T. and Shreeve, M. (2010) *Software Preservation Benefits Framework*,
www.software.ac.uk/attach/SoftwarePreservationBenefitsFramework.pdf.

Matthews, B., McIlwrath, B., Giaretta, D. and Conway, E. (2008) *The Significant Properties of Software: a study*, www.jisc.ac.uk/media/documents/programmes/preservation/significantpropertiesofsoftware-final.doc.

CHAPTER 10

How do I know that I have preserved software?

Brian Matthews, Arif Shaon and Esther Conway
e-Science Centre,[1]
STFC Rutherford Appleton Laboratory, UK

Introduction: software preservation

Software is a class of digital electronic object which is often a prerequisite to the preservation of other electronic objects. However, software has characteristics that make its preservation substantially more challenging than many other types of digital object. Software is inherently complex, dependent on the operating environment, and typically has numerous interacting components. Software preservation is rarely prioritized, and is thus a relatively underexplored topic of research. In this chapter, we consider some of the issues in software preservation. Software can be defined as:

> a conceptual entity which is a set of computer programs, procedures, and associated documentation concerned with the operation of a data processing system.[2]

Computer programs are sequences of processor instructions to permit the execution of a specific task. It should be noted that documentation is included, a crucial element in effective software preservation. We refer to a single collection of software artefacts that are brought together for an identifiable broad purpose as a software *product*.

The term software is sometimes used in a broader context to describe any electronic media *content* which embodies expressions of ideas stored on film, tapes, records, etc., for recall and replay by some (typically but not always) electronic device. For the purposes of this chapter, such content is considered out of scope.

Software represents a large and diverse domain which includes microcode, real-time control, operating systems, business systems, desktop applications, distributed systems and expert systems, with an equally wide range of applications. We can classify this diversity along a number of different axes, which impact on preservation requirements:

- **Diversity of application.** Software is used in almost every area of human activity: business office systems, scientific analysis applications, navigation systems, industrial control systems, electronic commerce, photography, art and music media systems. Each area has different functional characteristics and it is necessary to classify software according to some application-oriented classification or description of the domain.
- **Diversity in hardware architecture.** Software runs on a large range of different computer configurations. Assembler and micro-code are used to control the hardware directly, while at a higher level of abstraction applications are deployed on a wide range of computing hardware and architectures. In order to re-create the functionality of a system, the hardware configuration may need to be taken into account.
- **Diversity in software architecture.** Even within a common hardware configuration, there are different *software architectures*, requirements on the co-ordination of software components which need to interact using well defined protocols to achieve the overall functionality of the system. Accurate re-creation of the functionality of the entire system needs to take into account a number of interacting software components.
- **Diversity in scale of software.** Software ranges from individual routines a few lines long, through products which provide particular sets of library functions, major applications, such as Microsoft Word, to large multifunction systems that provide entire environments or platforms for complex applications that are required to work together as a coherent whole.
- **Diversity in provenance.** Software is developed by a wide range of different people and businesses. A single software product may, during its development lifecycle, pass through more than one organization, each having its own business goals, models and licensing requirements.

These different development models need to be reflected within attribution and licensing conditions.

- **Diversity in user interaction.** Some software is designed to have no interaction with users, while other systems have rich user interactions with complex graphical user interfaces requiring keyboard and pointer and high-resolution displays, or audio input and output. Clearly, in order to accurately reproduce the correct functionality of the software in the future, the appropriate level of user interaction will need to be re-created in some form.

This diversity and complexity present a number of barriers to preserving software. Consequently, although there are good reasons to preserve software, there have been only limited consideration of the preservation of software as a digital object in its own right; see for example Zabolitzky (2002) for early some early approaches. Nevertheless, we believe sufficient commonality exists for general principles of software preservation to be defined. Furthermore, although 'preservation' may imply availability for future generations, much software has a working life (without additional modifications or rewriting) of five years at best and so curation can be considered to be quite a short-term undertaking in the software domain. It is normal for the underlying data to have been created much earlier than the software used to manipulate it. It is the art of maintaining the underlying data by the way software systems are curated and migrated which is important in this sphere.

Software preservation approaches

Various approaches to digital preservation have been proposed and implemented. *The Cedars Guide to Digital Preservation Strategies* (Cedars Project, 2002) defines three main strategies, which we give here, and consider how they are applicable to software:

- **Technical preservation (techno-centric).** This approach maintains the original software (typically an executable binary file), and sometimes hardware, of the original operating environment. This is the preferred strategy in many legacy situations; otherwise obsolete hardware is maintained to keep vital software in operation. However, in the long term this approach becomes difficult to sustain, as the expertise and spare components for the hardware become harder to obtain.

- **Emulation (data-centric).** This aims to re-create the original operating environment by programming future platforms and operating systems to emulate the original operating environment, so that software can be preserved in binary and run 'as is'. This is a common approach, undertaken in for example the PLANETS[3] and KEEP[4] projects and also by groups such as the Software Preservation Society. The emulation approach for preserving application software is widespread, and particularly suited to those situations where the properties of the original software are required to be preserved as exactly as possible. Emulation transfers the problem to the (hopefully lesser) one of preserving the emulator. As the platform the emulator is designed for becomes obsolete, the emulator has to be rebuilt or emulated on another emulator. Thus, potentially a growing stack of emulation software will be required.[5]

- **Migration (process-centric).** Transferring digital information to new platforms before the earlier one becomes obsolete. Software migration (or 'porting' or 'adaptive maintenance') is, in practice, how software which is supported over a long period of time is preserved. However, the migration approach does not seek to preserve all the properties of the original, or at least not exactly, but as observed in the European project CASPAR,[6] only those up to the interface definition, which we could perhaps generalize as those properties which have been identified as being of significance for the preservation task in hand.

These approaches have been refined in Chue Hong et al. (2010) to the seven different approaches given in Figure 10.1, which considered the social approach of the developers engaging in the preservation as much as the technical approach, for example distinguishing between migration, a notion of an 'official' software port to provide a version on a new platform, and 'cultivation', which involves managing the software in the long term by opening it up to a wider developer community, which can maintain and migrate the software. In the rest of this chapter, we are neutral to the preservation approach, but consider how the preservation of the key properties can be identified and checked.

Software preservation has four major steps:

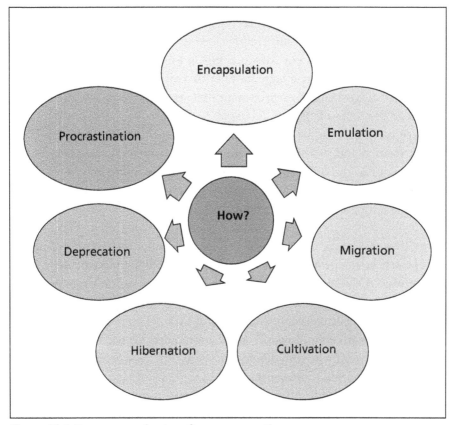

Figure 10.1 Seven approaches to software preservation

1 **Storage.** A copy of a software 'product' needs to be stored for long-term preservation. Whatever the exact items stored, there should be a strategy to ensure that the storage is secure and maintains its authenticity (*fixity* in OAIS terminology) over time, with appropriate strategies for storage replication, media refresh, format migration, etc., as necessary.

2 **Retrieval.** In order for a preserved software product to be retrieved at a date in the future, it needs to be clearly labelled and identified (reference information in OAIS terminology), with a suitable catalogue. This should provide a search on its function (e.g. terms from controlled vocabulary or functional description) and origin (provenance information).

3   **Reconstruction.** The preserved product can be reinstalled or rebuilt within an environment sufficiently close to the original that it will execute satisfactorily. For software, this is a particularly complex operation, as there are a large number of contextual dependencies to the software execution environment that are required to be satisfied before the software will execute at all.

4   **Replay.** In order to be useful at a later date, software needs be replayed, or executed and perform in a manner that is sufficiently close in its behaviour to the original. As with reconstruction, there may be environmental factors that may influence whether the software delivers a satisfactory level of performance.

In the first two steps, software is much like any other type of digital object type. However, the problem of reconstruction and replay is particularly acute for software. Digital objects designed for human inspection have rendering requirements that have issues of satisfactory performance; science data objects also typically require information on formats and analysis tools to be 'replayed' appropriately. However, software requires an additional notion of a software environment with dependencies to other hardware, software and build and configuration information.

Note that other digital objects require software to provide the appropriate level of satisfactory replay, and thus for other digital objects there is a need to preserve software too; as we shall see, there is also a dependency on the preservation of other object types (e.g. documentation) for the adequate preservation of software.

Thus in order to preserve software satisfactorily, we need to ensure that enough information is stored within the archival information package to support each of these steps in the future. We consider what kinds of information are required at each stage – see Matthews et al. (2009a) for full details.

What do we need to support retrieval?

In order to support retrieval from a software library or archive, we need to have an indication of software in general terms to determine whether it is the right software component to meet the requirements of our upcoming task in the future. Thus we are likely to want to know the following items:

- **Gross functionality.** This would include a description of the purpose of the software product in general terms, with a description of its major inputs and outputs, together with a discussion of how the software operates. This may also include an overview of the general software architecture principles under which the software operates (e.g. client-server architecture), and major dependencies.
- **Categorization.** The software archive may support a categorization under keywords or controlled vocabulary to support systematic searching of software.
- **Licensing.** There should be some indication of the ownership and legal control, and the licensing conditions under which the software is made available.
- **Provenance.** An indication of who developed the software for accurate attribution and possibly contact details for ongoing support.

This information is that typically found on the 'about' page of a software product's website, and gives enough information to be able to discover the software in a search, determine whether it is likely to be of interest, and whether the user is entitled to use the software and under what conditions. Note that this information is independent of the software preservation approach used. Note also that this information does not include operating system information, etc., which would typically be of interest to a user at this stage; strictly that would be reconstruction information (see below).

What do we need to support reconstruction?

Software products typically come in many versions, which typically support different sets of functionality, and variants for different platforms.[7] Versions are associated with a release with specific functionality. A variant is associated with an adaptation of a version for a specific target environment, usually associated with an executable binary, but also there could be additional source modules that are tailored to the target environment. Thus, in order to reconstruct the software, knowledge is needed of the precise environmental context in which the reconstructed software is expected to operate, so that dependencies can be tracked and satisfied on reconstruction. To reconstruct the software we would expect that the following information would be needed:

- a set of component version-specific source code and/or binary files and their dependencies, including installation, configuration and build scripts and instructions as necessary
- operating systems, version and modification details
- details of programming language and versions, with appropriate versions of compilers to reconstruct the executable
- details of software dependencies, including auxiliary software libraries used to build the executable, and other software packages that are used in conjunction with software
- details of hardware dependencies, including memory and processor requirements, screen resolution and peripherals.

Such material is what is usually supplied in the installation instructions supplied with software, and in well managed software development the versions and their relationships would be maintained under a version management systems such as CVS (Concurrent Versions System) or Subversion.

As a consequence of high dependency on the environment, preserving software is rarely a matter of preserving a single package of objects, but rather one of managing a collection of objects and their dependencies that need to be preserved in their own right.

What do we need to support replay?

Once the software product has been reconstructed, we need to know how to operate it. Thus, we need operating instructions and information on the expected inputs and outputs of the software. To support replay we need details of:

- the operation of the software
- valid input/output formats, and error handling
- programming interfaces
- user interactions, manuals and other documentation
- supported non-functional behaviour.

With this, largely documentary, information, we can operate the software in the future.

How do I judge now that what I have preserved is 'enough'?

Software preservation requires that the three stages of retrieval, reconstruction and replay must all be satisfactorily supported in order to provide a future user with the capability to use the software. But how much information is needed to guarantee that the preserved software product performs 'correctly'?

We introduce a notion of *performance* to demonstrate that a particular reconstruction adequately preserves the required characteristics of software. Performance as a model for the preservation of digital objects was defined by the National Archives of Australia in Heslop, Davis and Wilson (2002) to measure the effectiveness of a digital preservation strategy. Noting that, for digital content, technology has to be applied to data to render it intelligible to a user, they stipulate a *process* to be applied to source data to generate a *performance*, by means of which users extract meaning. Different processes applied to a source may produce different performances, and it is the properties of the performance that need to be considered to assess the value of a preservation action. Performance properties result from a combination of the source properties with the technology applied in the processing.

The notion of performance has been developed in the context of traditional archival records to identify the significant properties of different media types which compare the performance created by the original process of rendering with that created by later rendering processes on new hardware and software. The question that arises is how this model applies to software itself.

In the case of software, the performance is the execution of binary files on some hardware platform to provide the end experience for the user. However, the processing stage depends on the nature of the software artefacts preserved, which have differing reconstruction and replay requirements:

- In the case where binary is preserved, the emphasis is usually on performing as closely as possible to the original system.
- When source code and configuration and build scripts are preserved, we would expect that the performance would not necessarily preserve all the properties of the original (e.g. systems performance, or exact look and feel of the user interface), but have some deviations from the original.

- In an extreme case, only the specification of the software may be preserved, and we would expect significant deviation from the original and perhaps only core functionality to be preserved.

A software performance can thus result in some properties being preserved, and others deviating from the original or even being disregarded altogether. Thus in order to determine the value of a particular performance, we define the notion of *adequacy*: a software product can be said to perform adequately relative to a particular set of features ('significant properties') if in a particular performance it preserves that set of significant properties to an acceptable tolerance.

This notion of adequacy is usually viewed as an aspect of the established notion of *authenticity* of preservation. It is useful to separate these two notions in order to establish a more lucid requirement specification of long-term preservation of software. Thus, the term 'authenticity' in long-term preservation signifies the level of *trust* between a preserved software product and its future end-users. From the perspective of an end-user of a software product, this trust is primarily associated with the ability to trace the provenance, and verify the fixity information of the software. But this 'trusted preservation' does not guarantee a reliable behaviour from the software once reconstructed in future; it might incur a loss of some of its original features during its reconstruction process. An example of such software is the emulated version of the 1990s DOS-based computer game *Prince of Persia*.[8] While some of the instructions do not always work on the emulator and the original appearance of the game is also somewhat lost, it is possible to run the emulator to play the complete game on a contemporary computer platform. By measuring the adequacy of the performance, we can thus determine how well the software has been preserved and replayed.

The distinguishing feature of the performance model for software is that the measure of adequacy of the software is closely related to the performance of its input *data*. The purpose of software is (usually) to process data, so the *performance* of a software product becomes the *processing* of its input data.

The adequacy of different preservation approaches is dependent upon the performance of the final result on the end-use on *data*. As the software has to be able to produce an adequate performance for any valid input data, the adequacy can be established by performing trial executions against representative test data covering the range of required behaviour (including error conditions) against the significant performance property. As a consequence, it is also necessary to preserve test data to establish adequacy as part of the software preservation process.

This notion of performance can be applied recursively to software that processes other software. In this case, the performance of software is the processing of the application binaries or source code, which in turn is measured by its adequacy in processing its intended input data. The stages in the performance model can be related to the stages in the software preservation process, and the information at each stage to data in the OAIS information model. For more details see Matthews et al. (2009a).

The following list of examples illustrates how adequacy of software may be tested:

- **Scientific software.** Scientific software is usually concerned with the accuracy of calculations. Thus, conditions such as 'the system should calculate the Fast Fourier Transform', or 'the result must be accurate to eight decimal places' would be appropriate. So, typically, adequacy is established by processing some prespecified test data, and checking whether the output exceeds the acceptable level of error tolerance for the software.
- **Games software.** The emphasis here is on playability, so that the user graphics and user controls are the key factors. So in this case, adequacy is established by comparing its user interface (UI) with the screen capture of its original UI, against some predefined use cases.
- **Programming language compilers.** In the case of a compiler, we would need to check that it covers all features of the programming language that it supports, e.g. concurrency (i.e. threads) and polymorphism. For some programming languages (e.g. Fortran, C, C++), there exist ISO standards[9] that describe the correct behaviour of a piece of software written in these languages.
- **Word processing software.** The adequacy of a word processor may be measured on its ability to render existing supported documents with an acceptable level of error tolerance. In some circumstances, fonts, colours and page layout may be considered key properties to be preserved.
- **Digital art works.** In the case of digital art works, there are two standards of adequacy: the intention of the artist and the experience of

the audience. The software may change and it is arguable that as long as the user experience is adequately the same, the art work can be said to be preserved. However, the intention of the artist may mean that only the reconstruction of the original environment with the original source code is adequate.

Conclusion

In this paper we have presented some of the issues around preserving software and put forward a conceptual framework to express a rigorous approach to long-term software preservation. We believe that this is a general and principled approach which can cover the preservation needs of a wide range of different software products, including modern distributed systems and service-oriented architectures, which are typically built of pre-existing frameworks and have a large number of dependencies on a widely distributed network of services, many of which are outside the control of the typical user (e.g. DNS services, proxies). We also believe that the performance model presented here, which introduces a notion of *adequacy* of software performance as well as a notion of user feedback to influence the performance, represents an approach to preserving the user interface and the user interaction model, although work is required to further develop that notion.

Work is currently under way to incorporate the preservation of software within preservation planning processes, so that it can be managed in a cost-effective manner with the preservation of other digital artefacts. In addition, further work is required to evaluate the preservation framework, especially against a range of software types, to cover the diversity of software and to consider how to support the preservation of legacy software.

As a general principle, software preservation should ideally be considered within a software engineering process. Software developers, driven rightly by the immediate needs of developing and maintaining software, rarely consider the implications of the long-term preservation of their software. However, many of the disciplines which are part of good software development practice also make the task of preserving software much more tractable. These include: good version control; good configuration and build scripts and processes; good documentation for both the developer and user; and systematic and well documented testing and test cases, which ensure program correctness and are also the key to assuring adequacy of preservation. Further, many of the tools and techniques which promote software re-use in software engineering are also applicable to software preservation. Thus, we could say that good software engineering leads to good software preservation.

Acknowledgments

The work in this chapter arose from a UK Jisc-sponsored study into the significant properties of software for preservation[10] (Matthews et al., 2008), and subsequently in a Jisc project into methods and tools for software preservation[11] (Matthews et al., 2009a). Given the relative immaturity of the field, the project developed a framework to express the notion of software preservation and set out some baseline concepts of what it means to preserve software. The framework has been developed further, bringing in notions from the OAIS reference model (OAIS, 2012), and also developed tool support. The results of these two projects are reported in Matthews et al. (2009b, 2009c, 2010). The benefits of software preservation were considered in a further Jisc study between Curtis+Cartwright Consulting and the Software Sustainability Institute (Chue Hong et al., 2010) – see Chapter 9 of this book.

Further work has continued within the CASPAR, ENSURE[12] and SCAPE[13] European projects. We would like to thank our colleagues Juan Bicarregui, Catherine Jones, Jim Woodcock, David Giaretta, Steven Rankin, Matt Dunkley, Simon Lambert and Michael Wilson for their advice and discussions.

Notes

1 Now part of the STFC Scientific Computing Department.
2 http://en.wikipedia.org/wiki/Software [accessed 22 August 2011].
3 www.planets-project.eu.
4 www.keep-project.eu.
5 A problem addressed by the KEEP Virtual Machine, the bottom layer of which is simple enough to accommodate future emulators.
6 Cultural, Artistic and Scientific knowledge for Preservation, Access and Retrieval, www.casparpreserves.eu.
7 Note that this use of the terms 'version' and 'variant' is ours.

8   www.bestoldgames.net/eng/old-games/prince-of-persia.php.
9   www.iso.org/iso/iso_catalogue/catalogue_tc/catalogue_tc_browse.htm?
    commid=45202.
10 Joint Information Systems Committee (Jisc) Study into the Significant
    Properties of Software (2007), http://sigsoft.dcc.rl.ac.uk/twiki/bin/view.
11 Joint Information Systems Committee (Jisc)-sponsored project Tools and
    Guidelines for Preserving and Accessing Software Research Outputs
    (2007–9), www.stfc.ac.uk/e-Science/projects/medium-term/software-
    preservation/22426.aspx.
12 Enabling kNowledge, Sustainability, Usability and Recovery for Economic
    Values.
13 Scalable Preservation Environments.

References

Cedars Project (2002) *The Cedars Guide to Digital Preservation Strategies,*
    www.leeds.ac.uk/cedars/guideto/dpstrategies/dpstrategies.html.
Chue Hong, N., Crouch, S., Hettrick, S., Parkinson, T. and Shreeve, M. (2010)
    Software Preservation Benefits Framework,
    www.software.ac.uk/attach/SoftwarePreservationBenefitsFramework.pdf.
Heslop, H., Davis, S. and Wilson, A. (2002) *National Archives Green Paper: an
    approach to the preservation of digital records,* http://nla.gov.au/nla.arc-49636.
Matthews, B. M., McIlwrath, B., Giaretta, D. and Conway, E. (2008) *The Significant
    Properties of Software: a study,* www.jisc.ac.uk/media/documents/programmes/
    preservation/significantpropertiesofsoftware-final.doc.
Matthews, B. M., Bicarregui, J. C., Shaon, A. and Jones, C. M. (2009a) *A Framework
    for the Significant Properties of Software: Jisc Tools and Methods for Software Preservation
    Project report,* http://epubs.stfc.ac.uk/work-details?w=51076.
Matthews, B. M., Shaon, A., Bicarregui, J. C., Jones, C. M. and Conway, E. (2009b)
    Towards a Methodology for Software Preservation, paper presented at the *6th
    International Conference on Preservation of Digital Objects* (iPRES 2009), San
    Francisco, CA, 5–6 October,
    http://epubs.stfc.ac.uk/bitstream/4599/IPres2009_Matthews_swpres.pdf.
Matthews, B. M., Shaon, A., Bicarregui, J. C., Jones, C. M. and Woodcock, J.
    (2009c) An Approach to Software Preservation, paper presented at the
    *Proceedings Ensuring Long-Term Preservation and Adding Value to Scientific and
    Technical Data* (PV 2009), Villafranca del Castillo, Madrid, Spain, 1–3

December, http://epubs.stfc.ac.uk/bitstream/4790/PV2009_37_Shaon_
ApproachToSWPreservation.pdf.

Matthews, B. M., Shaon, A., Bicarregui, J. C. and Jones, C. M. (2010) Framework
for Software Preservation, *International Journal of Digital Curation*, **5** (1), 91–105,
www.ijdc.net/index.php/ijdc/article/view/148.

OAIS (2012) *Reference Model for an Open Archival Information: System: recommendation for
space data systems standard*, CCSDS Magenta Book,
http://public.ccsds.org/publications/archive/650x0m2.pdf.

Zabolitzky, J. G. (2002) Preserving Software: why and how, *Iterations: an
interdisciplinary journal of software history*, **1**,
www.cbi.umn.edu/iterations/zabolitzky.html.

Tools and techniques

CHAPTER 11

Digital preservation strategies for visualizations and simulations

Janet Delve
Future Proof Computing Group, School of Creative Technologies,
University of Portsmouth, UK

Hugh Denard
Digital Humanities, King's College London, UK

William Kilbride
Digital Preservation Coalition, UK

Introduction

The participants for each POCOS session were drawn from a wide range of professional contexts concerned with digital preservation (DP), including: scientific and cultural heritage projects; private consultancies; digital assets management, including creating digital preservation policy for, *inter alia*, 3D models and architectural drawings; digital repository management; DP research and development; development of research-based open-source tools; digital tool preservation; long-term digital preservation; emulation research; historical research; digital humanities research; and digital imaging and digital media technologies. With this eclectic mix of contributors from a variety of user and stakeholder communities, it was important not to make assumptions about prior DP knowledge, as some participants might be very knowledgeable about DP in general but be unaware of visualization and simulation initiatives, and vice versa. With this caveat in mind, William Kilbride reviewed the main categories of challenges regarding visualizations and simulations in the DP domain, and suggested initial key responses. The groups then discussed their ideas.

The main DP challenges and key responses

The first challenge to be faced is that the issue will not go away, nor will it resolve itself. A salutary note on this subject is delineated by Gartner's Hype Cycle on the introduction of new technology, which charts levels of optimism over time. The cycle starts on the trigger point of 'not my problem'; moves on through 'how hard can it be' to the Peak of Inflated Expectations; descends into misery at the Trough of Disillusion, when the scale of the task becomes apparent; then advances onto the Slope of Enlightenment followed by the Plateau of Productivity, when realistic progress is eventually realized. To avoid this roller-coaster experience, it is vital that DP plans be set out at the start of the project.

In general, digital objects such as software, simulations, visualizations and documents have value (however such 'value' is calculated), and they create opportunities. However, access to such objects depends on software, hardware and human intervention, and these are liable to change over time, thus resulting in technology creating barriers to re-use. Therefore it is vital to manage data in the long term to protect digital assets and create opportunities for their re-use. In particular, DP is not just about isolated topics such as 'data', 'access' and 'risk': rather it is paramount that DP is understood to be about outcomes, especially regarding *people and opportunity*. In a nutshell, DP should be about healthier, wealthier, safer, smarter, greener people and communities.

This is not always the case, however, as DP typically makes bleak reading. To take archaeology as an exemplar, it is the case that through excavation it destroys that which it studies, so DP is crucial for this field. The technical challenges in this domain are formidable; digital achievements and take-up to date are wholly inadequate and data loss is ubiquitous. For example, the Archaeology Data Service (ADS) *Strategies for Digital Data* reported that the archaeological record could be decaying faster in its digital form than it ever did in the ground (Condron et al., 1999).

Challenge 1. Access and long-term use of digital content both depend on the configuration of hardware, software, the capacity of the operator and documentation

Key responses:

1 **Migration** (changing the file format to ensure the information content can be read) is the most quoted, and most widely used solution. It is typically good for large quantities of data that is well understood and self-contained (with few or no dependencies), with there being a relatively small number of formats involved.

2   **Emulation** (intervening in the operating system to ensure that old software can function and information content can be read). This can be used in tandem with migration; in fact migration and emulation both often require, for their realization, deployment of elements of each other. *A vital step forward in the preservation debate is to embrace hybrid strategies deploying both migration and emulation, instead of seeing these as rival options* (Anderson et al., 2010, 10–18).

3   **Hardware Preservation** (maintaining access to data and processes by maintaining the physical computing environment, including hardware and peripherals). This is less fashionable, more expensive, but effective. It is often claimed that emulation obviates the need for preserving hardware, but this is not the case. In order to ensure that an emulation configuration is authentic, it is necessary to preserve hardware to set up benchmarks. This is particularly important for preserving the actual user experience of using the hardware and software. Computing history museums are key to this task (Anderson et al., 2010, 10), and the extent to which they can provide software, hardware, emulators and documentation is the subject of a scoping study in KEEP.

4   **Exhumation** (maintaining access to an execution environment or software services to that processes can be rerun with new data) also involves emulation and migration elements.

Challenge 2. Technology continues to change, creating the conditions for obsolescence

Key responses:
DPC Technology Watch reports/services give advance notice of obsolescence. Migration and emulation reduce the impact of changes in technology. File format registries such as PRONOM, UDFR and P2 also contribute by profiling file formats and their preservation status.

Challenge 3. Storage media have a short life and storage devices are subject to obsolescence

Key responses:
Storage media can be refreshed and in some cases can self-check, and storage densities continue to improve, offering greater capacity at reduced cost. It

must be emphasized, however, that storage may only be a minor part of the solution, but not the whole solution. (In fact, transferring bits from one medium to another is not necessarily inherently difficult – the problematic issues are often concerned with the *quantity* of information involved.)

Challenge 4. Digital preservation systems are subject to the same obsolescence as the objects they safeguard

Key responses:
Systems can be modular and conform to standards, and fitness for purpose can be monitored over time.

Challenge 5. Digital resources can be altered, corrupted or deleted without obvious detection

Key responses:
Digital signatures and wrappers are available that can safeguard authenticity. Also, security measures can control access to the digital material (although it must be admitted that digital preservation has not yet sufficiently well confronted security issues such as cyberattacks). It is also a real advantage that for digital as opposed to physical material, copies are perfect replicas with no degradation.

Challenge 6. Digital resources are intolerant of gaps in preservation

Key responses:
Ongoing risk management can provide vital monitoring to help deal with this problem, and there are significant economies of scale to be made. It is critical that we work with colleagues in computer science towards the end that processes such as metadata creation and harvesting, and media transfer where possible, be automated. We must also be aware that data is rapidly growing in scale, complexity and appetite or importance (that is to say, the expectations we have of data).

Challenge 7. We have limited experience

Key responses:

The rapid churn in technology accelerates our research, which has been transformed over the last decade. As noted in challenge 6, this is a *shared problem*: those at the forefront of DP research, such as memory organizations, need to be willing to appropriate solutions developed in other domains such as computer science (digital forensics, software lifecycle development) (Gladney, 2008, 14, 25).

Challenge 8. DP has to cater for widely varying types of collection or interaction, so different strategies are required for different types of collection or interaction

Key responses:
Where possible we need to develop strategies that cater for discrete categories of material, such as:

- simple v. complex
- large v. numerous
- gallery v. laboratory.

A helpful way of confronting the issues is to consider that DP involves three key components: technology, organization and resources. With this in mind, the following list indicates the pressing questions about complex digital objects in general, and visualizations and simulations in particular, currently facing the DP community:

1 Are the issues data size or data complexity, or both?
2 Which is the best preservation strategy: emulation, migration, hybrid or none of these?
3 Is it easier to re-create data than to secure it?
4 What does success look like and how will we recognize it (i.e. which metrics do we use)?
5 Will the material ever be used? How do we balance delivery and accretion?
6 Does the material fit with its original mission, and whose problem is this?
7 How do we find the necessary resources and expertise?
8 What is next on the horizon: more scale and more complexity?

9 Who is making DP tools and what are the dependencies between them?
10 Is visualization a special case for DP, or a special DP community?

Key issues in response to the DP challenges
Creating a proactive data management environment

Archives require active management, a fact that many institutions have not yet come to grips with. Indeed, most of the technological problems are soluble, but finding institutional resources or contexts for actively managing DP is much more intractable. In practice, many organizations – such as memory institutions – are not equipped to carry out active DP management, whether hindered by legal limits or by lack of resources (for example cash-poor cultural institutions cannot afford the requisite level of technical expertise). Where resources are the problem, ideally these institutions need to change their economic model to secure the technical services they need. This requires a change in mindset within the institutions, and in turn means the decision-makers need to have a sufficient understanding of the issues and the data management processes involved. It is crucial, therefore, that managers understand, and are enabled to understand, the 'value' inherent in their digital data. *Decision-makers need a way of calculating the value, to an organization, of their digital data.* This can, in turn, lead to better decision-making at an organizational or project initiation level with tangible practical outcomes, for example defining a more limited number of supported file types.

What should we preserve?

Historically, qualified people determined what data to preserve and what not to preserve: a process that in turn added to the value of the preserved data. In the digital domain, how do we determine the scope and nature of what is to be preserved, especially when the technical expertise needed to evaluate visualizations and simulations may be well beyond that of the curatorial staff, and relevant documentation may be too voluminous and therefore prohibitive to compile?

Digital art poses particular challenges. Many different contributors raise issues about ownership, while interactive and online art, which may dynamically change over time, and through various versions, poses questions about what actually constitutes the 'object' to be preserved. In the case of a theatre performance, it is the documentation that is preserved, rather than the performance itself. But art objects, and their various iterations, represent a somewhat different challenge. The key point is that the decision of what to preserve, and what not to preserve, ought not to be left to chance or (by default) to obsolescence, but should be a consciously deliberated strategic decision. A useful starting point is to create an inventory of what the holdings are, and systematically to prioritize objects, or categories of objects, for preservation. The Tate, for example, has started by asking key stakeholders (conservation departments, curators, artists, etc.) about the financial and legacy or heritage value of their holdings. Collection-holders always have had to make archival and preservation decisions on behalf of end-users, but we could also ask to what extent end-users (in the Tate's case, website users) might also be consulted? It is important to note that digital artists may have different priorities from preservationists, and so it is essential not to try to shoehorn artists' bespoke definitions into existing preservation standards, but rather to expand the latter sensitively according to this particular domain.

One of the challenges is how quickly decisions about preservation or destruction of resources need to be taken in the digital age: paper-based records could be warehoused for decades before decisions were made, whereas the reliability of hard disk drives (HDDs) or USB (Universal Serial Bus) drives is measured in a very few years only. This lack of temporal distance or perspective makes it very challenging to reliably determine what posterity will consider important. In particular, records of *processes* may not be rated highly at the moment, but may be viewed as crucial in the future. One option may be to preserve analogue versions of digital resources (e.g. print-outs onto acid-free paper, which indeed is done in some organizations). This becomes particularly challenging in the case of complex digital objects, but may bear further exploration in the future.

Whose responsibility is digital preservation?

This issue is not clear – is it down to the creators of simulations and visualizations, or archivists, or funding councils, or a mixture thereof? A suitable process for ascertaining such responsibility needs to be devised, otherwise the community is left with an unfunded mandate to preserve material but with no way of systematically carrying this out. Indeed, sound institutional and administrative processes are the key to making progress in this area. Mitigating against such advances is the fact that crucial technical skills are poorly distributed, making it hard for the cultural sector to recruit staff and obtain services. In short, it turns out that there are too many projects and too few 'services'. Added to that is the enormous difficulty in articulating the technical, practical and logistical requirements for simulation and visualization DP. Preservation from the outset would be a great asset, and this leads to the need for data creation tools for preservation-ready objects.

Another crying need is for greater documentation awareness in the communities. Currently data is created by people who do not have a document culture. It is critical to know before starting a project what you need to document in order to preserve the material created. The visualization and simulation communities could benefit from acquiring good engineering practice, where hard lessons have been learnt following on from data loss by e.g. NASA. To this end, the durability of digital objects, both complex and simple, should be inbuilt, and for this we can collaborate with and learn from the computer science and software engineering domains. In this respect, organizations such as the OPF and the DPC can play a vital dissemination role to IT students in universities by encouraging them to think about digital object sustainability. In tandem, the visualization and simulation communities should provide guidelines or standards and templates, following the example of, say, the SIARD standard for preserving databases.[1]

The problem of preserving 'everything'

In practice this means that the sector is not making strategic decisions to keep – or delete – objects. It is essential to define what is the boundary of a work, and then to go on to decide what should be retained or prioritized. Preservationists should be able to carry out confident deletion that would allow them to map resources against stated priorities for keeping material. To this end, a vigorous scholarly debate about what is important would be helpful in establishing what should be kept. A necessary prerequisite to achieving such a goal is to consider how to engage end-users in any discussion about deletion, especially where it impinges on long-term use. In practice, research is sometimes based on other people's perceived 'rubbish', for example, discarded maps of Pompeii. It may be hard to gauge the importance of such ephemera as a photo or map; to a researcher building a 3D visualization of Pompeii it could be really important. In an analogue world, we may feel sure that we know what future users would need. For digital documents, we do not know what future users will want to do, and how. There has been a paradigm shift in culture away from the physical: it seems that seeing a photo is as good as viewing the *Mona Lisa* (*La Gioconda*).

Also, it is expedient to see what can be learnt about digital preservation priorities by examining the various approaches to digitization. In terms of timescales, it is imperative to decide a suitable DP strategy early on, not later, as time constraints are then very narrow. It is also important to be flexible, and propose different solutions for different scales of preservation, whatever type of complexity these scales encompass. Unfortunately, in most cases, urgency leads to the wrong decisions being made.

The problem of scale

The issue of scale is indisputably a major problem. There are six types of complex visualization, so characterization is a problem of scale. We need a top-down solution, so that characterization can be undertaken systematically. The problem of scale may include not only the problem of preservation, but also the problem of access. Individual researchers in 3D visualizations may save everything, and this can result in an eclectic mess of floppies, Commodore files, tar files, etc., with everyone thinking they are doing things properly. While some standardization is necessary, it is evident that one system will not fit everyone – it is necessary to ascertain what stakeholders' needs are. Some archives preserve 5Tb per day in 1000 different formats.

Do the problems really only start with scale?

There are other problems concerning complexity that are not related to issues of scale. For example, preservationists of visualizations and simulations may not be able to identify the material they are given, as it takes considerable technical knowledge to be cognisant with the range of material covered by this domain. Where bespoke software or models are involved, customization is hard to achieve, and although standardization is desirable, it is also often an unreachable goal. A knowledge donor card or expert system would be most useful, where creators of such complex objects evince a desire or expectation to move on and leave their knowledge behind.

Do we understand the nature of the problem that we have?

It is unlikely that we can have entirely generic approaches for tackling the preservation of all complex objects, due to the fact that addressing more than one domain is hard. As observed in the abstract above, it can be argued that all objects are to some extent complex. For example, a PDF making a call on a tiff file represents a very complex file format. If complex objects require bespoke – i.e. expensive – solutions, who then is to be the arbiter of value? This again comes back to the question 'who decides what to keep?' Here, the designated community is a useful concept to establish the nature of the problem and hence the value of the data. For example the Arts and Humanities Data Service (AHDS) had context-specific rules that could not be transferred: they were only valid for the designated community.

Another salient approach involves determining the business case. In particular, the business cases for preservation will probably be different in different institutions. Two projects, CASPAR (Cultural, Artistic and Scientific knowledge for Preservation, Access and Retrieval) and SHAMAN (Sustaining Heritage Access through Multivalent ArchiviNg), looked at specific data to try to find a generic approach. However, it can be the case that even people looking for a single solution may end up with an integrated solution. For this POCOS symposium, it is important to establish what makes simulations and visualizations a different case. For these subject specialisms we need to understand digital preservation as a process 'in the present': encompassing good practice and assessment in the 'here and now' will be useful in the medium term.

What is the complexity in the object and what effect does it have?

This could be embedded material, as in the new PDF format, nested objects, obscure file types, extremely large objects, etc., or any combination thereof. An example of a complex digital object from archiving the web at the British Library highlights the difficulty of saving the commentary from the artist Anthony Gormley on the plinth of Nelson's Column in Trafalgar Square, London, together with the associated blog and video. The comments, the related structures and timings and overall experience were not preserved, so it was impossible to make sense of the commentary, blog or video.

One effect is that complex objects will cost more to preserve than their simple counterparts, as observed in the data security session. However, this does not necessarily mean that complex objects need complex governance. One suggestion is for e.g. a memory institution to save just one screenshot of an entire, complex digital scene (e.g. of a 3D visualization), whilst the creator should save all the digital components making up the whole digital scene. Here it is vital to recognize that complex objects have complex dependencies, thus it is advisable to carry out risk analysis and then prioritize problems, first ascertaining what the weak links in the chain are. Self-contained digital objects with inbuilt metadata, etc., play a key role in this task.

Another point to bear in mind is that complexity can differ depending on how an object is installed, e.g. under conditions of experimental extremism with flex glass panels and inputs from a person's sound, movement, etc. In this situation it may be sensible to try to preserve the system and the experience, noting whether it functions correctly or not. It may be possible to preserve a predefined sequence of events, whilst allowing for the fact that random effects cannot be reproduced. In this case it is necessary to decide what is important. Documentation can play a key part in re-creating a given technical environment necessary to re-create a particular experience. The data models behind the TOTEM database in KEEP/OPF[2] seek to provide metadata to allow robust descriptions of requisite technical environments.

To conclude, there is the general impression that complex objects may be categorized as just being too hard to deal with, so preservationists may be tempted to try just to archive them, to avoid dealing with the problems. Given that such an object has no clear migration path, then the next best thing is to follow a best-efforts path. In the end it is a case of preserving size, environment and experience.

Notes

1 Software Independent Archiving of Relational Databases,
   www.bar.admin.ch/dienstleistungen/00823/00825/index.html?lang=en.
2 www.keep-totem.co.uk.

References

Anderson, D., Delve, J., Pinchbeck, D., Konstantelos, L., Lange, A. and
    Bergmeyer, W. (2010) *KEEP Project: final document analyzing and summarizing
    metadata standards and issues across Europe.*

Condron, F., Richards, J., Robinson, D. and Wise, A. (1999) *Strategies for Digital
    Data: findings and recommendations from digital data in archaeology – a survey of user
    needs*, York, Archaeology Data Service, University of York.

Gladney, H. M. (2008) *Durable Digital Objects Rather Than Digital Preservation*
    (electronic version), ERPAePrints,
    http://eprints.erpanet.org/146/01/Durable.pdf [accessed 16 July 2009].

CHAPTER 12

The ISDA[1] tools: preserving 3D digital content

Kenton McHenry, Rob Kooper, Luigi Marini and Michael Ondrejcek

National Center for Supercomputing Applications,
University of Illinois at Urbana-Champaign, USA

Introduction

There are many different file formats to store any given content type. This is especially true in the case of 3D content, where it seems that nearly every vendor of 3D software tends to come up with their own unique file format. In our evaluation of a number of popular 3D software packages we have documented over 144 different file formats (McHenry et al., 2011). Having many different formats for the same type of data is a problem for a couple of reasons. The first reason is a matter of accessibility, in that having many formats makes it difficult to share data. If a particular format is obscure or used by only one particular software application, then content created in that application might be difficult to share with users who do not have that software. The second reason is a matter of preservation. If a software vendor uses a proprietary format and does not make the format's specification open, then if that vendor were ever to go out of business, any content stored within that format could be potentially locked away forever. This situation has been known to occur.

One might argue that in an ideal world there would only be one file format for each type of content. Having one format, a format that has a standardized open specification, would make archiving that content much easier, in that even if a viewer no longer exists in the future for that format, a new viewer could be created based on the available specification. Determining what this format could be is a problem. Even once this format is determined, converting from all the formats available today to that one format is also a problem.

As soon as the need for file format conversion arises we must begin to consider information loss. In Table 12.1 we list several 3D formats along the types of information they each support. While there are a variety of formats to store 3D content, each can store information a little differently.

As shown in the table, 3D files store a variety of attributes from geometry, to appearance, to scene properties and animation. Each attribute can also be stored in a number of ways. Not all file formats support all attributes. Converting between formats that do not support the same type of information will result in some sort of information loss. Even within individual attributes, information can be stored differently. For example the geometry of a model is often represented as either a faceted mesh, as parametric surfaces, as a boundary representation, or as constructive solid geometry. Converting from a format that supports one representation to one that supports another representation requires a conversion of the content itself. Some of these conversions are possible. For example B-Rep[2] surfaces can be transformed to faceted meshes by a process called tessellation. Doing this will alias an otherwise continuous surface and depending on the sampling drastically change the file size. The tessellation process will result in a loss of information, in that the inverse process, going from a faceted mesh to a B-Rep, will not result in the original content. In fact this inverse conversion is not trivial at all.

Keeping in mind that conversions will almost always result in some sort of information loss we can then begin the process of determining what is an optimal file format for long-term preservation.

We define this format as one that is standardized, open and results in as little information loss as possible when converted to from all other available formats. Such a format would have the best chance of keeping the bulk of an archive's data accessible in the future.

Below we present a number of tools that we have developed towards the end goal of empirically evaluating which format is optimal for long-term preservation for a given content type. We present these tools individually, as they possess useful qualities in their own right, separate from the overall goal of choosing an optimal file format.

3D Utilities

Our 3D Utilities are both a library and a collection of tools written in Java, created for the purpose of accessing content within various 3D file formats.

Table 12.1 Common attributes stored within 3D files

Format	Geometry				Appearance				Scene				Animation
	Faceted	Parametric	CSG	B-Rep	Color	Material	Texture	Bump	Lights	Views	Trans.	Groups	
3ds	✓	✓			✓	✓	✓	✓	✓	✓	✓		
igs	✓	✓	✓	✓	✓						✓	✓	
lwo	✓	✓			✓	✓	✓	✓				✓	
obj	✓	✓			✓	✓	✓	✓					
ply	✓				✓	✓	✓	✓					
stp	✓	✓	✓	✓	✓							✓	
wrl	✓	✓			✓	✓	✓	✓	✓	✓	✓	✓	✓
u3d	✓				✓		✓	✓	✓	✓	✓	✓	✓
x3d	✓	✓			✓	✓	✓	✓	✓	✓	✓	✓	✓

Like the NCSA Portfolio project before it, 3D Utilities provides a number of 3D file loaders. Unlike Portfolio, which was built on Java3D and loaded content in a Java3D scene graph, 3D Utilities takes a far simpler and less restrictive approach. 3D Utilities uses an extremely simple polygonal mesh representation for all its 3D content. File loaders for various formats are created so as to parse a 3D file type and load its content into a polygonal mesh. If a file format does not store its 3D geometry as a mesh, then it is up to the loader to convert between representations. This library of loaders can be used by any Java application to load 3D content from a file for the purpose of rendering or manipulating it through the mesh data structure (which is nothing more than a list of vertices and faces connecting them).

In addition to file loaders, the 3D Utilities library also contains a library of mesh signatures. These mesh signatures act as a hash, allowing one to compare two different 3D models and retrieve the most similar instance from a collection of 3D models. We have implemented signatures based on vertices statistics, polygonal face surface area (Brunnermeier and Martin, 1999), light fields (Chen et al., 2003) and spin images (Johnson and Hebert, 1999). Each signature allows for different aspects of the models to be considered during a comparison and each is best suited under differing situations. These signatures can be used within Java code to compare two meshes that have been loaded using the library of loaders.

3D Utilities also contains several tools: ModelViewer, ModelViewerApplet, ModelBrowser and ModelConverter. The ModelViewer is both a class extending a JPanel, which can be used within code to display 3D content, and a standalone application to view content within 3D files. The ModelViewerApplet is an applet version of the ModelViewer allowing 3D content to be viewable from within a web browser. The ModelBrowser tool uses ModelViewers to provide a convenient way of viewing all 3D files under a given file system directory (Figure 12.1). All 3D files found under a user-specified directory are shown. From here a user can select one of the files to be displayed in the top right panel. This panel, being an instance of a ModelViewer, allows a user to use the mouse to change viewing directions and manipulate the model. In the bottom right panel, the metadata of the 3D model being viewed is displayed. If multiple files are selected in the left pane, they are compared using a specified signature and shown simultaneously in the right pane, with distances along edges that connect them. This can be used as a means of visualizing how the various signatures emphasize different

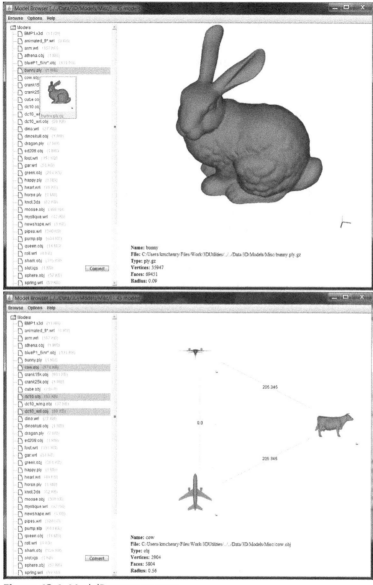

Figure 12.1 ModelBrowser screens

aspects of a 3D model during comparison. The last tool, the ModelConverter, utilizes the 3D Utilities file loaders to perform format conversions.

As all loaders load and save content to and from a mesh representation, it is a simple matter to convert between formats by loading the content using one loader and saving it using another.

The Conversion Software Registry

As stated previously, vendors have a tendency to create new file formats. For the sake of some level of portability, applications often allow content to be imported/exported to and from a handful of other formats. This feature allows many software applications to act as converters between different formats. As many formats are closed-source and proprietary, the software of the vendor responsible for the format is often the best means of getting into and out of that particular format.

As many applications only support a small number of imports and exports, it is also very likely that many desirable conversions from specific source formats to target formats will not be supported. However, it is very likely that multiple applications chained together can carry out conversions though intermediary formats that are not directly supported by any one application.

This information, in terms of software inputs and outputs, is essential in order to identify software to carry out a specific conversion. Determining what software is needed for a particular conversion, however, can be difficult without direct access to the software (i.e. without purchasing it). To aid users in this task we have created the Conversion Software Registry (CSR), an online database that indexes software based on the input and output formats they support (Ondrejcek, McHenry and Bajcsy, 2010). A user can type in the extension of a source format and target format to get back a list of applications that directly supports that conversion. By clicking a radio button below the query box, a user can tell the system to consider conversions using one or more intermediary formats.

The CSR also allows users to search through the space of possible conversions graphically. Applications selected in the left pane are represented in the right pane as an input/output graph. This graph has at its vertices file formats and directed edges connecting a pair of formats to represent an application capable of carrying out that particular conversion. Users can search for a conversion path between formats by using their mouse to select a source and target file format. An un-weighted shortest path algorithm is then used to find a conversion path with the least number of intermediary formats (Figure 12.2).

Other types of supported queries include: finding all the formats reachable from a given source format, finding all the formats that can reach a particular target format, and finding a set of file formats that can be commonly reached by a selected set of source formats.

Software servers

Ideally we would like to be able to support format conversions within code (e.g. Java). However, because of the many closed proprietary formats in existence, this is not at all feasible. Nevertheless, as pointed out in the previous section, software is available to carry out many conversions. A software server is a tool that attempts to bridge this gap between need and availability (McHenry et al., 2010, 2011; McHenry, Kooper and Bajcsy,

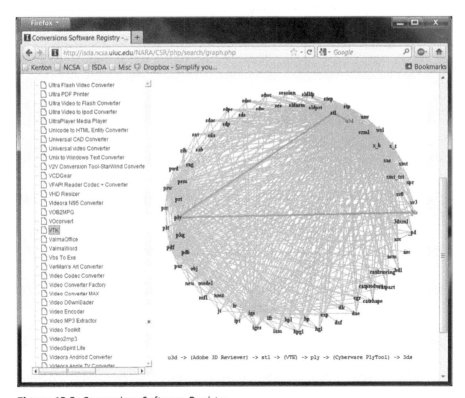

Figure 12.2 Conversions Software Registry

2009b). A software server running on a system allows functionality within locally installed software to be shared in a matter that is analogous to the way Windows allows one to share a folder. To share functionality within software (e.g. the open and save operations within a particular program), one needs only to right-click on the shortcut of the application and select 'Share Functionality' from the menu that appears.

Once this is done, information obtained from the shortcut is used to query the Conversion Software Registry, which serves as a repository for wrapper scripts that are capable of automating functionality within command line- and graphical-interface-driven software. These scripts can be written in any text-based scripting language. We tend to use AutoHotKey[3] and Sikuli (Yeh, Chang and Miller, 2009), as they allow for the scripting of graphical interfaces (making a large amount of software accessible from the Software Server). Wrapper scripts associated with the required software are downloaded and configured to run on the local environment.

Once a software server is running shared software, functionality can be accessed by simply pointing a web browser to the address of the hosting machine. When this is done, a user is presented with a page that mimics modern file managers with a number of icons representing available software. When a user clicks on a particular piece of software, they are presented with a form that allows them to call the remotely shared functionality from the browser. Tasks always take the form of a quadruple of the form: software, task, output format, input file. Though the form presents this in an easy to use graphical manner, the strength of the software server is in the RESTful interface[4] it provides to carry out these tasks.

Specifically, the same task can be carried out by posting a file to a URL on the host in the form of:

http://**<host>**:8182/software/**<Software>**/**<Task>**/**<Output>**/

where the final element of the quadruple, the input file, is the posted file. This simple, consistent, widely accessible interface to software allows software functionality to be used within new code as if it were a function within a library. Any language that supports accessing URLs can access this functionality, possibly wrapping it to look like a native library.

Polyglot

NCSA Polyglot (McHenry, Kooper and Bajcsy, 2009a) is a conversion service built on top of the previously described software servers. When software servers come online they begin to broadcast their existence. A Polyglot instance listens for these broadcasts. When a new software server is found, Polyglot will query it for all shared software functionality, looking for software with available input and output operations to carry out conversions. From this information Polyglot constructs an input/output graph. This graph is searched in order to carry out conversions across chains of software based on a given input format and desired output format.

Polyglot can be accessed through either a Java API or a web interface which allows a user to drag and drop a number of files from their local machine, select an output format, and carry out the conversions with the results being made available for download.

Versus

Versus is a framework or library of content-to-content comparison measures supporting raster images, vector graphics, 3D models (via the signatures from our 3D Utilities) and documents. These measures are used by Polyglot as a means of estimating the information loss incurred by converting from one format to another through a piece of software. Information loss is evaluated in Polyglot by using a sample set of files in a format that can be directly loaded by one of the loaders in our 3D Utilities library. These files are converted to every reachable format within an input/output graph and then converted back to the original. We are forced to execute through these A–B–A conversion paths in order to compare the file's contents before and after the conversion. Each before and after file is compared using a set measure from Versus, and the returned similarity is averaged along each edge representing software in the graph. This weighted graph can be used by Polyglot to identify conversions paths with minimal information loss. In addition, this weighted graph can be used to derive an answer to the question of which format would be best suited for long-term preservation (as described earlier).

Conclusion

The ISDA tools are a collection of libraries and software constructed for the purpose of providing solutions to problems in digital preservation. We have presented five of these tools: 3D Utilities, the Conversion Software Registry, software servers, Polyglot and Versus. These and others are available from our site at http://isda.ncsa.illinois.edu as free open-source software.

Acknowledgments

This research has been funded through the National Science Foundation Cooperative Agreement NSF OCI 05-25308 and Cooperative Support Agreement NSF OCI 05-04064 by the National Archives and Records Administration (NARA).

Notes

1 The Image and Spatial Data Analysis division, based at the National Center for Supercomputing Applications.
2 Boundary Representation.
3 www.autohotkey.com.
4 http://en.wikipedia.org/wiki/Representational_state_transfer.

References

Brunnermeier, S. and Martin, S. (1999) *Interoperability Cost Analysis of the U.S. Automotive Supply Chain*, RTI International Research Publications.

Chen, D., Tian, X., Shen, Y. and Ouhyoung, M. (2003) *On Visual Similarity Based 3D Model Retrieval*, Eurographics Computer Graphics Forum.

Johnson, A. E. and Hebert, M. (1999) Using Spin Images for Efficient Object Recognition in Cluttered 3D Scenes, *IEEE Transactions on Pattern Analysis and Machine Intelligence*, **21** (5), 433–49.

McHenry, K., Kooper, R. and Bajcsy, P. (2009a) Towards a Universal, Quantifiable, and Scalable File Format Converter, paper presented at the *Fifth IEEE International Conference on e-Science*, e-Science, 140–7.

McHenry, K., Kooper, R. and Bajcsy, P. (2009b) Taking Matters Into Your Own Hands: imposing code reusability for universal file format conversion, paper presented at the the *Microsoft eScience Workshop*, Pittsburgh, PA, 15–19 October.

McHenry, K., Kooper, R., Marini, L. and Bajcsy, P. (2010) Designing a Scalable Cross Platform Imposed Code Reuse Framework, paper presented at the *Microsoft eScience Workshop*, Berkeley, CA, 11–13 October.

McHenry, K., Kooper, R., Ondrejcek, M., Marini, L. and Bajcsy, P. (2011) A Mosaic of Software, paper presented at the *Seventh IEEE International Conference on E-Science*, e-Science, 279-286.

Ondrejcek, M., McHenry, K. and Bajcsy, P. (2010) The Conversion Software Registry, paper presented at the *Microsoft e-Science Workshop*, Berkeley, CA, 11–13 October.

Yeh, T., Chang, T. and Miller, R. (2009). Sikuli: using gui screenshots for search and automation, paper presented at the 22nd *Annual ACM Symposium on User Interface Software and Technology* (UIST), Victoria, BC, Canada, 4–7 October, http://groups.csail.mit.edu/uid/projects/sikuli/sikuli-uist2009.pdf.

Metadata, paradata and documentation

Ecologies of research and performance: preservation challenges in the London Charter

Hugh Denard

Digital Humanities, King's College London, UK

Introduction

This chapter has two primary concerns. First, it asks what the London Charter for the Computer-based Visualization of Cultural Heritage has to say that is relevant to the preservation of complex digital objects? Second, it looks at the nature of some of the complex objects (note, not just complex *digital* objects) that are produced by multifaceted projects – in this instance, projects with both humanities research and artistic dimensions – as well as projects that span digital and non-digital materials.

The London Charter

The London Charter started off in February 2006 with a symposium and workshop called 'Making 3D Visual Research Outcomes Transparent', which was held at both the British Academy and King's College London as part of our 'Making Space' AHRC ICT Strategy Project. There was, at that time, no international consensus or standard about the type or level of documentation needed to communicate to scholarly audiences the methods and outcomes of visualization-based research projects. A computer visualization of an historical monument or object is really no more than a picture unless we also communicate to people what has gone into the making of that visualization: what is the evidence, how reliable is the evidence, what decisions have been made in order to create this digital object. Without such information, the visualization cannot be properly understood or evaluated.

At this symposium in 2006, the question was posed: 'How do we move from the idea of good practice to a *culture* of good practice within the heritage visualization domain?' I suggested that we needed a 'Charter', which would enable us to draw the community's attention to a formal, consensus-based statement of best practice for heritage visualization. A working group was established and released the first version of the London Charter in March 2006, with a more detailed version (Draft 2.1) being published in February 2009 (London Charter, 2009). All the drafts of the Charter, together with its detailed history and an introduction, can be seen on the London Charter website.[1]

The Charter has six principles, each of which addresses a specific topic:

- Principle 1, 'Implementation', addresses the scope of the Charter's applicability.
- Principle 2 discusses the importance of making aims and methods cohere with each other.
- Principle 3, 'Research Sources', discusses the importance of publishing the evidence upon which research visualizations are based, and of demonstrating the systematic and rigorous evaluation of that evidence.
- Principle 4, 'Documentation', mandates that sufficient information should be documented and disseminated to allow computer-based visualization methods and outcomes to be understood and evaluated in relation to the contexts and purposes for which they are deployed.

There are two final principles, 'Sustainability' and 'Access', which I will discuss in more detail shortly, as they perhaps have the most direct relevance to digital preservation as it is conventionally defined.

The London Charter has had significant impact. It has been translated into a number of languages: Japanese, Italian, French, German and Spanish. The 100-member EU EPOCH (European Network of Excellence in Open Cultural Heritage) strongly endorsed the Charter, and it has attracted the interest of senior figures within the EU and UNESCO and in a number of national-level bodies. The UK's Archaeology Data Service has set the London Charter as a benchmark for the deposit of digital visualization. The Italian Ministry of Culture has also accepted the London Charter as a guideline for work in its domain. There is also a new set of principles emerging, called the Seville Principles, which the International Forum of Virtual Archaeology is working on, and which describes itself as an implementation of the London Charter specifically for the domain of archaeology.

Preservation issues raised by the London Charter

The core statement of Principle 4, 'Documentation', is:

> Sufficient information should be documented and disseminated to allow computer-based visualisation methods and outcomes to be understood and evaluated in relation to the contexts and purposes for which they are deployed.

The London Charter is not an absolute standard: it is a relational model which places the onus on the creators of the visualization to work out what quantity and quality of documentation is appropriate, according to community consensus on best practice.

From a preservation perspective, what we are dealing with is the preservation of, first, ephemeral processes and, second, the documentary traces that these research processes leave, which can appear in a wide variety of formats, from video diaries to illustrated scholarly articles.

The 12 sections of Principle 4 discuss a variety of important ancillary issues, which we can review briefly. These include the importance of taking account of the ways in which the process of creating documentation can enhance research practice (4.1–4.3), and of documenting knowledge claims (4.4) – i.e. making clear whether a particular visualization is recording evidence or is representing an hypothesis, and if the latter, then establishing how secure that hypothesis is.

The Charter stipulates the need to document research sources, processes and methods (4.5–4.9): to explain why we are using these methods – indeed, why we are using a visualization-based approach at all. In short, the Charter challenges us to consider rigorously, and to document our decisions.

Section 4.10 discusses the documentation of dependency relationships:

> Computer-based visualisation outcomes should be disseminated in such a way that the nature and importance of significant, hypothetical dependency relationships between elements can be clearly identified by users and the reasoning underlying such hypotheses understood.

So for example, if all I know is that a glass of water was in the Anatomy Lecture Theatre at King's College London at 12.30 p.m. on 17 June 2011, in precisely this position in three-dimensional space (expressed as X, Y, Z coordinates), then it follows that there must be some additional object upon which the glass is resting, otherwise the glass would be sitting in mid-air. So the position of the glass depends upon something being present to support it – a dependency relationship. If I am fortunate, my research sources may include a photograph of this lecture theatre showing a fixed desk in this location. If I do not have such a photograph, I might study images of comparable lecture theatres and hypothesize that the glass is likely to be resting on a desk, which may be supported by a review of types of objects which are both likely to be in this position and which would also result in a surface of the appropriate height. Put simply, each piece of evidence may imply certain other things, but in order for our visualization-based arguments to be intellectually transparent, we need to document and publish those detailed chains of reasoning.

The sections of the Charter covering the documentation of formats and standards (4.11–4.12) also relate to preservation issues, stipulating that:

> Documentation should be disseminated using the most effective available media, including graphical, textual, video, audio, numerical or combinations of the above. (4.11)

and:

> Documentation should be disseminated sustainably with reference to relevant standards and ontologies according to best practice in relevant communities of practice and in such a way that facilitates its inclusion in relevant citation indexes. (4.12)

The Charter aims to provide enduring, methodological principles, and so deliberately avoids entanglement in technical details, which are likely to become obsolete over time. So, without dwelling on the above two articles, we may note that they remind us of the importance of developing discipline-specific implementation guidelines.

Documentation is a means of preserving the ephemeral, and often intangible, aspects of highly complex research processes. Three-dimensional digital models are themselves complex digital objects which have technically challenging digital preservation requirements. But, equally, documenting in detail the process through which they were produced is also an important aspect of preservation – we need to create surrogates, through documentation, for research processes that unfolded over time. Of course, it is of central importance to determine what we think is important to preserve, which allows us to work towards a preservation strategy, and the London Charter provides a very strong framework for identifying documentation/preservation priorities.

Let us move on now to look at Principle 5, 'Sustainability', which opens as follows:

> Strategies should be planned and implemented to ensure the long-term sustainability of cultural heritage-related computer-based visualisation outcomes and documentation, in order to avoid loss of this growing part of human intellectual, social, economic and cultural heritage.

Here are some key concepts:

> The most reliable and sustainable available form of archiving computer-based visualisation outcomes, whether analogue or digital, should be identified and implemented. (5.1)

If digital data may be under threat in the future, consideration needs to be given to creating some sort of physical print, whether as an actual three-dimensional object through 3D printing or as a set of print images. If we cannot preserve the actual digital data, we can – and *should* – preserve an enduring, physical record of our visualization.

> Digital preservation strategies should aim to preserve the computer-based visualisation data, rather than the medium on which they were originally stored, and also information sufficient to enable their use in the future, for example through migration to different formats or software emulation. (5.2)

This recommendation was really designed for people within the humanities and heritage domain who had not yet made the distinction between medium and content; the aim was to get them to think about whether it really mattered if a CD, for example, would still be usable in ten years' time, or whether the important question was whether the bits would still be available and usable.

> Where digital archiving is not the most reliable means of ensuring the long-term survival of a computer-based visualisation outcome, a partial two-dimensional record of a computer-based visualisation output, evoking as far as possible the scope and properties of the original output, should be preferred to the absence of a record. (5.3)

Or, to paraphrase, some preservation is better than none.

> Documentation strategies should be designed to be sustainable in relation to available resources and prevailing working practices. (5.4)

This is to encourage institutions to provide resources and to facilitate working practices to enable us to carry out this best practice.

Preservation of mixed reality objects

The Charter's distinction between digital preservation and the preservation of digital objects (or between medium and content) is important, and brings us to the threshold of an even knottier set of problems, which is my second major theme, namely: what do we do when the object of preservation itself may have non-digital, as well as digital, elements? Some of our 'complex objects' live in both physical and digital worlds. In such cases, how do we even define the object of preservation?

To give an example: the art work *Vanishing Point(s)*[2] is based on a large-scale Roman fresco dating from the middle of the first century BCE, which is to be found *in situ* within the Villa at Oplontis (modern day Torre Annunziata, near Pompeii). This beautiful and complex fresco offers an imagined vista onto a sacred precinct, enclosed by monumental architectural colonnades and, in the foreground, a complex set of architectural framing features – including grand, golden columns, screen walls, coffered ceilings and arches – dressed with significant objects, such as theatre masks, peacocks, burnished shields and paintings. The entire composition is bookended by a quiet garden colonnade which subtly bends the apparent spatial coherence of the whole.

Vanishing Point(s) translates the compositional principles and the spatial rhythms of this ancient fresco into a different kind of space – that of the Great Hall at King's College London. Taking the idea that the Roman fresco invites the viewer to enter into a kind of imagined, virtual world, the contemporary art work is created by taking a snapshot of a fully realized three-dimensional environment specially created within the virtual world of *Second Life*; at the time the piece was created, one could go online, as an avatar, to walk around this virtual park in real time. This snapshot of the virtual realm was printed out onto 30m² of large-format digital transparency film, called Duratrans, and applied to 108 panes of the five-window array of the Great Hall's east wall, achieving a stained-glass-like effect. Once installed, the trees in the art work carried forward into virtual space the rhythm of the actual columns of the Great Hall, overlaying its architecturally constructed garden vista upon the actual view, which is of a drab, congested urban courtyard. In several subtle ways, which I will not detail here, the new art work draws upon the compositional principles of the ancient Roman fresco, involving an intricate network of social, philosophical, optical as well as aesthetic considerations.

This particular art work constructs a crossing point between humanities research (on Roman fresco art) and artistic practice (specifically, Michael Takeo Magruder's work combining elements of physical installation and virtual worlds technologies), and this intersection raises all kinds of issues regarding how we scope and prioritize our preservation processes. How, when we are dealing with a 'mixed reality' art work such as this, which comprises a blend of actual and virtual elements (a virtual landscape in *Second Life* and a physical installation in the Great Hall), do we define the object of preservation? And who do we identify as the intended beneficiaries of preservation, which would enable us to establish appropriate preservation priorities? How does London Charter-articulated best practice apply to blended entities such as these?

We might consider whether the question of intellectual transparency ought to have any purchase on our preservation strategy. The Charter:

> is concerned with the research and dissemination of cultural heritage across academic, educational, curatorial and commercial domains. It has relevance, therefore, for those aspects of the entertainment industry involving the reconstruction or evocation of cultural heritage, but not for the use of computer-based visualisation in, for example, contemporary art, fashion, or design. (Preamble)

However, *Vanishing Point(s)*, while it provides a pleasant, artificial view for the Great Hall, also becomes much more richly meaningful if its audience is aware of its intense, inter-textual relationship with the Roman fresco from the Villa at Oplontis – a relationship, however, which the art work itself does not overtly present to its viewers. And I hope I have indicated how an art work such as this becomes even more stimulating and enjoyable if the viewer has access to some of the thinking that explains how it draws on a deep, multifaceted interpretation of that Roman fresco and its social, cultural, as well as 'spatial', presence. And there are yet further strands to do with the reception of the art work, such as the decision by the College authorities to extend its initial six-week life indefinitely, all of which is part of the 'object' which merits consideration as part of a preservation strategy.

So perhaps this suggests is that preservation has a role, not only in recording, but also in creating what almost amounts to a new iteration of the art work in the 'medium' of documentation: documentation which not only records, but also actually augments, the art work in a significant way.

Preservation, access and enhancing practice

The final principle of the London Charter, which deals with issues of 'Access', reads as follows:

> The creation and dissemination of computer-based visualisation should be planned in such a way as to ensure the maximum possible benefits are achieved for the study, understanding, interpretation, preservation and management of cultural heritage.

This brings me to my third major theme: how can preservation (including, of course, preservation of ephemeral processes through documentation) contribute additional, valuable dimensions to historical research and creative practice? Let us review the sub-sections of the Access principle:

> The aims, methods and dissemination plans of computer-based visualisation should reflect consideration of how such work can enhance access to cultural heritage that is otherwise inaccessible due to health and safety, disability, economic, political, or environmental reasons, or because the object of the visualisation is lost, endangered, dispersed, or has been destroyed, restored or reconstructed. (6.1)

Projects should take cognizance of the types and degrees of access that
computer-based visualisation can uniquely provide to cultural heritage stakeholders,
including the study of change over time, magnification, modification, manipulation
of virtual objects, embedding of datasets, and instantaneous global distribution. (6.2)

Most cultural heritage visualizations are carried out by publicly funded bodies.
This implies an obligation to ensure the benefits of that work are shared with
the public.

Case study – the Abbey Theatre, Dublin

I will conclude by presenting a case study of a visualization of the Abbey
Theatre in Dublin. The Abbey Theatre, founded by William Butler Yeats,
Lady Gregory, *AE*, Edward Martyn and John Millington Synge, opened on
27 December 1904 in a theatre leased and renovated for the purpose by
Annie Horniman, which remained in use until fire damaged it in 1951. The
Abbey went on to become a world-famous theatre, producing playwrights
and plays of major international importance.

Everyone who goes to school in Ireland studies these plays. These are
major landmarks of international drama, but very little attention is given to
the physical space for which these plays were written. What, if any, is the
relationship between the tiny size of the original Abbey's stage and the
intimacy of the scenes that the early Abbey playwrights created, including in
the new genre of the 'peasant play'? Historians have tended to focus on the
Abbey's contribution to an emergent national (Irish) identity at the beginning
of the 20th century, as well as considerations of the literary, poetic and
dramatic merits of the plays written for the theatre. Scholars have found it
very difficult to break sufficiently free of these preoccupations.

One relatively neglected perspective is space. From January to April 2011,
while a visiting research fellow in Trinity College Dublin's Long Room Hub,
I investigated the physical properties of the original Abbey Theatre. Working
with a local digital communications company, Noho, I undertook to collect
and synthesize into a three-dimensional digital model all the evidence I could
find about the earliest phase of the theatre's stage and auditorium.

The research sources contributing to the visualization effort were quite
diverse, including: a painting by Jack B. Yeats (brother of W. B.) of the pre-
renovation theatre; the original, highly detailed, architectural plans for the

redesigned theatre by Joseph Holloway (who was also notable for having recorded, in 221 heavy volumes, his extensive observations on the cultural and theatrical scene of Dublin in the first half of the 20th century); black-and-white photographs of the interior of the early Abbey in the present-day Abbey Theatre's archives, as well as original portraits and artefacts that survived the fire of 1951; published descriptions of the theatre from varying dates; previously unpublished fire insurance maps showing the dramatic changes that the site underwent in phases between 1893 and 1961, with the theatre company's holdings expanding to include a variety of neighbouring buildings used as dressing rooms, green room, properties and scenery stores; and so forth. These maps also clearly indicate the social stratification that the new theatre design introduced; in place of a single entrance for the audience of the previous, popular, so-called Mechanics' Theatre, Abbey patrons with tickets to the Stalls and Balcony now entered through an attractive vestibule on Marlborough Street, while the cheap seats, known as 'The Pit', were accessed from an entrance on Abbey Street, passing through narrow corridors to enter at the very rear of the theatre.

The Irish Architectural Archive on Merrion Square contains drawings from a survey of the theatre by Michael Scott Architects carried out in 1935, which gives additional details that Holloway's plans omit, which are particularly useful when, as often occurs, it is difficult to ascertain which one of the many designs that Holloway created were actually implemented in the theatre. The original programmes from the Abbey, of which the Trinity College Library has a good collection, give us invaluable information about the tradesmen and companies that carried out the electrical installation, scene painting, upholstery, and so on. Honora Faul, Curator of Prints and Drawings in the National Library of Ireland, discovered in Joseph Holloway's vast collection of theatrical ephemera ticket envelopes from the early Abbey, which contained miniature plans of the seating in the theatre, showing the position and number of each individual row and seat, which, although they appear to contain some discrepancies with the early photographs – indicating that they are from a slightly later phase in the building's life – represent yet another extraordinarily valuable source of information.

My research into the history of the fabric of the original Abbey Theatre was full of these unexpected windfalls, of which none is more extraordinary than the following story. In 1961, ten years after the theatre building had been abandoned due to fire damage, it was finally decided to clear the site to make way for a new purpose-built theatre. At the time, former Dublin City architect Daithi P. Hanly realized that no steps were being taken to preserve for posterity the original, historic theatre building, despite its unquestionably iconic importance. He therefore persuaded Christy Cooney, the demolition contractor, to number the external stones and to remove them to Hanly's own garden, in Killiney, south County Dublin, where he would hold them in trust until a way could be found to restore the theatre's façade. Despite a strenuous campaign of several years, backed by numerous luminaries of the Irish theatrical world, the stones remain, to this day, in the late Daithi P. Hanly's garden, where his family continues to care for them in the hope that some day his great vision will be realized. When I visited the garden, and spoke to his family, a member of the film crew accompanying me tilted back one of the stones to find the original lettering of the Abbey Theatre still clearly visible, showing not only the green and cream livery of the later Abbey, but also the gold and red which, subsequent research verified, were the original theatre's decorative colours. In outhouses within the grounds of Hanly house, we found stored the original wooden window-frames, doors, and even billboards that flanked the Vestibule doors. Even the cash till for the Peacock Theatre – the smaller stage – has survived, thanks to Hanly's intervention. And there, on a side table, we found the detailed, scale wooden model of the original Abbey, thought to be lost, which had been photographed and published by James W. Flannery in 1976 in his book, *W. B. Yeats and the Idea of a Theatre*; again, a wonderfully rich research resource.

A project benefiting from such diverse research sources inevitably throws up quite a variety of documentation and preservation challenges. To ensure the project represented an exemplary implementation of the London Charter, it was necessary to devise an intellectually transparent approach, which captured the research process, rather than just the research outcomes. It was important to maintain a running record of the research and modelling activities, and consistent with the Charter's recommendations on access, this needed to be publicly visible. This was accomplished by creating a project blog.[3] Thus it was possible to document in an informal way the research process as it unfolded, showing , step by step, how the research process fed into the digital model that Noho were creating. A project Twitter account was used to notify people when the blog had a new update. The blog contained a simple title page indicating the project scope, and blog contents, together with outline information on London Charter compliancy. Detailed information was also made available for anyone wanting to drill down a little. Entries were categorized either 'Project', 'Research Sources' or 'Visualisation', but were also to be found in a manually created chronological index of entries, with journalistic-style by-lines giving a sense of their content. Under the 'Visualisation' category were video diary entries created by the project's 3D modeller, and founder of Noho, Niall O hOisin, in which he described each day's work and how information extrapolated from the various research sources were incorporated into the geometry of the digital model, a classic implementation of London Charter documentation/paradata.

There was also an entry explaining the project methodology in some detail, including the plan to create three different versions of the model, a forensic massing model, an artist's impression and a forensic textured model. The massing model would be un-textured but colour-coded green, amber and red – a 'traffic-light' system proposed by Daniel Pletinckx – to show the different levels of probability ('certain', 'probable' and 'plausible') accruing to different parts of the model. The artist's impression model was intended to give an impression of how the theatre may originally have appeared, while the forensic textured model was to indicate levels of probability about decorative, rather than architectural, elements. We did not implement this final version, because it proved impossible to source any colour photographs of the interior of the original auditorium, despite its having survived until 1951 – well into the age of colour photography. We therefore modelled and rendered the theatre in greyscale, in the style of a black-and-white photograph. It was several months after the modelling process was completed before the first textual description of the original colour scheme of the auditorium was located, and this was published, via the blog, as a freely downloadable PowerPoint presentation with rendered images of the model to make it easy for others to incorporate the project's outcomes into their own historical and cultural narratives.

The blog proved to be a great way to engage and reward stakeholders; when meetings or visits turned up something interesting or exciting, it would appear on the blog together with details for our contact(s) at the institution involved. It quickly transpired that the contacts, delighted to be getting such great publicity out of their contribution to the project, were tweeting the blog to all their friends and colleagues, so very quickly a social ecology began to circulate around the project. People were enthused and motivated to help, and established scholars quickly recognized that this was a new way at looking at this period of Irish cultural and theatrical history, one which highlighted the importance of thinking seriously about the architectural, material and spatial aspects of historical and literary/dramatic phenomena. Because of the old Abbey's key symbolic place within narratives of national identity and nationhood, the project was even taken up by the media, with an illustrated feature on the project appearing in the *Irish Times*, a radio interview with Niall and me on RTE's Lyric FM, as well as additional articles in an online arts magazine (Christopher Collins, 'SHIFTS in Sedition', *Vulgo*, February 2011), and even in a tourist industry magazine, *Ireland of the Welcomes* (Summer 2011). In fact, that the latter was part of a two-page spread of illustrated stories deemed of 'national interest', sharing billing with the historic visits to Ireland of President Obama and Queen Elizabeth II, says something about the status of the Abbey within the Irish cultural imagination. Together, these indications of both professional and wider public engagement provide a striking example of how documenting and publishing research and visualization processes can add very significant value, and benefit, to a project, helping it both to gain a lot of momentum in a very short amount of time, and to reach a wide range of stakeholders far beyond those one might have imagined at the start of the project.

But while there is clearly a set of interesting preservation issues around a blog such as this – with its combination of hypertext, still and moving images, drawn from a wide range of sources, and using the proprietary WordPress technology – the more intriguing challenge is capturing and preserving the social ecology of the research process, the complex set of relationships and interactions that circulated around the project. These, too, are highly important parts of this object called 'The Abbey Theatre, 1904 Project'.

To illustrate just how significant this challenge is, let me sketch for you one final 'moment' in the project. On 15 April 2011 we held an open-air, official project launch at the Samuel Beckett Centre, attended by around 200 people, including those who had contributed funding, as well as time, resources and expertise, and members of the wider academic community and of relevant cultural institutions. While guests perused the commemorative postcards and programmes created especially for the event, Professor Steve Wilmer, Head of the School of Drama, Film and Music, and the then Provost of Trinity, Dr John Hegarty, spoke about the project, putting it into the context of Trinity's flagship Creative Arts Technologies and Culture initiative, after which I introduced the project in more detail, with an outdoor data projection playing an animation of the model in the background.

These formal presentations were a prelude to an artistic intervention. Along with my research for the visualization project, I had been co-ordinating the creation of a new theatrical performance, designed – along the same conceptual lines as the *Vanishing Point(s)* art work discussed above – as a creative companion to the historical research process. Directed by Dan Bergin, *S H I F T* was a devised response, in performance, live music, video mixing, sound and light engineering, to the stimulus provided by both the new digital model and the notorious riots that took place within the old Abbey Theatre, in January 1907, in response to the first performances of J. M. Synge's iconoclastic play *The Playboy of the Western World*. Lasting just under an hour, it incorporated vignettes of Abbey architect and diarist, Joseph Holloway, period cinema segments, a new musical score by members of silent cinema band '3epkano', audience participation, and intertextual allusions to Synge's masterpiece. Without going into any detail, you can well imagine that there are as many stories to be told, and captured, about this theatrical facet of the project as there are about the visualization-based research process. We were fortunate that, in addition to my own blogging, documentary maker Colin Murphy had become interested in the project, and for some weeks had been tracking the progress of the project in both its research and performance aspects; we hope in time to find the resources to edit these up into a form suitable for publishing as short videos on the project website.

So this composite launch event/performance, too, and its constituent elements – publicity, scripts, projections, catering, ticketing, performance, video footage and so on – now become part of the social and material ecology of the project. In however small a way, it matters, I think, who was there and what was said. It matters, for example, that Daithi P. Hanly's grandsons, who must have played on those stones in the garden when they were children, were present; it matters, I think, that they were seeing that childhood playground transform itself into elements within a new narrative of the National Theatre. And it matters, perhaps, that people from the Abbey Theatre itself were there, including the Chair of the Abbey's Board, along with representatives of the various libraries and archives who had contributed to the project, and noted scholars and journalists who had previously written and broadcast on the history of the early Abbey. These are energies that we can pour into new initiatives, for example to create a new set of research and digitization initiatives, or a new generation of educational resources, or to attempt to revive Hanly's vision of the physical restoration of the original theatre façade, or further iterations of the *S H I F T* production concept. But they also matter, quite simply, in their own right, as part of the story to be told.

Such things are all highly intangible and ephemeral, but they are also essential, important parts and outcomes of the object called 'The Abbey Theatre, 1904 Project'. So what is the role for preservation in a case such as this? I'd simply like to conclude by suggesting that this is one of the challenges to which we could profitably turn our attention, exploring how we might define and undertake the preservation of 'objects' that involve a combination of digital and non-digital, tangible as well as intangible, artistic as well as scholarly facets. Processes and relationships need to be captured, or evoked, just as much as outputs. In short, should we ask what might be entailed in preserving the priceless, but elusive, social ecologies of our processes of exploration?

Notes

1 www.londoncharter.org.
2 *Vanishing Point(s)* by Michael Takeo Magruder and Hugh Denard, www.takeo.org/nspace/sl005. See also the description in Chapter 4 of this book.
3 http://blog.oldabbeytheatre.net.

References

Flannery, J. W. (1976) *W. B. Yeats and the Idea of a Theatre*, New Haven, Yale University Press.

London Charter (2009) *The London Charter for the Computer-based Visualisation of Cultural Heritage*, V. 2.1, February, www.londoncharter.org.

CHAPTER 14

A tangled web: metadata and problems in game preservation

Jerome McDonough

Graduate School of Library and Information Science,
University of Illinois at Urbana Champaign, USA

Preserving virtual worlds: an introduction

At the beginning of the first decade of the 21st century, the digital preservation community faced a world in which models for preservation were at best inchoate and functioning preservation systems practically non-existent. By the end of the decade, functional, data and economic models (CCSDS, 2002, 2008; Kejser, Nielsen and Thirifays, 2011; Hole et al., 2010) were developed and under active refinement, and open-source software for repository systems intended to preserve digital content, such as DAITSS, DSpace, ePrints, iRods and LOCKSS[1], were well developed and in production use at a variety of institutions. Our knowledge of digital objects and our ability to manage and preserve them has undergone a dramatic advance.

The inevitable price of these early successes, of course, has been the discovery of even more difficult problems. As we apply the models and tools developed to date to support digital preservation efforts, we encounter new and more complex problems in the technical, legal and administrative aspects of digital preservation. This is particularly true with respect to commercial digital media, where the complex technical nature of these objects, combined with their equally complex intellectual property status (and our occasionally challenging intellectual property laws), create an administrative headache for anyone trying to preserve these digital works in the long term. Web archiving, interactive fiction and multimedia and software of all sorts present a number of issues with which the digital preservation community has struggled, but cannot yet be said to have completely solved.

The Preserving Virtual Worlds project, a joint effort of the Rochester Institute of Technology, Stanford University, the University of Illinois and the University of Maryland, has been studying one sub-domain of these problems, the preservation of computer games, for the past four years. With support from both the Library of Congress' NDIIP Program and the Institute of Museum & Library Services, our team has investigated what makes digital games difficult to preserve, how we might approach the preservation of these complex objects using existing tools, and how the significant properties of these objects are defined by their creators and users. As might be expected, a close examination of computer games reveals that they pose a number of unique challenges to the digital preservationist.

One of the keys to confronting those challenges is creating and maintaining appropriate metadata for the objects to be preserved. It is fair, in fact, to say that generating adequate descriptions of the games we wish to preserve is as significant a preservation activity (if not more) than choice and implementation of a preservation strategy for the game. Preservation of computer games is in many ways a knowledge management problem, and without adequate metadata, managing the knowledge necessary to keep a game accessible *and understandable* is an insurmountable task. The remainder of this chapter will discuss in detail the problems our project has encountered in trying to preserve computer games, how properly designed metadata may help alleviate some of those problems, and some of the issues still waiting to be solved in the metadata realm.

Problems in game description

The Preserving Virtual Worlds project has adopted a case set methodology in our study of computer games. We have tried to select games from differing periods of computer history, for different platforms, and of different genres, in order to try to identify as wide a range of potential problems as possible. Games we have studied in our research include:

Spacewar! (1962) – one of the earliest computer games, developed at MIT as a demonstration program for the PDP-1 computer from DEC.

Adventure (1977) – originally developed by William Crowther and Don Woods, *Adventure* was one of the earliest text adventure games and had a significant impact on the culture of early internet users.

Star Raiders (1979) – originally released for the Atari 8-bit computers, *Star Raiders* became one of the more popular games for the Atari 2600 game console.

Mystery House (1980) – developed by Roberta and Ken Williams, this is the first work of interactive fiction to employ computer graphics as a significant part of the game.

Mindwheel (1984) – an interactive fiction work, authored by US Poet Laureate Robert Pinsky.

Doom (1993) – developed by iD Software, *Doom* popularized the first-person shooter game, and spawned an entire culture of third-party gaming development and modification.

Warcraft III: Reign of Chaos (2002) – the popular, real-time strategy game from Blizzard Entertainment provided the foundation for Blizzard's *World of Warcraft* multiple-player online role-playing game.

Second Life (2003) – the virtual environment created by Linden Lab has been one of the most successful of the 'social' (i.e., non-gaming) virtual worlds and presents numerous interesting issues around intellectual property and preservation. Given the large amounts of data involved in archiving all of *Second Life*, our project focused on three particular islands in *Second Life*: The International Spaceflight Museum, Democracy Island and LifeSquared.

Typing of the Dead (2000–present) – based on a Japanese arcade game named *House of the Dead*, this educational game for the Sega and Windows platform attempts to hone students' typing skills by using them to defeat attacking zombies.

Oregon Trail (1970–present) – one of the longest running game series, *Oregon Trail* is a simulation game challenging students to survive travelling the Oregon Trail in the mid-19th century. It has been used extensively in K-12 education in the USA.

The first problem to present itself in our study of computer games was the fact that computer games have very poorly defined boundaries. We tend to think of software as a relatively discrete item, something that has a completely independent existence from our operating system and computer. The underlying technical reality, however, is obviously quite a bit different. Games possess hardware and software dependencies that make separating them from the platform on which they are intended to run difficult or impossible. One of the older games we studied, *Adventure*, was developed by two separate individuals, initially by William Crowther and subsequently by Don Woods.

One of the first actions Mr Woods took to modify Will Crowther's original code was to reimplement a library function that existed on the operating system for the PDP-10 that Will Crowther used for development, but which was not part of the operating system on the Stanford University computers to which Don Woods had access. Modern computer games rely extensively on dynamic software libraries included in operating systems such as MS Windows and OS X. At the end of the day, a functioning computer game requires game software, an operating system and computer hardware operating together. Drawing a clear line and saying 'this is part of the game, and that is not' can be a challenging proposition. Without that distinction, however, we start the task of preservation with either an unfortunate lack of clarity as to what exactly we are preserving, or a commitment to maintaining complete systems, including hardware, which may profoundly hamper long-term preservation.

Related to this problem are the issues of versioning and version control, both at the game level and the component file level. Successful games such as *Doom* will become ongoing franchises with multiple versions of the game released over the years, and each version may be made available on a number of different platforms. Moreover, the individual component files comprising the game may each have multiple versions as the result of ongoing game enhancements or bug fixes. Producing a workable copy of a game is not just a matter of having all the software and data files necessary, it is also a matter of having the right *version* of all of the files. Tracking these version changes, and the relationships that exist between files in a game, and between files in the game and specific files in an operating system (e.g., a particular patch level of a dynamic load library), is essential if we are to maintain access to the game.

Maintaining access to the game itself, while obviously a necessary condition of game preservation, is not in itself sufficient. Our goal as preservationists needs to go beyond maintaining the technical interpretability of a game to ensuring what we might call its social interpretability, the ability of scholars in the future to ascertain the game's significance and meaning to its participants. This requires more than tracking just the game's component parts. I can preserve the client and server software used by *Second Life*, the database which tracks objects' location and ownership in-world, the modelling, texture and script files for objects in the virtual world, while still losing most of the information about what people *did* in those worlds. To ensure that we can continue to understand not just how a game functioned, but how it was used and what it meant, we must preserve information above and beyond the game itself.

Direct documentation of a game's use is one of the most important forms of information we can preserve. Fortunately, the gaming community excels at producing this. Screenshots of *Second Life*, videos of raids in *Warcraft* and websites documenting Guild activity, speed run files that users record of their quickest passes through levels in *Doom* – all of these provide information about game use and gaming culture that will assist scholars in interpreting these games in the future. Fortunately for game preservationists, all of these are readily available on the web today to add to their collections.

There are other forms of contextualizing information that may assist future scholars in interpreting games. Scholarly writings on games are one obvious source. Platform studies on systems such as the Atari 2600 (Montfort and Bogost, 2009) and digital humanities works on games such as Nick Montfort's (2005) and Dennis Jerz's (2007) examinations of *Adventure* provide vital information about games' history and evolution. Another, often overlooked, type of contextual information for games is the physical packaging and documentation that accompanies the game (including the licensing terms covering the game's use). This provides important information on how a game was marketed and promoted, and on occasion proves vital to basic technical accessibility of a game as well. One of our project team was stymied for months while attempting to play an old version of *Where in the World is Carmen Sandiego?*, as the copy we acquired on the secondary market proved to lack the encyclopaedia that shipped with the original, an encyclopaedia that provided keywords necessary to access portions of the game.

The problem of ensuring the social interpretability of games is therefore not typically one of a lack of information, but of an overload. Selecting among the numerous sources of information online and in print can be daunting. It also puts anyone interested in preserving games in the position of having to preserve a variety of digital and non-digital ephemera simultaneously. Critically, it requires that metadata linking all these items exists, so that both scholars *and* preservationists will be aware of the existence of all of the relevant material for a given game. This type of description is more akin to archival description, with its emphasis on collections, than it is to traditional library description.

I have already mentioned licensing information as being important contextual information for the preservation of games. Intellectual property rights and permission provided some of the most difficult issues for our project and in some cases these proved insoluble. Modern games are highly complex, composite artefacts, and any given game may have many rights holders controlling different assets within the game. Microsoft may hold the intellectual property rights to *Halo*, but it does not hold the intellectual property rights for all of the music contained within the game; most of it is used under licence from the musicians who created the music.

Second Life provides an extreme example of complex ownership, as each user retains copyright over any object they create inside *Second Life*. This, combined with the terms of service for *Second Life* (which dictate that you may not copy another user's intellectual property without their explicit permission), means that any attempt to make a preservation copy of an island in *Second Life* must start with obtaining the permission of all of the intellectual property owners for any object in that island. While our project experimented with this approach, it resulted in at best a 10% response rate from copyright holders. The ability to preserve 10% of a game's content is something like being able to preserve 10% of a book; it may be better than nothing, but it is a good deal less than perfect.

Within the USA, current intellectual property law poses additional obstacles to preservation of some games. The Digital Millennium Copyright Act (DMCA) made it illegal to defeat a technological protection measure on digital media, even to make a preservation copy of a work. Digital media have extremely limited lifespans; if a game cannot be legally transferred from its original media, its likelihood of survival is extremely low.

In theory, the DMCA's restrictions are not necessarily an absolute impediment to preservation activity on computer games. If the rights holder for a computer game is willing to grant permission for an archive to make a preservation copy of a work, despite the presence of a technological protection measure, the DMCA restriction is moot. Unfortunately, there is a significant orphan works problem in the world of computer games. While the vast majority of computer games are clearly still under copyright protection, identification of the rights holder can be a monumentally difficult, and occasionally impossible, task (Swalwell, 2009). Without a rights holder with whom to negotiate, libraries, archives and museums are helpless to make preservation copies of protected games or transfer them to new media. The combination of issues involving complex (and occasionally unknown) ownership of intellectual property rights, restrictive licensing terms, and strong protection for technological protection measures can make it difficult or impossible to preserve some digital games.

Other problems our project encountered resulted from trying to apply developing models for digital preservation to gaming materials, in particular the Open Archival Information System (OAIS) Reference Model (CCSDS, 2002). One of the key insights of the OAIS Reference Model was that preserving a piece of digital information requires preserving not only the digital bitstream, but also the ability for a human being to decipher the meaning of the bitstream. To ensure this, the OAIS Reference Model dictates that in addition to the bitstream, an archive should also keep and preserve what it calls representation information, the information necessary to interpret a string of zeros and ones as meaningful data. Representation information includes both structure information, which maps bit sequences into basic data types (e.g., characters, pixels, numbers), and semantic information, which establishes the context for interpreting the basic data (e.g., that a number represents the number of lives a player has at the beginning of a game).

The OAIS Reference Model states that representation information is part of the content information that must be preserved as part of an archival information package for an object of preservation. If I wish to preserve the FORTRAN IV source code file for the game *Adventure*, I should therefore also be preserving a copy of the character set standard used to record the textual information (e.g., in our case, ISO/IEC 10646) as well as the PDP-10 FORTRAN IV Programming Manual documenting the syntax and semantics for that version of the FORTRAN language. Preservation of digital information is therefore just as much a process of preserving standards documents as it is preserving the original object of preservation.

It is a rare standards document, however, which can be interpreted without consulting other standards. A data standard like the PDF specification, for example, incorporates various other standards to control aspects of the format such as compression or colour space. The full set of representation information necessary to decode a particular piece of data can quickly begin to resemble a small technical library. The OAIS Reference Model recognizes this dilemma, and allows an archive to limit the set of representation information it stores to the minimum necessary for the designated community the archive serves to independently understand the data object.

One of the responsibilities of an Open Archival Information System is to assess the knowledge base of its designated community on a regular basis to determine the level and extent of representation information that needs to be preserved along with a data object.

In the context of a scientific data archive (the original target for the OAIS Reference Model), where the members of the designated community (research scientists) can be assumed to be at least somewhat technically literate and have roughly consistent levels of technical knowledge, this is a reasonable approach to ensuring the interpretability of data in the long term. In the context of an academic library preserving computer games, it is extremely problematic. The 'designated community' for the University of Illinois library system is incredibly diverse, containing individuals with vastly disparate levels of knowledge and skill in dealing with digital data. Should the University Library collect the representation information necessary to support its least technical users, in which case the quantity of representation information needed will be immense? And if it does not, how will it ensure access in the future to those users?

One final problem with regards to representation information deserves mention. As mentioned previously, standards documents for file formats and the operation of computer hardware (e.g., instruction sets for computers' processor chips) are a critical part of the representation information needed for software preservation. If you wish to preserve a game like *Adventure* in its original FORTRAN IV source code incarnation, you should preserve a copy of the Digital Equipment Corporation's FORTRAN IV language specification (Digital Equipment Corporation, 1969) to document the source code's semantics.

The good news is that many research libraries already collect these types of standards documents. The bad news is that given current bibliographic practices in the USA, no one is ever likely to discover that fact (or those standards). A search in WorldCat, OCLC's shared cataloguing database, for the title term 'multimedia' and the author 'International Organization for Standardization' results in a set of 37 records covering a variety of ISO standards, including sections of ISO/IEC 11172 (MPEG-1), ISO/IEC 13818 (MPEG-2), ISO/IEC 14496 (MPEG-4) and ISO/IEC 21000 (MPEG-21). However, of the 37 standards documents present in WorldCat, only six records list holdings at libraries in the USA, and of those six, two are for draft versions of standards documents, not the final published version. Are research libraries in the USA utterly bereft of standards documents?

The answer is 'no.' Many research libraries hold standards documents. However, they do not make bibliographic records for those items publicly available. Grainger Engineering Library on the University of Illinois at Urbana-Champaign campus, for example, holds shelf after shelf of technical standards from the International Organization for Standardization, the Society for Motion Picture & Television Engineers and other standards bodies. But a search by a typical end-user of the library catalogue will not reveal any of those standards documents. Standards documents are often quite expensive; they are vital information sources for certain technical fields; and they also are often loose-bound and therefore difficult to tag with security strips. In short, they are perfect candidates for theft. As a result, most research libraries do not go out of their way to advertise their collections of standards documents.

While this is understandable, it presents the preservation community with a serious dilemma. Standards documents are vital to digital preservation, yet libraries try their best to limit widespread knowledge of their holdings of these materials. Unless research libraries develop procedures that allow them to advertise their holdings of standards documents more widely, digital preservation work will be severely impeded.

Preservation of computer games thus presents a large number of problems, and many of these problems have a significant metadata component. To preserve games, we need to be able to:

- clearly define the boundaries of digital objects and express links between them
- precisely identify digital objects, particularly with respect to versions
- link an object with related materials necessary to contextualize that object
- document complex intellectual property rights situations
- identify representation information needed to decode an object, and link to available copies of that information.

While there are a number of metadata standards in place that support some of the above requirements, our project needed to address all of them, and preferably in a manner that built on existing standards already in use in the library and preservation communities.

The wisdom of OWL

As the requirements above make clear, game preservation not only requires a substantial amount of metadata, it requires metadata of a variety of types. Clear identification of content is the goal of descriptive metadata standards such as MARC/XML or Dublin Core. Establishing the boundaries of a digital object and enabling links between materials is the province of structural metadata standards such as METS and OAI-ORE. Recording intellectual property rights information is the domain of administrative metadata standards like the Open Digital Rights Language and the Creative Commons Rights Expression Language.

There are a large number of existing standards for metadata in place within the library, archives and museum communities for different forms of metadata. Our project had no wish to invent new metadata formats when existing formats would do. However, existing standards by themselves did not provide a complete solution to the problem of metadata for game preservation, particularly with respect to the problems of carefully delineating versions of materials and providing clear links to other objects. We needed a data model for preservation description of materials to guide our use of existing standards.

The OAIS Reference Model provides the beginning of the data model in its description of an archival information package (AIP) (CCSDS, 2002, 4-18–4-47). An AIP contains the data object to be preserved along with the representation information to decode that object, and preservation description information that includes documentation of the system of identification used to refer to the content within the object, fixity information used to confirm that a digital object has not undergone unauthorized change, provenance information and context information. This data model addresses several of the key requirements we identified previously, but does not provide support for identification of versions of material necessary for game preservation.

Fortunately, the entity-relationship model developed by the International Federation of Library Associations and Institutions in its *Functional Requirements for Bibliographic Records Final Report* (Madison et al., 1997) provides the support needed. This model employs four entities to depict intellectual and artistic creations: the *Work* (a 'distinct intellectual or artistic creation'), the *Expression* (the realization of a *Work* in some form), the *Manifestation* (the physical embodiment of an *Expression*) and the *Item* (a single exemplar of a particular physical *Manifestation*). A Work may have one or more Expressions; the game *Adventure*, for example might be realized in both a FORTRAN language Expression and a C language Expression. A given Expression may be embodied in more than one physical Manifestation (the same FORTRAN version could be recorded to both an optical disc and to a magnetic disc), and a particular Manifestation may exist in multiple copies (Items). The FRBR (Funcional Requirements for Bibliographic Records) entity–relationship model was developed by the library community to support the fine-grained identification and description of editions of works needed for scholarly research, and thus enables the identification of versions needed by our project.

To meet the requirements for metadata for game preservation, what we needed was a mechanism for merging these two data models and to use the results in conjunction with existing metadata standards to describe the games in our case set. We achieved this by creating an ontology in the World Wide Web Consortium's OWL ontology language, which used the FRBR entity-relationship model entities as classes. Specific relationships between those entities, whether deriving from the FRBR entity–relationship model or the OAIS reference model, were set as properties for those classes. So, in addition to asserting standard relationships within the FRBR model (e.g., an Expression is embodied in a Manifestation), we might also assert OAIS relationships using FRBR entities as classes (e.g., a Manifestation has as representation information an Expression). Figure 14.1 shows a graphic depiction of our OWL ontology and the FRBR and OAIS relationships it establishes between the FRBR classes.

A formal ontology allows us to use existing structural metadata standards like OAI-ORE and METS, but in a way that conforms to our new data model and thus fulfils the requirements we have established for preservation metadata for computer games. Taking the case of the game *Adventure*, we might create separate OAI-ORE resource map files for *Adventure* as a FRBR Work, an Expression, a Manifestation and an Item. Each of these OAI-ORE aggregations would aggregate the OAI-ORE aggregation representing the next level down in the FRBR hierarchy, e.g., the Work aggregation includes the Expression aggregation, which in turn includes the Manifestation aggregation, etc. Each OAI-ORE resource map could include additional metadata appropriate to that level of the FRBR hierarchy. If a new Expression of *Adventure* is to be included in our archival information package, we can simply create a new OAI-ORE resource map for that aggregation (with new subsidiary

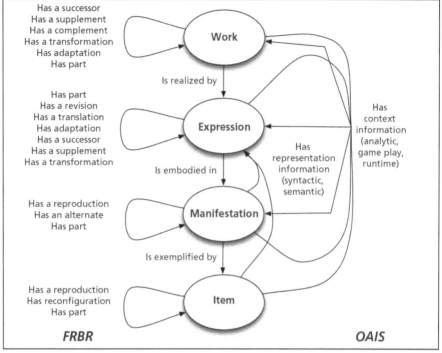

Figure 14.1 Preserving Virtual Worlds ontology

Manifestation and Item resource maps as appropriate), and add that Expression aggregation to the existing Work-level aggregation. Separate OAI-ORE aggregations could be created for digital content being used as representation information and context information, and appropriate links created in the aggregation resource map files using the terms from our ontology.

Graphically, we might depict the case of *Adventure* as we see in Figure 14.2. We have separate OAI-ORE aggregations for each level of FRBR hierarchy for all of the intellectual objects being stored in our repository. Each OAI-ORE aggregation has its own resource map file providing appropriate descriptive metadata about the object for that level, and which can also provide links to other objects as appropriate. Here we see the OAI-ORE vocabulary terms being used to indicate the links between FRBR levels and 'has_representation_information,' a term from the Preserving Virtual Worlds ontology, used to link the Item level aggregation for the game *Adventure* to the Expression level aggregation for the DEC FORTRAN programmer's manual. While the encoding details obviously vary, this same model of the

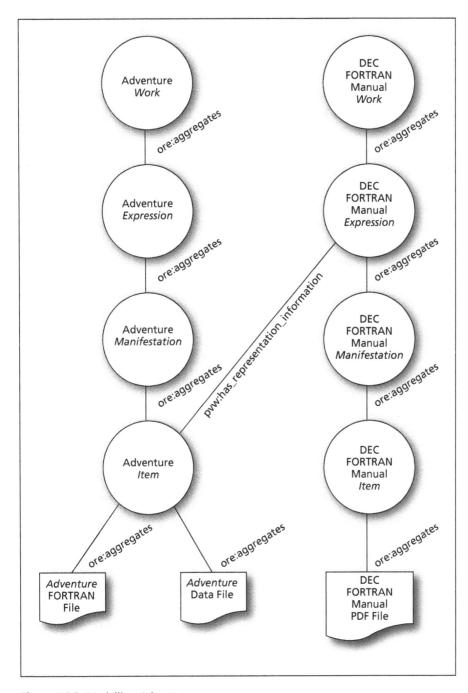

Figure 14.2 Modelling *Adventure*

objects for *Adventure* can be created using the METS metadata standard or any other structural metadata standard capable of following the RDF data model.

A few remaining problems

The combination of an OWL ontology with existing metadata standards provides us with a suitable mechanism for recording metadata for the preservation of computer games. However, based on our experiences in actually packaging games for long-term preservation in the Preserving Virtual Worlds project, this solution raises several new problems that need to be addressed. These problems include that of creating the metadata needed for game preservation, and enabling appropriate access to that metadata.

The metadata creation problem is simple in nature but may prove difficult to solve. Creation of an archival information package conforming to the model we have proposed involves generating significant amounts of metadata for even the simplest case. We created a visualization of the RDF graph from the OAI-ORE resource map files for the early Apple II text adventure game *Mystery House*. It should be noted that *Mystery House* is an extremely simple game by modern standards, and we included the absolute minimum of representation information and context information for this game. The OAI-ORE resource map files were produced manually in the Oxygen XML editor, and their creation took several days' worth of effort after the necessary files had been located and acquired. Creating archival information packages in this manner is simply not a scalable solution, particularly when you consider that a modern game, such as *Warcraft III*, may include thousands of files, all of which require description (including representation information links). If game preservation is to be conducted on a large scale, vastly improved tools for metadata creation are necessary.

Research also needs to be done on how to present these vast webs of information to users within an archival context. The RDF model utilized by our project lends itself to the linked open data paradigm being pursued by many libraries and archives in the higher education realm (Hawtin et al., 2011). But this web of data presents at least some difficulties for users trying to make sense of archival holdings. A user interested in the content of a game archive probably does not want to be presented with the entirety of the web of metadata, but rather an appropriately abridged version. Curators would presumably require a somewhat different view of this metadata. At this point, we do not really understand the issues involved in framing these webs of data for user consumption, but certainly neither the raw XML nor visualizations such as the above are going to be of much use to end-users.

Technologies such as SPARQL (W3C, 2008) provide a mechanism for selecting portions of this web, but how best to use such mechanisms for viewing and managing archival collections of game materials is an issue that will require much more exploration.

Computer games are some of the most complex digital creations in existence, technically, legally and intellectually. They are also arguably the first major new form of media to come along since the creation of television and have achieved a great deal of economic and cultural significance. Preserving these new art works of the digital era is critical, but if they are to survive, the metadata systems used by librarians, archivists and curators will need to undergo significant change.

Acknowledgements

The research described in this chapter was made possible through the support of the Library of Congress' National Digital Information Infrastructure and Preservation Program and the Institute of Museum & Library Services.

Note

1   DAITSS (Dark Archive in the Sunshine State) is a preservation repository for digital documents developed at the Florida Center for Library Automation for the use of libraries in Florida's publicly funded universities (http://daitss.fcla.edu). DSpace and ePrints are both digital institutional repository systems designed for universities to preserve scholarly content, e.g. papers, theses, teaching materials and white papers (www.dspace.org and www.eprints.org). iRods is a rule-based data management system targeted at the preservation of digital materials, and designed to operate as part of a data grid architecture (www.irods.org). LOCKSS (Lots Of Copies Keeps Stuff Safe) was created at Stanford University as a means of preserving web-based electronic journals (http://lockss.stanford.edu).

References

CCSDS (Consultative Committee for Space Data Systems) (2002) *Reference Model for an Open Archival Information Systems (OAIS)*, CCSDS 650.0-B-1 Blue Book, Washington, DC, CCSDS Secretariat.

CCSDS (Consultative Committee for Space Data Systems) (2008) *XML Formatted Data Unit (XFDU) Structure & Construction Rules*, CCSDS 661.0-B-1 Blue Book, Washington, DC, CCSDS Secretariat.

Digital Equipment Corporation (1969) *PDP-10 FORTRAN IV Programming Manual*, Maynard, MA.

Hawtin, R., Hammond, M., Miller, P. and Matthews, B. (2011) *Review of the Evidence for the Value of the 'Linked Data' Approach: final report to Jisc*, CC484D005-1.0, Surrey, UK, Curtis+Cartwright Consulting Ltd.

Hole, B., Wheatley, P., Lin, L., McCann, P. and Aitken, B. (2010) The Life³ Predictive Costing Tool for Digital Collections, *New Review of Information Networking*, **15** (2).

Jerz, D. G. (2007) Somewhere Nearby is Colossal Cave: examining Will Crowther's original 'Adventure' in code and in Kentucky, *Digital Humanities Quarterly*, **1** (2).

Kejser, U. B., Nielsen, A. B. and Thirifays, A. (2011) Cost Model for Digital Preservation: cost of digital migration, *International Journal of Digital Curation*, **6** (1).

Madison, O., Bynum, J., Jouguelet, S., McGarry, D., Williamson, N., Witt, M. . . . and Tillett, B. (1997) *Functional Requirements for Bibliographic Records Final Report*, The Hague, International Federation of Library Associations and Institutions.

Montfort, N. (2005) *Twisty Little Passages: an approach to interactive fiction*, Cambridge, MA, MIT Press.

Montfort, N. and Bogost, I. (2009) *Racing the Beam: the Atari video computer system*, Cambridge, MA, MIT Press.

Swalwell, M. (2009) Towards the Preservation of Local Computer Game Software: challenges, strategies, reflections, *Convergence: The International Journal of Research into New Media Technologies*, **15** (3), 263–79.

W3C (World Wide Web Consortium) (2008) *SPARQL Query Language for RDF, W3C Recommendation*, E. Prud'hommeaux and A. Seaborne (eds), Cambridge, MA.

CHAPTER 15

Metadata for preserving computing environments

Angela Dappert
Digital Preservation Coalition, UK

Introduction

Metadata is information about an object that is needed in order to manage that object. Preservation metadata (Dappert and Enders, 2010) for computing environments is the information that is needed in order to redeploy computing environments successfully in the future. Metadata for digital objects' computing environments constitutes essential representation information that is needed in order to be able to use digital objects and to make them understandable in the future. This is why metadata about computing environments must be preserved together with the digital objects as part of their core metadata. Furthermore, software components themselves may be the primary objects of preservation, and require a metadata description. Computer games can take either of these two roles.

Digital objects and the computing environments in which they function are continuously under threat of becoming unusable through deterioration, obsolescence or inadvertent damage during form or environment shifting. Computing environment preservation can happen, for example, through hardware and software preservation, emulation, reconstruction or porting to new environments. Depending on the nature of the computing environment, the nature of threats, the preservation approach and the community that wants to redeploy the computing environment, different metadata is needed.

The TIMBUS project (TIMBUS project, 2012), a three-year EU co-funded project, addresses the challenge of long-term digital preservation for business processes and services. This entails the preservation of computing environments. It entails definition of metadata needed to access processes and their computing environments in the long run. This chapter introduces the TIMBUS approach, illustrates how it can be applied to the preservation of computing environments and describes other efforts for defining metadata for preserving relevant aspects of computing environments. TIMBUS goes beyond the preservation of computer games and virtual worlds, but it is easy to see how the same approach can be used for them.

The TIMBUS project

The EU co-funded TIMBUS project addresses the challenge of digital preservation of business processes and services to ensure their long-term continued access. TIMBUS analyses and recommends which aspects of a business process should be preserved and how to preserve them. It delivers methodologies and tools to capture and formalize business processes on both technical and organizational levels. This includes the software and hardware infrastructures underlying these business processes and dependencies on third-party services and information. TIMBUS aligns digital preservation with well established methods for enterprise risk management (ERM), feasibility and cost-benefit analysis, and business continuity management (BCM).

TIMBUS explores this challenge with three scenarios: engineering principles for digitally preservable services and systems, civil engineering infrastructures and e-science and high energy physics.

It is executed by a consortium of industry, research and SME partners from across Europe. This involvement of industry is a sign that awareness of the need for preserving digital objects over the long term is spreading from the traditional champions in memory institutions and heavily regulated private sectors, such as pharmaceuticals and aircraft manufacture, to the general private sector.

This growth of awareness about the need for developing sound digital preservation methodologies and tools is accompanied by a growth in complexity of the digital objects that need to be preserved. Figure 15.1 illustrates the relationship between the fields of digital preservation and business continuity. The horizontal dimension expresses the degree of complexity of the digital objects that need to be preserved and the vertical dimension expresses the degree of concern for the longevity of the digital object. The digital preservation community has initially focused on relatively

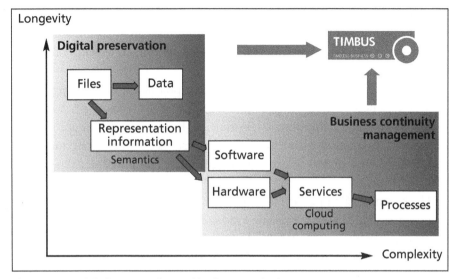

Figure 15.1 Digital preservation and business continuity management

simple objects, such as image files or documents, with a clear long-term access need. This was followed by scientific data held in databases and basic representation information that captures the semantics of files and data so that they can be interpreted in the long term. Obviously, these 'simple' digital objects sometimes are actually quite complex, especially if they contain embedded and linked digital objects or if there is a multitude of rare or customized file formats. Similarly, the representation information quickly becomes very complex, if one seriously thinks about preserving the underlying software and hardware that are needed to access a digital object. The situation becomes even more complex if there are dependencies on third parties, such as in service and licensing models, especially in the Cloud, where data and software may be outside the repository's immediate control, or if there are distributed computing environments. With increasing complexity and in the presence of non-digital preservation objects, such as hardware or processes, the actual object of preservation cannot always be digitally preserved; instead, sufficient descriptions of the object and its significant characteristics need to be captured in metadata to enable future redeployment. For example, hardware and business processes are not preserved directly, but their descriptions are.

BCM, as a discipline (Burtles, 2007), has focused on the lower right quadrant. Complete processes, including services and whole computing environments, need to be kept running. But traditionally BCM has dealt with immediate disaster response rather than with long-term aspects of digital preservation.

The TIMBUS project is shifting the emphasis into the upper right quadrant, where it deals with the long-term preservation of complete processes and their computing environments. It tries to combine approaches of digital preservation with those of enterprise risk management and BCM and investigates digital preservation need and potential in those new application areas.

The commercial imperative for business process preservation comes from several pressures. Heavily regulated industries, such as pharmaceuticals and aircraft manufacture, must fully document processes so that they can be audited, reproduced or diagnosed. This provenance information may be used as evidence in the case of litigation. Long-lived companies must manage services across multiple changes in technical environments; they may need precise process specifications to reproduce functionality on a new platform. If processes are outside an organization's control, such as in service and licensing models, especially in the Cloud, they may use an escrow service in order to mitigate the risk of losing access to the data or services they depend on. They must be confident that all of the necessary information is demonstrably included in the escrow agreement and services. This problem is isomorphic to the digital preservation of software. Organizations undergoing major staff changes must ensure that they retain the knowledge needed to operate or reinstate production processes.

In addition to publications and data, scientists need information about the software and processes that produced them to assess the validity of the data and the derived scientific claims. The same provenance information that can provide a key in regulated industries can also support credit assignment in academia. Process information provides a form of provenance metadata, which documents stewardship and the events that have impacted the resulting process products. This information is generally important to prove the authenticity or quality of process products. All industries benefit from analysis of processes that may lead to their continuous improvement. There is an example illustrating this latter use case later in this chapter.

The TIMBUS approach

TIMBUS breaks business process preservation down into three functions:

1 The **Planning** function performs risk analysis and determines the
   requirements for preserving the relevant business processes. It employs
   reasoning-based enterprise risk management to identify preservation
   risks, to assess their impact, to identify mitigation options and to
   determine the options' cost-benefit. This is integrated with a three-fold
   analysis:
   - *Determine the relevant process context*: what are the parts of the process
     and its environment context that need to be captured so that one is
     able to redeploy the process in order to successfully mitigate the
     risk?
   - *Determine dependencies*: what are the dependencies of these relevant
     process, object, software and hardware components to other
     process, object, software and hardware components in this context?
   - *Determine legal and regulatory restrictions*: what legislative, regulatory or
     licensing considerations impact the ability to preserve now or to
     redeploy later the context components that should be preserved?
2 The **Preservation** function virtualizes the business processes and
   services, together with their computing environments and relevant
   business documentation, and preserves them appropriately. This
   includes third-party and distributed services. It also validates the
   preserved process to ensure that it enables the redeployment of all
   significant functionality of the original process.
3 The **Redeployment** function reactivates and reruns the business
   processes. For testing purposes, this process is integrated with a testbed
   in which future potential scenarios are simulated. In the testing phase
   redeployed processes also are verified against the significant
   characteristics (Dappert and Farquhar, 2009) of the original process.

Example preservation of a business process

This section illustrates the TIMBUS approach by introducing an example
process and applying several of the TIMBUS preservation planning steps.
The process in case is a migration process: an organization holds millions of
images in the rather bulky TIF format. Management decides that it would be

preferable to migrate the files to a more compact file format in order to save on storage cost.

Following ingest of the original TIF files, a quality assurance step ensures that the ingested files are not damaged. The project team has to decide the best migration target file format and optimal configuration parameters, degree of lossiness, etc., based on the characteristics of the files. They chose the best tool suited to this migration task and perform the actual migration. This is followed by an automatic quality assurance step, and, since not all problems can be detected automatically, by a manual quality assurance step on a sample file set. The files are now stored, possibly over the course of decades. This may entail a need for data carrier refresh, copying to new locations and other preservation and administration tasks. The original files are deleted and the new files are made available for access.

The team would like to preserve the process in order to provide provenance information to future users that documents what changes have been performed to the original files. They also want to preserve the process, so that, should one later discover defective files, one could diagnose what part of the process may have caused this problem. This is part of their continuous improvement task. The diagnosis allows them to avoid repeating the same mistake in similar processes.

In order to determine which preservation metadata is needed to successfully redeploy or diagnose the process later, TIMBUS uses the four basic techniques discussed earlier (manage risks, determine the relevant process context, determine dependencies and determine legal and regulatory restrictions).

Manage risks

The enterprise risk management task might identify the following risks: the original received files may be faulty, the quality assurance steps may be insufficient, the new file format may be too lossy, the configuration parameters of the new file format may be chosen poorly, the migration software may be faulty or limited to a subset of files (for example of a limited file size), there may be manual handling errors, the files may be affected by unmitigated bit-rot, there may be file system errors, or the newest rendering software in use may not fully implement the file format standard and render the files in a way that they appear corrupted even though they are actually not at all damaged.

Determine the relevant process context

Each risk is related to a subset of the process metadata that is needed to redeploy or diagnose the affected process steps. The context capture step might, for example, determine that one would have to capture the following metadata in order to mitigate the risk of 'insufficient quality assurance': the sampling methods applied, the actual test sets used, the test methods used, the exception treatment applied when problems were detected, process descriptions, logs and quality criteria applied. Additionally, one might want to know the business requirements that drove the quality assurance step and the policies underlying it. For the risk of 'manual handling errors' one might wish to know the manual process steps, who were the actors, what training they had received and what processing logs were created. This illustrates that context components can be quite varied: process steps, software components, hardware components, virtual machines, networks, configurations, objects, documents, business requirements, etc.

Determine dependencies

In addition to identifying the relevant context components one has to determine which dependencies exist from the identified context components to other context components. The ones relevant for process redeployment need to be identified. For example, software used during the quality assurance step, the migration, or the manual quality assurance may depend on hardware or secondary libraries.

Determine legal and regulatory restrictions

Finally, legal or regulatory restrictions have to be captured for each process step that has been determined to be relevant during risk assessment. It is necessary to determine which preservation actions can be legally performed now and which restrictions may exist in the future on use of the preserved process and its computing environment. In the example shown in Figure 15.2, software licensing issues may affect the preservation of migration software used; data protection issues may affect the information that can be preserved about the actors in the manual handling steps; and copyright issues may affect the preservation of samples of the original data.

Finally, the expected impact of the risks and the cost of preserving the

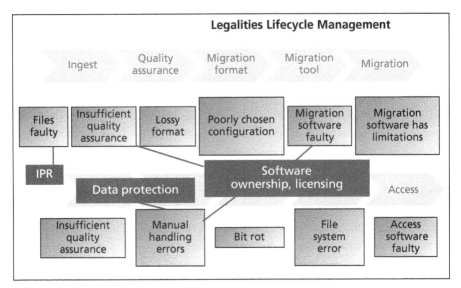

Figure 15.2 Example rights restrictions

context identified in this planning step need to be weighed against each other in order to derive the final preservation plan.

Metadata for preserving processes and computing environments

For each of these process description elements (processes, context, dependencies, regulations), suitable metadata definition has to be identified or created so that their descriptions can be captured in a uniform, repeatable manner. Their instances then need to be packaged, related to each other, and preserved for future redeployment.

Much relevant metadata work has been done in the past and is being done now on subsets of this domain. When determining metadata for computing environments and whole business processes the results of existing work should be re-used as much as possible. Some of it is discussed in the following sections.

Core digital preservation metadata and computing environments

The *PREMIS Data Dictionary* (PREMIS Editorial Committee, 2012), a *de facto* standard, defines core metadata for the digital preservation of any kind of digital object. 'Core metadata' is the metadata that is needed by most preservation repositories, rather than the application or content specific metadata defined for niche uses. Metadata for a digital object's computing environment is needed in order to be able to use the digital object and to make it understandable in the future. Furthermore, software components themselves may be the primary objects of preservation, and require a metadata description. Additionally, a computing environment can take the role of an agent that executes a preservation action.

The PREMIS Editorial Committee commissioned a working group in late 2011 to examine what computing environment metadata needs to be captured in order to describe computing environments in those varying roles and to be able to successfully redeploy digital objects and their environments in the long term. The goal of the group is to rethink the metadata specification for computing environments so that their capture meets the improved understanding of how they should be described in order to ensure their longevity.

In version 2.2 of the *PREMIS Data Dictionary* (PREMIS Editorial Committee, 2012), there are four key entities that need to be described to ensure successful long-term preservation of digital objects: Object, Event, Agent and Rights Statement. The Object entity provides two places to describe subordinate environments. For one, there is the 'environment' semantic unit that permits the description of software, hardware and other dependencies. Rather than being an entity *per se*, an Environment is modelled as a semantic unit container that belongs to an Object and is, therefore, subordinate to the Object entity. The second environment-related semantic unit is the 'creating Application', which also is subordinate to the Object entity. Creating applications are outside the scope of an OAIS repository and have therefore been historically treated separately from other Environment descriptions. In a generic digital preservation framework that is not restricted to OAIS use but supports the end-to-end digital preservation lifecycle, one would describe Environments uniformly, no matter in what context they are used.

Its subordinate position to Object means that Environment can only be captured to describe an Object's computational context. This has the following limitations:

1   Environments are too complex to be handled in an Object repository.
2   Environments are rarely specific to a single Object, resulting in their redundant spread across different Objects. This results in:
    • unnecessary verbosity
    • cumbersome management of Environment descriptions as they evolve.
3   Environments are unable to describe stand-alone environments and unable to be used for modelling an Environment registry that describes Environment components without the need for creating Objects.
4   They are primarily applicable to computing environments and do not include representation information in the broader sense. This restricts the description to a technical level rather than to a level that comprehensively enables redeployment.

The working group's use case analysis identified five desirable relationships. Because Environments are subordinate to Objects, it is impossible to express the last four of them:

1   An Object specifies its Environment, i.e. its computational context. This is the existing relationship in PREMIS 2.
2   An Environment (for example, games source code) is to be preserved as a first-class entity in its own right. It takes on the role of an Object.
3   An Environment takes the role of an Agent (for example, as software Agent involved in a preservation action Event).
4   An Environment is related to another Environment through inclusion, dependency, derivation or other relationships.
5   An Environment has an Event associated with it (for example, a creation or versioning Event).

Another limitation is that in PREMIS 2, Environments are unable to refer to external dedicated registries, which would enable the delegation of 'up-to-date and complete' information to an external source if needed. The identified shortcomings may be the reason that the Environment semantic container in PREMIS is rarely used.

A possible solution is to treat Environments as first-class entities that do not have the limitations listed here. Treating Environments as first-class entities also makes it more natural to model preservation actions that directly impact Environments, such as data carrier refresh or emulation, as easily as preservation actions that directly impact Objects – migration, say. This is particularly important for the preservation of computer games and other kinds of software. While describing those actions is possible with the PREMIS model in version 2, it is not do-able in a very natural way (Dappert et al., 2012).

Version 3 of PREMIS will address these limitations and requirements and introduce an improved platform for modelling computing environments.

Software preservation and technical registries

Specialized metadata has been defined to support the preservation of software. For example, *The Significant Properties of Software: a study* (Matthews et al., 2008) identified Functionality, Software Composition, Provenance and Ownership, User Interaction, Software Environment, Software Architecture and Operating Performance as basic metadata categories for software that could be applied on Package, Version, Variant and Download level. The Preserving Virtual Worlds project (McDonough et al., 2010), POCOS (POCOS, 2012), SWOP (SWOP, 2012) and DOAP (Dumbill, 2012) have also made proposals about preservation metadata needs for software preservation. Examples of software repositories, such as the NSRL (National Software Reference Library, 2012), MobyGames (MobyGames, 2012) and AMINET (AMINET, 2012), illustrate practically used metadata schemas, but do not necessarily support digital preservation functions. Likewise, Jhove (JSTOR and Harvard University Library, 2012), PRONOM (The National Archives, 2012), Unified Digital Format Registry (UDFR, 2012a) and the Library of Congress (Library of Congress, 2012) have defined metadata that is needed to technically or qualitatively describe file formats and have built repositories based on their metadata descriptions. This includes some software metadata specifications, which for PRONOM are now available in a linked data representation and for UDFR contain software description in the UDFR database (UDFR, 2012b).

Metadata that is used to capture complex dependencies is addressed in initiatives such as VRDF (Kadobayashi, 2010), which captures virtualized infrastructures, CDMI (SNIA, 2012) which 'describes the functional interface that applications use to create, retrieve, update and delete data elements from the Cloud' and the Web Service Definition Language (WSDL) (W3C, 2001).

The KEEP project on emulation (KEEP, 2012) designed a prototype schema for the TOTEM database (TOTEM, 2012) and is a recent move towards building a repository for describing the technical properties of computing and gaming environments, including software and hardware components. Similarly, the IIPC (IIPC Preservation Working Group, 2012) has developed a technical database using a computing environment schema as a foundation for web archiving, and TOSEC (short for 'The Old School Emulation Centre') (TOSEC, 2012) 'is dedicated to the cataloguing and preservation of software, firmware and resources for microcomputers, minicomputers and videogame consoles'.

All of these initiatives are relevant for the preservation of gaming environments and virtual worlds. TIMBUS additionally draws on metadata standards that capture business processes, such as BPMN (Object Management Group, 2011), and is defining other forms of supporting business documentation needed to redeploy processes and services.

Conclusion

When complex digital objects such as computer games, virtual worlds or even complete processes and services need to be preserved, redeployed and understood in future environments, a key task is to determine the metadata needed to support this goal.

Research has focused on specific environment metadata types, such as core preservation metadata, technical environment description, dependency descriptions and process descriptions. For complex objects it is necessary to identify the most suitable metadata descriptions available, to identify gaps that are not covered by existing approaches, and to determine the structural information that is needed to tie them together. This task should be driven by a thorough understanding of the components that make up the complex object's context, by the identification of risks and cost-benefits, by an understanding of the functions that are supposed to be supported through this metadata and the expectation of future needs of designated communities. Based on this one can then develop preservation actions if the need is identified.

The challenge of preserving computer games and virtual worlds is connected to the challenge of preserving complete business contexts. TIMBUS is working to define metadata categories, models and methodologies for identifying relevant metadata. The essential foundations in preservation metadata have been laid by PREMIS and are being extended to better support this and other complex use cases.

Acknowledgements

Thanks go to my colleagues on the PREMIS Environment Working Group: Sébastien Peyrard, Janet Delve, Carol Chou, Martin A. Neumann and Michael Nolan. This work has been funded by the TIMBUS project, co-funded by the European Union under the 7th Framework Programme for research and technological development and demonstration activities (FP7/2007-2013) under grant agreement no. 269940. The author is solely responsible for the content of this chapter.

References

AMINET (2012) http://aminet.net [accessed 8 May 2012].

Burtles, J. (2007) *Principles and Practice of Business Continuity: tools and techniques,* Rothstein Associates Inc., ISBN 978-1931332392.

Dappert, A. and Enders, M. (2010) Digital Preservation Metadata Standards, *NISO Information Standards Quarterly,* June, www.loc.gov/standards/premis/FE_Dappert_Enders_MetadataStds_isqv22no2.pdf [accessed 8 May 2012].

Dappert, A. and Farquhar, A. (2009) Significance is in the Eye of the Stakeholder. In Agosti, M. et al. (eds), *European Conference on Digital Libraries (ECDL) September/October 2009,* Lecture Notes in Computer Science 5714, Springer-Verlag, 297–308, www.planets-project.eu/docs/papers/Dappert_Significant_Characteristics_ECDL2009.pdf [accessed 16 April 2014].

Dappert, A., Peyrard, S., Delve, J. and Chou, C. (2012) Describing Digital Object Environments in PREMIS, paper presented at *iPRES 2012: Ninth International Conference on Preservation of Digital Objects.*

Dumbill, E. (2012) *DOAP – Description of a Project,* https://github.com/edumbill/doap [accessed 16 April 2012].

IIPC Preservation Working Group (2012) http://netpreserve.org/working-groups/preservation-working-group [accessed 16 April 2014].

JSTOR and Harvard University Library (2012) *JHOVE – JSTOR/Harvard Object Validation Environment,* http://hul.harvard.edu/jhove [accessed 8 May 2012].

Kadobayashi, Y. (2010) *Toward Measurement and Analysis of Virtualized Infrastructure: scaffolding from an ontological perspective*, www.caida.org/workshops/wide-casfi/ 1004/slides/wide-casfi1004_ykadobayashi.pdf [accessed 8 May 2012].

KEEP (2012) Keeping Emulation Environments Portable, www.keep-project.eu/ezpub2/index.php [accessed 8 May 2012].

Library of Congress (2012) www.digitalpreservation.gov/formats [accessed 8 May 2012].

Matthews, B., McIlwrath, B., Giaretta, D. and Conway, E. (2008) *The Significant Properties of Software: a study*, Science and Technology Facilities Council, http://bit.ly/eF7yNv [accessed 8 May 2012].

McDonough, J., Olendorf, R., Kirschenbaum, M., Kraus, K., Reside, D., Donahue, R., Phelps, A., Egert, C., Lowood, H. and Rojo, S. (2010) *Preserving Virtual Worlds: final report*, https://www.ideals.illinois.edu/bitstream/handle/ 2142/17097/PVW.FinalReport.pdf?sequence=2 [accessed 8 May 2012].

MobyGames (2012) www.mobygames.com [accessed 8 May 2012].

The National Archives (2012) PRONOM, www.nationalarchives.gov.uk/pronom [accessed 8 May 2012].

National Software Reference Library (2012), www.nsrl.nist.gov [accessed 8 May 2012].

Object Management Group (2011) *Business Process Model and Notation (BPMN) Version 2.0*, release date January, www.omg.org/spec/BPMN/2.0/PDF [accessed 1 August 2012].

POCOS (2012) Preservation of Complex Objects Symposia, www.pocos.org [accessed 8 May 2012].

PREMIS Editorial Committee (2012) *PREMIS Data Dictionary for Preservation Metadata, Version 2.2.*, www.loc.gov/standards/premis/v2/premis-2-2.pdf [accessed 8 May 2012].

SNIA (2012) Cloud Data Management Interface (CDMI), www.snia.org/cdmi [accessed 8 May 2012].

SWOP (2012) SWOP: The Software Ontology Project, www.jisc.ac.uk/whatwedo/programmes/inf11/digpres/swop.aspx and http://sourceforge.net/projects/theswo/files [accessed 8 May 2012].

TIMBUS project (2012) http://timbusproject.net [accessed 8 May 2012].

TOSEC (The Old School Emulation Centre) (2012). *What is TOSEC?*, www.tosecdev.org/index.php/the-project [accessed 27 April 2012].

TOTEM (2012) *Welcome to TOTEM – the Trustworthy Online Technical Environment Metadata Database*, http://keep-totem.co.uk [accessed 8 May 2012].

UDFR (2012a) Unified Digital Format Registry, www.udfr.org [accessed 8 May 2012].

UDFR (2012b) UDFR ontology,
   http://udfr.org/onto/onto.rdf [accessed 8 May 2012].
W3C (World Wide Web Consortium) (2001) *Web Services Description Language
   (WSDL) 1.1*, www.w3.org/TR/wsdl [accessed 8 May 2012].

CHAPTER 16

Preserving games environments via TOTEM, KEEP and Bletchley Park

Janet Delve
Future Proof Computing Group, School of Creative Technologies,
University of Portsmouth, UK

Dan Pinchbeck
School of Creative Technologies, University of Portsmouth
and thechineseroom, UK

Winfried Bergmeyer
Computerspielemuseum (Computer Games Museum),
Berlin, Germany

Introduction

Emulation has long been eschewed as a viable digital preservation (DP) strategy for mainstream memory institutions: it is seen as being possible in theory, but not actually practicable in real-life preservation situations. It is not surprising, then, that it took some lateral thinking to make inroads into the problem of bringing emulation to the fore as a viable DP strategy. To achieve this, the KEEP (Keeping Emulation Environments Portable) project included a somewhat eclectic mix of partners: traditional DP institutions such as national libraries, a computer games museum, and an academic partner with a background in computing history as well as games development and preservation. This rather unusual group has facilitated research and development into the use of emulation specifically to preserve, amongst other things, computer games: arguably some of the most complex digital objects for which memory institutions would expect to be responsible for preserving. In this chapter we discuss some of the tools and initiatives emerging from KEEP that support the preservation of computer gaming environments: including the Trustworthy Online Technical Environment Metadata database (TOTEM),[1] and the KEEP Emulation Framework[2] as deployed at the Computer Games Museum (Computerspielemuseum – CSM), Berlin. Whilst these new tools make a significant contribution to the practice of emulation, and therefore DP overall, there are still unfamiliar areas into which the community needs to look. Although software preservation has been accepted as important by the DP community for some while now, as witnessed by the work of the Software Sustainability Institute and the Science and Technology Facilities Council (STFC), hardware preservation has long been deemed to be unnecessary by proponents of both emulation and migration (see Chapter 2 in Delve and Anderson, 2012). This stance has the unfortunate effect that the DP community could then miss out on much sterling work carried out at computer history museums worldwide that could bring them important benefits: indeed, were they to collaborate across these different domains, it could result in valuable sharing of knowledge (database of hardware) and a plethora of computing resources (e.g. emulators) and documentation (e.g. manuals).

KEEP games initiatives

Emulation is well understood and practised by the computer gaming community, which is recognized as being at the forefront of developing emulators; e.g. the MAME (Multiple Arcade Machine Emulator) community,[3] which has developed emulators for computer games arcades. This was a key part of the rationale for including the games community in the KEEP project. The KEEP Co-ordinator, the French National Library, has arguably one of the largest collections of preserved computer games of any national library, as it is mandated (uniquely in Europe, it would seem) to do so due to its national deposit laws, obliging it to preserve computer games as cultural artefacts. Other KEEP partners include the Computer Games Museum, Berlin, the European Games Developers Federation (EGDF) and the University of Portsmouth, with academics researching games development and preservation, the history of computing and digital humanities. The digital preservation SME Tessella, together with the Dutch National Library (Koninklinke Biblioteek – KB), with their background in DP emulation (Dioscuri) were tasked with creating an emulation framework (EF), so that developers, particularly from the gaming community, could be made aware that their emulators could be used in order to render old computer games for both the DP and the gaming communities. The University of Portsmouth created the graphical user interface (GUI) for the EF, as well as the TOTEM database comprising technical environment metadata to support the emulation process on the EF. We will start with a brief review of the KEEP findings on the difficulties of preserving computer games (Pinchbeck et al., 2009; Anderson, Delve and Pinchbeck, 2010).

Games environments metadata: background to the challenge

The International Game Developers Association (IGDA) Special Interest Group on Preservation published a white paper (Lowood, 2009) detailing many of the specific issues facing game preservation. These include: rapid obsolescence of both software and hardware; media decay; access to material; legal constraints; lack of understanding or impetus; breadth of material surrounding any given title; and loss of cataloguing and descriptive information. They can be broadly grouped into three major problem areas: legality, cultural complexity and technical complexity. All of these require representation in any metadata schema aimed at the robust preservation of games.

In terms of technical complexity, migrating the quantity of code required to ensure runtime viability of a modern game is simply impractical (Pinchbeck et al., 2009a). Dondorp and van der Meer (2003) conclude of *Quake* (id Software, 1996) that 'Rebuilding such a game is a gruesome operation that might easily compare to the complexity of emulation of the computing platform. To preserve highly interactive objects such as games, emulation is probably the only solution.' It is worth noting that they are referring to a game nearly 15 years old and thus comparatively simple by contemporary standards. Guttenbrunner et al. (2008) present a case study on console videogame preservation using the Planets preservation planning approach for evaluating both migration and emulation as preservation strategies in a documented decision-making process. Their study included several different emulators and they conclude that emulation is well suited to preserving a variety of console games.

Guttenbrunner (2004) argues that emulation at a hardware level is the ideal solution for console games. The split of emulators into hardware and software is one also made by Tijms (2000) and Conley et al. (2004), who describe a 'window of opportunity' created by the lag in new console developments and PC hardware improvements that may even allow predictions to be made of when emulation technology will emerge for a given platform. Guttenbrunner et al. (2008) consider challenges such as proprietary hardware and the lack of documentation as well as the wide range of media and also non-standard controllers.

The technical issues surrounding games preservation do not stop at code complexity. Subtle aspects such as minor alterations in processing speed can affect qualitative experience. Tijms (2000) notes there is not a direct correlation between the actual processing power of an emulated system and the requirements of the emulating system, due to specificities and peculiarities of the underlying hardware components of the former. Many games include middleware and DirectX components, and an increasing number rely on internet connections for patches, updates and authorizations, some even requiring this to be active during play. Online multiple-player and LAN gaming all present further technical challenges, as in these instances it is not only a client-side emulation that is required, but emulation of the outlying environments with which the game may engage.

Equally problematic are the additional digital objects that develop around a commercial game. Lowood (2004) recognizes this when he states that 'Capturing the history of community-generated content and the mod scene is a huge challenge, and it will require special attention to the variability and modifiability of software, including provisions for carefully documenting version history through metadata.' We need to preserve not just a first or final version of an object, but its evolution through official patches and updates. But as well as these official add-ons, we need to ensure that we are also ingesting unofficial fan-community work as well. To put this into context, we should remember perhaps that *Counter Strike* (Valve Software, 2005), recognized as an important game in the history of online multiple-player shooters, spent its early life as a fan-community mod of the commercial game *Half Life* (Valve Software, 1998). Likewise, Media Molecule's *Little Big Planet* (2008) is less a game than an engine for the construction and sharing of user-generated content. More discussion of associated objects can be found in Pinchbeck et al. (2009a) and Lowood et al. (2009).

Barwick (2009), Lowood et al. (2009), Gieske (2002) and others have begun the process of understanding why games have been ignored by preservationists for so long, but at least the need is now generally recognized. However, the relatively late realization of what Gooding and Terras (2008) call the 'current preservation crisis' facing games means that we are confronted with the task of either retrofitting the specific preservation metadata we can infer from the above, or creating new metadata structures that can be easily assimilated into existing schemas. This introductory discussion makes clear that this specific metadata falls into three major areas not necessarily covered by existing schemas:

1   Technical metadata is required to describe the original runtime environment, middleware, add-ons, and aspects of performance that may affect the experiential qualities of the game, such as sound capabilities, processor speed, data delivery from disc in runtime, video outputs, I/O devices, etc.

2   Additional metadata and a robust network of associated objects (both games and other digital objects, such as video, audio, code, image and text) may be required to capture the cultural experience of a given game.

3   Legal information clearly describing the status of the disc image, runtime rights, and the potential legal status of embedded third-party requirements or associated material may be important, given the highly charged nature of the field.

Game-specific preservation metadata schemas

Previously, only Karsten Huth's Master's thesis (Huth, 2004) attempted to develop a systematic, game-specific schema. Current metadata on games tends towards simple cataloguing information, both in repositories and commercial/community sites such as MobyGames. While the latter are clearly vital in the preservation of games, the information contained is both patchy and mainly descriptive: title, date, platform, sometimes system requirements. This falls a far short of the level of detail, robustness and interoperability required by repositories.

Commercial organizations such as PEGI (Pan European Games Information), which maintain their own archives of games passing through the certificating process, are in a similar state, holding descriptive data to catalogue the titles, but little complex metadata that would allow a runtime environment to be selected or re-created. A recurring issue with descriptive data schemes is classification by type or genre, which has generated a substantial quantity of literature. Dahlskog, Kamstrup, and Aarseth (2009) and Bjork and Holopainen (2005) have both proposed alternative approaches to classification, for example.

Huth's solution is to draw from existing metadata schemas and supplement them with additional, self-generated, fields. The schemas he considers are:

• OCLC Metadata Elements (OCLC, 2003)

- the Dublin Core Metadata Element Set (DCMI, 2003)
- the Manual of Archival Description (Procter and Cook, 2000)
- DIN (German Institution of Standards) 66230
- Projekt Metadaten (DiGA, 2003).

Huth splits his fields into five groups: representation, reference, provenance, fixity and context. Additionally, he restricts his work to very early systems: the Atari 2600 and the Commodore 64 (one console, one computer). This means that his schema may not be particularly suited to dealing with some of the more complex issues noted above, as it predates them considerably. For example, user-generated content in the form of community 'mod' culture (literally, modification of a commercial game that is freely available for users to distribute, usually with the support or at least blessing of the developer) only really began in earnest following the release of *Doom* (id Software, 1993), as did network-based multiple-player gaming. Massively multiple-player online role-playing games (MMORPGs) such as *EverQuest* (Sony, 2000) or *World of Warcraft* (Blizzard, 2005) have their roots in the MUD systems first developed by Richard Bartle in 1991, but only really began to gather momentum in the late 1990s. However, even this falls nearly a decade after the C64's heyday.

In summary, Huth includes emulation and detailed run-functionality technical data. Of specific concern for preservation are: the complexity of the model and the consequent overheads of ingest; and cross-dependencies and object-extensions or alterations (in the form of patches, commercial extension packs, 'cracks', and 'mods' or modifications) which are common in the world of PC games. They can be quite extensive, more or less constituting entirely new games in themselves, but require the user to have the original game release in order to run. They typically include new items, weapons, characters, enemies, models, textures, levels, story lines, music and game modes. Huth's work was instrumental in informing the development of the technical environment metadata necessary for preserving games in the KEEP project.

Games' systems requirements

These days systems requirements can be found on the back of games' back covers, and if these could be garnered routinely by publishers, and shared via a community-wide database or similar resource, this would be a real step forward. Such an approach is currently under ongoing discussion with a major publisher: a sound business case to make this viable for all concerned is needed to move this initiative forward. The systems requirements cover necessary versions of software, operating system and hardware (sound card, graphics card, computer), and often include both minimum and required specifications. This can cause a dilemma for the digital preservationist, who may not know which one to include, and, additionally, abbreviations used are not always obvious (e.g. Windows Me – Millennium edition).

Having identified these various sources of games environment data, the issue is now to incorporate them into a metadata model. The point to note here is that a robust technical environment metadata model needs to capture a fine level of granularity: it should show how a version of a game can run on a particular hardware platform (Commodore 64, Commodore 65 or Commodore 128). Similarly for a PC game – a specific version of the operating system should be given (e.g. Windows 3.1) for a given PC, say x86. This level of granularity is not present in the excellent MobyGames site,[4] which does have generic platform information and images of the systems requirements from the games' back covers.

Technical environment metadata models

Within KEEP, a bottom-up approach was used to develop data models that would capture the technical metadata required to describe the technical environment needed to emulate five different digital objects from the German National Library. A detailed explanation of all steps of the analysis, including the data models created, is given in the TOTEM book (Delve and Anderson, 2012). In particular, there is a final generic data model comprising an enhanced entity relationship diagram on page 74 that also covers PC games (and also those for Apple II). This generic model delineates the relationships between the elements of a typical computing environment stack, with the full attribute listing on pages 76–87. The software libraries attribute can also be used to contain details of mods, cracks, extensions, etc. Similarly, the hardware part of the stack is given on page 75.

However, when it comes to games consoles, it has to be borne in mind that they are fundamentally different in structural design from PCs, as the operating system is not separate from the hardware as is the case with PCs. There are also many extra considerations to take into account in terms of the controller devices that are used with consoles: (joysticks, steering wheels, etc.). Hence a separate data model was created in KEEP just for console games, as shown in Figure 16.1. Here much thought was put into creating a generic model that could cope with any type of controller, which could be analogue, digital (or both, as specified by the 'o' for optional). So, for an analogue controller like a joystick or steering wheel, input would be captured in terms of degrees of movement, planes of movement, number of controls and whether it was pressure sensitive or not. For a digital controller, the number of buttons would be recorded. This approach has been subjected to initial testing by a HATII PhD student and was found to fare well. More user testing is envisaged using whole games collections.

TOTEM

These data models were translated into logical models for use in a relational database. TOTEM, the Trustworthy Online Technical Environment Metadata database, was developed, and to date it is populated, with a reasonable quantity of console game data. The use of the TOTEM acronym is inspired by the fact that totem poles are monuments created by First Nations of the Pacific Northwest to represent and commemorate ancestry, histories, people or events, and would be erected to be visible within a community. The TOTEM registry is used, analogously, to record the complex hardware and software relationships that apply to digital objects, and to make them visible to the digital preservation community. The aim of TOTEM is for a user to enter a version of one of the following – file format, software, software library, operating system or hardware – and then search to find compatible information down the stack. For example, entering the PDF file format version would produce a compatible Adobe Acrobat software version on which to run that particular PDF version, and similarly for an operating system version, a hardware version, etc. For the file formats, TOTEM contains PRONOM unique identifiers to ensure semantic interoperability. Johanna Puhl from the University of Cologne also created a linked data (RDF) version based on the data model (Delve and Anderson, 2012, 119–30).

   The *de facto* library metadata standard PREMIS[5] has recently set up an Environments working group to look at the need for a separate PREMIS Environment entity, and TOTEM was represented on this group, helping to ensure that the TOTEM registry work is adopted as part of this mainstream

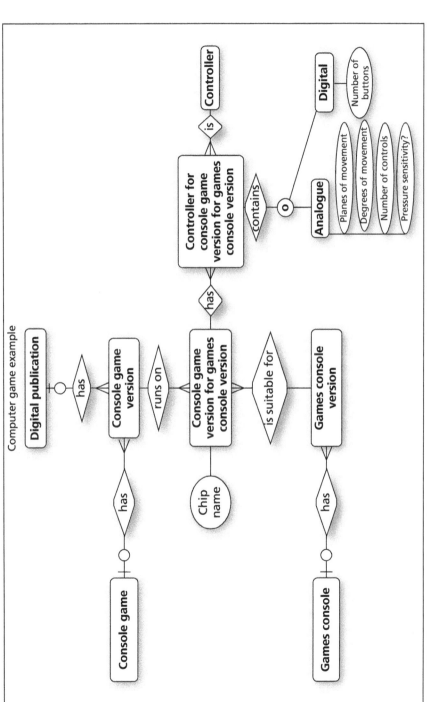

Figure 16.1 Console games data model

registry initiative. The TOTEM metadata schema (Delve and Anderson, 2012, 137–64) also contributes towards this, and contains XML mock-ups to aid those in memory institutions responsible for preserving games.

But TOTEM is not the only tool developed in KEEP to directly advance games preservation: the KEEP Emulation Framework provides a dedicated platform for various users (gamers, librarians, independent researchers, etc.) to render a plethora of different games via multiple emulation environments, the framework carrying out the analysis and selection necessary to determine which environment will suit which game. This framework has been installed at the Computer Games Museum, Berlin, for visitors to use.

The KEEP emulation framework

Using emulation for delivering various virtual environments in institutions today comes with a high amount of configuration and administration before anything is available for the user. To provide a variety of user-friendly emulators for different digital objects, the relevant metadata has to be stored in the digital archive and the different emulators have to be implemented and maintained. A process of automatization for the recognition and the verification of the data and the allocation of the appropriate emulation environment will inevitably facilitate the process of issuing them to the end-user while eliminating a number of intermediate administrative procedures.

The KEEP emulation framework has the resources to perform exactly this very process of automatization. Via a defined interface, a request for information will be addressed to the digital archive and will activate the EF. The data file (a single file or the image of a data carrier) is identified via file format registries and the appropriate emulation paths will be offered to the user. Selecting a specific pathway will start the emulator and the software package necessary for performing this task.

The EF software consists of three parts: a core application, a software archive and an emulator archive. The core EF is the technical heart of the system, performing the automatic characterization of file formats, selecting the required software and automatically configuring the emulation environment. It is delivered with a simple GUI to interact directly with the user. For selecting the software and emulator, the Core interacts with external services such as technical registries, e.g. TOTEM or PRONOM, containing file format classifications, etc., the software archive, which contains software captured in predefined disk images, and the emulator archive, which contains the emulators available for the EF.

The emulation framework software

The KEEP emulation framework is available on the SourceForge portal as a free download. The program and the GUI are written in Java, because it is executable on various computer systems; for the internal database H2 was chosen because of the small footprint and integrated web interface. An installation program simplifies the installation process. The full system requirements are shown in Table 16.1.

Table 16.1 System requirements of the EF software	
Processor	X86 32/64 bit 1.5 GHz or faster
Memory	At least 2 Gb of memory
Disk space	200 Mb of free available space for the base install Depending on the number of emulators and software images, from 1 Gb upwards
Operating system	Linux or Windows with compatible JRE and network support
Java Runtime Environment (JRE)	Oracle (Sun JRE version 1.6 or higher/compatible)

The download package contains the following emulators:

- Qemu (x86)
- Dioscuri (x86)
- WinUAE/Amiga)
- VICE (C64)
- JavaCPC (Amstrad/Schneider)
- BeebEm (BBC Micro).

It must be emphasized that this package may only contain open-source software. Thus it will not be possible to find an operating system such as MS Windows or an application such as WordPerfect to come along with the bundle. It is beyond the scope of the KEEP project to manage the software licences.

The emulation framework user interface

First we will take a look at the functionalities for the end-user. The EF starts with a graphical user interface. With the actual Java-based GUI, the user can select a digital object in the left column. A d64-image of a game designed for the Commodore 64 (*Ms Pacman*) is then selected (see Figure 16.2). Having selected the object by clicking on the icon, the lower region of the screen presents three different buttons (auto start, characterize and info). If you click on the button for auto start, a window will pop up presenting the VICE-emulator and the game. So the user is able to start the emulation from the digital archive only by clicking on a button. But in addition to this automatic procedure the user can select between several emulation pathways (if they are defined by the administrator). To illustrate this approach we will select a JPEG file. If the button 'Characterize' is activated, information in the right upper corner states that JHove has successfully identified the data format to be JPEG.

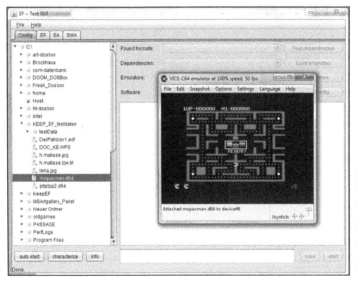

Figure 16.2
Commodore 64 Emulator VICE (Versatile Commodore Emulator) with *Ms Pacman* running

The next step, Figure 16.3, shows the current dependencies, i.e. which emulation paths have been allocated to this data format by the administrator. In this case the following two are available:

- the program Blocek under FreeDos on a x86 system
- the program XzgV under Damned small Linux on a x86 system.

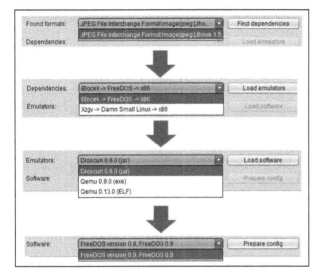

Figure 16.3
Choosing an emulation pathway

Now the user can select one of the paths and henceforth the emulators available; in this case the choice is between Dioscuri and Qemu. The next step consists in opting for the appropriate software package. FreeDos is being offered in connection with the Blocek-application. Finally the configuration is being prepared. This entails mounting the file as a disk (drive A). The system mounts every object with less than 1.2 MB as a disk, any file larger than that will be tied in automatically as a hard disk. Once on the level of the emulation environment, this integration is necessary in order to have access to the object. On clicking on the 'Start' button the process of emulation will commence. In contrast to the computer game example, it is necessary to start the program Blocek in the DOS emulation window and the file has to be selected manually. As a result the file will be rendered.

The emulation framework administration

The concept of the EF is based on employing three different archives that may operate on different servers. The EF-Core-Archive needs to be installed on the actual computer required to present the emulation. But the archives for both the emulators themselves and the appropriate software have only to be connected with it via LAN or WLAN. This facilitates a central administration of emulators and software for a number of computers or even for an institutional network. In addition to the two format registries contained in the download package, it will be possible to create customized registries as well as emulators or software packages and to integrate them in the EF. Thus, individual solutions can be created to fit the requirements of a particular organization.

To conclude, the EF will simplify the appropriation of emulators for the use of original digital objects substantially. By simply identifying the file format a range of appropriate emulation paths can be provided. Furthermore, the considerable range of configurations means that customized solutions for emulators, software and individual format registries can be integrated into a framework allowing a high level of automatization.

Software preservation and computer history museums

So far the challenges and complexities involved in preserving videogames have been reviewed, and it has been demonstrated how TOTEM and the KEEP EF have made inroads into addressing these serious issues in a way that is accessible to mainstream memory institutions. In facing up to such a vast challenge, the DP field is becoming aware of other domains from which it can draw support. More recently, DP professionals have recognized the necessity of preserving software, as witnessed by the dedicated Jisc 'Software Preservation' meeting on 7 February 2011.[6] On the basis of these talks, Neil Chue Hong of the Software Sustainability Institute and Brian Matthews of the Science and Technology Facilities Council were invited to participate in the POCOS events, and their excellent and comprehensive papers, drawn from the Jisc event, appear in this book as Chapters 9 and 10 respectively. The discussion of the KEEP EF above also highlights the need for software archiving.

But we need to go beyond software archiving and accept that we also need to know as much as possible about the hardware platforms used for running computer games. In this we are fortunate, because, as with the gaming community, it is mainly volunteers and amateurs who have kept old computers together in museums with all the attendant material: peripherals, documentation and also software. From these communities some formal bodies have sprung, and there are now a number of associations with which collaboration is possible on a number of fronts: providing data to inform, say, TOTEM or the KEEP EF and also direct knowledge transfer between computer history museums and memory institutions on e.g. media transfer.

Computer history societies have also created emulators for many past machines, large and small, which can benefit emulation research and practice.

For example, the UK's National Museum of Computing, at Bletchley Park,[7] contains old machines in working order, such as BBC Micros running old computer games.[8] This museum does not receive any government support. The Computer Conservation Society,[9] on the other hand, is part of the British Computer Society and has Royal Charter status. And from the other side of the pond, the Computer History Museum[10] in Silicon Valley, California, holds a vast amount of material and expertise. And last but not least, the IT History Society,[11] a worldwide association for those interested in computing history, has a database of hardware, and is developing two more databases, of software and of IT companies. These are of huge value to the DP community and can also be used to inform TOTEM. Some of this discussion has been written up by Anderson (2012) for the computer science and computer history communities, and more is forthcoming in that vein.

Conclusions

There are now a number of mature initiatives to move forward the work on preserving games environments and related metadata. These need to be harmonized and to achieve this all interested parties must continue to build bridges across the disparate communities, share resources and expertise, and together work with bodies such as PEGI (Pan European Game Information)[12] so that systems requirement data can be transferred directly into a suitable technical registry such as TOTEM at the point of publication or age and content rating and thus provide workable pipelines for harvesting the metadata we currently need.

Notes

1 www.keep-totem.co.uk.
2 http://emuframework.sourceforge.net.
3 http://mamedev.org.
4 www.mobygames.com.
5 www.loc.gov/standards/premis.
6 http://softwarepreservation.jiscinvolve.org/wp/2011/02/18/7-feb-outputs-key-points-from-the-participants.

7   www.tnmoc.org/about-us.
8   www.tnmoc.org/explore/pc-gallery.
9   www.computerconservationsociety.org/about.htm.
10   www.computerhistory.org.
11   www.ithistory.org.
12   www.pegi.info/en/index.

References

Anderson, D. (2012) The Future of the Past: reflections on the changing face of the history of computing, *Communications of the ACM (CACM)*, **55** (5), 33–4.

Anderson, D., Delve, J. and Pinchbeck, D. (2010) Towards a Workable, Emulation-based Preservation Strategy: rationale and technical metadata, *New Review of Information Networking*, **15** (2), 22.

Barwick, J. (2009). Where Have All the Games Gone? Explorations on the cultural significance of digital games and preservation. In *Proceedings of DiGRA2009: Breaking New Ground: innovation in games, play, practice and theory*, London, Brunel University.

Bjork, S. and Holopainen, J. (2005) *Patterns in Game Design*, Hingham, MA, Charles River Media Inc.

Conley, J., Andros, E., Chinai, P., Lipkowitz, E. and Perez, A. (2004) Use of a Gameover: emulation and the video game industry, a white paper, *Northwestern Journal of Technology and Intellectual Property*, **2** (1), 1.30, www.law.northwestern.edu/journals/njtip/v2/n2/3/conley.pdf [accessed 21 August 2007].

Dahlskog, S., Kamstrup, A. and Aarseth, E. (2009) Mapping the Game Landscape: locating genres using functional classification. In *Proceedings of DiGRA2009: Breaking New Ground: innovation in games, play, practice and theory*, London, Brunel University.

DCMI (2003) *Dublin Core Metadata Element Set, Version 1.1: reference description*, http://dublincore.org/documents/2003/06/02/dces.

Delve, J. and Anderson, D. (eds) (2012) *The Trusted Online Technical Environment Metadata Database – TOTEM*, Hamburg, Verlag Dr Kovac.

DiGA, e. V. (2003) *Projekt Metadaten: Ein Blick auf verschiedene Softwarearchive und deren Datenstrukturen.*

Dondorp, F. and van der Meer, K. (2003) Design Criteria for Preservation Repositories. In De Bra, P. (ed.), *Proceedings of Conferentie Informatiewetenschap*

2003, Technische Universiteit Eindhoven.

Gieske, J. (2002) *Avoid Missing Ball for High Score*, University of Salford.

Gooding, P. and Terras, M. (2008) 'Grand Theft Archive': a quantitative analysis of the state of computer game preservation, *International Journal of Digital Curation*, **3** (2), 19–41.

Guttenbrunner, M. (2004) Preserving Interactive Content: strategies, significant properties and automatic testing. In Babi, F., Parali, J. and Rauber, A. (eds), *Proceedings of Workshop on Data Analysis WDA'2008*, Dedinky, Slovakia.

Guttenbrunner, M., Becker, C., Rauber, A. and Kehrberg, C. (2008) *Evaluating Strategies for the Preservation of Console Videogames*, paper presented at the Fifth International Conference on Preservation of Digital Objects (iPRES 2008), London.

Huth, K. (2004) *Probleme und Lösungsansätze zur Archivierung von Computerprogrammen – am Beispiel der Software des ATARI VCS 2600 und des C64*, Humboldt-Universität Zu Berlin.

Lowood, H. (2004) *Playing History with Games: steps towards historical archives of computer gaming*, paper presented at the Annual Meeting of the American Institute for Conservation of Historic and Artistic Works, http://aic.stanford.edu/sg/emg/library/pdf/lowood/Lowood-EMG2004.pdf.

Lowood, H. (ed.) (2009) Before It's Too Late: a Digital Game Preservation White Paper, *American Journal of Play*, **2** (2), 139–66, www.journalofplay.org/sites/www.journalofplay.org/files/pdf-articles/2-2-special-feature-digital-game-preservation-white-paper.pdf.

Lowood, H., Armstrong, A., Monnens, D., Vowell, Z., Ruggill, J., McAllister, K. et al. (2009) Before It's Too Late: preserving games across the industry/academia divide. In *Proceedings of DiGRA2009: Breaking New Ground: innovation in games, play, practice and theory*, London, Brunel University.

OCLC (2003) *Digital Archive Metadata Elements* (policy document), Dublin, OH, Online Computer Library Center.

Pinchbeck, D., Anderson, D., Delve, J., Ciuffreda, A., Alemu, G. and Lange, A. (2009) Emulation as a Strategy for the Preservation of Games: the KEEP project. In *Proceedings of DiGRA2009: Breaking New Ground: innovation in games, play, practice and theory*, London, Brunel University.

Procter, M. and Cook, M. (2000) *Manual of Archival Description*, British Library R&D Report No. 5965, Gower Publishing Ltd.

Tijms, A. (2000) *Binary Translation: classification of emulators*, Leiden Institute for Advanced Computer Science.

CHAPTER 17

Documenting the context of software art works through social theory: towards a vocabulary for context classification

Leo Konstantelos

Digital Scholarship, University Library (Research),
The University of Melbourne

Introduction

Whereas digital preservation – as a field of knowledge and as a practice – mandates the long-term appraisal, definition and management of the content and context of digital information, it has been repeatedly signalled that context can be elusive and difficult to pin down in meaning (Giaretta, 2011). In the world of software art, this danger is magnified by the temporal, ephemeral nature of art works whose intrinsic value derives from the *sociotechnical framework* in which they are created, rendered and experienced. Lovejoy, Paul and Bulajic (2011) argue that – although context has been 'traditionally understood as subordinate and supplemental' – the use of digital media in artistic output blurs the boundaries between content and context, so much so that interpretation and documentation depends on 'the thematic lens under which [an art work] is examined'. What are the ramifications of this interconnectedness for preserving digital art? Is our long-term ability to preserve the meaning, value and impact of digital art works impaired by the elusiveness of context documentation and interpretation?

In an effort to investigate platforms for explicitly documenting contextual dimensions of digital art works, this paper presents an approach towards defining a vocabulary for context classification that builds on the theory of social informatics. Software art is perceived here as a sub-genre of digital art, which in turn pertains to the broader domain of new media art. Hence, the analysis transcends the confines of software art and approaches the definition of a context classification vocabulary from the 'new media art' perspective.

The result is by no means definitive, but rather a vehicle for deliberation and placement of software art in a historical context.

The context of software art as a sociotechnical system

What is *context?* One definition would be the discourse, facts, circumstances, environment, background or settings that surround a phenomenon and help to determine, specify or clarify its interpretation. From an empirical analysis perspective, this reflection on context is rather too vague to allow us to deploy any classification scheme for contextual characterization of new media art. If the computability – as in *digital,*[1] *computer-based* – and interactivity characteristics of software art are considered as dimensions in the context equation, a parallel can be drawn to sociotechnical theories that define a context for computer-based technologies. Viewing software art as a sociotechnical system – where the development of art work binds people, processes and technology in a joint and collaborative effort – could lead to a (re-)appraisal of our understanding of context. Kling (1987) situates the baseline for understanding the *social* aspect of context in three elements:

1   *Social relations between actors* that influence the adoption, development or use of the technologies
2   Supporting *infrastructure*
3   *Historical evidence* of actions taken to develop, operate and showcase related technologies.

The possibility for mapping these elements to a context classification scheme for software art is evidenced in relevant literature from the broader domain of new media art.

The Inside Installations project, an effort focusing on conservation of installation art, has identified the contribution of social interaction between actors (artists, preservation experts, curators and end-users) within the broader interdisciplinary framework of new media art preservation, in the 'observation/participation/communication' triptych (Scholte and Hoen, 2007). New media art – in its interactive, time-based sense – requires the creation of platforms of exchange that are manifest through technological devices and aim to stimulate a two-way interplay between an individual (or indeed a group of individuals) and a given art work (Popper, 1997). This interaction is expressed by Weight (2006) as a *trilogical* relationship formed when technology is used to mediate creative communication, its constituents being the human programmer/artist, the executing apparatus, and the human interpreter.

However, Weight's concept marginally touches on the blurring distinction between user roles, which often resembles Allan Kaprow's notion of a 'happening' (Kaprow, 2003), where the artistic motivation lies in 'increasing the "responsibility" of the observer and finally eliminating the audience altogether as each individual present [becomes] part of the event organised by an artist' (Cornwall, 1993). From the preservation standpoint, contextual classification needs to move beyond the art work developer/end-user level, by allowing for the representation of relations of such roles as new media art curators, conservators, commissioners and collectors (Morris, 2001). However, actors and their relations should be studied within the setting(s) where people and the new media art apparatus meet. These apparatuses encapsulate not only any programmed or programmable machine, either networked or standalone (Weight, 2006) employed by the art work, but also the plethora of additional parts (frames, stands, etc.) used to deliver the intended (or at times unintended) experience of the work. The entirety of these parts constitutes the 'supporting infrastructure' element in Kling's definition of 'context'.

But if new media artefacts are in themselves complex agglomerations of virtual and physical characteristics, which are further dependent on environmental – spatial and temporal – factors, what *state* of infrastructural context should a classification scheme reflect? If we accept the parallelism of redefining new media as tendencies in modern art and computing, technologies are not only the enabling factor to materialize the artistic imagination; they are a medium that extends the original idea of a project and as a result have become art works in their own right (Manovich, 2003). In this sense, the intrinsic characteristics of computer-based technologies – evident in their application within or outside an art template – form the core for providing contextual characterization. On the other hand, the variety of artistic approaches and the boundaries between what is *art* and what is *technology* blur too much to make terms like 'dynamic', 'interactive', 'collaborative', 'networked' or 'customizable' define precise characterization of context. What is missing here is the logic behind the sequence of events orchestrating a new media artefact, which directs what is communicated to the audience, when and why.

As Paul (2007) explains, '[w]hile every art project is embedded in its own specific context, the shift towards a dependency on context increases with new media works that require information about which data (in the broadest sense) is being shown, where it is coming from, and according to which logic it is configured.' Paul pinpoints two additional issues that must be included in the identification of infrastructural context. The first is an account of the different manifestations that new media art works can have and speaks to the medium's variability and modularity. Indeed, the same work can potentially be instantiated as part of an online exhibition, as an installation or a projection within a physical space, or form part of digital archival material. The second issue is the definition of the physical environment as dictated by the specification of art work requirements in terms of physical and virtual space. In this sense, *context* should describe how the connection – if any – is established between the physical and the virtual. The introduction of manifestations and physical environment in the classification scheme can be based on the experience and assumptions of the preservation and documentation professionals about the ways in which a work could be presented; or can draw on historical evidence collected from existing experience with presentation, instantiation and documentation of a set of related works.

In Kling's definition of social context for computer-based technologies, this historical evidence describes three distinct entities: development, operation and showcase of technologies. A number of existing publications offer a historical roadmap to the emergence and evolution of new media art (Berwick, 2001; Castle, 2000; Montfort and Wardrip-Fruin, 2003; Rush, 2005). Other scholars have focused on historical facts about presentation and curation of new media art in the museum and gallery context (Candy and Edmonds, 2002; Greene, 2004; Morris, 2001; Paul, 2003, 2007; Rugg and Sedgwick, 2007). Candy and Edmonds (2002) and Greene (2004) provide a comprehensive overview of the history of the field, which shows that the use of digital technology for artistic creation is not a new phenomenon and in fact dates back to the 1960s.

What we understand today as new media art is the combination of traditional cultural conventions – which stem from human experience and visual reality – with new conventions of data representation, which are numerical, computational data (Manovich, 2003).

From this perspective, the points of convergence between historical cultural forces and digital data use through human–computer interaction (HCI) can inform the definition of contextual elements for new media art works. Consider, for instance, Mark Napier's *Feed*,[2] a net art piece that appropriates raw material on the web, not with the goal of providing information, but instead '[consuming] information, reducing structure, meaning and content to a stream of text and pixels'.[3] This type of work challenges, indeed redefines, cultural conventions and implicit assumptions regarding conventional perception of technologies whose everyday use has become ubiquitous in our (developed-world) society. The aesthetics of new media art, which assume the existence of historically particular characteristics of artistic and cultural production (Manovich, 2003), point toward a shift of focus from the digital and technical to the visual and stylistic aspects of digital art works. In order to promote how human–computer interaction can be understood as an aesthetic discipline, Bertelsen and Pold (2004) have introduced the *Interface Criticism Guide*. The guide draws on media and digital aesthetics theory to discern operational perspectives that can be used for the study of visual aesthetics of new media art, so as to address the definition of a vocabulary for *cultural context* that takes into account 'the dynamics of interaction in new and relevant ways' (Bertelsen and Pold, 2004).

A vocabulary for context classification

How can the different expressions of context reviewed above be situated within an operational definition of a vocabulary for contextual classification? Kling (1987) suggests the use of *situations* as a methodology to encapsulate different contextual facets in a scheme that is dependent on:

- the number of participants (individuals or larger collectivities) that engage with a computer-based technology
- the set of artefacts involved
- the spatial scale and arrangements of activity
- the time periods of activity
- the primary social processes that shape critical behaviour.

Using a *situation* as the primary unit of analysis is suitable for defining a context classification vocabulary, particularly because it allows for scalability within and among these five dimensions. Mapping again to new media art, specific situations can be located along, for instance, the first two dimensions, based on the number of users who can view or interact with a piece simultaneously. Other situations may be located by the amount of space their equipment occupies and/or the amount of space the participants take up when engaging with the artefact. Time periods of activity can describe the amount of time over which key events of the art work take place, the total possible duration of interaction between user and art work, or other temporal components – such as scheduled tasks programmed in a software art work. Social processes can describe critical relationships between 'participants' – and by this we refer to all kinds of stimuli for co-operation or conflict between actors involved in the creation, presentation and preservation of a work; social processes also include beliefs, critiques, resources, common practices, procedural elements and constraints associated with new media art works. In addition to this scalability advantage, situations are open-ended in the sense that the above-mentioned dimensions and their characteristics are extensible and flexible enough to permit augmentations and tailoring to particular needs. Table 17.1 summarizes these situational dimensions and some of their characteristics, which can be used as a starting point for building a vocabulary for context classification for new media art (and, by extension, software art) works.

Population scale

Starting with population scale, the most basic contextual element involves the transient encounter between an individual and an art work. For instance, Antonio Mutandas' *This Is Not an Advertisement* (1985) was an animated sequence of words created for the Spectacolor Electronic Billboard in Times Square, New York; as it momentarily subverted the public space – its position manifest in the urban context (Alonso, 1998) – the interaction of vehicles and passers-by with the work was equally brief. A larger scale of the population dimension is that of an individual assuming a role within the greater new media art environment; an artist, a museum curator, a preservation officer, a collector, an art historian or an art work observer are all roles that affect to varying extents the meaning of context. Although not new media art-specific by nature, the type of participation of these roles in a *situation* is influenced by the more new media art-specific characteristics of other dimensions. Moving from the individual to the more collective entities,

Table 17.1 Situational dimensions related to new media art (adapted from Kling, 1987)

Dimension	Characteristics		
Population scale	Encounter Role Institutional subunit Institution Community Social world		
Equipment (infrastructural context)	Simple Obsolete Disconnected Single owner Open-source Manifestations: Monolithic Invariant	↔ ↔ ↔ ↔ ↔ ↔ ↔	Complex State-of-the-art Closely-coupled Multiple owners Proprietary Modular Variable
Spatial context	Local Compact (distributed) Environment: Physical	↔ ↔ ↔	Global Geographically dispersed Virtual
Temporal context	Timescale: Picoseconds Scheduled Perishable	 ↔ ↔ ↔	 Centuries Random Time persistent
Aesthetical context (cultural/historical context)	Stylistic references Materiality Remediation Genre Hybridity Representations		
Social processes (behavioural context)	Critical relationships: Co-operation Direct Beliefs and critiques: Isolated Common practices: Standardized Procedures: Community-adopted Constraints: Political Legal Physical Cultural Financial	 ↔ ↔ ↔ ↔ ↔	 Conflicts Mediated Widespread Ad hoc Institution-specific

the population scale ranges from an institutional subunit or an entire institution, to a community.

At the highest end of this dimension is the social world, which describes the entire set of entities that constitute the social environment where new media art is created, disseminated, presented and preserved. Population scales influence the remaining contextual elements of a work, particularly in terms of social processes that bind together a behaviour setting that surrounds new media art objects and the relationships of the group(s) that populate this setting. Social processes derive from and shape participants' actions in relation to infrastructural, temporal, spatial and cultural characteristics (Kling, 1987).

Infrastructural context

The equipment and infrastructure necessary to create, present and interact with new media art work are key elements in defining situations. Infrastructural characteristics for a given art work refer to the associated resources that are needed to realize or perform a work and achieve the original artistic intentions. Although these characteristics can potentially be static, they are unlikely to remain unchanged for a long time because new media art is still evolving (Manovich, 2003). To represent this in the vocabulary, pairs of related characteristics are presented in Table 17.1 as two ends of a continuum on which specific situations can be placed; as a work evolves, its position on each continuum can change respectively. Hence, the supporting infrastructure for an artefact can range from:

- **Simple to Complex**. The positioning of a work on this continuum depends on such requirements as staff, supporting documentation, equipment contracts, programming skills or working hardware/software. For instance, a multi-part installation that requires assembly of physical parts and configuration of computer-based parts calls for skilled staff and equipment to install the piece, accurate and complete construction documentation and the provision of related software and hardware to render the coded components. The complexity of infrastructure can also be an indicator of the population layers that are involved in the management processes related to an art work. Generally, a work is considered more complicated when the requirements for its support cut across many institutional sub-units or many institutions (Kling, 1987).
- **Obsolete to State-of-the-art**. This continuum represents the potential of digital art works with obsolete components to be migrated to or

emulated on contemporary media, and its converse – i.e. the efficiency and suitability of modern infrastructure for supporting the requirements of obsolete equipment through migration or emulation or other digital preservation techniques. An example of defining this situational characteristic is the exhibition *Seeing Double* (2004) which featured 'a series of original art installations paired with their emulated versions'.[4]

- **Disconnected to Closely-coupled**. This pair of characteristics refers mainly to the relationship of a new media art work with networked environments. At this level, the requirements for equipment – and interrelated entities that ensure the proper handling and operation of the equipment, as described earlier – can vary significantly. In their effort to push the boundaries of technologies, artists can employ systems and computer infrastructure of high sophistication. This continuum is wide enough to encompass all types of technical dependence on networks: from disconnected, stand-alone artefacts to 'art works-as-information-systems', characterized by large numbers of processing elements interconnected by some scalable high performance network (Schlichtiger, 1991).

- **Single to Multiple owners**. The issue of ownership is addressed here from a supporting infrastructure perspective, rather than from an intellectual property perspective for the art work itself. Single ownership is perceived as a case where all the associated resources needed to experience a work ensue from a single role, institution or community. An art installation commissioned, managed and curated exclusively by one museum is such a case. On the other hand, multiple ownership of resources refers to cases where the infrastructural prerequisites to realize a work come from different sources. For instance, the supporting infrastructure for net art works stems from multiple owners: one might be the provider of storage space on a server for the web pages; another is the internet service provider (ISP) company that offers access to the internet so that people can view the work; a third might be a private company commissioned to maintain the website of the hosting institution where the net art work resides.

- **Open-source to Proprietary**. The creation of computer-based art works inevitably requires the use of equipment (software and hardware) that can vary between open-source, protected by intellectual property rights, or a combination of both. From this standpoint, the nature of the equipment influences the interpretation of the supporting infrastructure. A digital work administered in the native format of software can only be rendered by use of these applications and therefore requires the obtainment of a licence from the parent company; proprietary software is licensed under limitations, which further forbid processes such as reverse-engineering for preservation purposes.

- **Monolithic to Modular**. A work is perceived as monolithic when it is made up and fabricated as a single, one-piece, integral structure. This structure is unchanging and therefore only allows for one manifestation. Le Corbusier's *Poême Électronique* (1958) is such an example. The work consisted of black-and-white video, colour light ambiances, music moving over sound routes and visual special effects and was created specifically to be installed within the Philips Pavilion building; it has never been reprised after the end of the exhibition (Lombardo et al., 2006). On the other hand, a modular work is composed of units or sections that can be reconstructed or permit flexible (re)arrangement. The work of the *Soul Condenser* team for the 3rd Workshop of the Design Department at Domus Academy (2007) is a modular installation that uses water and therefore the walls are made of different materials that are readapted according to the environment in which the work is exhibited (for instance, ice would be used in cold weather, transparent thermoformed plastic filled with water for indoors exhibition and water fountains for warm climates).

- **Invariant to Variable**. New media art that uses computerized resources can take inputs and/or produce outputs whose values are liable to change while the work is being experienced by an audience. Within this definition of context, the position of such works tips toward the variable end of the continuum. The distinction between invariant and variable art works addresses the issue of capturing the logic behind the artistic piece which dynamically processes inputs and generates related outputs. The common denominator of variable works is that a singular experience – i.e. the way that one specific user interacts with the work and the outputs produced by this interaction – cannot be duplicated. For instance, in Ken Feingold's *Sinking Feeling* (2001)[5] and Stelarc's *Prosthetic Head* (2003)[6] the art works respond to human feedback and engage in a dialogue with the observer that depends on the inputs provided. Leeson's *Synthia Stock Ticker* (2003) and Joshua Portway and Lise Autogena's *Black Shoals Stock Market Planetarium* (2004) produce varying results and representations of data coming from stock market figures reported on the web. In contrast, invariant works are characterized by either unchanging outputs – as in a video recording – or preconfigured logic; the outputs in this case can be duplicated if the input provided by any user is the same. An example of the latter is Barbara Bloom's *Half Full-Half Empty* (2008),[7] where the viewer can choose between events in the past, present and future but the resulting scene is always the same.

Spatial context

Equipment and infrastructural context are closely related to the spatial dimension of a situation, because they are manifest through some kind of physical existence. However, in new media art *space* can take the form of a virtual environment as well – and this is particularly true for virtual reality, immersive projects. The characterization of the spatial setting of new media art works is the result of a process that is based on evidence and objectives that derive from the overall framework surrounding a work's commission, acquisition, exhibition, presentation or preservation strategies. These strategies reflect the decision-making mechanisms for identifying priorities, programmes, policies and space allocations alongside the resources necessary to deliver them. Such decisions may include:

- the confirmation that the space occupied by a work is available at the right time and in the right place and that it accords with the requirements for social and physical infrastructure
- the accordance of costs incurred by the use of a space with institutional policies and availability of funds; in cases where a work is installed in a public space,[8] the understanding of policies extends beyond monetary terms and requires co-operation from public services and authorities
- the contribution to local distinctiveness and community-specific objectives, which – from an institutional viewpoint – justify the investment in a work and promote economic, environmental and social benefits for a community.

Building on the above, the characteristics of the spatial dimension can be mapped to new media art as follows:

- **Local to Global.** The spatial dimension is characterized as *local* when the incentives to deal with or create an art work (depending on whether the issue is perceived by an institution's or an artist's side respectively) serve the concerns of a local community. The aim is to generate 'critical socio-cultural context, as well as [promote] public critical discourse and new forms of creative collaboration in the local community' (Šukaityte, 2008). Based on the nature of the environment where the work is situated, these communities can belong to both a physical and a virtual sphere. Examples of local spatial context include events like the *Fertile Ground* exhibition[9] and the creations of such artists as Judy Baca[10] and Suzanne Lacy.[11] At the other end of the continuum, the spatial dimension is characterized as *global* when the outreach of an art work is universal and not confined by any kind of boundaries.
- **Compact to Geographically dispersed.** The operational requirements of a work influence not only the amount of space that the artefact occupies, but also the amount of space and spatial arrangement necessary for observers to experience it. Hence, a *compact* art work is understood as one that is arranged within a single space that can be relatively small compared to the entire environment within which it is situated. In contrast, a *geographically dispersed* work is comparable to a distributed system architecture, with the artistic experience being provided by components scattered in different locations that collaboratively run tasks in a transparent and coherent manner. Examples include *Hole-in-Space*[12] and Jeffrey Shaw's *The Distributed Legible City* (1998).[13]

Temporal context

Similarly, we can discern temporal characteristics of new media art that describe a situational dimension related to time periods of activity. These include:

Timescale:
- **Picoseconds to Centuries**. Although *time* has been a recurring theme and notion throughout the history of fine arts in general, the arrival of

computerized means to create art has revolutionized the way that artists can exploit temporal qualities to produce highly time-based art works. The limits of the timescale continuum represent two extremes, which are nonetheless potentially achievable and evident in new media art works. Sadie Benning's video installation *Play Pause* (2006)[14] displays a narrative through gouache illustrations, with each image appearing only for a couple of seconds.[15] At the other end of the continuum, John F. Simon Jr's *Every Icon* (1996) needs approximately six billion years to reach the end of the second row of a 32x32 square grid (Wands, 2006).

- **Scheduled to Random.** This continuum refers to the time sequence of events unfolding as part of a new media art work. While in *scheduled* works this sequence is predefined and hence the experience received from the piece by different users is theoretically the same, artefacts characterized by randomness in the temporal dimension expose their events in no specific fashion or in a non-linear manner. The latter differ from *variable* art works, because they do not necessitate some kind of user input to produce a result (in which case the event is not random, it is 'user-driven'). An example of a scheduled work is Janet Cardiff and George Bures Miller's *The Telephone Call* (2001),[16] a video walk that leads visitors through the museum on a meandering tour up the central staircase, taking them briefly into a nearby gallery, and then into a service stair normally off limits to visitors; the path that the walk follows is predefined.[17] On the other hand, in Nam June Paik's *Participation TV II* (1969), signals sent from video cameras to television sets were manipulated randomly by acoustic signals, and the result was that viewers could see images of themselves distorted in random ways, interacting with the abstract forms and patterns on the screen (Decker-Phillips, 1998).

- **Perishable to Time-persistent.** The advent of new media art – and contemporary art in general – has marked a new era in the materials that artists use to bring their creativity to life. This pair of characteristics addresses the emergence of works that may be (intentionally or otherwise) short-lived due to their construction from *perishable* materials, as opposed to works whose deterioration, ageing and wear is at a par with traditional art forms and thus considered more *persistent* to the passing of time. Within a context classification scheme, this issue is of particular importance as institutions and collectors have been struggling to preserve and ensure perishable new media art pieces (Benedictus, 2004; McQueen, 2007). Examples are numerous: from Sarah Lucas's *Two Fried Eggs And Kebab* (1992) and *Au Naturel* (1994)[18] to Damien Hirst's *Love Lost* (1999)[19] and Dan Peterman's *Store (Cheese)* (1991–3) (Coulter-Smith, 2006).

Aesthetical context

Aesthetics can provide a solid representation of the cultural and historical context that spans a work's lifetime. The original situational dimensions for computer-based technologies defined by Kling (1987) do not include a cultural dimension as such – although glimpses and traces of it can be witnessed among the characteristics of the remaining dimensions. The theory and guide developed by Bertelsen and Pold (2004) provides the basis for an initial vocabulary for aesthetical context, which is based on six operational concepts:

- **Stylistic references**, whose source can be found in three areas. One is inheritance from predecessors and normative guidelines in the HCI field. For instance, Char Davies' work *Ephémère* (1998) is an interactive, fully immersive visual/aural virtual art work, which furthers the work begun in an earlier project called *Osmose* (1995).[20] Jeffrey Shaw's *The Distributed Legible City* (1998) is a new version of his 1989 project, which extends the original's aesthetics with multi-user functionality. Similarly, human interface guidelines proposed by Apple,[21] Microsoft[22] or Nokia[23] influence the aesthetics of software and create a coherent look and feel among – otherwise dissimilar – applications.[24] Stylistic references can also be found in art and architectural history; the aforementioned Bertelsen and Pold suggest a number of ways that interface style can be characterized as baroque, renaissance or romanticist. Lastly, stylistic references can be expressed through 'fashions' in application design. In the new media art paradigm, such cases include avatars created for virtual worlds (Liao, 2008) and artistic customizations for application software – such as skins and wallpapers for mobile phones, and themes for operating systems' graphical user interfaces.
- **Materiality** seeks to identify the materiality and remediation of the interface through which the audience experiences and communicates

with a digital art work. Materiality is used here to describe the constituents of a digital work's interface, such as code, algorithms and pixels. In new media art, there are examples of deconstructive interfaces which expose their own construction or that of other resources. Perhaps the best specimen of this type of work is the art of Joan Heemskerk and Dirk Paesmans – a collaboration established under the title *jodi*.[25] Jodi's net art is famous for '[stripping] away the reassuring navigation bars and identifiable pictograms of the everyday website to let loose the HTML behind the façade' (Ippolito, 1999).

- **Remediation**, a new media theory by Bolter and Grusin (2000), proposes the logic of remixing older media forms with newer ones and vice versa; the theory sheds light on the interdependency of all media and highlights the ways that reality itself is mediated by and for social actors.[26] New media art is often the product of mixing together text, video, audio, machinery and digital technology. Game art offers a good example of remediation and its many facets, with such works as Mike Beradino's *Atari Painting* (2008)[27] and Michael Bell-Smith's *While We Slept* (2004),[28] which appropriate vintage videogames to create a remediation of the original with a new scope. The converses of these works are the creations of artist and sign-maker Melissa Jones, who creates original wood carvings of classic arcade characters.[29]
- **Genres**. The issue has been explored in a number of publications (Lichty, 2000; Strehovec, 2009; Tribe and Jana, 2006; Wands, 2006). Although there is no standard genre vocabulary, the linchpin of the scholarly approaches is the understanding that a classification of genre builds on traditional art practice and can only be temporary – based at each time period on the contemporary state-of-the-art technology and evolving or being redefined as new technologies emerge and 'become more refined and familiar' (Wands, 2006). At the same time, genres can further 'define roles for the user and his interaction' (Bertelsen and Pold, 2004), with new media artefacts that vary between, say, an interactive installation and a digital imaging piece.
- **Hybridity** exposes the agglomeration of functional and cultural interfaces that surround new media art. Consider for instance *Crank the Web* (2001)[30] by Jonah Brucker-Cohen, a browser that allows people to physically crank their bandwidth in order to see a website. The idea behind *Crank the Web* is to combine ancient forms of automation with

today's digital telecommunications technology, thus creating a hybrid between mechanics and digital technology.

- **Representations**. The above-mentioned concepts of stylistic references, materiality and remediation, genre and hybridity reflect features of aesthetic theory and how these contribute to an understanding of a cultural context shaped by historical evidence. Bertelsen and Pold (2004) hold that these features contribute towards an awareness of issues and related analysis methods pertaining to *representations* of new media. Based on this logic, they distinguish two types of representations: realistic or naturalistic versus symbolic and allegorical. This idea is not new; representation in the arts has been the subject of many philosophical debates from Plato and Aristotle to Duchamp, McLuhan, Adorno and Dutton. For instance, Dutton (Dutton, 2008) has expressed seven signatures in human aesthetics, which include virtuosity, non-utilitarian pleasure, recognizable styles, criticism, imitation, special focus set aside from ordinary life and imagination. However, many new media art works are essentially exceptions to these signatures. For instance, in jodi's net art, virtuosity of web technology is deliberately avoided; Cohen's *Crank The Web* contradicts non-utilitarian pleasure. These characteristics of the cultural dimension in identifying a *situation* – and therefore classify contextual elements – might not be immediately observable and possibly difficult to represent and use as part of a vocabulary, but influence the nature of the other dimensions.

Social processes

How do the above-mentioned dimensions and their related characteristics fit into a grander scheme of things, which initiates, motivates or discourages and dissuades certain behaviours in the participant ecology? Social processes are perceived here as a means to work towards addressing the issue of *behavioural context*. Kling (1987) offers the view that the way participants in a situation conceptualize their actions, adopt practices and procedures, form coalitions and deal with constraints is influenced and dictated by another situation that is larger on at least one of the other dimensions. The boundaries of this *defining situation* used to interpret the *focal situation* are defined by criteria that regulate how limited or encompassing the boundaries will be. Building on these views, the characteristics of social processes are summarized in Table 17.1. Mapping social elements to new media art is by definition prone to exclude certain elements or lack depth, simply because these processes are complex and often very specific to particular contexts. The following points attempt to illustrate how these elements could be interpreted within a context classification vocabulary:

- **Critical relationships** between participants are essential for understanding the environment surrounding the creation, commission, etc., of new media art. To this end, two continuums are suggested. The first ranges from *co-operation* between participants/populations scales to *conflicts*; it represents agreements, debates, joint actions, oppositions or controversy surrounding either individual pieces or new media art in general. An example that has become ubiquitous in modern discourse is the ongoing debate in the institutional art world on whether new media art constitutes a distinct field, whether it should be considered 'just art' or even whether it is art at all (Dietz, 2005). On the other hand, community art is a case where the social environment promotes or at least strives for co-operation between participants. At an institutional level, co-operation and conflicts represent the relationships between roles or sub-units within the institution or among institutions. The second continuum describes the nature of these relationships, based on the distinction between *direct* and *mediated* contact. For instance, a common occurrence in modern museum practices is for a curator and a new media artist to collaborate closely, often exchanging ideas and helping each other to understand their role in the lifespan of the work. In other cases, communication between artist and audience is mediated by some third party. Such cases include online art galleries that provide artists with a platform to promote their work to potential buyers/collectors without the necessity of interpersonal contact.
- **Beliefs and critiques** describe the discussion or evaluation of new media art and can range from *isolated* – as in the body within the arts community engaging in art criticism – or *widespread*, which can extend as far as encompassing the social world. The breadth of this characteristic depends on the level of population scale under which a particular instance of the classification scheme is viewed. Similarly, procedural elements can be studied anywhere between institutional and community

levels. These procedures may describe the manner that a work is acquired and installed within an institution's physical space, management decisions over funding for an art commission, assessment procedures in order to evaluate the impact of a work on the target audience, surveillance procedures to ensure the security of an exhibit, or conservational methods.

- Akin to procedures are the characteristics of a situation that refer to **common practices** in dealing with new media art and can range from standardized to ad hoc. From an institutional standpoint, these may include the process and policies adopted for documentation and preservation. From an artistic point of view, these practices describe situations where the methodology of the artist has a direct effect on some aspect of social life (e.g. hacking-as-art of everyday tools, communication platforms, etc.)[31]

- **Constraints** position the role and consequences of limitations and restrictions placed on all the aforementioned dimensions, and can stem from a variety of sources. Constraints are possibly one of the most difficult facets of context to include in a vocabulary, particularly when the suggested terminology needs to be rigorous and thorough. In this sense, it would be unrealistic to provide an inclusive account of examples; constraints are very 'situation-specific' and can vary between cases, so much so that what constitutes a limitation in a particular context might be negligible in another. A reasonable – and definitely more thorough – account of potential constraints with new media art is given in Middlebrooks (2001).

Conclusion

The contextual dimensions presented in this chapter and their characteristics are not orthogonal. Many are mutually dependent and require combined consideration in order to describe fully the contextual background of a work. This study provides a first step towards reaching the objective of a vocabulary for context classification by use of sociotechnical theories. The approach needs to be empirically validated so as to gauge its suitability and understand its potential impact on situating the much sought-after, but thus far eluding 'pinning down', software art context.

Acknowledgements

This work was supported by the Planets Project (IST-2006-033789), funded by the European Commission's IS&T 6th Framework Programme. The work was conducted at the Humanities Advanced Technology & Information Institute (HATII), University of Glasgow, with valuable contributions by Prof. Seamus Ross and Andrew McHugh.

Notes

1   Given the ambiguity of the term 'digital', it is used here to describe art works where the computer has been used as 'a primary tool, medium and/or creative partner' (Wands, 2006).
2   http://potatoland.org/feed.
3   Source: http://potatoland.com/feed/about.html.
4   Source: http://variablemedia.net/e/seeingdouble.
5   www.kenfeingold.com/catalog_html/sinking.html.
6   http://stelarc.org/?catID=20241.
7   www.diacenter.org/bloom.
8   For instance, see Kit Galloway and Sherrie Rabinowitz's *Hole-In-Space* (1980), installed at the Lincoln Center for the Performing Arts in New York City, and 'The Broadway' department store located in the open-air Shopping Center in Century City, LA. (Source: www.ecafe.com/getty/HIS.)
9   http://rhizome.org/editorial/fp/reblog.php/1756.
10 www.judybaca.com/now/index.php.
11 http://en.wikipedia.org/wiki/Suzanne_Lacy.
12 See note 9.
13 www.jeffrey-shaw.net/html_main/show_work.php?record_id=102.
14 http://whitney.org/Exhibitions/SadieBenning.
15 Source: http://rhizome.org/editorial/2642.
16 www.sfmoma.org/multimedia/audio/aop_tour_421.
17 Source: www.cardiffmiller.com/artworks/walks/telephonecall.html.
18 Source: www.bbc.co.uk/dna/collective/A6641318.
19 www.artnet.com/artwork/58443/414/damien-hirst-love-lost.html.
20 www.immersence.com/ephemere/index.php.
21 https://help.apple.com/asg/mac/2013/.
22 http://msdn.microsoft.com/en-us/library/aa511258.aspx.

23 http://developer.nokia.com/resrouces/library/LWUIT/lwuit-for-nokia-asha-software-platform.html.
24 For instance, see Liliana Porter's *Rehearsal*, Barabara Bloom's *Half Full–Half Empty* and Dorothy Cross's *Foxglove* (all in Dia's Web Projects page: www.diabeacon.org/webproj). The three art works share similar features in their interface that are inherited from the common use of Adobe Flash. These features are distinct from, say, Napier's *Net Flag* (http://netflag.guggenheim.org/netflag) interface – developed in Java and presented online as a Java applet.
25 www.jodi.org.
26 Source: http://en.wikipedia.org/wiki/Mediation_(Marxist_theory_and_media_studies)#Remediation.
27 http://mikeberadino.com.
28 www.foxyproduction.com/artists/421/works/10131.
29 Source: http://technabob.com/blog/2008/03/15/awesome-arcade-game-art-by-melissa-jones.
30 www.mee.tcd.ie/~bruckerj/projects/cranktheweb.html.
31 Source: http://web-archive-it.com/page/1139786/2013-01-13/http://www.neural.it/art/2008/02/plink_jet_plucking_inkjet_prin.phtml.

References

Alonso, R. (1998) *This Is Not an Advertisement: an essay on Muntadas' work in video and internet*, www.roalonso.net/en/videoarte/muntadas.php.
Benedictus, L. (2004) Here Today, Gone Tomorrow?, *Guardian Online*, www.guardian.co.uk/artanddesign/2004/oct/09/friezeartfair2005.friezeartfair2.
Bertelsen, O. W. and Pold, S. (2004) Criticism as an Approach to Interface Aesthetics, paper presented at the *Third Nordic Conference on Human-computer Interaction*, Tampere, Finland.
Berwick, C. (2001) The New New-Media Blitz, *ARTnews*, www.artnews.com/2001/04/01/the-new-new-media-blitz.
Bolter, J. D. and Grusin, R. A. (2000) *Remediation: understanding new media*, Cambridge, MA, MIT Press.
Candy, L. and Edmonds, E. A. (2002) *Explorations in Art and Technology*, New York, NY, Springer.
Castle, N. (2000) *Internet Art and Radicalism in the Digital Culture Industry*,

http://video.lulu.com/items/volume_1/89000/89324/2/preview/netart_
preview.pdf.

Cornwall, R. (1993) From the Analytical Engine to Lady Ada's Art. In
Druckrey, T. and Stainback, C. (eds), *Iterations: the new image*, Cambridge, MA,
and London, MIT Press.

Coulter-Smith, G. (2006) *Deconstructing Installation Art*, www.installationart.net.

Decker-Phillips, E. (1998) *Paik Video*, Barrytown, NY, Barrytown Ltd.

Dietz, S. (2005) Collecting New Media Art: just like anything else, only different.
In Altshuler, B. (ed.), *Collecting the New: museums and contemporary art*, Princeton,
NJ, Princeton University Press, 85–101.

Dutton, D. (2008) Aesthetic Universals. In Gaut, B. N. and Lopes, D. (eds.),
The Routledge Companion to Aesthetics, 2nd edn, London and New York, NY,
Routledge, 203–14.

Giaretta, D. (2011) *Advanced Digital Preservation*, Heidelberg and New York, NY,
Springer.

Greene, R. (2004) *Internet Art*, London and New York, NY, Thames & Hudson.

Ippolito, J. (1999) Deconstruction or Distraction? *Artbyte* (New York), **2** (1), 22–3.

Kaprow, A. (2003) 'Happenings' in the New York Scene. In Wardrip-Fruin, N. and
Montfort, N. (eds), *The New Media Reader*, Cambridge, MA, MIT Press, 83–8.

Kling, R. (1987) Defining the Boundaries of Computing across Complex
Organisations. In Boland, R. J. and Hirschheim, R. A. (eds.), *Critical Issues in
Information Systems Research*, New York, NY, Wiley & Sons, 307–62.

Liao, C. L. (2008) Avatars, Second Life® and New Media Art: the challenge for
contemporary art education, *Art Education*, **61** (2), 87–91.

Lichty, P. (2000) The Cybernetics of Performance and New Media Art, *Leonardo*,
33 (5), 351–4.

Lombardo, V., Valle, A., Nunnari, F., Giordana, F. and Arghinenti, A. (2006)
Archeology of Multimedia, paper presented at the *14th Annual ACM
International Conference on Multimedia*, Santa Barbara, CA, USA.

Lovejoy, M., Paul, C. and Bulajic, V. V. (2011) *Context Providers: conditions of meaning
in media arts*, Bristol, UK, and Chicago, IL, Intellect.

Manovich, L. (2003) New Media: from Borges to HTML. In Wardrip-Fruin, N.
and Montfort, N. (eds), *The New Media Reader*, Cambridge, MA, MIT Press,
13–25.

McQueen, M. P. (2007) Perishable Art: investing in works that may not last, *Wall
Street Journal Online*,
http://online.wsj.com/news/articles/SB117927768289404269.

Middlebrooks, K. (2001) *New Media Art: a new frontier or continued tradition?* Good Work Project Report Series, Number 9.

Montfort, N. and Wardrip-Fruin, N. (2003) *The New Media Reader*, Cambridge, MA, MIT Press.

Morris, S. (2001) *Museums and New Media Art*, www.issuelab.org/resource/museums_and_new_media_art.

Paul, C. (2003) *Digital Art*, New York, NY, Thames & Hudson.

Paul, C. (2007) Challenges for a Ubiquitous Museum: presenting and preserving new media, *NeMe*, www.neme.org/571/preserving-new-media.

Popper, F. (1997) *Art of the Electronic Age*, London, Thames & Hudson.

Rugg, J. and Sedgwick, M. (2007) *Issues in Curating Contemporary Art and Performance*, Bristol, UK, and Chicago, IL, Intellect.

Rush, M. (2005) *New Media in Art*, London, Thames & Hudson.

Schlichtiger, P. (1991) Closely Coupled Systems. In Karshmer, A. and Nehmer, J. (eds), *Operating Systems of the 90s and Beyond*, Lecture Notes in Computer Science, Vol. 563, Berlin and Heidelberg, Springer, 44–7.

Scholte, T. and Hoen, P. (2007) *Inside Installations: preservation and presentation of installation art*, Amsterdam, ICN, SBMK.

Strehovec, J. (2009) New Media Art as Research: art-making beyond the autonomy of art and aesthetics, *Technoetic Arts: a Journal of Speculative Research*, **6** (3), 233–50.

Šukaityte, R. (2008) New Media Art in Lithuania, *Athena: Philosophical Studies*, **3** (21), 173–86.

Tribe, M. and Jana, R. (2006) *New Media Art*, Cologne and London, Taschen.

Wands, B. (2006) *Art of the Digital Age*, New York, NY, Thames & Hudson.

Weight, J. (2006) I, Apparatus, You, *Convergence*, **12** (4), 413–46.

PART 4

Case studies

CHAPTER 18

The Villa of Oplontis: a 'born-digital' project

John R. Clarke

Professor, Department of Art and Art History,
College of Fine Arts, University of Texas at Austin, USA

Introduction

In 2005, the Centre for the Study of Ancient Italy at the University of Texas entered into a collaboration with the Archaeological Superintendency of Pompeii, a branch of the Italian Ministry of Culture, to study and publish one of the largest ancient Roman luxury villas buried by the eruption of Vesuvius on 24 August AD 79. Known officially as Villa A at Torre Annunziata – the modern town built on top of the ancient town of Oplontis – the Villa of Oplontis lies under 8.5 metres of volcanic material, and is about three miles north of Pompeii. Its importance rests on three facts: it is enormous, with 99 excavated spaces; its decoration is exquisite; and it may have belonged to Nero's unfortunate second wife, Poppaea Sabina.

Advantages of the e-book

To develop a research strategy, I assembled a small group of experts, including an architect, a photographer, an art historian and an archaeologist. Our questions included: How did the current reconstruction of the Villa come about? What can archives and excavated artefacts tell us about the Villa? What lies beneath it? What are the meanings of its vast and complex decorative apparatus? How did its residents, including the masters, guests, and slaves, use the Villa? To answer these questions we established the Oplontis Project team, and embarked on a six-year campaign of research and excavation (Oplontis Project website[1]).

Since the principal goal of the Oplontis Project is the definitive publication of Villa A, the question was how to publish. Over the past 30 years, two acclaimed print series had set the standard: the German series, *Häuser in Pompeji*, or *Houses in Pompeii*, and the four-volume publication *The Insula of the Menander at Pompeii* edited by Roger Ling. Both of these print series aim to document the houses in question to the fullest possible extent: architecture and construction techniques, decorations – including pavements and wall and ceiling paintings – statuary, small finds, and much more.

Presentation of such complex materials is a problem. Even in the folio format used by the *Häuser im Pompeji* volumes, illustrations often represent a large wall painting inadequately (Strocka, 1991). To create the drawings that illustrate all the walls of the house, whether decorated or not, draftspersons actually traced the walls on huge sheets of mylar. They then redrew them, using various graphic devices to make them legible. Despite the great pains taken, these drawings remain schematic. To complete lacunose wall decorations, the graphic artists propose conservative reconstructions, drawn into the actual-state tracing in faint outlines. Black-and-white photographs document the actual state of each wall. Often, especially in narrow spaces, the actual-state photographs must be taken from an oblique angle, making them difficult to understand.

In the smaller-format volumes for *The Insula of the Menander*, the editor often utilizes long gatefolds to show – again in a schematic way – the positioning of the decorations of their respective walls (Ling, 2005). In order to save space and paper, drawings from different spaces sometimes appear together on the same gatefold. A scholar wanting to investigate the decoration of a particular room must first find its number on the plan at the back of the book, then consult the catalogue description, then find the appropriate foldout, then go to a separate plates section to find the colour illustration, and to yet another section to find the black-and-white photos. She will also have to take the scale markers seriously, for the drawings are reproduced at different sizes.

Was there a better way to publish Villa A at Oplontis? Since its inception in 1999, I had been following the successes of the Humanities E-Book (HEB) series published by the American Council of Learned Societies (ACLS) in New York (2014). The ACLS, created in 1919, represents 81 societies in the humanities and the social sciences, providing leadership and funding for scholarly initiatives. The HEB Series is an online collection of approximately 4000 books of high quality in the humanities, accessible through institutional and individual subscription. These titles are offered by the ACLS in collaboration with 30 learned societies, over 100 contributing publishers, and the Michigan Publishing division at the University of Michigan Library. The result is an online, fully searchable collection of high-quality books in the humanities, recommended and reviewed by scholars. These are works of major importance that remain vital to both scholars and advanced students, and are frequently cited in the literature.

In addition to the scanned page-image books forming the bulk of the collection, the HEB Series features a number of XML-encoded titles from established scholars who wish to take full advantage of the possibilities of digital publication. These are the so-called 'born-digital' e-books. In contrast to books that are image-based, the XML books (88 as of February 2014) are text-based, a format that allows for features such as image enlargement, internal and external links, interactive maps, audio and video files, databases and archival materials. All of these are things that the Oplontis Project publication wants to do.

The publication is complex. At this point, we have 42 authors whose contributions will cover, in four volumes: the ancient setting and modern rediscovery, the decorations, the excavations, and the architecture of the villa. The current plan shows the 99 spaces, including beautifully painted rooms, gardens, and a 61-metre swimming pool, including our excavations since 2006, consisting of 20 trenches in all (Figure 18.1). In addition, we need to document the excavations from 1783 to 2010 on the basis of texts, drawings and photographs. We have 19 large-scale sculptures, marble columns and capitals, ceramics and bronzes. And we have to make clear what is ancient and what is modern.

We have to organize this mass of information for a born-digital e-book. This is where the digital model comes in. Our goal is to take the finding tools of the print book and locate them within a navigable, 3D model of the Villa of Oplontis. Scholars agree that the effectiveness of the scholarly print book rests of the accuracy and effectiveness of the finding tools: the table of contents, the index, figure call-out numbers, notes and – above all – cross-references. All of these tools allow a reader to find information. From the author's point of view, these tools are the building blocks of his or her argument. They allow the author to take the reader from text to image and back, and to compare one set of information (such as bibliographical

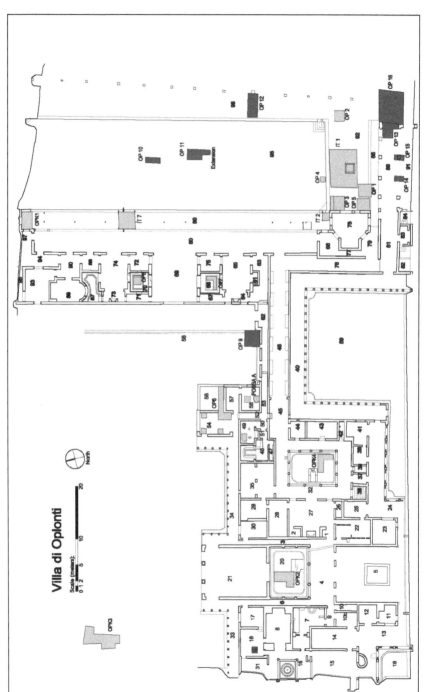

Figure 18.1 Villa A, Torre Annunziata, plan 2010 (drawing Jess Galloway)

references or visual comparisons) with another set of information. Clearly, recasting these traditional finding tools in the born-digital environment provides faster access to a much greater quantity of information, all of it located in the actual spaces of Villa A. In short, the 3D model becomes the index to the digital book.

Linking the 3D model with the database

To make the model function as the index, we had to create a database, and make access to the database possible by clicking on images or spaces within our index – i.e. within the digital model itself. We have spent considerable time and effort refining the database to make it represent our research well. The fields include the major types of information we have. The platform is Microsoft Access, and all of the fields are searchable by keyword. Most importantly, it allows us to upload high-resolution photos of each item, and it automatically associates photographs of items in categories 1 through 8 with category 9, photographic archives. The database assigns each item a unique number. For archaeological finds, that unique number becomes the inventory number; the same is true of any item that the Oplontis Project catalogues and describes: wall paintings, whether in situ or unassociated with a specific wall; archival photographs, plans and drawings; and documents such as the excavation journals. The full description appears in a searchable field; a thumbnail image appears at lower right. Clicking on the thumbnail allows the user to download a high-resolution image. An important feature of the database is that when there exist many images of the same artefact – say of a wall painting discovered 45 years ago – the database will associate all the images of that artefact contained in the database. As I hope to demonstrate in what follows, photographic archives are extremely important to the success of this project.

Although from the beginning we knew we wanted to publish a born-digital e-book, it was in the third year of our work that we met with Richard Beacham and decided to partner with the King's Visualisation Lab (KVL). Our collaboration found success in two substantial grants, one a collaborative research fellowship from the National Endowment for the Humanities, and on the British side a grant from the Leverhulme Foundation. As the reviewers for both of these granting agencies acknowledged, it was important, as part of the e-book publication, to create a 3D digital model. In addition to its role of disseminating the results of our studies of the ancient Villa of Oplontis, the model must also preserve the Villa itself for posterity. In light of the severe damage the Villa has suffered from exposure to the elements and improper care, a digital actual-state record is essential for all future work. Creating this model from the resources at hand has proven an exciting and often daunting task.

We began with the idea of scanning all 99 spaces of the villa using available laser-scanning technology, but this proved too costly. We then decided to build the model in 3D Studio Max, based on the electronic plans and sections created by our architects. We assigned one of our architects, Tim Liddell, to provide resources for KVL's Drew Baker, so that together we could make an accurate 3D Max model. The Oplontis Project engaged an experienced architectural photographer, Paul Bardagjy, to create the most accurate possible photographs of walls, floors, ceilings and colonnades – and to oversee stitching the photographs to scale. The stitching proved particularly demanding and time-consuming. Many long spaces, such as the Villa's porticoes (33, 34, 24, 60), had to be stitched together from numerous shots, and required the work of several professionals to create an accurate, undistorted record of just what is there. Because of the scholarly nature of the project, reproduction of the actual state of the Villa remained the fundamental demand of our publisher, and an absolute criterion for our professional readers: archaeologists, architects and art historians.

With much work, determination and considerable expense, we have arrived at the alpha-state model. Three features are especially exciting from the point of view of the digital humanities. First, the Unity interface allows real-time exploration of all the spaces of the Villa. Second, the user can click on features to find out more about them. Third, the user can switch from the actual-state model to accurate reconstructions of complex rooms. These three features, we believe, put new tools in the hands of scholars and the public alike. Currently, Heriberto Nieto, Research Engineer at the Texas Advanced Computing Center (TACC), is configuring the Villa A model to function in Oculus Rift, a fully-immersive 3D virtual environment.

From archives to digital reconstruction

In what follows, I wish to highlight one particular aspect of the e-book: the use of archival material. The most straightforward kind of enquiry that the model can answer is what the villa looked like in antiquity. Although they might not know it, the structure that visitors see when they come to the site at Torre Annunziata is largely a fabrication. When modern excavations began in 1964, the aim of the Italian Government was to make the Villa of Oplontis into a tourist site. To make it look like a 'real' ancient villa, contracting companies were called in to use any means available to turn the rubble into a living museum. The photo of the unearthing of the north portico of the Villa (33) in Figure 18.2 demonstrates the enormous size of this task. We see the columns cut down by a pyroclastic surge, made of superheated volcanic mud that sped along the ground at speeds up to 450 miles an hour. These surges cut down everything in their path. The construction company used the remaining pieces to make whole columns and piers that to support new architraves and roofs. It is the duty of the Oplontis Project to provide photos like these to demonstrate the true nature of the artefact known as the Villa of Oplontis.

Archival research can greatly expand our knowledge – not only of reconstruction techniques but also of the Villa's decorative apparatus. In 1986, I became aware, through a drawing executed in 1971, that there once was a painting in the tympanum above the north alcove in room 11. After years of searching, in 2008 the archivist at the Superintendency of Pompeii found 30 black-and-white photographs taken in 1967. Figure 18.3, clearly shows the subject of that painting, illegible today. It is a beautiful rendition of a harbour surrounded by turreted walls, populated by graceful figures.

Figure 18.2
The discovery of porticus 33, c.1967 (Photo: Soprintendenza Archeologica di Pompei D106)

Figure 18.3
Room 11, north wall, tympanum, c. 1967 (Photo: Soprintendenza Archeologica di Pompei B1244)

Using PhotoShop, Martin Blazeby of KVL has been able to create an accurate colour restoration of this important painting, allowing us to integrate it into the room's decorative scheme. It is worth mentioning that this painting is the only existing example of a landscape used as a tympanum decoration in this period, c. 50 BC and that it has attracted much scholarly attention.

We get a sense of the chaotic situation the workers faced in another early archival photo (Figure 18.4), when excavations have got down to the upper

Figure 18.4
Oecus 15 and toppled wall of 14 (Photo: Soprintendenza Archeologica di Pompei B1284)

third of the standing walls. We are looking at the upper left section of the east wall of room 15. But perhaps the most dramatic photograph is this one, of oecus 15. It reminds us how violent the cataclysm was, and that violent earthquakes accompanied the eruption. Two sides of the same wall appear in the photograph. We see the portion of the wall of oecus 15 that is still standing. We can recognize the image of the tragic mask and just the head of the famous Oplontis peacock sitting on a ledge. But at the bottom of the photograph we can see the image of a goddess in her circular shrine from the opposite side of this wall: a piece of the west wall of triclinium 14 overturned by the cataclysm.

Fortunately, a conscientious draftsperson, Ciro Iorio, recorded these fragments before they were lost forever in the failed attempts to recompose them and reattach them to the reconstructed wall. Today the entire upper left quadrant shown in Iorio's drawing is lost, including the frieze decoration consisting of shields and armour, the ornate capital at the top of the large pier that runs from floor to frieze, as well as the shield image, the so-called *imago clipeata*, to the left of the goddess in her circular shrine.

We have used these archival photographs and drawings to create reconstructions of the original states of these and other decorations. Thanks to the work of Blazeby, the digital model allows the viewer to switch back and forth between actual-state and reconstructed views of the frescoes in many of the rooms of the villa. The digital model also allows us to distinguish separate phases of decoration in several rooms. In AD 45 the owners decided to convert room 8 from the hot room of a bath to a dining and reception space. The back wall had to be partially demolished; the owner then got an artist to imitate quite carefully the original – and by now, old-fashioned – wall scheme. He or she did not want lose this period-style room – painted in AD 10 – when the room was remodelled 40 years later. By far the most dramatic find from our excavations is a piece of the demolished part of this very wall. It is a piece of the original frieze of the Third-Style decoration of AD 10 found in Oplontis Project trench OP3, about 100 metres away and buried along with lots of other plaster fragments at a depth of 1.5 metres (Clarke and Thomas, 2009). Once again, this is the kind of scholarly information that we can embed in the 3D model and explain clearly through the database documenting our excavations.

By coupling archival photographs with the 3D model we can also recover the original architectural configurations of spaces lost in the hasty and sometimes inept modern reconstruction process. In a photograph of the excavation of room 23 around 1967 (Figure 18.5), we see workmen exploring the standing the north and west walls. They are clearing the rubble as best they can. They have put cloths weighted down by stones on the tops of the walls, and there are lots of wooden poles at the ready to build a temporary tin roof. Two important features are about to be lost in an undocumented but certain collapse: the remains of a tympanum on the north wall and the beginning of another on the west. In other words, the original covering of this room was a suspended cross-vaulted ceiling. The room got restored with a flat ceiling in reinforced concrete, no trace of either tympanum to be found. In its original form it would have resembled a well preserved cross-vaulted room of the same period (c. 50 BC) in the House of Ceres at Pompeii. Given the information provided by the archival photograph and the House of Ceres, we have with certainty restored properly the cross-vaulted ceiling of this beautiful space. This reconstruction demonstrates how archival photographs combined with archaeological research can create new knowledge.

In addition to filling in losses and correcting inept reconstructions, the digital model can provide a home for the hundreds of orphaned fragments in the villa. When workmen found a detached fragment of wall painting, they placed it face down on a table. They cut down the ancient plaster backing to create a regular surface; then they put down galvanized steel wire for reinforcement. They also formed this wire into loops so that they could hook the fragment back onto the reconstructed wall. They then built up modern cement around the reinforcing wire. Once the fragments from a room were consolidated in this way, they would cement them into the reconstructed wall – presumably in the right position.

Figure 18.5
Room 23, excavation of north and west walls, c.1967 (Photo: Soprintendenza Archeologica di Pompei, De Franciscis 945)

Archival photographs from the early 1970s document many of these consolidated fragments that were never integrated into their original walls. Particularly in the atrium (5), many fragments of its decoration turned up after the hasty reconstruction, in reinforced concrete, of its roof – an imitation of the typical Roman compluviate type.

We located most of these fragments belonging to the Second-Style scheme of the atrium in a storage area of the Villa. One of our architects, Timothy Liddell, worked with the puzzle. Using Photoshop and Illustrator, he was able to place a number of these orphaned fragments into a plausible scheme that fits with the architectural perspectives of the standing wall. Since the only column-capital among the atrium fragments is Ionic, Liddell hypothesized an Ionic upper order. The pieces fit quite well; however, it is impossible to calculate the exact height of the lost Ionic columns. Liddell's reconstruction is deliberately quite conservative, and for this reason only some of our orphaned fragments have found a home. A full, intelligently imaginative reconstruction of the decoration recently completed by Blazeby takes Liddell's Ionic architrave and elaborates an upper storey. These two reconstructions come from combining two kinds of archives: photographs and the actual fragments found in deplorable conditions of storage in one of the rooms of the Villa that had become a rubbish heap.

Work continues on the many other fragments that constitute a physical archive of the Villa's decoration. Recently we found numerous fragments of a Fourth-Style scheme that was partially consolidated but never fully restored. These fragments were extremely delicate, not only because the plaster was so friable but also because the painters applied the costly cinnabar red pigment like a watercolour wash rather than allowing the pigment to carbonate in true fresco fashion. After careful study by team members Erin Anderson and Zoe Schofield, these fragments turned out to be part of the lost ceiling of room 8 – the same room as that where we found a match for our excavated frieze fragment. Back in 1967, excavators made only a half-hearted attempt to restore this ceiling. There are many other diagnostics that make it certain that this ceiling fragment, after wasting away for 44 years in a dust-heap, has finally found a home. This major discovery restores a ceiling to one of the most important rooms of the Villa. Another group of fragments may allow reconstruction of the lost ceiling of porticus 60. As work continues, we hope to find more pieces of this decoration as we wade through the remaining orphaned fragments, and we hope to find a home for them – at least in the digital model.

Another invisible element of the Villa is its sculpture. The pieces found in situ, in the north garden (56) and along the eastern side of the 61-metre swimming pool, have never been exhibited at the archaeological site. We hope to put the sculpture found in these gardens back into place, after languishing for 40 years in the storerooms. Now and then a few pieces get pulled out of storage to illustrate a theme of an exhibition. We intend to put them into the digital model, so that a viewer will be able to see them from various vantage points in the villa, walk around them, and contemplate them as an ancient Roman would have done. Recently the Oplontis Project commissioned Marcus Abbott of ArcHeritage, UK, to record all of the sculptures using laser scanning and photogrammetry so that we can put them back in their original setting in the 3D model.

The model will not only be a perfect medium for studying the sculptures, it will also allow us to demonstrate, finally, just how Villa A fitted into the ancient landscape. The modern coastline has changed dramatically over the centuries. The masses of materials blasted from the cone of Vesuvius in AD 79, as well as the many subsequent eruptions, have changed its shape dramatically. Over the past years, geologist Giovanni di Maio conducted a series of cores, most of them going 15 metres deep, to determine the shape of the ancient coastline. Along it, archaeologists have noted the foundations of several ancient villas in addition to Villa A. In di Maio's aerial view, he has marked the remains of these villas with white crosslets (Figure 18.6). Today, Villa A lies about half a kilometre inland, at the depth of 8.5 metres below the level of the modern city. In a second view, we see the outline of the ancient coast, the position of Villa A marked with a crosslet (Figure 18.7).

Figure 18.6 Modern coastline at Torre Annunziata, with sites of ancient Roman villas marked (Photo: Giovanni di Maio)

Figure 18.7 The ancient coastline highlighted, with site of Villa A marked (Photo: Giovanni di Maio)

In 2009–2010 the Oplontis Project commissioned di Maio to conduct cores around the Villa to determine just what it stood on. The result is rather dramatic as the section reveals (Figure 18.8). The Villa was not on flat land, not even on sloping land. It stood on a cliff 13 metres above the sea. It would have commanded a dramatic view. We have already explored this ancient panorama as seen from various rooms overlooking the sea using Google Earth and other GIS imaging tools.

Conclusion

The excavations at the so-called Villa of Poppaea stand at a crossroads in the long history of excavations in the region buried by Vesuvius. They aimed, as Amedeo Maiuri had at Herculaneum, to make the Villa into a living museum that the public could visit. This meant creating a new building that looked ancient. Walls had to be rebuilt and colonnades had to be reconstructed to support modern concrete beams and new tile roofs. In the process much of what made the Villa so attractive in antiquity had to be sacrificed. The sculpture had to be removed to safekeeping, as well as all objects subject to vandalism or theft. Archives, such as precious excavation daybooks, disappeared. When funds dried up, restorers gave

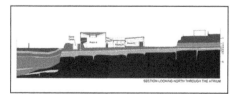

Figure 18.8
Section of Villa, south to north, at atrium (Photo: Giovanni di Maio)

up on the fragments of painting that did not easily fit back on the walls. The gardens were never restored properly, despite the wealth of evidence discovered by the American garden archaeologist, Wilhelmina Jashemski.

We can now, through virtual means, put the pieces of this puzzle back together. As we have seen, the idea of the archive of an excavation is changing from that of a catalogue of objects classified according to their materials into an interwoven – and indeed an interactive – experience. The ideal archive is one that allows us, and future generations, to find material easily electronically, and to study it in the context of the place where it originally functioned. We hope to facilitate just that kind of retrieval and study with the Oplontis Project, linking our database with the interactive 3D model, putting the fragments back in place, showing what came from our trenches and cores, and making this information – as well as the four-volume publication – available free on the web. In this way, if and when excavation of the Villa continues – and I estimate that another 40% of the structure still lies buried – scholars of the future will be in much better shape than we were when we began our study. They will have at their fingertips all of the information they need to complete the study of this rich and complex Villa.

Note

1   http://oplontisproject.org.

References

American Council of Learned Societies (ACLS) (2014) Humanities E-Book Series, www.humanitiesebook.org.

Clarke, J. R. and Thomas, M. L. (2009) Evidence of Demolition and Remodeling at Villa A at Oplontis (Villa of Poppaea) after A.D. 45, *Journal of Roman Archaeology*, **22**, 201–9.

Ling, R. (2005) *The Insula of the Menander at Pompeii, Vol. 2., The Decorations*, Oxford, Clarendon Press.

Strocka, M. V. (ed.) (1991–) *Häuser in Pompeji*, 12 vols, Munich, Hirrmer Verlag.

CHAPTER 19

Preservation of complex cultural heritage objects – a practical implementation

Daniel Pletinckx

Visual Dimension bvba, Ename, Belgium

Six issues to deal with

The London Charter[1] provides a very complete and well structured framework to carry out documented 3D visualization of complex cultural heritage (CH) objects, such as objects of art, man-made structures and historical landscapes. When focusing, however, on the practical implementation of the preservation of such digital visualizations, we need to deal with six major issues, which are:

1 lack of methodology for documenting and exchanging 3D CH objects
2 lack of communication methodology
3 lack of stimuli to document and preserve
4 lack of long-term storage and digital preservation strategies
5 lack of business models for re-use and exchange
6 lack of updating methodology.

Lack of methodology for documenting and exchanging 3D CH objects

The **first issue** is still very basic: *we still do not have any traditional or adopted methodology or standards for how we document the creation of a 3D visualization.* Although the London Charter[2] outlines the principles very well, we need a more practical methodology that can be adopted by the majority of people involved in 3D visualization. There are already some initial guidelines, for example on implementing heritage visualization in *Second Life*[3] or on general documentation of interpretation processes (paradata) in 3D visualization[4] developed within the EPOCH European Network of Excellence in Open Cultural Heritage.[5] But we need more good examples and best practices on how to take on such documentation activity, on what tools to use, on the workflow to follow. We need major involvement by the community to reach consensus that 3D visualization and its documentation is a normal part of cultural heritage practice.

But these guidelines need to deal not only with the lonely researcher who creates such 3D visualizations of complex cultural heritage, but also with teams, multidisciplinary and geographically distributed. In other words, *exchange* of such documentation and methodology to *collaborate* are essential elements in the practical implementation of a documentation and preservation strategy. This is clearly linked to the capabilities of the tools used. The InMan methodology[6] as developed within EPOCH used a wiki as medium for the documentation process, because of its discussion and versioning capabilities. Recent experiments for the 3D visualization of the Abbey Theatre in Dublin[7] and the Etruscan Regolini-Galassi tomb[8] used a blog to record the interpretation process and related visualization issues and to stimulate discussion and consensus creation amongst the group of 3D experts and a wide variety of cultural heritage experts. Although the idea of a peer review process of 3D models was coined several years ago now by Bernard Frischer in the SAVE concept,[9] very little experience is already available on how exactly to implement such a review process, including source assessment, evaluation of 3D models, discussion amongst peers and improvement of the 3D model. Moreover, a peer review process should be based upon the London Charter and use metrics that reflect the London Charter principles. This process still needs to be defined and a sufficient degree of consensus needs to be built on the methodology and implementation.

Lack of communication methodology

This brings us to the **second issue**, which is the *communication of 3D models of cultural heritage objects for collaboration, scientific publication and public use*. We need to make a clear distinction between these three goals, as they have different dynamics and requirements.

Within *collaborative research*, 3D models and their linked paradata need to be passed on from one expert to the other, for study, review and adaptation. In practice, this turns out to be quite difficult, not only for technical reasons (ownership and knowledge of tools and 3D software) but also for organizational and psychological reasons. Our experience is that it works much better if one central person or team deals with the 3D models and paradata, while experts are consulted to contribute in their domain of expertise. This is also how the multidisciplinary team of Robert Vergnieux at the Ausonius Institute[10] deals with 3D visualization projects with great success. Using a blog is a useful instrument in this process (see above), but our preliminary observations are that the blog needs to be private (limited to the research team), as experts are reluctant to contribute on a public blog, which they see as a kind of publication with final conclusions, while the contributions are ongoing research, of a volatile and progressive nature.

Scientific publication of 3D visualization projects is quite common, but very few of these publications allow one to see the 3D results in 3D. As most publications result in a PDF file, we can use the 3D capabilities of PDF, which have matured significantly since 2008. PDF is an open format, standardized as ISO32000-1 (an update of this ISO standard, i.e. ISO32000-2 aka PDF2.0, was in preparation at the time of writing). When authoring PDF documents, one can easily add 3D models into a publication[11] from a wide range of 3D formats. Other technologies to publish 3D online, such as WebGL, are beginning to be available. The uptake of this simple approach, however, is hampered on one hand by the lack of 3D models in archaeological and historical research, and on the other by the lack of education in the cultural heritage domain on how to use 3D in research and documentation.[12] Once a sufficient number of 3D models has been created and used within the cultural heritage domain, there will be much more pressure to deal with proper 3D publication and digital preservation processes.

However, the most common purpose for 3D cultural heritage data is *public use*. This means that a certain body of scientific results is used to show cultural heritage objects to the public in exhibitions, online or on TV. In this *public use* phase, the focus needs to be on the translation of those scientific results into a 3D visualization that uses a certain medium (website, serious game, video, TV programme, etc.). Each medium has a specific language and the creation of results for public use from 3D cultural heritage objects needs specialists who master that language. For example, a director of a video can switch from

3D rendered images to animated drawings when the reliability of the visualization of a certain object is too low. If we have, for example, insufficient data for making a reliable 3D model of a Phoenician ship, we still can show it as an animated line drawing (which also clearly conveys the message that we do not know these boats that well).

The CARARE project[13] is delivering cultural heritage objects (archaeology and monuments) to Europeana, partially in 3D. All of this 3D content does exist already but needs to go through a publishing cycle in which PDF is used for most content. Although part of the content will use 3D PDF[14] simply as a file format that can be displayed on every computer and operating system, another part will need curated objects into which 3D is integrated in a document, with links from the text or the photographs to the 3D.

Many cultural heritage objects need to be reduced in resolution or complexity to be viewable online. Practice shows that too little effort is made to preserve the original high-resolution data, while the low-resolution public version is preserved, probably because it has much more visibility.

Efforts for establishing an *implementation framework* for 3D cultural heritage objects, such as the Seville Charter need to make a much clearer distinction between these three uses, and identify the different processes that are involved. In the research phase, the focus needs to be on collaboration tools to support annotation, discussion and consensus building. In the publication phase, the focus needs to be on optimal communication, linking the argumentation to the 3D models and passing on the 3D models for further research within the cultural heritage community. In the public use phase, the focus needs to be on transferring the 3D models and their relevant paradata to communication specialists, and using the right visual language of a particular delivery medium to convey the story that is told by these cultural heritage objects.

Lack of stimuli to document and preserve

The **third issue** is how to *ensure that documentation and preservation of complex cultural heritage is made*. Practice shows that in most projects, over 90% of the work goes into the analysis and interpretation of the data, while less than 10% goes into 3D modelling and texturing. Hence, failing to document and preserve the visualization process results in the loss of at least 90% of the money invested. For research projects that receive funding, documenting the visualization process should be compulsory. Other projects within a more commercial context (for example commissioned by a museum from a company) can do the same, as most or all of the budget for 3D visualizations is public money. In other words, we need to focus today on creating regulations that make documentation and preservation of digitally born cultural heritage objects a condition for funding or commissioning.

Lack of long-term storage and digital preservation strategies

The **fourth issue** is how to *ensure that all these 3D visualizations, 3D models and their related paradata are stored for long-term use.* This issue of course deals directly with several technical preservation issues, such as the file format of the 3D models and the documentation of all related files (textures, bump maps, etc.), for which strategies are in hand. But technical preservation issues are only a part of the problem. Although universities and companies can exist for a long time, research teams and company teams are normally quite transient. This means in practice that universities or companies are not the right place to store complex cultural heritage objects. In our opinion, storage in a repository at the national level should be compulsory (see for example the ArcheoGrid repository[15] at the national level in France). Storage at such a repository should be subject to a selection and prioritization procedure on what to preserve and what to let go, to limit the cost of registration and storage. Ownership and IPR should be clear, at least at the moment of storage.

Lack of business models for re-use and exchange

The **fifth issue** is the *creation of a model for possible re-use.* It is conceivable that 3D cultural heritage objects should be available free in low-resolution to the public (for example in Europeana[16]) but can have a paid use for high-resolution versions. Museums can use and exhibit digital museum objects from other museums, digital publications can incorporate high-resolution 3D digital objects (for which royalties will be paid, just as for professional photographs today), even film companies and game developers could pay significant fees to use scientifically correct 3D models of historic buildings and objects. The V-MusT.net project[17] is developing a business model and practical implementation for exchange and re-use of digital museum objects and virtual environments.

Lack of updating methodology

Finally, the **sixth issue** is *how to keep 3D visualizations of cultural heritage objects and their related paradata up to date*. Nearly all digitized cultural heritage objects are static, as they represent the physical object as truthfully as possible. Practice shows, however, that 3D visualizations are not static at all, they are based upon sparse data, hence they change because of the availability of new research, better excavations or new insights in the use and meaning of objects. The ideal situation would be that any 3D visualization research by a certain team could be taken up by any other team that improves and complements the results of the first team. If that ideal situation were present, updating 3D visualizations would be quite a natural thing to do. However, this ideal situation is still a distant dream. We can bring that ideal situation a bit closer by dealing with all the issues described above. But there will still be an important issue of cost, as we need to balance the available resources. What is the use of documenting the finest detail of a 3D visualization project if that documentation is never used again? In other words, we still need to find out what the optimal amount of documentation and preservation should be, so that long-term overall costs are minimized. This is still uncharted territory and needs more research and practice.

Conclusions

The conclusions of this short paper are quite simple: the London Charter provides an excellent framework for the digital preservation of complex cultural heritage objects, but we need to focus now on putting the principles of the London Charter into practice.

This means that we need to collect *best practices* by analysing existing projects to find out which approaches do work and why.

This also means we need – based upon the conclusions of these best practices – to define *optimal workflows and specific requirements*, so that documentation and preservation of complex cultural heritage objects becomes an integrated part of cultural heritage practice. Crucial in this process is the definition of *quality* for the documentation, communication and preservation steps, as described above, and taking care of an appropriate balance between resources, results and the impact of those results.

Finally, we need to realize the *uptake* of such workflows and requirements, first of all by integrating them as soon as possible into the *curriculum* of students of subjects in the cultural heritage domain, such as archaeology, history, anthropology, monument care and muscology. The emergence of *Competence Centres*, such as those being established by the European projects V-MusT.net and 3D-COFORM,[18] to support cultural heritage institutions and their partners, represents another major step towards such uptake of documentation, communication and preservation strategies.

And why not look into *expanding the London Charter* with clear guidance on these processes, based upon a wide consensus in the cultural heritage domain, so that it can acquire the status of a real Charter that governs documentation, communication and preservation of digital cultural heritage objects?

Notes

1   See also Chapter 13 of this book.

2   www.londoncharter.org.

3   The London Charter in *Second Life*.

4   *Interpretation Management: how to make sustainable visualisations of the past*, EPOCH Knowhow book, http://media.digitalheritage.se/2010/07/Interpretation_Managment_TII.pdf.

5   www.epoch.eu.

6   *Interpretation Management: how to make sustainable visualisations of the past*, EPOCH Knowhow book, http://media.digitalheritage.se/2010/07/Interpretation_Managment_TII.pdf.

7   Abbey Theatre blog: http://blog.oldabbeytheatre.net. See also Chapter 13 of this book.

8   3D Visualisation of the Etruscan Regolini-Galassi tomb: http://regolinigalassi.wordpress.com.

9   Serving and Archiving Virtual Environments (SAVE): http://vwhl.clas.virginia.edu/save.html.

10   www2.cnrs.fr/en/442.htm.

11   Ni (www.nino-leiden.nl/doc/Annual Report NINO-NIT 2010_3D.pdf.

12   Presentation on 3D technologies for Cultural Heritage in 3D PDF: www.faronet.be/files/bijlagen/blog/visual_dimension_v3.pdf.

13   Connecting ARchaeology and ARchitecture in Europeana, www.carare.eu.

14   3D PDF – CARARE: http://carare.eu/eng/Resources/3D-Virtual-Reality.

15   http://archeogrid.in2p3.fr.

16   http://europeana.eu.

17   V-MusT.net Network of Excellence: http://v-must.net.

18   www.3d-coform.eu.

CHAPTER 20

In homage of change

Vicky Isley and Paul Smith

boredomresearch, National Centre for Computer Animation,
Bournemouth University, UK

Introduction

As artists we build on a heritage that extends back over millennia. However, many aspects fundamental to our practice trace their origins to the more recent detonation of the first atomic bomb at Hiroshima. The Manhattan Project was the code name for a research programme that produced the first of only two nuclear bombs ever to have been detonated in war. Significantly, it was also the first serious use of computer modelling. The natural world is a beautiful place and we humans have spent our entire history struggling with its complexity. This struggle took a massive leap forward in the years following World War 2, as the relevance of computers expanded beyond the domain of code-cracking and bomb-building to offer insight into almost every aspect of nature's wonderful mystery. Computers and computer modelling are now fundamental to our artistic practice.

Swords to ploughshares

There are many riddles of nature that are best understood through computer modelling, for example, the ability of unintelligent ants to solve complex problems such as finding the shortest route between two points. The simplicity of the rules required to solve what scientists call shortest path optimization has not only been revealed by computer modelling but has become a field of research in its own right. As we started our career, the computational tools necessary for this type of study were, for the first time, freely available to artists like ourselves. We, too, had a fascination with the complexity that exists in natural systems and were keen to find a deeper way to embrace this in our practice. We did not wish to create mere representations of the fascinating forms that exist in nature. We were moved by the way forms, behaviours and patterns come into being and appreciated how the techniques and tools, used by scientists to understand the natural world, were equally relevant to us.

In many ways our practice builds on established practices of artistic endeavour taking at its centre the observation and study of nature. However, we incorporate in all our works the power of computer modelling to go deeper than the surface image into the mechanics of nature's intricate systems. As a consequence, our art works rely on technology both for their production and display. This move from canvas to code has significant ramifications both for the creative process and the life of art works once they leave the studio. Before we struggle with the problems this adds to conservation, let us first explore the relevance of this medium to our practice.

Computational death and renewal

The diversity present in nature is staggering. In the order Lepidoptera alone, over 600 new species are discovered each year. Those who perceive the value of diversity are rightfully mindful as extinctions erode its reach. Separate from those extinctions arising from our selfish exploitation of the planet are those that form the natural process of evolution. All the diversity that currently persists is a consequence of countless annihilations in the endless competition between species. This natural process of change informs many of our art works.

With scientists we share a fascination both for the mechanisms and processes that create this rewarding diversity and for our use of computational technologies. Many of our art works model the behaviours and growth of imagined beings, which through their artificial lives explore a similar diversity to that found in nature. The artificial life-forms represent a study of a narrow facet of diversity – they live and die, with each new instance exploring a seemingly infinite range of song, colour, form and pattern. Because their ability to change is constrained, they will always look recognizably similar. Like the order Lepidoptera they present a vast amount of diversity while maintaining an overall visual consistency. Within this tiny slice of diversity there are still more possibilities than anyone could view in a lifetime.

As we view these art works we witness a process – liquid, uncertain and irresolute: a familiar process, as change is more a part of contemporary life than ever before. We understand the world not as a stable constant but as fluid, dynamic and unpredictable. We thrive on the richness and excitement change brings, pausing occasionally to worry. For there is a tension, a fear. We appreciate more than ever before the messy conflict between our accelerating pursuit of the new and anguish over its consequences. Computers allow us to place this battle at the centre of the creative process; making works that are not safe, fixed and stable but that reflect the complexity and conflict in the world around us. Significant to this approach is the move from rigidity to fluidity. Here our concern is not in maintaining what is present but allowing the freedom necessary for flux. In contrast to many art works that exist as static moments, time becomes the dimension through which the work lives and breathes. Even we, the authors, are not sure what form they will take, finding ourselves shifting from creator to spectator as we watch some unexpected event unfold.

Restless concerns

In 2005, we created our art work *Biomes* (Figure 20.1), a series of computational systems that use artificial-life algorithms to remain open to change. The life-forms in the *Biomes* use a rule-based system to form intricate patterns on their bodies. The rules are generated randomly from a vast range of possibilities so each life-form viewed is unique. We value the life this brings to the *Biomes* – adding surprise with a procession of new forms. This excites us but there is a price to pay. The more freedom we give the art works to change, the greater the chance for unexpected outcomes. We invest a lot of time testing to ensure the art works will run for extended periods without problem. We balance the reward of freedom with the risk of collapse, erring on the side of caution. Despite our every effort, complex systems can have emergent properties that, like the weather, are impossible to predict in the long term.

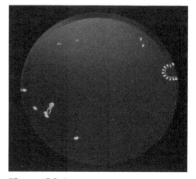

Figure 20.1
Biomes, image of the computational art work, 2005

The life-forms in the *Biomes* have natural cycles of activity, not dictated by us, but emerging from their behaviour. Normally this behaviour alternates from moderate periods of tranquillity to intense action. Time spent testing assured us this range was within bounds that would make for a rewarding experience. There was, as we later discovered, the possibility of the art work slipping into a mini ice age of inactivity. This, albeit rare, occurrence illustrates the risk of allowing independence and autonomy in an art work. Some see a fascinating and fitting expression of complexity in a lifelike system, others an undesirable bug. In the studio we are concerned with realizing the creative possibilities of fluidity; handing works over to a collector or a gallery, we are faced with the paradoxical challenge of preserving artefacts that are made to change:

> This art does no longer hold on to the safe properties of the final object, the ultimate manifestation of a creative process. In its production, it responds to the major shift from an industrial culture based on the concept of the final product to a post-industrial, networked culture. It explores the variety of form and behaviour of systems and objects without limiting itself to the rules of an art market that favours the single specimen. Becoming more work-in-progress than finalized matter, this art bears the possibility of the infinite series, of the unfinished and open-ended oeuvre.
>
> Jaschko and Evers (2010)

The dynamic nature of this work fidgets nervously in the quiet of the unchanging gallery. Presenting art works within this context allows us as viewers to perceive the works as stable. The clinical white space, like the inside of a refrigeration unit, reassures us that its contents are safely preserved. This image is misleading – things change, varnish yellows, inks fade, paper oxidizes. Change, but all beyond the casual perception of the viewer. In contrast, the sign apologizing that a digital exhibit is temporarily out of order also begs pardon for rupturing this sense of stability. A computer's hard drive does not fade or yellow, it dies – sudden, abrupt, blank. Having worked with a public collection, we are fully aware of the activity beyond the viewable galleries, ensuring the public enter an exhibition where everything seems ordered, fixed and permanent. How do we rationalize these two conflicting worlds? Do we ensure that works are made to accommodate the desire to preserve or do collections embrace the nature of change and variance? Is the frozen gallery no longer relevant in our frenetic changing world?

Time is the devil

David Hancock, chief of the Hitachi Corporation's portable computer division, drove his team with the slogan 'Speed is God, and time is the devil'. Software product cycles, already short at eighteen months to two years, have begun to evaporate. Instead of distinct, tested, shrink-wrapped versions of software, manufacturers distribute upgrades and patches that change within months or even days.

Gleick (1999)

As we type this quote, another Java update beckons us from the task bar, reminding us that we are out of date again. We often wonder how many developers are pounding away at their keyboards in order to produce such an unrelenting stream of revisions. Does this affect the expectations of those commissioning, purchasing and exhibiting digital art? The pressure to make work robust enough to survive beyond the studio boils over in the last moments before an exhibition deadline, as we endeavour to resolve any last moment glitches. But is this work finished or the first release, Beta 0.0.1? In addition to facing the same challenges as the software industry we also need to interface with the established arts institutions. Do they imagine we, too, have a team of developers, working on update after update? The speed, at which the wheels of technology spin, does little to ease our hurry sickness as we struggle to keep up. Product cycles are equally nauseating as they rush out new hardware models, bigger, better, faster. A specific monitor or motherboard may no longer be commercially available before the work has even left our studio. What about spares and repairs? Some of our art works have already outlived the natural life of their computer hosts. In the intervening years the shifting sands of software and hardware have added complexities to this problem. In almost all other commercial situations, revisions and upgrades are produced to support the latest hardware. In the art world it is normal practice for public collections to trawl eBay, hunting down and archiving an ever-diminishing stock of redundant technology to preserve hardware-dependent art. Surely this can only delay the inevitable? Even so, we can increase the longevity of software art, as we learnt with one of our early computational art works, *System 1.6* (see Figure 20.2). This generative animation creates its own sound score through the interactions of a large number of digital creatures.

To achieve fluidity in this art work, we had to optimize, cut corners and find compromises; pushing the boundaries of what was possible on the chosen platform and hardware. In our attempt to squeeze every last cycle from the processor, we set everything to run as fast as possible. This was a race we could not win. Within a couple of years technology thundered past. Appearing from the dust cloud left in its wake were our creatures, whizzing about manically at supersonic speeds far beyond our intention. This simple blunder, easily corrected with a single line of code, reminds

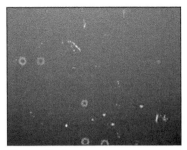

Figure 20.2
System 1.6, a detail from a screen grab of the computational software, 2001

us we are not the only authors of change. We have to follow good programming practice to ensure the future of our work, if not for future generations at least for future presentations.

We are not the first to make this mistake. In his book *In Praise of Slow*, Carl Honoré talks of a small group of musicians who think we play classical music too fast. Many of these rebels belong to a movement called Tempo Giusto. They believe that at the start of the Industrial Revolution, musicians started speeding up with the accelerating pace of life. Speed and dexterity of virtuoso performers gave them the edge, but resulted in a gradual acceleration. Many believe works of composers like Beethoven are now played too fast:

> But surely the great composers laid down what they considered the 'right' tempo for their music? Well, not exactly. Many left behind no tempo markings at all. Almost all the instructions we have for the works of Bach were added by pupils and scholars after his death. By the nineteenth century, most composers denoted tempo with Italian words such as presto, adagio and lento – all of which are open to interpretation.
>
> Honoré (2004)

Some feel even if these works should be played slower, doing so is pointless, as we are geared up to experience life at an accelerated pace. Slowing down would simply make them lose relevance. Considering the fluid adaptable nature of digital art, to what extent should we honour the author's original intentions? Is it acceptable for future audiences to tinker with the tempo, finding what feels right to them?

Disentangling the art from the architecture

In the same way that recordings of musical performances provide additional documentation, video documentation of computational works could likewise help. However, as these works change and morph, never repeating, this only captures how the work once appeared rather than how it should be. Contrary to increasing the clarity of documentation, we have grown comfortable with the intrinsically plastic nature of the medium. Over time, we have increased the number of preferences, allowing flexibility after authoring, after the point at which convention encourages us to see the work as finished, correct and definite. On many occasions we have been unable to resist temptation, opening and fiddling with these parameters. In order to preserve work of this nature one must disentangle the definite from the malleable.

Not only do we wish to leave some aspects of our art work free and unbound, the very nature of the medium makes it impossible to cement the visible expression of the work. Lurking in the shadowy corners there is a deceit which we will explore through our art work *Lost Calls of Cloud Mountain Whirligigs* (Figure 20.3).

The whirligigs are imaginary beings that inhabit the peaks of a craggy mountain. They swish their long plume-like tails as they propel themselves around their world with intricately patterned propellers. Tired, the whirligigs come in to roost, extending a single arm to grab wires that span the view. From these wires they hang and rest, occasionally singing their melancholy songs, with chirps that emit puffs of luminous smoke. Curling tails tightly around their bodies, they slip into a deep sleep, replenishing spent energy. This is what a viewer sees but it is not the work. In the same way as the nuclear detonation modelled during the Manhattan Project is separate from the bomb that explodes and destroys, a viewer of *Lost Calls of Cloud Mountain Whirligigs* sees an expression of the work made by a machine – a reflection or mirage that has the potential to distort. The whirligigs we made are abstract in the form of a computer model. Everything they can and will do is a product of this description – absolute, precise, even though the expression itself can be complex, messy and unpredictable. Each whirligig has values embodying every aspect of its being. Anything not represented by a discrete symbol does not exist. One number represents how much its tail is curled, another, how much it should be curled. Every cycle the tail's actual curl is adjusted by 0.125 times the difference between these values. Never more, never less. Every grain of a whirligig being is manipulated using the same

Figure 20.3 *Lost Calls of Cloud Mountain Whirligigs* (view left and right), a screen grab from the computational art work, 2010

maths we all learnt at school. The order in which these manipulations take place is described by the model with inexorable precision.

At the level of the model the art work is the ideal object for conservation, its abstraction allowing the freedom to move from one programming language to another, or even escaping the computer in favour of paper and pen. After all, the term 'computer' used to be a job description before it became a machine. Depending on ability, it might take days to compute one small moment in time, but it could be done.

A haze develops as we follow the whirligigs on the path from model to screen. Definition is lost between the model and its sustaining software and hardware. At their creation, whirligig body parts are assembled from libraries of images. These source images share the stability of all digital imagery, being easily moved between formats without change. However, when we composite them into new and unique versions we employ algorithms not described by us. The fog thickens as authorship is shared. These algorithms are part of the open-source environment in which we make the work. We could look under the hood to see how each pixel is manipulated. Unperturbed, let us carry on, for you will see nothing unless our whirligigs appear on screen. We calculate locations, rotations and scales until all is ready. Now vanishing in the fog, our atomized whirligigs have their numbers crunched and munched by a library interfacing with the graphics card. Here we lose all sight until, by magic, they materialize on screen. As we make art works like *Lost Calls of Cloud Mountain Whirligigs*, we shift back and forth between the model and its expression created by the graphics card. Even we forget to maintain a healthy distinction between them. The model depends on this supporting software and hardware to come alive but can also be separated, uncoupled and transplanted into a new body.

Exploring the possibility of re-authoring one of our early art works on a different platform, we noticed an improvement to the rendering quality. The model translated without change but its representation on screen was subtly different. The spinning flowers present in the art work appeared smoother, more delicate. This was due to the platforms using different rendering engines – the former DirectX and the later OpenGL. Although fundamentally the same, this small shift in appearance reinforces the separation between model and visible manifestation. How far beyond the bounds of the model must we go to preserve that which is quintessential to a computational art work?

In order for custody of a work to have true value, a greater range and depth of material should be included with diminished significance given to the compiled software. We feel that the art work is embodied in the source code, extending beyond the model written by us, to encompass the platform and libraries employed. Our departure from Macromedia Director, the platform used to make our early works, was impelled by the restrictiveness of the licence and black-box concealment of its inner workings. This obstruction prevented us from passing this crucial component of the work into the care of a collection. We now opt for open-source platforms allowing us to include not only the compiled software but also more importantly the source code for the work, its platform and supporting libraries.

Emancipation

We would like to foster an appreciation, less centred on the tangible fixed and final. In the same way that it would be madness to conserve a piece of music by keeping the performer alive, it must surely be equally foolish to rely on archiving and preserving hardware in order to maintain digital art works. However, artists must carefully consider the extent of material required by a collection, enabling them to embrace effectively the challenges of translating software art for future technologies.

What we need is a new perspective if we are to relax and enjoy the potentials of this exciting medium. We hope here to encourage emancipation from our obsession with the fixed tangible object, that which is traditionally favoured by collectors. In preference, we suggest a philosophy that accepts the complex interrelationships between myriad providers of software and hardware – one that appreciates change as a vital component of life. Hardware like our mortal selves will die but ideas expressed in code that is open and visible can pass uninhibited through successive technologies, like culture, flowing through the generations.

Acknowledgements

National Centre for Computer Animation, Bournemouth University, UK; Arts Council of England; DAM Gallery, Berlin. All images courtesy of boredomresearch and DAM Gallery, Berlin.

References

Gleick, J. (1999) *Faster: the acceleration of just about everything*, London, Little, Brown and Company.

Honoré, C. (2004) *In Praise of Slow : how a worldwide movement is challenging the cult of speed*, London, Orion Books.

Jaschko, S. and Evers, L. (2010) *Process as Paradigm: art in development, flux and change*, Gijón, Spain, LABoral Centro de Arte y Creación Industrial.

CHAPTER 21

Archiving software and content in visual film effects: an insider's perspective

Paul Charisse

School of Creative Technologies,
University of Portsmouth, UK

Introduction

The commercial world of feature film computer graphics exists on the frontiers of new technology. In an industry that can make or lose tens of millions of dollars in an afternoon (*Harry Potter and the Deathly Hallows* took US$91,071,119 on its opening day) the quality and implementation of its cutting-edge visual technology matters. Since the inception of computer graphics in the movie industry, with films such as *Tron* and the *Last Star Fighter*, Hollywood, particularly with the summer blockbuster, has come to rely on the emerging technology of computer graphics as a way to make ever more visually extravagant eye candy, keeping the public hooked on escaping to places that were once the preserve of the avid bookworm.

These graphical toys give the director the ability to create previously unseen worlds. It was only possible, for example, to undertake a complete film adaptation of the epic *Lord of The Rings* once graphical technology had advanced to the level where it could try to match the imagined visual richness of the books, creating a creature like Gollum, fully realized with all his mannerisms, or giant winged serpents battling with mythical armies on a scale not even Cecil B. DeMille would have contemplated.

The profit motive

In modern movie-making, profit margins drive everything. This gives rise to immense pressure to produce the best, most visually stunning graphics. Visual effects studios are in a constant cycle, bidding against one another to secure work, promising higher and higher quality for shorter and shorter production periods, while trying to balance out the age-old struggles between time, quality and expense. At the forefront of this is the graphical tools and software innovations that give visual effects companies and the films they serve the visual and financial edge at the box office. Where it was once enough to have the presence of Liz Taylor or Fred Astaire sell your film, now, in what might reasonably be thought of as an infantilized post-*Star Wars* film market, films also need all the bells and whistles of a fully realized fantastical world; *Transformers* without any skyscraping robots or Roland Emmerich's apocalyptic *2012* without a collapsing Manhattan would have been left with little more than a predictable plot held together with merchandizing tie-ins, a string of stereotypes and a collection of unmemorable one-liners.[1]

Archiving in a competitive environment

So in this culture of competiveness, with the constant need to produce the biggest and best, how are these emerging technologies to be archived? The very nature of cutting-edge technologies dictates that they are in a constant state of flux. It is not just the content created that changes, it is the software that creates them and the environments and practices within which the software operates. As the whole process is driven by money, there would need to be a financial imperative for the VFX (visual effects) companies to archive their own software materials. There isn't, indeed quite the reverse. As with all aspects of capitalism, renewal and improvement is the bottom line. Things have to get better to continue to be productive. So there is little or no incentive to keep software or techniques that are outdated and of no further financial value.

There is another problem, also resulting from the economic aspects of production, and that is ownership. As mentioned earlier, the visual effects companies compete for work; owing to the massive scale of modern features film they often end up working on the same titles. As they are still essentially competing companies, the level of collaboration and sharing of assets can differ from production to production. I have worked on a film where the same assets where created twice (for twice the cost) by two companies working on the same shot. This is still standard practice on some productions. As it's imperative for companies that they don't let their rivals get the edge over them by copying their technologies, a culture of secrecy has become the norm. This is clearly not unique to the movie business, as it's a necessity in all commercial sectors that rely on technological innovations to have the edge over their competitors. So on a practical level, getting hold of things to archive would be problematic, as by the time a company would be happy to release work into the public domain, it is unlikely they would still have it all in a useful coherent form. I have known companies to use software methods to ensure work would not be usable beyond the facility, for all the reasons mentioned above.

A well known company I worked for took a uniquely physical approach to protecting its data: as this was before the internet could realistically accommodate large transfers of data from personal users, the only way to take work off-site was by cutting it onto a CD. However, the company had removed all the CD drives from the artists' computers, meaning that the only way to remove work was with a floppy disk. This meant, for those desperate to get showreel material out to secure work after the film had wrapped, a lot of late nights accompanied by a very large box of floppy disks and a suspiciously long coat!

In addition to the actual software and tools used on a production, which are generally either owned by the VFX company or the third-party software provider, the actual film assets, the images and designs used in the film are owned by the film production company. Film companies are notoriously protective over their property and the legal web of intellectual and property copyright issues that surround this content would possibly provide the biggest challenge of all to archiving materials.

Bespoke solutions and the chaos of production

There is another more fundamental and technical issue in archiving VFX work, arising from the level of complexity and the constantly evolving nature of the VFX software pipeline. Methods employed on one film may be improved for a subsequent film; a piece of software may be rewritten, or a new team member might arrive, bringing with them a different approach. As VFX is basically bespoke problem-solving, this dynamism is at the very core of the process. In the chaos of production the only thing that matters is finishing the work for the client. It's unlikely that these constantly evolving processes could be documented effectively during the production, and it would require a sustained effort to interview all the people involved afterwards. Even then, the actual software is likely to have evolved. Even if the software was retained, a complete history of all its interdependent software and methodologies would be required to effectively archive it as a usable technology. As companies often write their own software, as well as augment existing packages, the correct versions of all the individual pieces of software would be required just to open the file.

The numbers of assets required for a particular shot on a particular film mean that a system called 'instancing' is used on many productions. Multiple assets are called from multiple locations and loaded onto a local computer. An example of this might be a file that an animator is using to create a giant battle with hundreds of different creatures. For the animator to animate these creatures he will need separate items such as a rig (a computerized puppet to animate with), a model of the creature, and a model of the film set. These items are all loaded onto his local machine for him to work on, but when the file is saved, only the address of the assets used and the information relating to how the assets are employed are recorded, not the actual assets themselves. With the advent of Cloud computing and the increasing speed of the internet, there is good reason to believe that this method of working will become more prevalent, and more complex to deconstruct. This means post-production collation of actual assets into one readily archival form will become increasing difficult, if not impossible.

Third-party software producers

Third-party producers of commercially available VFX software also present a problem. Many of these companies have historically had a bad record in supporting old files, as the majority of people, certainly in the consumer market, rarely need to work with them, so there is no financial imperative to support them. A recent example is Apple's Final Cut Pro, which has announced it has stopped supporting all previous versions:

> While Apple's bold decisions on hardware and software design usually pay off, in the audio/visual market where things move a little more slowly, rapid changes such as Apple's decision to discontinue support for previous Final Cut Pro file formats was not welcome.'[2]

3D packages such as Maya, XSI and 3ds Max do support previous versions of work, but again there are often interdependencies specific to the asset (for example the images loaded in to texture a model or a third-party plug-in which adds a feature such as hair) or occasionally deeper aspects of the core software platform.

Often specific software updates in the newer versions will make an old file crash or not even load, and supporting these problems is not always at the top of the list for the software providers. I have, on more than one occasion, witnessed the chaos resulting from updating to newer version of software midway through a production.

Conclusion

Archiving VFX software, content and methods provides a massive challenge. The economic factors that restrict the release of content and the complexities of an ever-evolving technology, constantly in a state of flux, mean that archivists are going to have come up with some very creative solutions to keep a record for future generations. There is, in all likelihood, the possibility that much of what has been achieved in software and development for films in the last 20 years will exist only as shadows in the present iterations of the technology, recollections of those who have worked on them and in the final finished film prints. The assets and software themselves have long since been overwritten by newer, shinier and more realistic 1s and 0s.

Notes

1 *Transformers* made US$29.5 million in its first weekend. *2012* grossed US$65,237,614 on its first weekend.

2 *The Inquirer*, © Incisive Media Investments Limited, 2012, www.theinquirer.net/inquirer/news/2106316/apple-quietly-sells-version-final-cut-pro.

CHAPTER 22

Preserving interaction

Daisy Abbott
Digital Design Studio,
Glasgow School of Art, UK

Introduction

As early as 1992, Brenda Laurel noted that the operation of computers is a performative activity (Laurel, 1993). The use of digital technologies to create interactive and immersive art works is continually increasing as hardware and software becomes more available and affordable to artists and the conceptual and aesthetic opportunities offered by digital media continue to inspire. Interaction with technology is the virtual and conceptual equivalent of a man walking across Peter Brook's famous 'empty space' (Brook, 1968) and is both performative and ephemeral. In terms of their inherent characteristics, digital arts are very similar to performing arts: artistic experiences that are manifested physically yet do not rely on a static materiality to communicate meaning or emotion, that have a life beyond the moment of their enactment, and that, crucially, require active interpretation and interaction. As such, it is useful to consider interactive art works through a dramaturgical framework and to draw parallels between their similar challenges for documentation and curation and the preservation of these art forms into the future.

Interaction as performance

Like the performing arts, interactive art works are characterized by **ephemerality, variability,** and an individual and two-way mode of perception that defines their **interactivity**.

Ephemerality refers to time-based enactment and the audiences' experiences of it. Any live or interactive work of art is irreproducible; each experience is unique and cannot be replicated in another space or time, even if both the work's author and the audience/user (or 'spect-actor', to borrow a term from Augusto Boal's Forum Theatre) wishes it.

Variability refers to the separation of the concept of the artistic work from the physicality of its manifestation. Just as there have been many thousands of performances of *A Midsummer Night's Dream* with different casts, sets and even texts (not one of which can be considered to be the 'original' or definitive performance), the core of software art is typically much more about what it does rather than what it is made out of. Function has primacy over material; performance and behaviours are more important than format. This reinforces the idea of art as being something you *do*, not something you *make*.[1]

Interactivity is about a mode of perception that leads to active influence on the art work. While multiple interpretations of a 'static' art work such as a film or painting are certainly possible, the art work itself remains unchanged by these interpretations. Software art often moves the interpretation of meaning outside the mind of the spect-actor and incorporates it as an inherent part of the enactment of the work, with the work itself changing and adapting to user inputs. Depending on the design of the art work and the technological framework surrounding its delivery, interaction may be crucial to the aesthetics and semantics of the work, or a much more subtle influence. Furthermore, both performance and interactive art are shaped by the audience's tacit knowledge, hidden decisions and learned behaviours (for example clapping or double-clicking). In fact, interaction itself is a performative activity, requiring an audience to willingly suspend their disbelief (deliberately ignoring the technology of the proscenium or computer screen) in order to engage with the work in an active and rewarding way. One of the principal goals of interactive art works is to motivate the audience to take action (Utvich, 2004, 225).

Interactive art, therefore cannot be defined as discrete objects – the type of computer monitor or a text file containing the code – but as an 'arrangement of possibilities' or 'sum of possible narratives' (Grau, 2003, 205); their ephemeral and malleable nature becomes a deliberate feature of the art work. The work becomes less about delivering a particular message and instead about creating a system of communication:

Ultimately the creative process itself becomes an open-ended work: production and reception merge into a single, mutually conditioning cycle.

Hagebölling (2004, 16)

As the framework of the artistic experience, software develops these characteristics further than much of live performance, as it can offer a non-linear or segmented, hypermedial experience, often requiring further competencies from spect-actors such as navigation, decision-making and individual action. The form or narrative of the work may only develop through incremental actions by users, based on individual motivations or by other interactive inputs such as live datastreams. It is at these points of interaction that the dramaturgical design of the work becomes most clear. Furthermore, as dramaturgy is a formative, aesthetic and communicative lens, and above all creates the overall experience for the audience (Hagebölling, 2004, 9), it is useful to apply this framework when considering the design of interactive art works.

Interactive works can also add further layers of narrative and aesthetic complication when making use of networks which can overlay spaces (e.g. two remote users occupying the same virtual space, or a mixture of physical and virtual space), time (e.g. replaying the effect of an interaction long after the user has gone), and identities (e.g. when a user takes on a different character in order to engage more fully with the work). Of course, it is these very characteristics and complexities that make documentation and curation of both performance and interactive media art works so challenging:

Only fixed artworks are able to preserve ideas and concepts enduringly . . . an open work, which is dependent on interaction with a contemporary audience, or its advanced variant that follows game theory – the work is postulated as a game and the observers, according to the 'degrees of freedom', as players – effectively means that images lose their capability to be historical memory and testimony. In its stead, there is a durable technical system as framework and transient, arbitrary, non-reproducible, and infinitely manipulable images. The work of art as a discrete object disappears.

Grau (2003, 207)

Complexities of interaction and documentation challenges

Spect-actors experience interactive works through a two-way, iterative process of reception, interpretation and action. Interactions themselves are extremely problematic to document, as they are typically based on a decision made within the user's brain and while techniques exist for documenting the interactions themselves (for example recording mouse clicks, data input, tracking eye movements, or even full body motion capture within 3D environments), they are time-consuming and expensive. Furthermore, it is more difficult to capture the user's intent: why a particular action was undertaken and what sparked that decision. The alternative is to embrace qualitative, subjective methods of capturing tacit knowledge, opinions and intent such as conducting feedback interviews with spect-actors, but this is similarly resource-intensive. Each approach has its own challenges and demands from even the most expert of documenters and the choice of approach (or balance between multiple methods), preparation and resources required are all factors which need to be considered well in advance.

As well as the fine detail of audience–user interactions such as the examples mentioned above, it is useful to consider an overview of the entire experience that spect-actors have with software art. The concept of **trajectories** has emerged in recent human–computer interaction (HCI) research into interactive applications. A trajectory through an art work is the whole user experience, the 'narrative' of the work as defined jointly by the work itself and its interfaces, and spect-actor knowledge and choices. Mapping these trajectories of interaction and the reasons why the experience unfolded as it did (i.e. the dramaturgy of the interactive experience) is, again, a serious challenge for documenters.

Trajectories are, of course, partially defined by the works and their creative and technological framework: 'journeys are steered by the participants, but are also shaped by narratives that are embedded into spatial, temporal and performative structures by authors' (Benford et al., 2009, 712). A user can be manipulated into moving at a particular speed through the arrangement of possibilities open to them or even forced to engage with certain elements of the work at certain times (for example, pre-timed events which do not rely on user action to occur). Designing how much free exploration of the work an audience can undertake is, of course, part of the process of creating any interactive experience. Trajectories can be applied to spatial and temporal experience, as well as the shifting roles and identities of the spect-actors. For example, a visitor to a gallery could spend some time watching another visitor interacting with a work before making the decision to directly interact herself, using knowledge built through this observation and in turn creating an effect on other spect-actors (Benford et al., 2005). Many art works are designed to deliberately encourage this type of passive engagement – and the documentation of these effects adds yet another layer of complexity on understanding these works.

Typically, the creator of an interactive work will have an 'ideal' trajectory in mind for participants: a starting point, an end point which allows the spect-actors to disengage, some experiential goals, and an expected time-range for the process of interacting. Spect-actors can diverge (in space, time or type of engagement) from the expected path and the creator could choose to encourage divergence or encourage (or even force) them to re-converge, using a variety of dramaturgical or technological techniques built into the interaction design of the software framework.

Defining the essence of interactive works

After centuries of the development of knowledge of conservation sciences, it is easy to fall into the trap of treating the curation of interactive art works as similar to that of other pieces of art. In archival terminology, a curated painting must have both authenticity (i.e. it is what it purports to be) and integrity (i.e. it still communicates the basic 'essence' of the original art work). However, given the inherent variability of software art installations – and the fact that often the essence of the art work itself exists wholly outside tangible objects – this object-based approach cannot possibly preserve interactivity. Simply put, there is no single 'authentic' version of a work. Attempts to store interactive works as authoritative, static, self-contained objects that are anything other than examples of the framework of possibilities set out by the software are doomed to failure:

> The idea of capturing a static snapshot as a faithful (or even reasonable) representation is somewhat incongruous. Moreover the possibility that one viewpoint or interpretation could be valued over others and presented as the single authoritative account by virtue of being archived is strongly opposed.
>
> Abbott, Jones and Ross (2008, 83–4)

Therefore, the question becomes: how then can we define (and communicate to future audiences) the essence of interactive works? The essence of an interactive work is defined by both the artistic intent of the creator and the implementation of that intent: its physical or ephemeral manifestation. It may rely on physical objects but is not those objects. It may rely on interactions from human users or technological actors (e.g. underlying operating systems) but is not those interactions.

Interactions lead to inherent variability at the level of the manifestation of the art work which must be somehow captured and represented – or at the very least acknowledged – in curation efforts, but too much variability in representations may lead to a loss of coherency and therefore reduce the integrity of the curated work. As well as in its ephemeral manifestation, part of the essence of interactive art work lies in its trajectories of user experience. Appraising what aspects of user experience to capture to most accurately represent the core essence of the work is a very skilled documentation task. Furthermore, there are interactions that can affect the aesthetics or function of software art that are not defined by human actors. Machine interpretation of, for example, a section of code is more easily defined, predicted and repeated than that of human actors, and as such the technical and procedural aspects of curating software art can occlude the other aspects of a work's integrity: its core essence. Again, there is a danger of relying on the heritage of conservation studies and fixating on the curation of the more manageable, tangible and static aspects of the work at the expense of the more difficult (and resource-intensive) but more meaningful representations.

Automated interactions can raise other important issues. For example, *System 1.6*, a work created by boredomresearch,[2] showed sprites moving around a monitor screen. The speed of the movements was an important aspect of the work's visual and sonic aesthetic and at the time was limited by the graphical processing power of the technologies used, so in terms of coding the sprites' behaviour instructions were to move 'as fast as possible'. Enactments of the curated version, however, have much greater underlying processing power, which results in increased speed described by the creators as 'comedic' and 'manic' (Smith and Isley, 2011). The lack of hard-coded behaviour leads, therefore, to a *reduction* in the integrity of the curated work over time: too much variability. This raises the potentially controversial issue of whether curators should make changes to the components of an interactive work in order to preserve, as best they can, its artistic essence. If behaviour is more important than material and function/interaction has primacy over the code, should a curator edit the original code to enforce a maximum speed closer to the first manifestations of this art work? Other interactive works draw in external interactions which form an intrinsic part of their essence, for example data from the internet, gallery environment or specialist data feeds. Is it necessary to record these datastreams alongside other representations of the work (and perhaps to document how the data interacts with the framework to produce a particular manifestation observed in, say, a video recording)? Or is it enough to simply acknowledge the fact that data form an inherent ingredient of the work? A particularly important scenario is when an art work collects data from user interactions as it runs, each user's interactions feeding into future experiences and adding to the overall art work. When user influence is crucial not only to their individual experience but is captured and accumulates as an inherent part of the work, questions are raised about not only the 'richest' version of the work (e.g. is the last enactment any more valid than all those that came before it, as it benefits from the accumulated interaction data of previous instantiations?) but also of authorship and ownership.

One final issue of how to define and document the essence of interactive works is the relationship between single works and the whole body of work produced by a particular artist, group or institution. Interactive behaviours can evolve and be learned over one or multiple instantiations, changing user trajectories both within one art work and over several pieces by the same creator. Spect-actors integrating knowledge of specific control mechanisms to achieve particular interactions can be clearly observed in computer games and their sequels, but from the perspective of the user can be hard to identify – in fact these learned behaviours can seem so natural to users with previous experience that they are baffled when new users demonstrate a lack of interaction knowledge. Given that creators of interactive art are, almost by definition, 'expert' users of their own interactive frameworks, there could be a risk that over-assumption of the mechanics of interaction in their audiences leads to unintended user trajectories, which may well occlude the intended artistic experience. While the dramaturgy of the experience is a core concern for most software artists, not all are, or wish to be, expert interaction designers in terms of specific input/output mechanisms. One danger of removing an individual work from its context in the artist's body of work is a failure to acknowledge that this act could inherently change the modes of interaction an audience has with the work.

So, capturing interaction is a task which requires high levels of skill and understanding in both the artistic and curatorial domains in order to document both intent and manifestation of a work, avoid misrepresentation, reflect variability and adaptation over time, and acknowledge variation in human and machine behaviours. The essence of the interactive work may exist simultaneously in multiple layers of reality: a live gallery space, a virtual space, and a networked or conceptual environment. These challenges lead to an incredible burden of documentation and uncertainty about who (if anyone) has the responsibility for ensuring the integrity of interaction is preserved.

Strategies for approaching documentation

Research into digital representations of various types of live art works has shown that academic researchers value documentation about the process of creating art works as highly as documentation of the work itself (Abbott and Beer, 2006, 31–2). Neither performance and interactive art ever reach a state of completion: both are open-ended creative endeavours, experienced uniquely, and continually being re-formed as part of an ongoing creative process. The decisions of the creators in setting up these works are as critical to inform future understanding, as are the decisions of the participants who shape the work on each instantiation. Museums and galleries have understandably struggled with the curatorial strategies necessary to create collections of media or interactive art works at both a conceptual and a practical level (Grau, 2003). Therefore, the preservation of these art forms has been neglected until relatively recently, and even if communities are actively embracing the conceptual challenges, there are still financial and organizational issues to overcome.

Simply put, it is impossible to capture every aspect of an interactive work. This means that creative and interpretative choices are a necessity in order to appraise the art work and define which of its many facets are the most important (or the most representative), while working within the confines of the time, money and expertise available for documentation and curation. This process of realistic appraisal is one that demands a deep understanding of the work, and is arguably best performed by the creating artist, although it is noted that the perspective of someone without close ties to the work can be exceptionally useful in helping to define how best to capture particular elements. Appraisal is itself a time-consuming task; therefore a useful strategy for managing documentation is to define the drivers for documentation, and choose on which to focus curation efforts. Some common drivers and the questions that surround them are outlined below:

1 **Preserving the essence of the work:** a major driver is to preserve the integrity of the art work over time. Issues here include how the artist wishes the work to be preserved and what is the most 'accurate' way in which it can be captured (which may sometimes conflict), which (if any) stage is the most important (e.g. process of creation, live enactment, subsequent interpretation), behaviours and aesthetics, and context, including place and significance in the artist's wider practice and society in general. Recording one instantiation of interaction could be vital, as could suggesting how the work 'might have been'.

2 **Establishing rights and permissions for re-use and curation:** clear statements of intent about if and how the artist wishes the work to be re-used in the future, and what rights a curator may have to make changes in order to preserve the work.

3 **Enabling reconstruction or adaptation:** might include near or far future enactments, or instructions for installing the art work in another physical or virtual space, or by another artist. What are the crucial/desired/irrelevant elements of the work and what information must be recorded to facilitate reconstructions? The desire or need to collaborate with other artists or technologists is a major driver (e.g. providing clear comments in software code to allow other people to understand it).

4 **Extending the reach of the work:** good documentation can be used as a research tool, even if the work is itself not re-enacted. This driver encourages the production of high-quality documentation that would significantly help a curator. It can even be seen as useful to introduce new creative elements into representation that are a 'surrogate' for the type of interaction experienced in the work, although artists must be aware of the limitations of documentation (cf. Gray, 2008, 414).

5 **Increasing reputation and facilitating further work:** a major driver for artists is to have a collection of past work on which to draw in ongoing practice and also to demonstrate their particular skills and

artistic concerns. Attracting funding for further work is another major driver and relies not only on presenting a portfolio seen to be valuable by the funders, but potentially on documentation which helps to validate previous work, such as project reports and budgets. In addition, re-usability of elements of the work (e.g. a section of source code) can be of particular importance to save the artist time in the future.

As can be clearly seen from the examples above, adequate documentation must be an ongoing process, throughout all stages of the creation, instantiation, interpretation and even curation of an interactive work. Documentation is not a task that can be left until the 'completion' of a work or installation. Commenting code is an ongoing task, not something that is easy or useful to undertake several months later, and retroactive documentation is in many cases simply impossible; if preparations are not made in advance to capture, for example, users' behaviours and reactions when interacting, this information is gone forever. Therefore, a useful strategy is to give thought not only to the most important drivers for documentation well ahead of time, but also how to plan the timeline of creative documentation decisions: when will particular elements be recorded, collected or reflected on; who can/will take on the task; who will be responsible for storing (and possibly adding metadata to) the documents; are there any skill gaps for desired evidence collection; how will each documentation decision relate to the overall representation of the work and its context?

Another critical element of documentation is to increase the value of representations by striving for **transparency** in the creative decision-making related to appraisal and documentation processes. In the same way that a file format migration would be recorded as part of digital preservation, transparency of more subjective curatorial choices is not only necessary to demonstrate or validate some level of archival authenticity for curated works, it also helps to illuminate the curation process, which can only be valuable in bringing different communities of expertise to a shared understanding.

In a situation where there is an almost infinite amount of information that could be collected, the strategies above will help artists and curators to analyse and prioritize those aspects which will be most meaningful in the preservation of interactive art. As our understanding of the critical issues in this domain grows, so does the opportunity to create higher-quality representations with greater long-term value. Nevertheless the issue remains that documentation of interaction is a considerable drain on the resources of artists and curators alike. The first step therefore should always be to investigate ways of *sharing the burden* and to maximize use of existing work, resources, services, methodologies and expertise in this field.

Researchers into interaction design have identified a notable gap in the techniques, tools and expertise to assist documenters in capturing and preserving interactive works (Benford et al., 2009, 717). However, recently developed tools and techniques are opening up those areas which have been neglected by a 'traditional' understanding of archiving works and addressing notions such as the documentation of process; collaborative, shared or networked art works; and multiple intents, interpretation and user experiences. For example, the Media Art Notation System offers a conceptual model similar to that of a musical score, that is, a non-prescriptive, structured set of information about works, which explicitly allows for multiple subjective interpretations (Rinehart, 2007). Furthermore, the development of holistic, high-level curation strategies in recent years, such as the Digital Curation Centre's Curation Lifecycle Model (Higgins, 2008), offers a structured approach which is more appropriate to open-ended works such as performance and interactive art works. The explicit acknowledgement of an ongoing cycle of curation which includes elements of transformation[3] is particularly useful for addressing the challenges of work in this domain.

Several national initiatives in the UK offer resources designed to reduce the burden of documentation and curation for practising artists and much of the information provided could be extremely useful for planning and achieving efficient and high-quality documentation processes. The resources available range from the highly technical (e.g. file formats and standards, registries of representation information) to general best-practice guides, case studies and briefing papers aimed at non-experts. There is also a range of templates for planning documentation and preservation (e.g. data management plans, usage rights declarations).[4]

Finally, the DOCAM (Documentation and Conservation of the Media Arts Heritage) Research Alliance has a series of research outputs and practical resources aimed specifically at the documentation and conservation of media arts heritage. They span cataloguing, conservation, the history of relevant technologies and a complete documentation model based on the whole lifecycle of an art work. These resources are an excellent starting point for planning the best possible ways in which to preserve interactive works.

Conclusion

Documentation of interaction, whether 'real' or virtual, can be difficult, time-consuming and expensive, often leading to the production of data that is just as complex as the art work itself. It is crucial to have a clear and realistic strategy for producing appropriate, accurate and evocative representations of interactions within art works and their relationship to the aesthetics, form, function and context of the overall work. Professional artists and curators have different skills and knowledge and must work together on this challenging task with a clear understanding of both the reasons for producing documentation, and the creative decision-making that underlies the entire process. Creating an interactive art work is an open-ended activity and includes documentation strategies within it. To successfully open up the possibilities for future interpretation, re-use and preservation of interactive works, artists and curators alike should be familiar with both the intellectual and the practical challenges of documentation, as well as the existing methodologies and resources that can be used to produce the best possible outcome.

Notes

1   Cf. Richard Rinehart, Artworks as Variability Machines, and Simon Biggs, Make or Break? Concerning the value of redundancy as a creative strategy, presentations at the *Preservation of Complex Objects Symposium* (Software Art, Glasgow, 11–12 October 2011), www.pocos.org/index.php/pocos-symposia/software-art. Variability is discussed more fully in Rinehart's forthcoming book (Rinehart and Ippolito, *New Media and Social Memory*).

2   www.boredomresearch.net/system16.html. Presentation available online at http://vimeo.com/31447537 (accessed 16 November 2011). See also Chapter 20 of this book.

3   Cf. Digital Curation Lifecycle Model: www.dcc.ac.uk/resources/curation-lifecycle-model.

4   Examples of freely available resources can be found at www.dcc.ac.uk/resources; www.jisc.ac.uk/whatwedo/services.aspx; www.dpconline.org; and, of course, www.pocos.org.

References

Abbott, D. and Beer, E. (2006) *Getting to Know Our Audience: AHDS performing arts scoping study*, Glasgow, UK, AHDS Performing Arts.

Abbott, D., Jones, S. and Ross, S. (2008) Theoretical Discussions on Digital Representations of Performance. In Leclercq, N., Rossion, L. and Jones, A. (eds), *Capturing the Essence of Performance: the challenges of intangible heritage*, Oxford, P. I. E. Peter Lang, 81–8.

Benford, S., Giannachi, G., Koleva, B. and Rodden, T. (2009) From Interaction to Trajectories: designing coherent journeys through user experiences, paper presented at the *CHI 2009, Conference on Human Factors in Computing Systems*, Boston, MA.

Benford, S., Reeves, S., O'Malley, C. and Fraser, M. (2005) Designing the Spectator Experience, paper presented at the *CHI 2005, Conference on Human Factors in Computing Systems*, Portland, OR.

Brook, P. (1968) *The Empty Space*, London, MacGibbon and Kee.

Grau, O. (2003) *Virtual Art: from illusion to immersion*, Cambridge, MA, MIT Press.

Gray, C. (2008) Can Documentation Re-Create and Enhance Theatre? In Leclercq, N., Rossion, L. and Jones, A. (eds), *Capturing the Essence of Performance: the challenges of intangible heritage*, Oxford, P. I. E. Peter Lang, 409–19.

Hagebölling, H. (2004) Introduction, Elements of a History of Interactive Dramaturgy. In Hagebölling, H. (ed.), *Interactive Dramaturgies: new approaches in multimedia content and design*, Berlin, Springer, 1–16.

Higgins, S. (2008) The DCC Curation Lifecycle Model, *International Journal of Digital Curation*, **3** (1), 134–40.

Laurel, B. (1993) *Computers as Theatre*, Reading, MA, Addison-Wesley Longman.

Rinehart, R. (2007) The Media Art Notation System: documenting and preserving digital/media art, *Leonardo*, **40** (2), 181–7.

Smith, P. and Isley, V. (2011) Best Before . . . Software Artworks May Be Seen after This Date; However Their Quality May Be Affected by Improper Storage, presentation at *Preservation of Complex Objects Symposium* (Software Art, Glasgow, 11–12 October 2011), www.pocos.org/index.php/pocos-symposia/software-art.

Utvich, M. (2004) The Circular Page: designing a theatre of choice. In Hagebölling, H. (ed.), *Interactive Dramaturgies: new approaches in multimedia content and design*, Berlin, Springer, 221–9.

PART 5

A legal perspective

The impact of European copyright legislation on digital preservation activity: lessons learned from legal studies commissioned by the KEEP project

David Anderson

Professor of Digital Humanities and
CiTECH Research Centre Director,
University of Portsmouth, UK

Introduction

Digital preservation activity in the European Union takes place within a complicated and often contradictory legislative landscape. Over and above national law stands the European Community (EC) framework – which, although meant to be incorporated into member state legislation, is not uniformly or completely implemented across the whole of the EU. Finally, certain non-EU legislation, as well as international understandings and treaty obligations such as the Paris Convention for the Protection of Industrial Property (1883), and the Berne Convention for the Protection of Literary and Artistic Works (1886), all play their part in determining the precise legal status of preservation actions. During the first year of the KEEP[1] project two legal studies were commissioned[2] to explore the impact of European law on the project's proposed programme of work. The purpose of the present document is to articulate, as far as is possible, the main conclusions of the KEEP legal studies in layman's terms. Naturally, this involves some diminution of legal rigour, in consequence of which the present document should not be regarded as legally definitive.

The KEEP project

The KEEP project was the first EC-funded project to concern itself primarily with an emulation-based approach to digital preservation. From the outset it was recognized that there was some potential for the project to encounter unique legal issues. Emulation involves the creation of software that permits one hardware platform (computer) to 'mimic' the behaviour of an entirely different hardware platform. In a preservation context this has enormous potential, as it offers the possibility of running software originally designed for a now-obsolete computer on the latest hardware, although there are, of course, considerable technical challenges which need to be addressed before this potential can be achieved. There are also obvious copyright issues which need to be considered when writing or using software that attempts to reproduce exactly the behavioural characteristics of third-party code.

An emulation-based approach to preservation has the advantage of avoiding any need to make alterations to preserved files in order to make them accessible on modern machines. In this respect emulation is very different in character from 'migration'-based preservation techniques that 'convert' old file formats into forms which run on new platforms. The primary problem which the KEEP legal studies sought to address concerns 'media transfer', which is the process of moving computer files from their original storage medium (5.25 in floppy, magnetic tape, etc.) onto a managed storage system within a library context. This is essentially a process of copying software.

The KEEP project initially proposed to create a framework which would agglomerate a number of distinct media transfer tools, with the aim of creating a 'one-stop shop' for media transfer within a digital preservation context. It was recognized from the outset that transferring copyrighted material from one medium to another was subject to legal regulation both with respect to what might legitimately be transferred, and what use might permissibly be made of material after transfer had taken place. One aim of the legal studies was to delineate more precisely the legal boundaries of such a framework.

Rights holders very frequently look to protect their rights over digital material by means of encryption, password protection or other so-called 'technical measures of protection' (TMP). There are a number of situations in which a library or archive may have a need, or even a legal responsibility, to bypass TMP but cannot agree with the rights holder a means by which this might be achieved. On some occasions the rights holder cannot be identified or has ceased trading or may be unwilling to co-operate. The legal studies therefore sought to clarify the state of the law with respect to bypassing TMP.

The KEEP consortium contains three national libraries, each of which has a 'legal deposit' responsibility within its own legislative framework. Unsurprisingly, therefore, one of the topics which our legal advisers were asked to explore was the degree to which 'legal deposit' is recognized at the Community level and how far exercising legal deposit responsibilities might attenuate the operation of the law on copyright.

The stakeholders in the KEEP project were particularly interested in so-called 'complex digital objects', such as multimedia works[3] (e.g. computer games) and interactive educational software, and sought greater clarity about whether the complexity of digital objects has any consequences in law. Furthermore, the KEEP project sought legal clarification on any restrictions that might apply to the use of computer files following media transfer. Finally, the project sought clarification about any limitations that the law might place on batch (i.e., large-scale) transfer of software, since the national libraries likely to be involved in this activity have vast numbers of software titles that need to be preserved.

The KEEP legal studies threw up two important issues: making copies of digital materials (media transfer) and making these copies available to users. Libraries and archives have no general right of reproduction but may reproduce (or transfer) digital material only in certain specified cases. The exemptions that libraries enjoy are sufficient to permit at least some of the activities necessary for preservation. However, the inconsistency between national and Community laws and the lack of clarity on key terms (e.g., multimedia works) give rise to confusion at the margins. There is a tendency for national legislation to be both more permissive than Community law, and for it to provide a greater degree of detailed governance. Unfortunately, this leads both to inconsistency between member states, and to national regulation that is, in certain key areas, almost certainly incompatible with Community law.

Complex though the legal landscape is, a number of consistent and clear messages have emerged from the investigations carried out both into EC law and the three national jurisdictions.

European copyright law: a very brief overview

Copyright laws have generally attempted to balance ensuring a reward for creativity and investment with the dissemination of knowledge. The preamble to the Directive 2001/29/EC of the European Parliament and of the Council of 22 May 2001, on the harmonization of certain aspects of copyright and related rights in the information society, makes clear that the overriding purpose of harmonizing copyright regulation within the EC is to ensure that competition in the internal market is not distorted. This is fully in line both with the Treaty establishing the European Community, and with the general notion that the primary purpose of copyright law is to promote knowledge by establishing, for authors and creators, a temporary monopoly over their output, thereby permitting them to protect and stimulate the development and marketing of new products and services, and the creation and exploitation of their creative content.

The rights granted to authors, while very extensive, are not unrestricted, since there is recognition that creating an absolute monopoly would have the effect of stifling rather than promoting markets. Where the rights of authors are seen as conflicting with a public interest, various exemptions are provided. However, the onus is on those who wish to make use of exemptions to copyright protection to demonstrate clearly that they are properly entitled so to do, and that they have complied with any restrictions placed on the use of material reproduced under a copyright exemption. This is, in practice, somewhat difficult to accomplish.

While the purpose of the KEEP legal studies was to come to a view about the legal status of the work proposed to be carried out within the KEEP project, the findings have implications for any institutional programme of digital preservation. Something of the complexity that examining the legal issues involved in digital preservation involves may be conveyed by carrying out a keyword search at legislation.gov.uk to see how many pieces of UK legislation touch on a given topic. The results are shown in Table 23.1.

The complexity indicated by the result of this search should make us hesitant in assuming that it is possible, within the context of the KEEP legal studies, to arrive at anything other than the most tentative of conclusions.

Table 23.1 Search results, legislation.gov.uk

Keyword	Pieces of legislation
Copyright	>200
Software	>200
Database	167
Intellectual Property Rights	163
Trademark	74

The Community legal corpus

Principal legislation at the Community level includes:

- **The Information Society Directive** (Directive 2001/29/ EC of 22 May 2001 on the harmonization of certain aspects of copyright and related rights in the information society)
- **The Computer Programs Directive** (Directive 2009/24/EC of 23 April 2009 on the legal protection of computer programs; codified version replacing the abrogated Directive 91/250/ EEC of 14 May 1991)
- **The Database Directive** (Directive 96/9/EC of 11 March 1996 on the legal protection of databases)

(the above collectively referred to as the 'Community Framework')

- **The Resale Rights Directive** (Directive 2001/84/EC 27 September 2001 on the resale right for the benefit of the author of an original work of art)
- **The Rental Directive** (Directive 92/100/EEC/EC 19 November 1992 on rental right and lending right and on certain rights related to copyright in the field of intellectual property).

The following general rights are protected:

- **reproduction** for authors, performers, producers of phonograms and films and broadcasting organizations
- **communication to the public** for authors, performers, producers of phonograms and films and broadcasting
- **distribution** for authors and for performers, producers of phonograms and films and broadcasting organizations
- **fixation** for performers and broadcasting right of rental and/or lending for authors, performers, producers of phonograms and films
- **broadcasting** for performers, producers of phonograms and broadcasting organizations
- **communication** to the public by satellite for authors, performers, producers of phonograms and broadcasting organizations
- **reproduction, distribution and rental** for authors of computer programs.

The 'three-step test'

Critical to understanding the general framework within which IPR legislation operates is the so-called 'three-step test', which first appeared in the Berne Convention and has come to be regarded as a cornerstone of international copyright regulation. It imposes constraints on the possible limitations and exceptions to exclusive rights under national copyright laws. The three-step test applies to limitations and exceptions to copyright protection and specifies that they will:

- be confined to certain special cases
- not conflict with a normal exploitation of the work
- not unreasonably prejudice the legitimate interests of the rights holder.

Limitations and exceptions within Community law: the Information Society Directive

The Directive permits member states to make provision exceptions or limitations to the right of reproduction and/or communication in some 20 cases. Of these, the following four are of direct relevance to organizations responsible for digital preservation:

- in respect of specific acts of reproduction made by publicly accessible libraries, educational establishments or museums, or by archives, which are not for direct or indirect economic or commercial advantage (Art. 5, 2(c))
- incidental inclusion of a work or other subject matter in other material (Art. 5, 3(i))
- use in connection with the demonstration or repair of equipment (Art. 5, 3(l))
- use by communication or making available, for the purpose of research or private study, to individual members of the public by dedicated terminals on the premises of establishments referred to in paragraph 2(c) of works and other subject matter not subject to purchase or licensing terms which are contained in their collections (Art. 5, 3(n)).

The Directive therefore permits limited rights for memory institutions to make copies for the purpose of preservation, but not for general communication. For reproduction to be permissible it must be permitted under national law, and should not conflict with a normal exploitation of the work, nor unreasonably prejudice the legitimate interests of the rights holder.

The Information Society Directive is typically regarded by the academic community as a victory for copyright-owning interests (publishing, film, music and major software companies) over content users' interests. The list of exceptions outlined in the Directive has achieved a certain degree of harmonization but it is important to note that member states have no power to introduce new limitations not already included in the Directive. This has the unwelcome effect that member states possess no independent ability to keep their legislative frameworks up to date with unforeseen technological developments.

The KEEP legal study concluded that media transfer should primarily be assessed under the Computer Programs Directive and the Database Directive.

Limitations and exceptions within Community law: the Computer Programs Directive

The Computer Programs Directive gives the rights holder exclusive rights to authorize:

- **the permanent or temporary reproduction of a computer program** by any means and in any form, in part or in whole; in so far as loading, displaying, running, transmission or storage of the computer program necessitate such reproduction
- **the translation, adaptation, arrangement and any other alteration of a computer program** and the reproduction of the results thereof, without prejudice to the rights of the person who alters the program
- **any form of distribution to the public**, including the rental, of the original computer program or of copies thereof.

However, the legal owner of a program is assumed to have a licence to:

- create any copies *necessary to use the program* and to alter the program within its *intended purpose* (e.g. for error correction)
- make a *back-up copy* for his or her *personal* use
- decompile the program if this is necessary *to ensure its operates* with another program or device, *but not for any other purpose.*

None of the exceptions set out in the Directive expressly serves the purpose of institutional digital preservation and the Directive does not provide for actions related to legal deposit requirements or for scientific, study or education purposes that would be similar or close to those set out by Article 5.2 (c) and 5.3 (n) of the Information Society Directive.

As a result, reproduction of computer programs carried out by institutions like libraries and museums, even when authorized under national laws, is in conflict with the Directive.

Limitations and exceptions within Community law: the Database Directive

The Database Directive harmonizes the treatment of databases under copyright law, and creates a new *sui generis* right for the creators of databases that do not otherwise qualify for copyright protection. A database is defined as 'a collection of independent works, data or other materials arranged in a systematic or methodical way and individually accessible by electronic or other means' (Article 1).

The overall objective of the Directive is to provide:

- copyright protection for the intellectual creation involved in the selection and arrangement of materials
- *sui generis* protection for an investment (financial and in terms of human resources, effort and energy) in the obtaining, verification or presentation of the contents of a database, whether or not these have an intrinsically innovative nature.

The Database Directive gives the rights holder the exclusive right to authorize:

- temporary or permanent reproduction by any means and in any form, in whole or in part
- translation, adaptation, arrangement and any other alteration
- any form of distribution to the public of the database or of copies thereof (subject to the exhaustion of rights)
- any communication, display or performance to the public
- any reproduction, distribution, communication, display or performance

to the public of a translation, adaptation, arrangement or other alteration.

Member States are allowed to provide limitations of rights in the following cases:

- reproduction for private purposes of a non-electronic database
- for the sole purpose of illustration for teaching or scientific research, as long as the source is indicated and to the extent justified by the non-commercial purpose to be achieved
- for the purposes of public security
- for the purposes of an administrative or judicial procedure.

It is reasonable to assume that a significant proportion of databases, whether made available on a standalone basis or embedded in a multimedia device, will be protected by copyright. Databases put on the market or otherwise made available to the public on tangible media generally offer more than a simple list or catalogue of items or data and are likely to be eligible for copyright protection under national laws within the EU.

None of the copyright-related exceptions or *sui generis* rights offered by the Directive is relevant for the purposes of institutional digital preservation.

Implications of the rules on technological measures of protection

Many works are made available in a form to which technical measures have been applied to prevent or restrict the use that may be made of them. This might take the form of a simple password protection scheme or may involve considerable technical sophistication.

Provisions related to technological measures and rights management information originate from the World Intellectual Property Organization (WIPO) Copyright Treaty (WCT) and the WIPO Performances and Phonograms Treaty (WPPT). The WCT and WPPT mandate the provision of adequate and effective legal remedies against anyone knowingly performing an act that may induce, enable, facilitate or conceal an infringement of any right related to rights management information.

The Information Society Directive (2001/29/EC) recognizes the 'need to provide for harmonized legal protection against circumvention of effective technological measures and against provision of devices and products or services to this effect'. It stipulates that 'Member States shall provide adequate legal protection against the circumvention of any effective technological measures, which the person concerned carries out in the knowledge, or with reasonable grounds to know, that he or she is pursuing that objective.' However, it also permits member states to be given the option of 'providing for certain exceptions or limitations for cases such as educational and scientific purposes, for the benefit of public institutions such as libraries and archives'.

Our investigation has shown that the potential for exemptions is quite limited and does not extend to permitting the creation or use of tools by individuals to bypass TMP. It should be noted that even in the limited situations where TMP may legitimately be circumvented, subsequent use of the transferred or copied material is extremely limited.

Other key legal issues examined
Online dissemination of digital material

In line with the general approach to the knowledge economy, libraries and others increasingly try to bring information to users rather than requiring users to come to information. Our research clearly indicates that the current legislative framework on copyright and digital material does not support this approach and contains restrictions on making digital material available online or off-site.

Legal deposit status

Community law provides no specific exceptions in respect of legal deposit. National legislation which grants special exemptions to legal depositories permitting them to engage in preservation activities not open to others is almost certainly inconsistent with EC law.

Multimedia works

No definition of 'multimedia works' exists either in Community law or in the national jurisdictions examined. There is, however, general agreement on taking a distributive approach in which each component part of a multimedia work – audio, graphics, software, database, etc. – is considered separately. Since multimedia works are not, in general, made available on computer platforms in such a way that individual elements can be removed from the whole, this means that, in practice, multimedia works enjoy the strongest protection under law that is available for any of their constituent parts. This has a significant impact on the preservation of multimedia works. Libraries (and others) are placed under a responsibility to perform a detailed assessment for each individual multimedia work they intend to preserve (or transfer from one storage medium to another) to establish the level of legal protection it enjoys. Given the scale on which national legal depositories are required to operate, such an individual assessment is impractical.

General conclusions of the KEEP legal studies

The KEEP legal studies concluded that with respect to Community law:

- None of the exceptions set out at the Community level serves adequately the purposes of memory organizations in going about their digital preservation activity.
- Community law does not provide for legal deposit requirements.
- Community law does not provide for scientific, study or education purposes across the full range required for memory organizations.
- Reproduction of computer programs and databases even when carried out by memory organizations and authorized under national laws, is in conflict with Community law.

Acknowledgements

The Keeping Emulation Environments Portable (KEEP) Project is co-financed by the European Union's Seventh Framework Programme for research and technological development (FP7), Grant Agreement number ICT-231954.

Notes

1   Keeping Emulation Environments Portable.

2 The legal work was sub-contracted to Bird & Bird and was presented to the
   KEEP consortium in the form of detailed reports.

3 For the purposes of the legal study, the term 'multimedia works' is
   understood as combining audiovisual, software and, as the case may be,
   database elements along with off-the-shelf software programs and databases
   considered on a standalone basis.

CHAPTER 24

Issues of information security applicable to the preservation of digital objects

Andrew Ball and Clive Billenness

The British Library, Boston Spa, UK

Introduction

Eyes front

The IT industry looks forward, not back. Smaller, faster and with increased functionality are the industry's focus; nostalgia is a rare indulgence. This focus on the future creates recurrent issues with backwards-compatibility; using old data with new systems or integrating old and new information systems can be problematic. Backwards-compatibility is often an afterthought or simply ignored and information security tends to concern itself with the current information and system lifecycle. Archived or offline data can result in less emphasis on information security; this presents challenges for digital preservation. Information security controls and risk assessments tend to be diminishing concepts in archive information systems.

Taking notes

Digital preservation arises in many forms – electronic musical instruments are a good example. Many of the older synthesizers from the 1970s and 1980s had unique sounds which still have a place in modern music. However, many almost became extinct as newer instruments with more accurate samples were produced. The sounds made by these early instruments have been rescued, remastered and are now available to the current and future generations of musicians.

Ticking boxes

Organizations talk about 'governance' but they often really mean 'compliance'. A lack of empathy with the business results in controls that create unnecessary barriers to normal operations. These controls, when combined with business targets, can create perverse incentives for staff to circumvent procedures rather than comply with them in order to 'get the job done'. This is not good governance. 'Tick-box governance' is a serious problem for a business and arises where there is no sound basis for the compliance framework that has been adopted. Tick-box governance creates an illusion of compliance and false sense of security. Identifying the right standards to comply with and clearly defining the scope and application is critical to achieving good governance.

Breaking barriers

There will always be tensions between end-users, IT operations and information security specialists. A lack of communication and mutual understanding exacerbates this. Dialogue between the parties can help to create a consensus approach that will encourage informed compliance and some common objectives. People are at their most creative when seeking ways to bend the rules, so making rules that make sense and are attuned to the business are essential for true compliance.

A principled approach

Information security is built on three founding principles:

- confidentiality
- integrity
- availability.

All three principles must be in balance. Confidentiality is often well understood and complied with; legislation and regulation makes responsibilities clear. Integrity is similarly well understood, particularly as it relates to data quality. Any disconnect between information user and information providers will degrade data quality. Information providers (e.g. clinicians) have to understand the value of clinical data to accountants so that activity is correctly coded and billed; this drives the health economy. A failure to make that connection leads to careless coding and incorrect billing. The financial errors that result ultimately impact clinicians and patients – it is in their interests to get it right. The impact of data error is important to understand – its reach can be considerable, compounding as it spreads across organizations and over time. The least well understood principle is availability. There is an inevitable tension between the principles of confidentiality, integrity and availability. The more effective the controls to secure data and protect it, the less accessible it becomes. When data is archived, the question of long-term continuing accessibility is not always considered.

Relevant standards

Extensive standards exist that cover information security. The ISO27000 series of standards alone cover information security in six separate standards (ISO27001–ISO27006).[1] One standard in the ISO27000 series – IS027037, *Evidence Acquisition Procedure for Digital Forensics* – has potential relevance to digital preservation activities, as its summary explains:

> This International Standard provides detailed guidance that describes the process for recognition and identification, collection and/or acquisition and preservation of digital data which may contain information of potential evidential value.[2]

Published in October 2012, this standard is narrowly focused on digital preservation and the law, so its wider applicability is limited. Standards are attractive to organizations that wish to demonstrate certification of compliance. However, scope and timing are critical: how much of the organization is certified and how recently (certification should be renewed every three years)? ISO/IEC 27002:2005 (*Information Technology – Security Techniques – Code of Practice for Information Security Management*) contains a number of sections that may be relevant to digital preservation specialists.

Security policy

Policies must be about your organization and your business. Avoid cloned policies taken from one organization and applied to another without customization and engagement. There is very little chance that a cloned policy will prove effective if simply imposed – even for similar organizations. Consistency is laudable and templates or frameworks can help deliver this; however, it is important not to be too constrained by this approach and fail to reflect the operational needs of the organization. Ground-up is definitely the best way to making an effective policy that works and will be complied with.

Security organization

High-profile losses of media carrying sensitive data in both the public and private sectors have helped to raise the profile of information security and governance within organizations. Board-level engagement is critical to success. Few organizations are unique, so it can be very helpful to seek analogues with which to benchmark in order to secure improvement. We can all learn from the mistakes of others.

Third-party suppliers are another important component of an organization's security arrangements. Security arrangements most work through the supply chain to ensure that data can be retrieved following mergers, contractual changes or an organization going into administration. Information security arrangements need a 10–20-year horizon to adequately serve digital preservation specialists; very few security plans look this far ahead.

Asset management

Ownership, classification and management of digital assets is an important consideration. Where a digital object is access-controlled or restricted, definitions of that classification may change over time. If an object is archived while classified with a restriction on access, does an adequate procedure exist to revoke the classification at a later date? For complex objects, where only a part of it is restricted, storing different components of the object at different security levels can be challenging. This process will need to take account of how links between the different components are maintained. In addition, a procedure must be created to allow for classification changes. This may not be well recognized at the point of archiving, leading to difficulties in retrieval in the distant future.

Arrangements for ownership and succession over an extended period must be established and documented, covering the context and meaning of any classifications that have been applied.

The widespread use of digital rights management (DRM) to protect digital intellectual property – e.g. games – can also present a challenge where an object is retrieved and the holder of the digital rights is not easily identifiable. The intent of an archivist or another later user of preserved digital may differ from that of the original owner and must also be taken into account. An original owner will want to use digital content for its original intended purpose and so DRM restrictions are appropriate; but the intended use by an archivist may differ to the extent that the DRM is no longer appropriate.

People security

People have a strong link to information security – people represent the greatest risk. One example is 'tacit knowledge' – the operationally important, but undocumented, information that staff acquire over time. When considering long-term digital preservation, this 'tacit knowledge' may no longer be available. When a future user of a digital object attempts to withdraw it from archive the know-how is lost. Barriers to documentation of tacit knowledge can be cultural, where knowledge is power, or due to a simple lack of facilities. Changing cultures to encourage knowledge-sharing and providing adequate mechanisms to gather and organize this information are vital to guarantee future access to archived data.

Physical and environmental security

Few organizations are now in control of their own 'tin'. Outsourcing and Cloud capabilities mean that no assumptions can be made on information security; providers must demonstrate certifications and their applicability. Experienced and reliable providers will routinely offer accredited security standards but these cannot be taken for granted or at face value. Due diligence is the purchaser's responsibility. Obsolescence is another consideration: while enthusiasts still have the ability to source obsolescent equipment via online auction sites and used equipment dealers, this is a high-risk strategy for an organization with a heavy investment in digital objects. Two options exist:

- Maintain a hardware library, complete with all necessary associated software on which the original environment of a digital object can be retained.
- Create an emulation environment on which the original environment can be replicated.

Mechanical hard disks typically suffer failure after around three to five years of regular use but can last up to ten; solid-state drives have a far greater lifespan, as life expectancy for solid state memory is between 10 and 30 years. Optical disks are similarly perishable with an experiential life expectancy of two to five years[2] according to The National Archives (UK), although manufacturers claim much higher lifespans, in excess of 100 years. A hardware library can only provide a time-limited solution, with an ever-increasing risk of both hardware failure and partial or complete media failure.

An emulation framework to enable the original hardware/software configuration to be replicated in software within a modern environment can continue to evolve with each subsequent generation of computer system. Recent European projects such as Planets and KEEP have undertaken substantial research in this area – work that continues to be developed by the Open Planets Foundation (OPF).

Communications and operations

Security should be considered as part of the operational lifecycle, right at the outset. While security considerations are now frequently considered at the early stages of IT system projects, archiving and long-term preservation issues are rarely discussed and usually as part of decommissioning. Archiving and preservation should also be designed into the system and into operations from the beginning.

Access controls

If access controls apply to information in a live system, that information may also be access-controlled in an archive environment, and so documenting and storing the authentication is part of digital preservation. It is poor practice to store authentication keys with the object to be protected: there should be a separation between the two. This may require complex arrangements that are sustainable over an extended period of time. Access rights tend to accrue and are rarely revoked when the need expires; the preservation stage is the last chance to ensure that access rights are appropriately managed and any legacy or expired access permissions are deleted. Failure to correctly manage access rights for complex objects creates a risk to the integrity of the entire object if relationships between objects based on access controls is compromised.

Information systems security

Information systems security relates to the information systems lifecycle. Security risk assessments should consider long-term preservation issues, but rarely do so. Typically, such assessments focus on confidentiality and integrity but less so on availability, even though this is an equally important aspect of security. The earlier that long-term preservation is considered within any project, the more likely it is that the solution will meet the long-term preservation needs of the organization. Would a failure to meet preservation and archiving requirements ever result in a solution being rejected? If not, perhaps we are not asking all the right questions at project start-up.

Security incident management

Organizations should monitor and report security incidents to learn the lessons and improve their security arrangements. These lessons tend to be applied to live systems but not to digital objects in long-term preservation. Hackers frequently target back-up systems, and for good reason – they are less likely to be patched and access controls are often less robust. Archives offer an easier route in than the live operational environment; however, a back-up system – by definition – contains all the data held in the live system and so merits equal security.

Business continuity management (BCM)

This is risk-based, covering:

- **disaster recovery:** restoring the technical environment
- **business continuity:** maintaining business as usual until the technical environment has been restored.

Business continuity relies on the availability of documentation and back-up data – even if main buildings are inaccessible. An alternative site is of no use to you if you have no back-up media, no recovery plan and no idea how to configure it.

For digital preservation, there are special long-term risks to be considered, such as climate change. Long-term preservation activities demand a long-term approach to risk assessment. Forecasts of the levels of future flood plains and impacts of rising sea levels on coastal areas over a ten-year timeline or longer should form an important part of planning activities when identifying the locations of long-term archiving and preservation sites. Testing arrangements should include the retrieval of archived information, otherwise there is no assurance of successful recovery.

Compliance

Compliance focuses on people. It is the cultural and behavioural norms in an organization applied to policy and legislation. Few organizations make sufficient effort to really communicate policies to staff or monitor their effectiveness. Experience shows that people will notionally commit to a security policy and yet their observed behaviours are regularly in breach. This is rarely deliberate malpractice, more often a failure to appreciate risk and a desire to get the job done. Education is the key to combating these vulnerabilities; sanctions and disciplinary action remain popular organizational responses but incentives and engagement are generally more effective.

Beyond ISO27002, new information tools have created new threats to the integrity of organizational data and its long-term preservation. Web 2.0 technologies have led to rapid growth in user-generated content and archiving this content is a complex process. User-defined taxonomies (folksonomies) can create challenges where complex objects are created by interconnecting internal and external data sources. Recognizing and maintaining these connections when archiving using unstructured metadata is difficult. The documentation of object structures and relationships becomes an essential requirement if accessibility is to be maintained. E-mail systems can have a wide variety of formats of digital objects embedded within individual messages. In the event that an organization changes its e-mail service, it can be very difficult to retrieve the contents of individual e-mails or to re-create message threads. Many organizations do not even retain licences or software for obsolete systems, reducing probability that content in proprietary formats can be recovered and accessed in the future. The adoption of open data standards can help combat this risk.

It is easy to become reliant on large-scale but often transient brands of web-based software without any real consideration of how the corporate data stored by them can be backed up and retrieved in the event of the service provider ceasing operations. The rapid growth of hosted 'blogs' is one example of how information is gathered very quickly but is very hard to manage and preserve; according to Wordpress, tens of thousands of new blogs are created on their platform every day. Modern brands like Twitter and Facebook are dynamic and there are regular announcements of services merging, dividing or simply being switched off, with the attendant difficulties in maintaining links between objects created by them. Overall, the pace of technological redundancy is accelerating, and this presents new difficulties for organizations concerned with digital preservation.

Summary

Availability is the key principle for digital preservation, although integrity and confidentiality are also important. Information security often tends to favour confidentiality and integrity over availability. Those managing long-term digital preservation must challenge the balance between these three principles to ensure that their business needs are adequately catered for. Projects tend to treat the preservation of legacy data as an end-of-lifecycle process: this is a mistake and often leads to such preservation being de-scoped from new systems on cost grounds. If a requirement exists to ensure the long-term preservation of digital objects, this is a 'business-as-usual' cost that should not be deferred. Risk assessments must look beyond the operational life of systems and data to a longer horizon and risk must be part of the preservation space, with up-to-date controls in parallel with live data.

Notes

1 www.27000.org.
2 Source: The National Archives, frequently asked questions (FAQs) about

optical storage media: storing temporary records on CDs and DVDs, www.archives.gov/records-mgmt/initiatives/temp-opmedia-faq.html.

PART 6

Pathfinder conclusions

CHAPTER 25

Pathfinder conclusions

Janet Delve

Future Proof Computing Group, School of Creative Technologies,
University of Portsmouth, UK

David Anderson

Professor of Digital Humanities and CiTECH Research Centre Director,
University of Portsmouth, UK

Introduction

The preservation of complex materials and associated environments presents the digital preservation (DP) community in general and the Jisc community in particular with considerable intellectual and logistical challenges. While many of the techniques that have been developed within the context of migration-based DP approaches are of continuing value, others cannot be applied so well, given the extra complexity presented by, for example, interactive videogames. Recent work undertaken in the Planets and KEEP projects has shown that the problems involved in preserving such materials and their associated environments, while substantial, are by no means intractable, but in order to continue to make progress in this area it is important to engage and energize the wider DP community. A vital aspect of this process comprises articulating the state of the art in:

* simulations and visualizations
* software art
* gaming environments and virtual worlds.

Digital preservation strategies for visualizations and simulations

It can be argued that there are robust and well defined digital preservation strategies to deal with migrating simple digital objects such as single files. The question is: can these strategies extend practically for complex objects in general, and for visualizations and simulations in particular?

During POCOS I, eight challenges were identified and a number of responses suggested.

Challenge 1: Access and long-term use of digital content both depend on the configuration of hardware, software, the capacity of the operator and documentation

- **Migration** (changing the file format to ensure the information content can be read) is the most quoted, and most widely used solution. It is typically good for large quantities of data that are well understood and self-contained (with few or no dependencies), within a relatively small number of formats.
- **Emulation** (intervening in the operating system to ensure that old software can function and information content can be read) can be used in tandem with migration; in fact migration and emulation both often require, for their realization, deployment of elements of each other. A vital step forward in the preservation debate is to embrace hybrid strategies deploying both migration and emulation, instead of seeing these as rival options.[1]
- **Hardware preservation** (maintaining access to data and processes by maintaining the physical computing environment including hardware and peripherals) is less fashionable, more expensive, but effective. It is often claimed that emulation obviates the need for preserving hardware, but this is not the case. In order to ensure that an emulation configuration is authentic, it is necessary to preserve hardware to set up benchmarks. This is particularly important for preserving the actual user experience of the hardware and software. Computing history museums are key to this task[2] and the extent to which they can provide software, hardware, emulators and documentation is the subject of a scoping study in KEEP.
- **Exhumation** (maintaining access to an execution environment or software services so that processes can be rerun with new data) also involves emulation and migration elements.

Challenge 2: Technology continues to change, creating the conditions for obsolescence

DPC Technology Watch reports and services give advance notice of obsolescence. Migration and emulation reduce the impact of changes in technology. File format registries such as PRONOM, UDFR and P2 also contribute by profiling file formats and their preservation status.

Challenge 3: Storage media have a short life and storage devices are subject to obsolescence

Storage media can be refreshed and in some cases can self-check, and storage densities continue to improve, offering greater capacity at reduced cost. It must be emphasized, however, that storage may only be a minor part of the solution, but not the whole solution. (In fact, transferring bits from one medium to another is not necessarily inherently difficult – the problematic issues are often concerned with the quantity of information involved.)

Challenge 4: Digital preservation systems are subject to the same obsolescence as the objects they safeguard

Systems can be modular and conform to standards, and fitness for purpose can be monitored over time.

Challenge 5: Digital resources can be altered, corrupted or deleted without obvious detection

Digital signatures and wrappers are available that can safeguard authenticity. Also, security measures can control access to the digital material (although it must be admitted that digital preservation has not yet sufficiently well confronted security issues such as cyber attacks). It is also a real advantage that for digital, as opposed to physical, material copies are perfect replicas with no degradation.

Challenge 6: Digital resources are intolerant of gaps in preservation

Ongoing risk management can provide vital monitoring to help deal with this problem, and there are significant economies of scale to be made. It is critical that we work with colleagues in computer science towards the end that processes such as metadata creation and harvesting, and media transfer where possible, be automated. We must also be aware that data is rapidly growing in scale, complexity and appetite/importance – that is to say, the expectations we have of data.

Challenge 7: We have limited experience

The rapid churn in technology accelerates our research, which has been transformed over the last decade. As noted in Challenge 6, this is a shared problem: those at the forefront of DP research, such as memory organizations, need to be willing to appropriate solutions developed in other domains, such as computer science (digital forensics, software lifecycle development).[3]

Challenge 8: DP has to cater for widely varying types of collection or interaction, so different strategies are required for different types of collection or interaction

- Where possible, we need to develop strategies that cater for discrete categories of material, such as:
  — simple v. complex
  — large v. numerous
  — gallery v. laboratory.
- A helpful way of confronting the issues is to consider that DP involves three key components: technology, organization and resources. With this in mind, the following list indicates the pressing questions about complex digital objects in general, and visualizations and simulations in particular, currently facing the DP community:
  — Are the issues data size or data complexity, or both?
  — Which is the best preservation strategy: emulation, migration, hybrid or neither?
  — Is it easier to re-create data than to secure it?
  — What does success look like and how will we recognize it (i.e. which metrics do we use)?
  — Will the material ever be used? How do we balance delivery and accretion?
  — Does the material fit to its original mission, and whose problem is this?

— How do we find the necessary resources and expertise?
— What is next on the horizon: more scale and more complexity?
— DP tools: who is making these and what are the dependencies between them?
— Is visualization a special case for DP, or a special DP community?

Practical issues in preserving software art

The preservation of software art is both a research field in its infancy and an emerging field of practice. Software art is gathering a critical mass in museums, galleries and arts funds, which has prompted debates on the issues of collecting, curating and preserving unstable media art. Recognizing the challenges deriving from this changing landscape, the POCOS Symposium on Software Art invited participants to actively engage in sharing knowledge and expertise through breakout sessions. Participants at POCOS II examined four key challenges for delineating and advancing the state-of-the-art in preserving software.

Challenge 1: The role of the artist

• defining and preserving the integrity of software art works
• responsibilities and rights of the artist.

In summarizing the role of the artist in preserving software art works, the symposium participants felt that the focus should be on preserving the essence of the work rather than the objects and technologies that manifest that essence. At present, the onus remains with the artist to help preserve the art work. This is partly because the technological complexity of software art works can only be fully comprehended by the creator. Intrinsic to this realization (for both artists and curators) is the sense of urgency in that degradation of a software art work can have immediate effects (as opposed to, say, a slowly degrading painting). Artists are aware of the benefits of facilitating the curation and preservation process of their work, but are at the same time challenged by the time, cost and expertise burden and the underlying feeling that – without taking the initiative – no one else will.

Challenge 2: The role of cultural institutions: storage, access and preservation technologies

The group of participants studying this area concluded that software art does stand out as a unique case, with hybrid physical/digital art works, the primacy of the artist's intentions and the effect the file formats and storage media may have on the performance and pecuniary and cultural value of the artefact. There does not appear to be a single one-size-fits-all preservation solution.

Challenge 3: Legal and ethical responsibilities

- An organization with responsibilities for curation of digital art should only make commitments to preservation which it is within their power to fulfil. Failure to do this would in itself be unethical. The institution should also possess a framework to enable it to calculate the relativities of harm in different preservation approaches, and ensure that its preservation activities are entirely consistent with the ethics of its institutional mission.
- 'The development of complex digital objects leads to the creation of complex ethical models' – William Kilbride, Digital Preservation Coalition.

Challenge 4: Developing a preservation strategy

- With preservation of software art being a field in its infancy, it is no surprise that exploring the requirements for a preservation strategy generates more questions than answers. POCOS II highlighted, in the most generic terms, the repeated signal from both communities of software artists and curators for a continuing dialogue that reflects an appreciation of the issues involved in preserving complex visual art work. For this dialogue to be meaningful, there is a growing demand for extensions beyond the artist/curator microcosm that will reach decision-making and policy construction in culture heritage institutions. This dialogue between artists and institutions (either mediated by curators or otherwise) must allow for information flow both horizontally and vertically and result in a continuous stream of dissemination and information exchange regarding innovative research, emergent artistic practices and forthcoming curatorial and preservation processes.

- At present, it becomes evident that an immediate, all-encompassing solution is idealistic. Competing positions – and their repercussions – tip the balance in software art preservation. From the one hand, the adherence to recording comprehensive metadata and thoroughly documenting the process of scientific research behind software art for the sake for re-instantiation is viewed by cultural institutions as part of the return in their investment. On the other hand lies the defiance of performance arts (of which software art can be seen as a genre) against the obligatory 'institutionalization' and the obligation to become reproducible.

- With an array of hardware and software dependencies – and the torment of obsolescence that these entail – the only viable parameters in a preservation strategy are the realization that experimentation with new techniques such as emulation and virtualization is required (let alone inevitable) and the need to work with 'acceptance parameters' that indicate how much of the art work can be reasonably expected to become lost, and what can realistically be saved. These parameters imply an underlying 'community consensus' on the content and extent that preservation parameters are considered acceptable. The need for community support has been signalled repeatedly, and in many instances has worked well, but also generates a host of questions:

  — Who would initialize and co-ordinate communication within and among communities? The paradigm of fan-based communities (predominantly in the realm of videogaming) has offered digital preservation some remarkable lessons, but can it work within the context of software art?

  — What are the requirements for central facilities, expertise and training in preserving software art? For some of the participants, the responsibility in these areas lies with cultural institutions; but do they have the technological capability to act as the arbiters of expertise?

  — Crowd-sourcing has been cited as a potential solution, to conglomerate expertise and alleviate costs from individuals and institutions to document and understand technologies. Can crowd-sourcing present a valid approach to preserving software art? The public must perceive that software art should be saved, in order to be brought into the curation and preservation process. In such a case, should we hand them the 'can of worms', shifting the responsibility from the traditional custodians of cultural heritage?

• Besides raising these questions, the POCOS symposium reached a provisional solution toward approaching a preservation strategy for software art: to work at present on a case-by-case basis, within broad rules. In the pages of this volume, some of these 'rules' are presented and explained and can hopefully shed light on the grey areas of software art preservation. By collating these rules, ideas and research outputs, the symposium has provided a platform for raising awareness and setting the groundwork for a future formulation of standards and construction of institutional policies that explicitly appreciate the issues pertaining to software art and the requirements for its long-term preservation. Specifically, the symposium recommended the forming of a strategic grouping of all interested parties that would work together to bring these aims into practice.

Practical issues in preserving gaming environments and virtual worlds

Only very recently have games been officially recognized as part of our cultural heritage, and so official links between memory institutions and gaming communities are not well developed. Thankfully, this is changing, and more and more national libraries are starting to archive games and virtual worlds. For example, the British Library holds games collections in its personal digital archives, and the Royal Library, Copenhagen, Denmark, has a sizeable games collection. Representatives from both these institutions were present at the third POCOS event. Previously the only groups leading games preservation were the games fans and developers themselves (the French National Library being a significant exception here).

The games industry is young and dynamic, production companies are formed and disappear quickly, sometimes leaving their IP 'orphaned', with no one knowing who, if anyone, owns it, and creating difficulties when ascertaining what can be preserved legally. IPR problems also arise in the virtual worlds space, but in this case the major difficulty arises from the practical problems surrounding securing permission from all the users to preserve their avatars and other digital assets. Without universal consent, the best that can be achieved is partial preservation of virtual worlds, and depending on the exact configuration, this represent a barely functional subset of the whole.

Another pressing topic is the technical complexity of the games and virtual worlds and their attendant environments. At the scale required by memory institutions, it is technically and financially unfeasible to assure future access to this material using a migration-based preservation approach. Even recording the many parts of these games (including mods, cracks etc.), plus details of their computing environments, so that they can be emulated or virtualized in future, poses a significant challenge. The founding of the dedicated New Media Museum, UK, has been a real boon in this respect, with its games environments and associated material, as has the Computer Games Museum in Berlin, Germany, which allows access to old games via the KEEP Emulation Framework.

At POCOS III, discussion centred around:

- the role of the developer in curating and preserving games and virtual worlds
- the role of cultural institutions, especially with respect to technical registries, metadata, software, hardware and online issues, interpretation and documentation
- the role of the community, especially with respect to abandonware, orphan works, greyware and preserving *Second Life* – content owners' permission issues.

Challenges from the developers' standpoint

From the key discussion between developers, academic researchers and those in memory institutions, some fundamental needs emerged. As a backdrop, it was important to explore the issues in terms of preservation in the games industry in order to establish the expectations coming from the memory institution and preservation side. This is so that those in industry will be able to determine the practicality of such requirements, so as to determine what developers would need in terms of support to bring such ideas into fruition. There is a tendency for those in the private and public sector to have perhaps somewhat unrealistic expectations regarding what the private sector is both capable and willing to do under their various business pressures. In terms of a perfect world for preservationists, it is important to identify what are the key materials and information that are needed but are not currently available. Are there lacunae in the actual games themselves, or their paradata, or the preservation process surrounding them?

Challenge 1: Establishing controlled vocabulary for computer games

A critical prerequisite to any research is to establish a controlled vocabulary for computer games: otherwise it is difficult to classify and specify the material in question. Terms like 'first-person shooter' and 'role-play' games need to be commonly understood and accepted across all relevant communities.

Challenge 2: Establishing provenance and ownership

Establishing provenance and ownership information is absolutely vital, so that researchers can access the work and memory institutions can catalogue it. Researchers will want the material that has been created in the studio to the point where a game is published – the algorithms, source code, storyboard, designs, maps, etc. – indeed, all the elements of the game itself. Walkthroughs of the game can be garnered from the gaming community who create this resource. Credits provide vital bibliographic data, but can only be obtained once the game has been completed.

Challenge 3: Gameplay metrics and functionality

- Moving on to the data that researchers, in particular, require from developers, gameplay metrics and functionality stand out as key. Here companies like Bungie[4] and Infinityward[5] aid the researcher by providing the facility to record statistics within the game.
- With *World of Warcraft*,[6] a massively multiple-player online role-playing game (MMORPG), it is the socialization aspects of the game that are important to record, as well as technical run-time data and requirements. Hence it is necessary to establish which techniques and types of data relate to which genres or groups of games.

Challenge 4: QA documentation

Quality assurance documentation is required to show how the game should be run: at what pace, with what effects? If it is really robust, it will delineate how versions of the game progressed.

A developers' charter?

Given this preservation wish list, what can we realistically hope for from games developers, and how can we go about achieving these aims and objectives? Provenance or ownership details are lacking for some older games, and this is a real problem in terms of IPR. But developers should be able to specify middleware. Going forward, there are ways developers can work today that will avoid the nightmare of abandonware recurring (see list below). Developers, like anyone else in industry, need a good business case to encourage them in this area.

Here is a possible developer's charter of what developers could provide:

- The source code, documentation, etc. to re-create the game build. This can be kept in an SVM (support vector machine) repository, but there may be IPR issues.
- A list of the tools used to build the games. This could be provided in a Word document, and would include the build requirements specification. It would be not be too onerous for a developer to participate in this.
- The 3D engine models, and the pre-builds in 3D outside the game in 3D Max or Maya, together with the concept art or design documents. Access needs to be allowed to these artefacts.
- The launch materials: press releases, etc.
- The assets for the game, and the provenance of the game.
- The game objects such as the source code. It is possible to re-create a game from the components of the game, and there is the question as to whether the game objects are different from the final legal product, as it takes a lot of effort to create a game from the components.
- The names of games workers, so that they can be properly credited. The same applies to middleware developers' credits.

From the publishers' standpoint

From the publishers' standpoint, preservation represents a business cost. In the absence of some legislative or regulatory requirement to preserve, it will be necessary to produce a business case which shows that preservation can be made profitable.

Key elements of this case are likely not only to include the opportunities for publishers to generate income from selling back titles, but also to develop new markets, perhaps by offering design documentation as add-ons, e.g. released stories, concept art and everything else actually buried within the game release. The infrastructure to support this is already in place: for example, the Valve Corporation (Steam online store)[7] make it possible not just to sell a game, but also the add-ons and the soundtrack on the same Steam page, etc.

Challenge 1: Facilitating collaboration

Computer games are now increasingly recognized as a part of our cultural heritage, as witnessed by the fact that growing numbers of national libraries are preserving such material as part of their legal deposit law remit. Such initiatives make it ever easier for the previously disparate communities to work together more closely, opening the way for specialist games archives, games museums, games developers and publishers, fan communities and academic researchers to join forces with national libraries and other memory institutions. Jisc is also keen to collaborate, especially in the areas of shared infrastructure, common business models and metadata. This joint effort across all communities great and small should greatly increase our capability to preserve games. The associated issue of trust is also paramount: for example, publishers and developers need to be assured that their IPR is respected and protected by curators.

Challenge 2: For whom are we preserving games?

This is a complicated issue, as there are potentially a myriad of different users wanting to use different games' artefacts or paradata, from a variety of standpoints. It is important to identify where the demand is coming from: who exactly wants to use computer games and related paraphernalia, and why, in order to ensure the correct material is available for them.

Challenge 3: What do we preserve?

The spectrum of interest in different kinds of games-related material is very wide but, practically speaking, it is impossible to preserve everything. Several different aspects emerged here. First the performance aspect – how were the games played? What were the ludological elements of the games engineer? What was the psychological impetus behind the game, and what were the benefits of play? The story and narratives are also important components. It is vital to record the acts of playing computer games on particular hardware platforms, and videoing players – recording players on YouTube can play a key role here. For example, would researchers playing *Quake*[8] in 1000 years time know about the Rocket Jump? Information on interaction and immersion needs to be recorded. After all, we have very well preserved physical examples of Roman games, but not a clue how to play them. All aspects of games' paradata were also deemed to be of great interest to various communities: fan fiction, wall art, exhibitions, etc. Survivor stories from games developers are of interest: is there an equivalent of a war poet for games? The ethnographic aspect of games studies is also relevant, and it is important to reward developers who preserve their material, in the same way that the film industry, led by Martin Scorsese, preserved old films. There is deemed to be a conceptual shift from preservation to a live public games archive or museology. The game's cover or box is a critical starting point for recording data, and other paradata such as mods, discussions and competitions can all be downloaded from games sites.

Challenge 4: Preserving hardware

Preserving computer hardware was established as crucial. A key question was: how many do we need of each piece of hardware – are three sufficient: one to use, one for spares and one for future use when the first breaks down? This was felt to be an absolute minimum. Detailed information on the hardware platforms is necessary in order to be able to emulate them. In big institutions such as broadcasting, there can be as many as 400,000 tapes and dozens of machines to play them on. In situations such as this, it is crucial to break down hardware issues into layers. For institutions that receive donated hardware, it needs to be established whether it is in working order. This is important for memory institutions, such as the British Library, that accept whole archives from games developers into their digital archives. Also, what are the significant properties of the hardware environment? Entropy comes into play here, and we should not get rid of hardware that we need, for example, to understand 3D objects. Collaboration with computer history museums can come into play here, as outlined in Chapter 16. What other steps are there to take all the above initiatives forward?

Challenge 5: Orphanware

What about the problems of orphanware? A positive step here would be to reward developers and publishers who preserve their games. An interesting case study is Charle's Settle's (Revolution Software) *Beneath a Steel Sky*,[9] which has no IPR attached. This included a virtual machine and the response to the game was very good indeed. It was distributed by scummVM,[10] amassed many sales and was easy to preserve, having been released to the games community, then rereleased commercially. The quality of the games is important here: *Beneath a Steel Sky* was successfully preserved because it was so good: mediocre games may not have fared so well. Similarly, rare games may be seen as being worthy of special attention. But we need to preserve games that failed as well as the top ones, so perhaps a multi-community-based ranking system of games might be useful? Attention also needs to be paid to where games appear and under which marketing strategy: for example, games available on the front of magazines might easily be overlooked. A Noah's Ark of games might be something to aim for, with representative samples of different games genres, etc.

Challenge 6: What do we mean by 'preservation strategy'?

There are issues which arise in understanding what is meant by the term 'preservation strategy'. This might be understood narrowly in an organization-specific sense, broadened out to embrace collection management issues, or taken as implying the development of a 'national' strategy for digital preservation. It was this latter sense which the panels agreed was most appropriate in the POCOS context.

Challenge 7: Gap analysis

It is standard research and development practice to establish prior art before committing resources to new developments. However, among the delegates there was consensus that work still remained to be done on gap analysis. Key foundational tasks remain either incomplete or yet to be started. One of these was the development of controlled vocabularies to assist preservationists in harvesting information from developers and publishers. This is necessary in order to establish a standardized starting point for collaborative activity. Similarly, considerable work remains to be done on building trust with stakeholders external to the preservation community. There is little knowledge of the preservation activity, problems and practices in countries outside Europe, North America and Australasia.

Challenge 8: Co-ordinated approaches

A very strong theme which emerged was a clear recognition of the need to develop co-ordinated approaches to the preservation of digital games and virtual worlds. This will involve developing productive working relationships with organizations and individuals who come from communities far removed from academia and memory organizations. Much of the preservation activity which currently takes place in the games and virtual world domain is led by 'enthusiasts' and is somewhat piecemeal. It is quite usual for enthusiasts to restrict their interests to a single hardware platform, or a few software titles. Within these restricted areas coverage can often be very extensive, well researched, and may deploy robust and effective software tools, such as emulators, or media transfer services. Mainstream preservationists will potentially need to work with many different enthusiast groups to ensure general coverage of the domain. In addition to preserving software, there is also a need to produce 'ancillary' or related items, such as manuals, reviews, walkthroughs and cover art.

Challenge 9: Community-specific needs

In seeking to form new alliances with other stakeholder communities, it is important to recognize that enthusiasts, developers, publishers and others are distinct not only from preservationists, but also from each other. Thus, for example, developers are much more likely to be relaxed than publishers about sharing information and data. However, developers (in general) almost certainly retain less IPR, and (probably) have fewer infrastructural resources to support information transfer, than is the case with publishers.

In order to reflect the concerns of these different stakeholder groups, it was suggested that (at least) two strands be identified in preservation activity. First, an access strand, where preserved material should be made available only to designated people, or types of user. Restrictions might also be imposed on accessing certain hardware or software platforms, or imposing a period of 'purdah', before material can be accessed. There would, in most cases, also need to be constraints placed on giving access to 'supplementary' material, such as source code, in recognition of the fact that such material lends itself much more easily to 'abuse' than does 'executables'. The second strand would concern itself with preservation. While this strand would need to allow availability to much more material than is required simply to ensure reasonable access, this would be held securely in order to meet the legitimate concerns of rights holders, as well as the preservation priorities set out in the appropriate national strategy.

The details of these arrangements would, naturally, need to be worked out carefully with the stakeholder communities.

Challenge 10: Lessons from the print industry

While there are superficial differences between the practices and concerns of the games industry and the print industry, there are also similarities. Lessons learned in engaging with the print industry can be carried over to interactions with the games industry, and common approaches are possible. It is important to identify clearly the remit and scope of any policy of software submission, as well as the barriers which must be overcome in order for it to be successful. Central to our approach should be a commitment to work with the industry, in partnership. While stressing the commonalities which exist between the print and games industries, it is important not to overlook the fact that the media themselves have unique attributes and issues, and that this will inevitably need to be reflected in preservation policies, and access arrangements.

Challenge 11: Broader perspectives

We must avoid the temptation to see preservation solely from the perspective of preservationists. Progress is likely to be much swifter and more efficient by working collaboratively with other stakeholders. This will, in turn, be facilitated by giving attention to the value which memory organizations and the wider preservation community can bring to other stakeholder communities. Attention needs to be directed at the creation of advocacy material, particularly using multimedia approaches. It would be helpful to produce clear guidelines on, for example, ingest, preservation and digital forensics. In these 'outreach' activities there are clear roles for the Digital Preservation Coalition, the Digital Curation Centre and the Open Planets Foundation. The Library of Congress 'Open Days' and the public interest they generated were offered as an exemplar of the sort of activities in which memory organizations ought to engage.

One useful service which the preservation community could try to develop is a 'one-stop shop' for clearing permissions on digital deposits. It was felt that additional help could be provided to support 'bottom-up' archiving activity. This could perhaps take the form of the creation of an archiving hub, with related website (for resource identification and community building), and associated organizational infrastructure. Institutions engaged in preservation might also lend support to enthusiast-driven preservation activity. Costing out these proposed activities was suggested as the topic of a POCOS follow-up meeting.

Challenge 12: Improving the perception of value

An important precursor to getting the games industry to engage with a preservation agenda is fostering an appreciation of their past. The IGDA (International Game Developers Association) white paper *Before It's Too late*,[11] was highlighted as representing a significant step along this path. The paper, which comes from within the games industry, argues that games are worth preserving because:

- games are history
- games are property
- games are design
- games are art
- games are culture
- games are fun.

Challenge 13: Building on success

It is important to encourage an early sense of success in order to stimulate further success. To this end, it makes sense to begin by setting targets which are relatively easy to accomplish. The resulting 'quick wins' will promote further, more challenging, work.

Consistent with this approach is a recognition that we may have to concentrate less of our attention on the past, where we may already have suffered irretrievable loss. It might be better to concentrate more on current users and contemporary challenges such as Facebook games, iPad applications, etc. A profitable place to begin might be in web archiving, because we enjoy the advantage of an existing and significant infrastructure.

Challenge 14: The law

Discussions of the impact legislation has, or may have, on digital preservation came up in many of the sessions. There was a widespread recognition that the law has not kept pace with the rapid progress of technology, and that IPR law stands in need of revision. Among the points made were:

- The notion of legal deposit should be widened to include digital material:
  - This would require significant consideration to be given to the scope of mandatory submission.
  - Consideration needs to be given to the secondary material which ought to be submitted along with the 'digital object', e.g., source code, user manuals.
  - The issue of DRM needs further thought, as DRM software is an interesting class of digital object in its own right.
- Libraries often do not approach the games industry for material because they have no legal or obligatory right to have it. Thus, the lack of an appropriate legal framework is having a distorting effect on the collections policy of libraries, and is hindering the development of productive dialogue between the games industry on the institutional preservation community.

Recommendations

POCOS was a flagship Jisc project about complex digital objects, specifically focusing on visualizations and simulations, digital art and computer games and virtual worlds, all of which evince a high level of complication. Right from the outset of the project, the intention was not to seek to pin down and define the nature and scope of a complex digital object: instead, waxing lyrical about Cantor's levels of infinity, it was to at least partly cover the problem space in terms of scope and level of detail. KVL's Drew Baker constantly highlighted the fact that POCOS was hosting symposia, which by their very nature set out to stimulate debate and glean opinion, rather than specify already established axioms and approaches. At the end of the project, the expectation was to be able to provide some sort of a clear definition of a complex digital object that would suffice for the near to mid term. However, after the comprehensive discussions surrounding each event, and having read the excellent material from the contributors, there is a sense of being no nearer to precisely delineating this elusive subject. Stephen Hawking's ever-expanding universe seems an appropriate analogy here – the possibilities for complexity in digital creation are so very wide indeed and seem to be ever-increasing.

Definitions

The Digital Curation Centre provides a good starting point with:

> Digital Objects: simple digital objects (discrete digital items such as text files, image files or sound files, along with their related identifiers and metadata) or **complex digital objects** (discrete digital objects made by combining a number of other digital objects, such as websites). Databases: structured collections of records or data stored in a computer system.[12]

Similarly, in Hunter and Choudhury[13] we find discussion of 'composite, mixed-media digital objects, a rapidly growing class of resources'.

Building on these baseline definitions, here are the main aspects of complexity that have come to the fore in the POCOS symposia. For a complex digital object comprising many different components:

- There are interdependencies between the components. These can be:

  — nested
  — embedded
  — interactive
  — encrypted
  — any permutation or combination of the above.
- Interaction can take a plethora of forms: real-time or with another temporal aspect; physical with any kind of platform, network, subject, object or data; virtual; etc. The possibilities are truly endless here, as exemplified by the software artists who streamed live financial data into their art works, or followed the winding path of humble snails.
- Each element of the object is affected by legal constraints, various institutional policies, etc.
- A complex digital object may be hybrid – part-physical, part-digital, as is the case with a 3D model of an archaeological fragment, as in the Villa of Oplontis project. This has significant implications for the curation of such interlinked objects.
- For any object such as digital art with a performance aspect, there is the issue of 'inter-subjectivity of meaning and the contexts of performance which defy simplistic approaches to documentation and representation. It crosses the boundaries of institutional genre and raises disconcerting questions about policy and competence.'[14]

Preserving technical environments

A key feature of many complex digital objects is the technical environment in which they were created or are rendered. For digital art works, it is vital to fully document the initial technical environment and conditions, in a manner which is comprehensible for curators, artists and other stakeholders, and which also specifies the artist's intent as to any changes permitted in any part of the environment (e.g. in one art work the printer type might be irrelevant, in another it might be paramount that the same printer be retained). For computer games, to get the original look and feel of playing them, information is needed regarding the whole computer platform, together with all of the accompanying mods, patches, joysticks, etc. The software preservation community has already made an impressive start towards preserving technical environments.

Preserving software

The Software Sustainability Institute[15] is doing an excellent job in this area, and there is a comprehensive chapter from Neil Chue Hong (Chapter 9) in the present volume; likewise in Chapter 10, by Brian Matthews and colleagues from the e-Science Centre, Science and Technology Facilities Council (STFC), Rutherford Appleton Laboratory.[16] This is a fiendishly difficult area, and both organizations and chapters mentioned above set out the issues in a clear and thorough manner. Work is under way in the software preservation community not just to enumerate the challenges, but also to create a software archive, together with accompanying licences and documentation.

Preserving hardware

This is an area of concern that has only just begun to be appreciated. There are many computer history museums worldwide that hold computing environment artefacts, documentation and data. For example, the IT History Society[17] holds several valuable online databases (hardware, IT companies), and the National Museum of Computing[18] in the UK holds original computers capable of playing old computer games. There needs to be a concerted effort by the DP community to work with colleagues from the computer history domain to share resources and know how, while we still have them.

Preservation practice

Following the KEEP and Planets projects, many in the DP community now see emulation as a viable strategy, and for some complex digital objects, such as computer games, it is the prime candidate. Much more work needs to be done to test and develop the prototypes created in these projects (the TOTEM technical environment metadata database, the KEEP Emulation Framework, the Emulation Workflow currently being built in the bwFLA project at the University of Freiburg, Germany), against collections of games, digital art, visualizations, simulations, etc. Here researchers and memory institutions can work together to determine the efficacy of emulation and virtualization techniques for preserving this wide range of disparate collections, and point towards the gaps in knowledge and technology to inform future research.

Community input

We need to form new groupings to tackle these new domains:

- A **Digital Art Preservation Forum** comprising artists, museums, collectors, researchers, legal bodies, etc., to debate and forge policy surrounding the entire digital art lifecycle.
- A **Computer Games and Virtual Games Preservation Forum**, comprising games developers, games publishers, memory institutions, legal bodies, games companies and researchers to debate and forge policy surrounding the entire computer games and virtual world lifecycle. In particular, it would be very valuable for such a group to organize a seminar for memory institution professionals on legal issues surrounding computer games and virtual worlds, given by a legal expert in this area.

Notes

1 Anderson, D., Delve, J., Pinchbeck, D., Konstantelos, L., Lange, A. and Bergmeyer, W. (2010) *KEEP Project: final document analyzing and summarizing metadata standards and issues across Europe*, 10–18.
2 Ibid., 10.
3 Gladney, H. M. (2008) *Durable Digital Objects Rather Than Digital Preservation*, ErpaePrints, http://eprints.erpanet.org/146/01/Durable.pdf, 14, 25 [accessed 16 July 2009].
4 www.bungie.net.
5 www.infinityward.com.
6 http://eu.battle.net/wow/en.
7 http://store.steampowered.com.
8 www.quakelive.com/#!home.
9 www.revolution.co.uk/games/skyr.
10 http://scummvm.org/downloads.
11 Lowood, H. (ed.) and Monnens, D., Vowell, Z., Ruggill, J. E., McAllister, K. S. and Armstrong, A. (2009) Before It's too Late: a Digital Game Preservation White Paper, *American Journal of Play*, **2** (2), 139–66, www.journalofplay.org/sites/www.journalofplay.org/files/pdf-articles/2-2-special-feature-digital-game-preservation-white-paper.pdf.
12 www.dcc.ac.uk/resources/curation-lifecycle-model.

13   Hunter, J. and Choudhury, S. (2006) Panic: an integrated approach to the preservation of composite digital objects, using semantic web services, *International Journal on Digital Libraries*, **6** (2), 174–83, doi: 10.1007/s00799-005-0134-z.

14   Kilbride, W. (2012) *The Preservation of Complex Objects, Vol. 2, Software Art*, preface. (Series Editors: Anderson D, Delve J, Dobreva M, and Konstantelos L.)

15   www.software.ac.uk.

16   www.stfc.ac.uk/e-Science/People/22343.aspx.

17   www.ithistory.org.

18   www.tnmoc.org.

Index